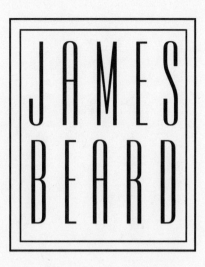

James Beard in Portland, Oregon, to promote *Theory & Practice*, 1977.
(© *Claudia Powell, 1977*)

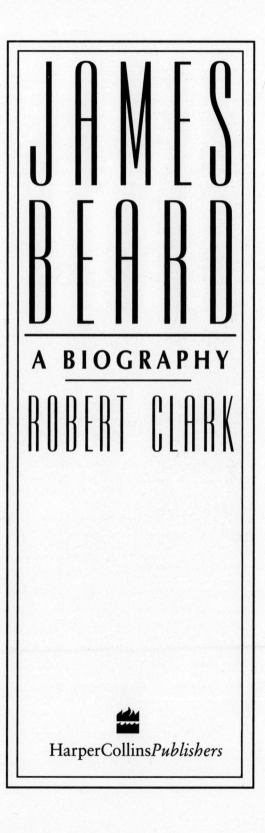

JAMES BEARD

A BIOGRAPHY

ROBERT CLARK

HarperCollins*Publishers*

Grateful acknowledgment is made to the Oregon Historical Society for use of the photograph of James Beard (*frontispiece*) and to Reed College to publish portions of the unpublished letters of James Beard.

HarperCollins books may be purchased for educational, business, or sales promotional use. For information, please write: Special Markets Department, HarperCollins Publishers, Inc., 10 East 53rd Street, New York, NY 10022.

FIRST EDITION

Designed by C. Linda Dingler

Library of Congress Cataloging-in-Publication Data
Clark, Robert, 1952–
   James Beard: a biography/Robert Clark.—1st ed.
     p. cm.
   Includes bibliographical references and index.
   ISBN 0-06-016763-7
   1. Beard, James, 1903–85. 2. Cooks—United States—Biography.
I. Title.
TX649.B43C57   1993
641.5'092—dc20   92-53322
[B]

94 95 96 97 ❖/HC 10 9 8 7 6 5 4 3 2

For Kirsten M. Bolin
1963–1991

Contents

Acknowledgments		ix
Prologue		1
One	1882–1902	5
Two	1903–1915	29
Three	1916–1923	53
Four	1924–1938	77
Five	1939–1949	105
Six	1950–1954	133
Seven	1955–1959	161
Eight	1960–1964	191
Nine	1965–1969	219
Ten	1970–1974	245
Eleven	1975–1979	275
Twelve	1980–1985	305
Afterword		329
Bibliography		335
Index		343

Acknowledgments

Throughout his life, James Beard was noted for the generosity and support he accorded virtually everyone who came to him for help or advice. In writing this book I found that spirit very much alive among his dozens of friends and colleagues, who scoured their files for documents and willingly submitted themselves to hours of sometimes fumbling questions. My thanks to all of you.

I want to single out several friends of James Beard whose assistance and encouragement were extraordinary and without whom this book could not have been written: John Ferrone, Mary Hamblet, Barbara Kafka, Peter Kump, and Caroline Stewart.

The following libraries and institutions also played a vital role in the research for this book: the University of California, Davis; the University of California, Berkeley; the University of Washington; the Seattle Public Library; the New York Public Library; the Library of Reed College; and the Multnomah County Public Library. In addition the staffs of *The Oregonian*, the Oregon Historical Society, and the American Heritage Center of the University of Wyoming were exceptionally helpful. My heartfelt appreciation especially goes to the Schlesinger Library at Radcliffe College.

For their support and forbearance I want to thank the following people: Rick Allstetter, Phyllis Clark, Tessa Clark, Schuyler Ingle, Patricia Unterman and Tim Savinar, Alice Waters and Stephen Singer, Susan Weiss and Dennis Wheaton, and Sarah Ames Yarmolinsky.

At HarperCollins I've had the good fortune to work with Richard Kot as my editor, as well as his assistant Sheila Gillooly and his colleague Susan Friedland. Sallie Gouverneur has acted with selflessness and dedication not only as my agent but as my chief critic, coach, and confessor. Anne Mendelson generously took time off from her important work on Irma Rombauer and *The Joy of Cooking* to provide an invaluable critique of the manuscript as well as to share the fruits of her research. Finally, my deepest thanks to Nancy Harmon Jenkins, whose encouragement, aid, and friendship from the very beginning of this project were quite simply indispensable.

Prologue

August 1940

In the last days he had tried to make her eat. Not the fat Columbia salmon of summers past or the sweet Dungeness crab, bolstered with butter and cream from the Yamhill Market and celery from the Foltz family, but only a little broth or cold chicken. The house was small and wooden, and the heat that had beaten down on Portland for the last week penetrated the walls and clung to the ceilings like stale incense. Mary had been wasting since before James had arrived six weeks earlier, and her appetite and her life withdrew together like a waning tide, exposing her great bones under translucent skin. Still, she craved nothing so much as talk—gossip and intelligence from worlds she had once known and now viewed through the gauze of memory—talk of things she herself might have seen, done, or been and that, after a lifetime, had evaded her.

But there was news enough for her with James sitting by her bed; news from the papers of London where she had grown up seventy years before, now hammered by German bombers in that knife-edge August of 1940; and news of food. It was the eve of canning time, with peaches, berries, and tomatoes rolling into Portland by the lugload, sales on jars and lids, and the incipient promise of autumn's game and the sweet, salt-metallic taste of oysters. Finally, there was news of New York, where James, now thirty-seven, had settled a little less than three years earlier. As he—and she, too—had always wanted, he had left Portland to make his way in the theater or the opera. He told her, in his dry, weary, wry baritone, of the things she loved to hear; of Upper East Side parties, of opening-night bashes at "21," of actors and producers and people he knew in the chorus at the Met. And then there was the food: the grandest restaurants in the country, markets bursting, and a whole legion of people who not only enjoyed eating but approached it with intelligence and verve.

It was the world that Mary had hungered for James to make his way in, and, after a fashion, he had. She had wanted him to know the best, most fascinating people, and more importantly, to be one of them—to be shamelessly famous. She had always been convinced that he would do so as an actor or a singer and had brought him up accordingly. From his fifth birthday onward, they saw the best plays and operas as they came through Portland, glimmerings of a world beyond Oregon through which she taught James to feel the grandeur within him, which fame alone could loose upon the world.

But fame had thus far eluded him, and in the last few years he had found himself casting off his aspirations like old, ill-fitting clothes. James, like Mary, had always dreamed of fleeing the rose-festooned little city that was Portland but also of being embraced by its uppermost castes of Episcopalian pioneer families. But neither Oregon society nor the stage completely accepted or fulfilled him, and James tended the pot of his resentments and frustrations assiduously. He often imagined himself evening the score but settled for gossip, for knowing what people had wanted, what they had deserved, and what they had gotten.

The theater had in fact defeated him, just as the opera had seventeen years before. With his voracious charm, James had friends and connections in the business, but no work despite a long list of credits in Portland theater, West Coast radio, and small roles in two Hollywood films as well as in an eminent theater touring company. His body had dwarfed his talents: His height was over six foot three and his weight fluctuated between 240 and 300 pounds. The two together wrecked his opportunity of ever becoming what he and Mary desired.

The truth had settled over him for the better part of 1938, and even James's habitual unconcern for the morrow could not assuage the dread of a homeless, jobless, and loveless life on the verge of middle age. So he had turned to cooking, which—although hardly a career worthy of the name—had in the form of the occasional catering job or home cooking lesson tided him over before. It was only an avocation—something instinctive and effortless, as when he swam in the ocean and the water bore his weight, free from all gravity and resistance. In that respect it was a further reminder of his failures. But food was also his perennial comfort, a thing apart from ambition, achievement, and the interpersonal commerce of a career; a castle set in the sand of a perfect childhood beach.

By 1939 James had discovered he that he could actually earn a living of sorts by catering hors d'oeuvres to parties and wine and food society receptions. That had led to an offer to write a book on hors d'oeuvres which was being published even as he sat with Mary. So he cooked, dredged his considerable memory of meals from long ago for inspiration, and found himself attaining, oddly enough, a small measure of fame. He didn't refer to his work as a career to Mary; it was never what either of them had planned. But she listened, her face taking on the quizzical expression that for James forever mingled both concern and disapproval.

She and James did not talk long that Thursday. James's father, John, was home. John was never really comfortable in what was more Mary's house than his, and he moved amid the shadows and along the edges of rooms. Then Mary said a very curious thing to James—what would be the last words to pass between them—"a bitter thing, a biting thing," as he was later wont to remark. She said, "You know, if we weren't related, we might have been friends." She slept then, and died at dawn the following day because of her heart, which was inflamed and which, when it could bear no more, at last gave up. The doctor explained that she had been dying for years of heart disease—of what today would be blamed on a surfeit of fat and cholesterol—and more recently of a succession of small, sometimes imperceptible heart attacks.

They buried her Monday at Lone Fir Cemetery among the Oregon pioneers and many of the city's best families, and then James and his childhood friend, Mary Hamblet, went through her things— bits of brass, candlesticks, and tea caddies—selling some and distributing the rest to friends. The house now belonged to James, although Mary's will stipulated that his father might live there until his death. Within a few weeks the house was emptied of most of its contents, John Beard had installed his current mistress in the bedroom, and James had returned to New York, to the rest of his life—to the business of becoming, as he would later say, "the world's great gastronomic whore."

ONE

1882–1902

Writing not long ago of the eighties—the 1880s, in this case—someone said, "The social flavor of that period was expressed largely in dining out." It was a time of food for showing off and for striving; of sleek new money preening in restaurants and at dinner parties; of the middle classes earnestly assaying fashionable and exotic ingredients, implements, and recipes; of the melding of the adolescent, swaggering culture of America with the venerable, refined traditions of Europe. It was a time so swollen with ambition and so sated with money that to take great pains over very little indeed became the art of the age. It was a decade made for eating, interior design, and entertaining; for being seen and being *seen* to be seen; and, despite its habitual pose of nonchalance, for keeping score—a time that was fat but still a bit too diffident to be sassy.

Beneath the gourmandizing, the decorating, and the rush of the middle classes simultaneously to emulate and exceed one another, greater forces stirred. The role of women had changed drastically, as had the nature of the family. The middle class had grown and consolidated its position, but so too had a restive underclass, living in an urban squalor on which the general economic prosperity of the decade had no impact. But the public mood evinced little interest in either economic or social equality, lulled by a personable, unreflective, and unflappable political leadership. Instead the urge for reform was manifested in further concern about food and drink—in middle-class worries over diet, personal health, the purity and safety of foodstuffs, and the abuse of alcohol and drugs.

At least one source of that anxiety lay in the knowledge that even as the middle and upper classes strove to serve food of a distinctive and artisanal quality, the nation's food supply was growing more homogeneous and industrialized: Agriculture seemed increasingly to be dominated by corporate power and distribution networks; regional cooking traditions eroded; and the flavor of food was increasingly a function not of its own inherent qualities but of its processing and packaging by industrial conglomerates.

None of this should be taken as evidence that the eighties were a particularly callous, empty-headed, or narcissistic era. For food—in its production, preparation, and consumption—is the matrix on which culture and agriculture intersect, the field on which humans stake their claim to be civilized. We give up hunting and gathering; we cultivate the countryside; we establish markets, kitchens, and cities and make and trade goods and services; and so we become peoples and nations. Accordingly, for all its apparent and necessary banality, the subject of what people eat and how they eat it is at the center of their lives and of their civilization. That was true in the 1880s, and, although nothing and everything has changed, it is true today.

Mary Elizabeth Jones, English, twenty-one, and nearly six feet tall, was made for that era and made for Portland, Oregon. Her face was a broad oval with deep, bemused eyes and a strong, handsome chin; she had only a few loose black curls to soften the impatient heft and determined forward motion of her body. Built like a Victorian railway terminus—big-boned and ruddy, brick in the fundamentals, cast-iron filigree in the details—she was fit for dependable service yet redolent of travel and exotic places and persons. Or at least that is how her son James would see her: a formidable domestic machine who ran her family and household like a general but who also lived another life of sudden and mysterious journeys into a cosmopolitan, bohemian world peopled by actors, artists, celebrities, and others with extraordinary cultural, culinary, and sexual tastes.

One of twelve children, she was born on January 7, 1861, in Wiltshire in southern England to Joseph Jones and Charlotte Prangley. Joseph Jones's prospects were never steady, and the family lived an itinerant if not impoverished life, shuttling between his jobs in Ireland and England. As the household grew more crowded and its resources thinner, the decision was reached to send Mary, then about ten, to London to live with an aunt and uncle. As her son would one day do, Mary would claim later in life that these relatives inhabited Mayfair or Belgravia—two of London's toniest neighborhoods—but the house was in fact middle class, the routine regimented and dull, and the religion uncompromisingly Low Church evangelical. It was a solidly Victorian life in Victorian London, all gray mutton and electric green mint sauce, and the adolescent Mary hated it.

Still, she made friends easily through a mix of enthusiasm, outspokenness, curiosity, and charm, and while her size and manner excluded her from much she might have aspired to as a woman, they also allowed her to cross boundaries unthinkable to the easily scandalized, ever upright, delicate, neurasthenic middle-class Victorian female. At seventeen, with the connivance of several friends who worked at the same steamship company as her uncle, she arranged passage—probably free passage at that—to North America. And without a word to her family, fashioning herself to suit herself, she simply left for another life in another world.

She turned up in Toronto in 1879, encamping with a generous and tolerant relative. Through a newspaper advertisement she located a position as governess to a well-connected Canadian family planning immigration to and an extended trip around the United States. In early 1882 the party arrived in Portland, Oregon, where the Canadians numbered themselves friends of many of the city's better families, with whom Mary was able to ingratiate herself. When her employers reversed their decision to immigrate and decided to return to Toronto, Mary made up her mind to remain in Portland.

It was a good match. Where Mary was strong, Portland, an ingenue of a city scarcely thirty years old, was insecure but—in her love of principle at the occasional oversight of persons—decent if not quite kind. Outwardly pleased with herself and her circumstances, Portland stocked her hope chest with plans at whose disruption by flood, bank failure, and recession she was inclined to panic: Possessed of neither San Francisco's gilded insouciance nor Seattle's go-to-hell vulgarity, Portland knew she was good but wondered, in frequent bouts of self-consciousness, just how good. In any case Portland was pretty and entertained suitors, lovers, gigolos, and jilters with a vengeance in the 1880s. Railways, banks, real estate developers, and entrepreneurs fought for her hand—for control of her trees, her rivers, and the abundant Willamette Valley that trailed two hundred miles southward.

Both outside observers and citizens likened Portland to New

England, a place that was well-ordered, decorous, and appreciative of community and culture and from which many of the city's founders had indeed come. The rapacious scramble for resources and money, so evident in every other corner of the American West, was less apparent there—if hardly at all less fervent—than in other cities. At the same time, looming over the city like Mount Hood and Mount Saint Helens was a palpable appetite for gracious living; albeit perhaps not an appetite so much for pleasure as for status and acceptance, for the outward signs of a society that knows itself and is known by the world.

In that respect Portland was not very different from much of the United States, or indeed any emergent society at any time. Portland reveled in and exalted the largess conferred on her by nature, and more than most places, her claims to be something approaching heaven on earth were justified. But beauty and abundance do not of themselves produce the eminence Portlanders coveted, nor did they quickly foster the richness of culture that in the nineteenth century differentiated Europe from America. By populating and exploiting a new land and building a society that owed very little to Europe, America made itself into a land of plenty whose foremost achievement was the steady assimilation of laborers and immigrants into a new and unprecedented middle class.

But if that new class was economically blessed, it was culturally insecure and consequently sought to emulate the very European way of life that made its own emergence impossible in Europe. So while meat—and in particular beef, whose consumption rocketed in tandem with the burgeoning of the middle class—and potatoes remained the fundamental constituents of the American diet, food as an expression of culture and social attainment needed to pay homage to Europe.

Americans' relationship with French cooking in particular has been long standing but ambivalent. The wealthy and powerful, as in every other Western country, were on familiar terms with it, and the first book explaining French cooking to Americans generally, Louis Eustache Ude's *The French Cook,* appeared in 1828—a date at which few cookbooks of any description had been published in the United States. Four years later the most popular cookbook author of the first half of the nineteenth century, Eliza Leslie, produced a volume, translated from French, called *Domestic French Cookery*, which was reprinted at least six times in the following twenty-three years.

Europeans and European culture, then, held an irresistible lure for Americans of a certain class, and Portland's claim—with a copy of the *Atlantic Monthly* in every drawing room worthy of the name—to be more like New England than most of the West was ultimately an assertion of a more Old World character. Despite the glassy-eyed Anglophilia of Portland's upper crust, that claim was more a wish than a fact, but it did make the city highly amenable to the presence of Europeans—and particularly Englishwomen—like Mary Jones; Europeans who, being middle class rather than aristocratic, were unthreatening but who knew how to do things with food, hospitality, and entertaining as they were done in London and Paris and who would, without condescension, be happy to show Americans how to do it themselves.

Mary, of course, was a particularly American kind of European in her openness to novelty and easy passage across class boundaries, and, in her independence and assertiveness, she was a most un-Victorian Victorian woman. But she was also utterly possessed by the era's largely male passion for exploration and travel. After holding a succession of genteel domestic positions around Portland, Mary left in 1884 for New York, where she made friends among the city's bohemian set: actors and theater people, artists, and tolerant socialites with a taste for the bizarre. In 1885 she returned briefly to London, where she saw her now-estranged family for what would be the last time and considered but rejected a marriage proposal from an old friend.

For the next six years, never entirely settled in one place, Mary shuttled between the domestic world of cooking, housekeeping, and childminding in which she could earn a living and that of the arts, celebrity, and sophisticated society to which she had always been drawn—two worlds that for a Victorian woman might never be genuinely integrated. But when she worked she worked hard, and when she traveled, she took her pleasures as she pleased and built her extensive network of friendships without much regard for convention or propriety. During that time she returned to Portland at least once, recrossed the Atlantic, consolidated friendships in New York's arts community, and took an extended tour of the Caribbean and Central America with an actress who was also her lover.

Before the rise of late-nineteenth-century scientific culture and its obsession with the creating and cataloging of psychological and physiological pathologies—homosexuality among them—intense same-sex friendships were routine. So, too, were "Boston marriages," in which women, usually members of the professional classes such as college teachers, lived together in long-term relationships. The sexual component of such friendships was of course unacknowledged, but then sexuality itself tended to be viewed as amorphous in character, consisting more of a series of desirable or undesirable acts than of an integral component of personality that might be deemed sick or healthy. Mary's own sexuality seems to have been less a matter of ambivalence or repression than of ranging freely among a spectrum of partners and possibilities. Her closest attachments were to members of her own sex, but she also wanted the accoutrements that only heterosexual marriage could provide, and eventually she managed to maintain both. By her son's later reckoning, her interest in sex was intense and her conversation about it was frank and funny. She was a passionate advocate not only of women's rights but of what would eventually be called sexual and gay liberation.

On one passage along the Pacific Coast, she met and befriended Frances Curtis, a San Francisco woman who owned several residential hotels, one of which was in Portland and at which work was always found for Mary between her excursions. After a short-lived marriage to an engineer named John Brennan, followed by yet another European tour, she returned to Portland to stay in 1892. She took a room on Washington Street on the fringes of Chinatown, moved again a few blocks north, and by 1894 was the full-time resident manager of Mrs. Curtis's hotel at Twelfth and Morrison.

More a high-class boardinghouse than a genuine hotel, under Mary's direction the Curtis laid a decent table in a city that increasingly wished to eat with some refinement and distinction. Not much that life required could not be provided by Oregon's benign climate, proximity to fertile soil and sea, and manifold natural resources, and that was especially true of food. Salmon of eighty pounds or more beat their way up the Columbia River every month of the year, while the river's mouth and the adjacent Pacific shore teemed with oysters, crabs, and ocean fish. The fields were full of berries and game, and the valleys below the coast range and the Cascades lent themselves to cultivation and in a few decades became famous for their abundance: the Tillamook for milk, cream, butter, and cheese; the Hood for apples, pears, cherries, and other orchard fruit; and the Willamette for every conceivable foodstuff from wheat to garden vegetables.

Blessed with such raw materials, Portland had by the 1880s dozens of restaurants, most admittedly attached to boardinghouses and wooden hotels pitched a sill's height above the city's muddy streets and wooden sidewalks. Many ran on the "American plan," under which meals, eaten en masse at one sitting, were included in the bill, and not a few advertised their adherence to "Strict Temperance Principles." Others appealed to customers on more fundamental grounds, such as the place that published the following handbill in the 1860s:

> Thompson's Two-Bit House, Front Street between Main and Madison. No deception there. Here is your bill of fare: Three kinds of meat for dinner; also for breakfast and supper. Ham and eggs every other day, and fish, hot rolls, and cake in abundance. Hurry up and none of your sneering at cheap boarding houses. Now's the time to have the wrinkles taken out of your bellies after the hard winter. Board and lodging, $5; board, $4. Six new rooms, furnished with beds the best in town at my branch house, corner First and Jefferson Streets. I am ready for the bone and sinew of this country.

By the eighties, when Mary first arrived, Portland also had hotels and restaurants of greater sophistication and pretension, places that were more than louche appendages of boardinghouses and bars. There was the Louisville on First Street, the Vienna Coffee House on Washington Street, the Aurora on Alder Street, the French and Italian on Oak Street, and, inevitably, a place that called itself Delmonico's. By the 1880s and 1890s, probably every large American city boasted a restaurant of that name, though none was connected with the original Delmonico's in New York, the archetype for every serious dining room in the country for one hundred years.

Founded as a Lower Manhattan chophouse in the 1820s, Delmonico's was reincarnated as a deluxe dining establishment in the

1850s, when it began, in step with New York society, a succession of moves up Fifth Avenue that would end only with the century. By the 1860s it was the leading restaurant not just in New York but in the United States. Three achievements brought Delmonico's its fame: It made dining an event, a piece of grand theater complete with music, stunning decor, and a seeming cast of thousands; it introduced European chefs, service, and food to the restaurant-going public; and it made the restaurant a leading social venue and, in particular, one in which women were both welcome and comfortable.

That women should previously not have felt at home in restaurants seems paradoxical, given their dominance of food and hospitality in the domestic sphere. But the world of restaurants, hotels, and bars was, for most of the nineteenth century, purely an extension of the world of business and commerce, which is to say the world of men, joined by whores and fast women together with such disreputables as actors and actresses. It was the unalterable view of the day that those two worlds, occupied exclusively by each of the sexes, not only could not but *should* not meet; that women, the family, and the home must be inviolate from intrusions from the public world of male commerce and vice. The measure of any man's success was the making and possession of a fortune, but even more the possession of a wife and home whose virtue, privacy, and refinement offered a haven from the heartless, amoral world of business and trade. The family Sunday dinner and a meal eaten in a men's chophouse might bear some superficial resemblance to one another as food, but socially and morally they were as the marriage bed is to the brothel. That a middle- or upper-class woman should dine or, as in Mary's case, work, at a restaurant remained a controversial idea for the rest of the century.

By the 1880s, however, notions of what constituted success and a happy, fulfilling life had begun to change, perhaps principally as a result of rising incomes, technological and cultural innovation, and a growing dissatisfaction among women and the young with the narrowness of private life and their exclusion from the public world. As restaurants, amusements, and, later, movies and nightclubs, became increasingly acceptable and popular places for the middle classes to spend their time, success had less to do with production of wealth or the possession of Victorian virtues than with consumption: the use and enjoyment of the fruits of technological enterprise, what would become known as mass media and popular culture. In effect, leisure was reinvented as a consumer commodity, making spending as important as earning and pleasure as economically important as work. The public world was no longer to be shunned—indeed, the whole point of the Waldorf-Astoria's Peacock Alley and other such most-favored-table locations (a feature of New York high-society restaurants to this day, each with its corresponding "Siberia") was to see and be seen by one's fellow diners. And with the embrace of public places came a fascination with public faces—with actors, celebrities, style setters, and experts who created popular culture and determined what it was fashionable to consume. Artists, homosexuals, and other members of the bohemian fringe began to achieve both influence and power.

So, too, did women. The rise of consumer culture was likewise felt in the domestic realm, and what once were the banal necessities of life—food, clothing, and shelter—became the objects of middle-class consumer aspirations and fashions promoted and provided by food processors, national brands, and large-scale retailers. The home, formerly a private refuge, became a place to display the status, wealth, and stylishness of its owners to the world. In particular, the dining room, once either nonexistent or of little consequence in middle-class homes, became the target of enormous energies and expenditure for decor and furnishings. The kitchen, in the past a jumbled workshop, was now consciously designed for efficiency and pleasure. These two rooms and the home generally were the one arena in which Victorian women wielded some genuine autonomy and power. Now, as the home became the focus of so many cultural and economic interests, women were a force to be reckoned with, not only as consumers but as producers and professionals—as teachers, home economists, cooks, writers, journalists, social and political activists, and managers and entrepreneurs.

In Portland in the 1890s, Mary Jones was therefore a woman who exemplified the rise and confluence of these changes in American society: an inherently independent and dynamic woman; one who had always taken an interest in public life, the arts, and those who peopled them; one to whom social, cultural, and sexual boundaries meant little; and one who had taken her interests and skill in the domestic sphere and translated them into a career. In truth, of course, such positions as she held with Mrs. Curtis were among the few jobs available to middle-class women who wished to remain respectable and represented little more than the extension of women's work into the commercial world, enjoying little or no status. Hospitality and cooking as practiced at Delmonico's or the Waldorf-Astoria—particularly by such figures as Delmonico's chef, Charles Ranhoffer, or Oscar of the Waldorf—were by late in the century increasingly viewed as an art; as practiced by women like Mary, they were simply paid housekeeping.

But housekeeping, and in particular food and cooking, was the one arena of economic life in which women had a foothold, and they sought to raise its stature by professionalizing it. Home and kitchen chores were recast as home economics or domestic science, professional disciplines with schools and research facilities, textbooks, degrees, and a growing legion of experts. By the 1890s home economics had been taught at colleges like the University of Iowa for nearly twenty years, and the urban cooking schools in Boston, New York, and Philadelphia that would produce the groundbreaking, hugely popular cookbooks of the late eighties and nineties, such as *The Fannie Farmer Cook Book* (known as *The Boston Cooking School Cook Book* on its publication in 1896), were well established.

While the home economics movement was born of feminism, of nineteenth-century scientism, and of the changing roles and economic status of women, it survived and prospered through the unlikely joint support of corporate capitalism and progressive politics. Early home economists like Ellen Swallow Richards, a chemist at MIT, attempted to improve the lot of women and of the poor. In the nineties, the foundation of community kitchens; the promotion of the inexpensive, slow-cooking Aladdin oven; and the formulation of what were felt to be improved dietary guidelines closely paralleled the efforts of Jane Addams of Chicago's Hull House and other social activists and reformers. Like other progressives and reformers of the period, the home economists were convinced not only of the need for the program they advanced but of the irrefutable scientific logic that underlay it.

But to change people's diets is to try to change them at a very fundamental level, and the American poor and working class were not much interested in having their food habits reformed. Immigrants were attached to the ethnic cuisines that home economists saw as a bane to both their health and their assimilation into the American way of life. Nor did workers see why they should give up their aspirations to eat the beef-laden diet that epitomized success American-style in favor of the bland (and actually not, in light of subsequent nutritional discoveries, very healthy) diet advocated by the reformers.

Home economists, though they did not entirely abandon the lower classes, began to see that their future lay elsewhere. Wrote Richards: "I believe . . . that the well-to-do classes are being eliminated by their diet, to the detriment of social progress, and they and not the poor are most in need of missionary work." As home economics moved inexorably into every high school and home in the country, and its leading proponents, such as Boston's Fannie Farmer or Philadelphia's Sarah Tyson Rorer became bestselling authors, its influence became considerable, a fact not lost on food processors and retailers who sought to associate their products with domestic science and its luminaries.

Considering home economists' potential as sales and marketing vehicles, it is unsurprising that such corporate interests should court them; what is harder to understand, given the movement's roots, is why the relationship should be one of mutual attraction. But home economists loved science and progress—whose embrace would surely achieve the feminist goals of status and legitimacy for women—and big food business represented both. The food processors' ideal of food mined, milled, refined, and standardized to be sold in uniform packaging to a national market was appreciated by domestic scientists committed to bringing efficiency and scientific rigor and practice to the American home. Under the banner of progress, domestic science's reformist urge and corporate capitalism's incessant need to innovate and thereby create new markets became intertwined. By the turn of the century, the enthusiasm of leading home economists and cooking teachers for the products of the nascent food industry was so great that many became paid endorsers of products ranging from stoves to cornstarch to Jell-O. Home economics had not only created what in our time is known as the food professional—the food and cooking teacher, writer, or consultant— but also the perennially uneasy ethical relationship between such professionals and those who sell, distribute, and process food and drink.

. . .

By 1896 Mary—running a kitchen and dining room and overseeing the needs of perhaps three dozen guests—was by any account a
professional. Although she cared passionately about the quality of
domestic life—"She has no right to those airs. She doesn't know a
thing about a home and less about food!" she said of another
woman to the young James—"professional" or "domestic scientist"
was not a description she herself would have chosen. She had little
use for authority, no matter how credentialed or well intentioned,
and to the formidable but fun-loving Mary, the home economists
would have seemed an achingly dull and starchy lot. Moreover, she
was deeply suspicious of their approach to food, which was heedless
of both flavor and of the social and cultural pleasures of eating well.
Railing against "King Palate" and "the pampered diet," the leaders
of the movement asserted that taste and pleasure were inimical to the
kind of scientific cooking consistent with good nutrition, health,
economy, and ease of preparation. The menus promoted by home
economists too often featured stews or boiled meat or fish generally
accompanied by two boiled vegetables, all to be served and eaten
with more efficiency than gusto.

Such food was rooted in the New England clams, corn, and codfish background of much of the home economics movement, and in
its no-nonsense, Yankee austerity it exemplified not only the dietary
but intellectual and moral values food reformers felt were important.
Despite their links to New England, however, Portlanders were
unlikely customers for such a cuisine, as were most Americans.
Much as the poor and working classes refused to forsake their traditional diets, most members of the middle class were disinclined to
take up the manifesto of domestic science in its entirety: The general
spirit of home economics was vastly influential, but its particulars
were lacking in appeal. American women might applaud its general
goals of dietary reform, efficiency, and frugality, but they also
wanted their own oak dining tables and china-, pewter-, and silver-
laden sideboards to brim—at least for guests—with food that
revealed them to be successful, sophisticated, and stylish: oysters,
inevitably, to start, but perhaps rendered "dainty" by cream; beef, of
course, whose rich, red, bloody tang was the foundation of the
American good life; accompanied by potatoes and a green vegetable,
every hint of earth fulminated away on the stove; a molded dessert—a

rhomboid-studded, crenellated tower or crown of gelatine or blanc-mange—to finish; and perhaps the entire meal unified by a theme of some kind, a single color or a "favor" at each place setting.

In the eighties and nineties this was a menu any wife would have been happy to serve and any husband pleased to preside over, but it was in truth not recognizably American, French, ethnic, or regional and would have won the approval of neither restaurant chef nor home economist. Rather than representing any particular cuisine or domestic principle, it was an amalgam of tradition and fashion designed to send an implicit but clear set of coded messages about its purveyors. All the food was comparatively simple, save the dessert, whose construction was more a feat of engineering than a culinary achievement. But it required some learning beyond what the typical American girl might normally possess, and no little labor to produce, at a time when the "servant problem" had clearly begun to afflict the new middle class.

The new class wanted new food: food that necessitated cooking methods and materials that were mysterious and had to be mastered through study and practice by either a cook or her employer. But the servant problem—a shortage of cheap domestic labor—meant that most housewives would be lucky to employ a single maid and entirely precluded the possession of a cook. Moreover, the painstaking requirements of new, highly refined, "dainty" cooking collided with the housewife's urgent need to save time, money, and labor. Technology—in the form of mass-produced iron ranges, utensils ranging from eggbeaters to flour sifters, and processed food of all kinds—was one answer. Education and the systematizing of culinary and domestic lore were another, a development felt in the appearance of the home economics movement, in the establishment of cooking schools to train both servants and housewives, and, perhaps most important, in the rapidly growing market for cookbooks and what would come to be called food journalism.

Before 1850 cookbooks published in America numbered in the dozens, and the extent of their influence was fairly narrow; thereafter they appeared by the hundreds, with sales in some cases reaching the one-hundred-thousand mark by the turn of the century. There were two genres. The domestic encyclopedia was commercially published and usually authored by a self-described expert (for example, Mrs. Lydia Maria Child, author of *The American Frugal*

Housewife [1832]) and promised comprehensiveness with recipes of every description and advice on housekeeping, child rearing, the management of servants, and family health (for example, the anonymous *The New Family Book, or Ladies' Indispensable Companion and Housekeepers' Guide* [1854]). With comprehensiveness also came appeals to fashion and modernity based on Americans' habitual cultural insecurity, including one volume produced on the then American frontier entitled *Every Body's Cook and Receipt Book: But Being More Particularly Designed for Buckeyes, Hoosiers, Wolverines, Corncrackers, Suckers, and All Epicures Who Wish to Live with the Present Times* (1842).

The other, less noticed but no less important, genre consisted of "community" cookbooks, privately published for fund-raising by women's or church groups, with recipes contributed by individual members. Still flourishing today, in their characteristic spiral bindings, such cookbooks rarely pretended to be comprehensive; rather, they reflected local and regional tastes at the moment of their publication and revealed what might be called "food trends" that never penetrated the consciousness of New York publishers or national writers and experts.

In 1885 the San Grael Society of the First Presbyterian Church of Portland produced *The Web-Foot Cook Book,* the first such in the Pacific Northwest, which was offered to "those who are desirous of succeeding in preparing attractive dinners and excelling in delicate cookery." A two-hundred-page selection of what upper- and upper-middle-class Portland women were cooking (or telling their servants to cook), it reveals a culinary universe that had a dozen ways with oysters; where vegetables were boiled for from twenty minutes to an hour, but where meat was served fairly rare; that consumed astonishing numbers of puddings ("have your tinner make you a tin mould fives inches wide by nine inches long"); and that washed it all down with eight varieties of root beer and something called Pineapple Pop.

It was, with the exception of desserts, plain food customarily enlivened with an array of sauces, pickled vegetables, and catsups. In the pre-Heinz year of 1885, tomato catsup, which was to become the nation's supreme condiment, was not much in evidence, although it was allowed that some persons liked it added to deviled crab, an eternal Portland standby whose only real competition in popularity was chicken salad. But the national penchant for mayonnaise-based

salad dressings was apparent, as was one for pies, cakes, and cookies, with some seven recipes for ginger cookies and snaps alone.
Main dishes tended toward boiled, roasted, or baked fish and meat:
These well-to-do women universally owned stoves at a time when
many still cooked in the fireplace.

New England influences are reflected in recipes for cod balls,
baked beans, brown bread, and the like, though their number were
small in relation to the book's near torrent of baked desserts and
salmon, crab, and oysters. Of the more than 500 recipes, perhaps a
half dozen have foreign names, including a perfectly honorable
Boeuf (mangled by the typesetter to "Bocup") à la Mode. Others
reveal that pasta had been discovered (mostly as a bed for melted
cheese) and that the addition of a foreign place name to a recipe title
was a clue to the presence of tomatoes and other brassy flavors.
There is, for example, Macaroni Italian Style, a sort of bastard
lasagna of ground meat and tomatoes familiar to this day, and a
Puree of Tomates Parisienne, in which pulverized canned tomatoes
are married to garlic.

Food of this kind—much of it not to Mary's taste—was
undoubtedly served at the dining room of the Curtis, although it was
unlikely to be patronized by contributors to *The Web-Foot Cook
Book,* some of whom—Mrs. H. W. Corbett, wife of Oregon's Sena-
tor Corbett, or Mrs. S. G. Reed, whose family established Reed College—were married to the wealthiest and most powerful men in
Portland. It was a world Mary would have loved to penetrate and
around whose fringes she moved with some success. She attended
Trinity Church, the parish at the top of Portland's Episcopalian heap,
and, as ever, made friends there easily. Among these were Col. Owen
Summers and his wife, Clara, whose family's mercantile business,
Olds & King, was an advertiser in *Web-Foot.* The Summerses did
not have money on the scale of the Reeds or the Corbetts, but Clara
came from a pioneer family, something that still had considerable
cachet at a time when the pioneer era had ended barely thirty years
before. From the secure financial base of Olds & King, Colonel Summers was able to pursue a distinguished military career—fighting the
Sioux in the Dakotas and the Spanish in the Philippines—and
another as an Oregon legislator.

By 1896 Mary had decided to go into business for herself, and it was apparently the Summerses who helped her finance the lease of a three-and-a-half-story wood building with a mansard roof literally around the corner from the Curtis, at 174 Thirteenth Street. Aspiring to the status of a grand hotel, Mary christened it the Gladstone, although it appeared in the city directory under her name with the label "furnished rooms," a description somewhat closer to the reality of the twelve-room, four-bath, gentlefolk's boardinghouse it was. But that did not prevent Mary from running it as though it were the 326-bedroom Stanford White–designed Portland Hotel six blocks to the east. Up at 5:00 A.M. and firing orders like cannonades, she careened down Yamhill Street and then south on Third to the Metropolitan Public Market, sending stall holders running for cover.

Mary was an exacting shopper and withering in her criticisms of what she felt to be the less than the best. She instinctively understood the principle that good food is first and foremost a function of good ingredients and that mastery of techniques, recipes, or equipment cannot rescue a dish based on second-rate materials from its inherent mediocrity. The food she served at the Gladstone was probably never outstanding but always interesting and appealing: a vol-au-vent with creamed Olympia oysters, a sauté of wild mushrooms and chicken, salmon with Russian dressing, chicken pot pie, veal in aspic, roast lamb with mint sauce, a Welsh rabbit of Oregon cheeses, pot-au-feu, a medley of curries, sundry steaks and stews, and the inevitable crab and chicken salads. Such tastes were wide ranging, if not spectacularly more so than what Portlanders were used to, and reflected Mary's English background, her travels, and an unself-conscious appreciation of local materials in a style that might be called Anglo-Oregonian. For the most part it was hearty, direct, and varied food tempered—like the woman who cooked it and the city that ate it— by sometimes conflicting, sometimes complementary urges toward both propriety and sophistication.

The respect in which her approach to food differed from that of most of her contemporaries—whether old-fashioned home cooks or the new domestic scientists—was her frankly sensual and critical appreciation of its aesthetic qualities. For most women cooking was at best a craft, and the preparation and enjoyment of food as an art had largely been the province of male gastronomes and chefs. That a woman should enjoy her food with the same gusto as a cigar-smoking, cognac-quaffing gourmet at Delmonico's was as unthinkable as her embarking on adventures for their own sake, circulating between the well-to-do and the avant-garde, or acting on her own sexual desires and preferences.

Mary's unconventional attitude to food was mirrored in that of a book, *The Feasts of Autolycus: The Diary of a Greedy Woman,* published in London in the same year Mary began the Gladstone. An account of the pleasures of the table, with chapters ranging in subject from breakfast to oysters, tomatoes, partridges, and bouillabaisse, the female author urged women to embrace gastronomy and make it as much their cause as universal suffrage:

> gradually the delicacy of women's palate [has been] destroyed; food to her perverted stomach was but a mere necessity to stay the pangs of hunger, and the pleasure of eating she looked upon as a deep mystery, into which only a man could be initiated. . . . [But] gross are they who see in eating and drinking nought but grossness. The woman who cannot live without a mission should now find the path clear before her. Let her learn first for herself the rapture that lies dormant in food; let her next spread abroad the joyful tidings.

Beyond the exhortation that women should become gastronomes, neither the substance nor the style of the remainder of the book is especially striking: The genteel if barely contained lip smacking; the simultaneously stuffy, orotund, and gushing prose (*"poulet sauté à la Hongroise,* the clash of the Czardas captured and imprisoned in a stew-pan"); and the insistence on high seriousness of purpose characterize food writing of the gourmet tendency to this day. But *The Feasts of Autolycus* was likely perceived to be shocking because of its author's sex, and although an editor is credited on the title page, the author herself is anonymous. However pompous and silly the presentation in this particular instance, the idea that women should freely pursue the "rapture" of food seemed dangerously akin to their freely pursuing that of sexuality. In its prototypical stage, gastrofeminism of the gourmet rather than the domestic science school was not far removed from sedition or pornography, an underground and for the most part closeted passion.

Mary also had definite ideas about labor and management, and she grew frustrated by the incessant turnover and tantrums of her largely European staff. Her solution was to take over the stoves herself and to train, from the ground up, a complete staff that would be loyal, obedient, and reliable. Whether by deliberate choice or by accident, the result was an all-Chinese three-man kitchen—Jue-Let and two assistants, Gin and Poy—which Mary quickly taught to meet her standards of food and service. To employ members of Portland's ubiquitous Chinese community (more than a tenth of the city's 1890 population of fifty thousand) in such backstage roles was normal, but at a time when many hotels in Oregon advertised their "all-white" staffs, Mary's relationship with her new employees was striking: Jue-Let—easily Mary's equal if not superior as a cook—soon became not so much Mary's chef as her unacknowledged partner, her collaborator in matters of food and taste generally, who teased, cajoled, and fought with her with total ease.

The Chinese began arriving in Oregon in the 1850s, trickling up from California or across the Pacific by ship direct from Canton, to work in mines, on railroads, or as cooks and domestics, most with a view to saving a good sum of money and returning to China. In Portland they established themselves along First, Second, and Third avenues, and by the 1880s Chinatown stretched some seven blocks from Taylor to Pine. But the eighties also saw a ferocious explosion of anti-Chinese racist feeling along the Pacific Coast, beginning with the Chinese Exclusion Act of 1882 and culminating in riots, lynchings, and, in Portland in 1886, a series of mob attacks, fire settings, and dynamitings calculated to force the Chinese out of the city. Nonetheless, by the standards of California and Washington, Oregon was relatively tolerant and soon became a refuge of sorts for Chinese Americans.

Although racial tension subsided, racism itself did not, and at the best of times, white and Chinese Portlanders coexisted in discrete, parallel universes. Although Portland was a city of immigrants—the best-established and most secure families in town could claim at most perhaps forty years of residence—the Chinese were not considered ethnic but wholly and utterly alien. To white people (who often arranged to be escorted by a policeman) a visit to Chinatown seemed a descent into a miasma of opium, piercing aromas, bizarre foods, rare silks, and rich furniture, in which voices were sharp, smoke and vapors drifted through the air, and candles and lamps guttered and hissed. But in fact Chinatown was neither dangerous nor impoverished, and along the wharves of Front Street, Chinese merchants and traders were a force to be reckoned with, however distasteful.

It was a neighborhood Col. Owen Summers became familiar with in the autumn of 1897, when he was appointed U.S. Customs appraiser for Portland, three years after an opium-trafficking scheme jointly operated by his predecessor, James Lotan, and a powerful Chinese merchant had been exposed. One of the examiners, whom Summers rapidly promoted to be his assistant, was John Beard, a dapper, florid-faced man of thirty-six who had joined the department four years earlier and been widowed in August 1896.

Like Summers, Beard was of pioneer stock, born in Iowa and brought to Oregon by covered wagon when he was five. His parents and fifteen brothers and sisters settled in Linn County, seventy-five miles south of Portland in the Willamette Valley. John, bright, charming if taciturn, and handsome, seemed the son most destined for success and was the first and only Beard child to attend college. He studied pharmacy, returned to Lebanon in Linn County to work as a druggist, and married a local girl named Emma when he was twenty-three and she twenty-five. They had a daughter, Lucille Bird, the following year and a second, Genevieve, two years later.

In 1891 diphtheria raged through Lebanon, killing Genevieve, who was five. In distress, and with John's pharmacy business doing poorly, the Beards moved to Portland, where John found work for the next two years as a stockman and buyer for a local drug company. Exactly how John acquired his position at the Customs House in 1893 is unclear. Under Lotan's administration the department was blatantly corrupt—shockingly so for Portland, where kickbacks, patronage, and deal fixing were traditionally managed discreetly— and John's qualifications were not self-evident.

In any case John survived the scandal and the subsequent political housecleaning only to lose Emma to tuberculosis. Alone, habitually short of money, and the sole parent of a sullen twelve-year-old, he took refuge in work; in the clublike company of waterfront cronies and ships' crews from as far away as Hong Kong, Calcutta, and Constantinople; and in sexual liaisons in Chinatown and points north in Portland's gaming and whoring districts (much of which was owned and operated at arm's length by the city's leading families). But Owen Summers, ten years older than John, was impressed with the young examiner. John Beard had a grace under pressure, and an intelligence not usually found at the Customs House, which brought out the older brother and mentor in Summers, and John in turn taught him the ways of the wharves. In 1897 Owen and Clara introduced him to their friend Mary.

It seemed an unlikely match, albeit perhaps a practical one in the Summerses' eyes. Mary was thirty-six and growing less marriageable by the day, even as she grew in self-confidence, success, and career satisfaction. She was also less fit for childbearing, an ambition that increasingly preoccupied her: She had in large part gotten what she wanted from life, but she did not yet have a child. John Beard was not worldly or well traveled, and he did not share her interest in the arts or the art world, but he was attractive in both his demeanor and his person (although at five foot ten slightly shorter than Mary) and by Portland's lights was not a negligible prospect for a husband. For Mary, John represented a chance to join, to become a Portlander by becoming married, middle class, and a mother to a genuine Oregon family.

Although not a love match, it was a relatively quick courtship. John and Mary were married on April 12, 1898, at Trinity Church, with Owen Summers and E. R. Krieger, a colleague of John's from the Customs House, as witnesses. Despite its venue, it was not a society wedding; it was a tying of two loose ends by well-meaning friends and mutual need. John packed himself and Lucille out of the unprepossessing quarters on East Eighth Street they had tolerated since arriving in Portland and moved into the Gladstone, a place now in the family and with room service, after a fashion.

Other Beard friends and relations followed, moving as semipermanent guests; siblings from Linn County, who came to enjoy and be impressed by brother John's good fortune and hospitality in the big city—hospitality for which, most presumed, there would be no bill. Close relations like John's brother Harold took up residence for weeks at a time. Paying guests in turn were displaced, and the Gladstone's revenues dropped. Moreover, not only did John's salary have a habit of getting spent before he reached home—it was not Mary's place to ask how—but he also had debts, due mostly to his persistent and expensive tastes in clothes, entertainment, and sex.

His appetite for these was matched only by his hunger for respectability: Within the next three years, for example, he would order the body of the now-deceased Harold disinterred from its rest-ing place in Lebanon to be buried in the family plot he insisted be purchased in Lone Fir, Portland's pioneer cemetery. Fortunately Mary had capital. By dint of her own hard work and Portland's good fortune through the late nineties, the Gladstone had appreciated in value. The time had come, all sensible minds insisted, to cash out; to give up this last vestige of Mary Jones, to build and have a home, and with her fortieth birthday but three years hence, to produce a child. It was, like her marriage to John, a decision that swept Mary before it, all the while believing that she could keep control of events but in truth being carried away by a tide of friends' good intentions, social convention, and her own ambivalence.

Two young women, in their dynamism and ambition not so much unlike Mary a few years before, were in the market for a business like the Gladstone. In 1899, only a year after her marriage to John Beard, Mary sold the business to Miss Murphy and Mrs. Cornell, who would within six years triple its size and rebuild at a new location. But the staff drifted away, notably Jue-Let, who disappeared into the warrens of Chinatown, where he could be reached by John or Mary only if they left notes at preappointed spots.

The Beards once again followed the lead of the Summerses, who had built an imposing house occupying an entire block at Twentieth and Madison on the east bank of the Willamette, now readily accessible by three bridges and a network of streetcars. In 1900 the Beards—or rather Mary, with about fifteen hundred dollars of the proceeds from the sale of the Gladstone—bought a house two blocks away at Twenty-first and Salmon, in a development called Hawthorne Park. A shingled Victorian cottage of two stories and a basement, with small porches at the front and rear, a front parlor, and a large kitchen, it was in every respect a modest, middle-class home with flowers in front and fruit trees behind.

In the suburban isolation of Hawthorne Park, the reality of Mary's situation became plain to her. She had already learned to keep her finances separate from John's and placed the title to the house in her name alone, an arrangement she followed in all money matters for the rest of her life. But the solid, comfortable Oregonian life she imagined she would attain seemed to have eluded her entirely. Her life was, she now understood with increasing bitterness, nothing like that of Clara Summers, who had society, servants, and

the kindness and dependability of Owen as a bulwark. Mary, by contrast, once a woman of affairs and of the world, found herself playing housekeeper to a vain, selfish, and irresponsible husband and his
daughter, a teenager who was simultaneously imperious, diffident,
and utterly lacking in energy or curiosity.

But Mary had no capacity to admit defeat, particularly to the
very friends and neighbors on whose terms she had so abjectly failed.
She set about to make the best of a bad lot: to create a modus
vivendi with John, a marriage of convenience as palatable as conditions and their respective characters would permit; to travel when
she could and pursue her interests in the theater and the arts; to have
a child; and to construct the best of all possible domestic worlds. She
told John she felt he had entered into the marriage under false pre-
tenses, and therefore she owed him little or nothing. She wanted to
have a baby, and thereafter they would lead separate lives, albeit
under the same roof, where they would behave as a family. But what
each did was to be, barring a gross breach of propriety, none of the
other's business. For Mary living well—or at least as well as circumstances and constraints allowed—would be the best revenge.

Two years later, in the autumn of 1902, when she was forty-one,
Mary found herself pregnant. Thus—the marriage finished save in
name—began the pattern of days that would round out John and
Mary's lives together. John, anointed with cologne, his collar fixed,
his tie knotted in a four-in-hand, his hair pomaded, his mustache
waxed, a cigar in his pocket, and a carnation in his lapel, closed the
door behind him and commenced his two-mile walk down
Hawthorne Boulevard and across the Willamette to the Customs
House and the wharves. Lucille was shunted out the door and down
the street to Washington High School. Then Mary, dressed since
dawn and her hair piled up atop her head—perhaps already having
done her marketing—strode back to the kitchen and rounded the
great oak table, a sewing machine anchored at its nether end. She
tied an apron, fetched alder from the porch, and fed the fire box of
the cast-iron range. In the tiny pantry she stood before the pastry
marble, her great wrists arching, her delicate hands kneading, and
was soon covered to her elbows in flour.

TWO

1903–1915

On May 5, 1903, Mary gave birth to an enormous baby, James Andrews Beard, weighing by various accounts thirteen or fourteen pounds. The child inherited from his forty-two-year-old mother her considerable height, big bones, pinkish complexion, and knowing, soft, round features; from his father, yet more girth, stretching to outright portliness, and perhaps a measure of debonair owlishness. But in later life James would not acknowledge even that measure of heredity from his father: For him as for Mary, he was the product of a near virgin birth, an act of sheer willpower on Mary's part. James was less an offspring of two parents than a clone of one.

He was also in his body—as he would be only fitfully in mind—a product of his time and place, the distilled image of the nation in its heedless, hungry, expansionist aspect; a fat, impudent, baron of a baby, spoiled and incapable of countenancing or comprehending lean times. He was a baby fit for a nation poised for prosperity and plenty, a nation that could not only satisfy the appetites of every consumer but whose entire purpose was increasingly consumption and the creation of new and better consumers. The body literally incorporates the facts of its age—its sexuality, its notions of the beautiful, and its health and diet—as well as its contradictions: to truly make flesh the physiognomies of the round-faced, tomato-cheeked Campbell Kids, the hourglass-figured beauty, or the tycoon with his moneybag-shaped potbelly was inadvisable if not impossible. By 1903, moreover, Americans were becoming ambivalent about both dietary and bodily fat, and in that respect James was something of a throwback: Born fat to a food-obsessed mother to whom fat, both in the diet and on the body, was the essence of food, he was the succulent incarnation of the home economists' dreaded "King Palate."

James's first memory of food was in keeping with this. Recovering from malaria at age three, he was spoon-fed pot after pot of chicken jelly—the very essence of chicken clarified and blended with egg white: "I craved its rich, salty flavor and smooth texture which seemed to line my throat with a cool, palate-tickling film," he wrote nearly forty years later. The spooning was done not by Mary but by Jue-Let—whose swinging queue was once again a household fixture and whom James could unreservedly and openly adore—a grown-up unencumbered by either John's distance or Mary's formidability.

The birth of James had resuscitated the manager in Mary. Lucille was now enrolled in a teacher-training course, and was in any event less than useless around the house. In the interim Owen Summers had arranged John's appointment as chief assistant appraiser at the Customs House at a higher salary, some small portion of which found its way back to Salmon Street each week. Mary's drive and domestic skills meant the house could be run on a sort of barter economy for very little cash, and household help was found in Chinatown. A nurse was hired to mind the infant James, followed by a Chinese amah. Jue-Let was a constant presence, although he valued his independence as much as Mary did hers and was therefore wise enough to her ways to refuse to become a regular employee or submit to a schedule. As ever, notes were passed or messages left beneath the hanging ducks, lanterns, and high, stilt-columned porches of Chinatown, and sometime thereafter Jue-Let would reappear at Salmon Street.

James was pampered by the amah and by Jue-Let while Mary administered her middle-class cottage like a chatelaine, arranging deliveries, supervising the help, and stocking the garden. There were eggs and sweet Jersey cream and butter from Mrs. Harris; celery from Foltz's; vegetables and fruit from Joe Galluzo and Delfinio Antrozzo; cheese from La Grande Creamery; and specialty and exotic groceries from Mayer's and Sealy-Dresser. What wasn't delivered was bought on streetcar or bicycle forays—Mary businesslike in a cape, boots, and fedora—at the Metropolitan Public Market downtown. Mary, too, was nearly as comfortable in Chinatown as John, picking up preserved ginger, candied kumquats, fresh water chestnuts, bean sprouts, and mandarin oranges just off the clipper.

The home garden held three Gravenstein apple trees, five cherry trees, a walnut and a plum, and a patch that yielded chives, shallots, onions, radishes, potatoes, peas, and sundry herbs. Inside the house was an endless round of domestic production: canning and preserving through the summer and into October; sausage making and ham curing in the autumn; mince and pudding manufacture before Christmas and tea blending thereafter; and always baking and more baking—all in addition to routine sewing, washing, ironing, cleaning, and firewood hauling and stoking. Through it all James scuttled about the kitchen floor in an easy, walruslike crawl, testing the flour bin; opening cupboard doors and banging iron skillets, bread pans, and baking sheets with a spoon; and sampling whatever food came into reach—once ingesting an entire onion.

In most of these domestic details, the Beard house was not so very different from other middle-class homes in Portland or anyplace else in the country. It was the form of Mary's household that was distinctive—the sensibility and attitude that permeated the place and its products, endowing them with an aura of superiority based not on class or wealth but Mary's conviction that she, like few others, knew and understood quality, the way in which things ought to be done. Unlike the majority of homemakers, Mary knew exactly what she wanted and how to get it. For most women running a house was a Sisyphean grind, but for Mary it was a career to be pursued with calm, professional competence. On Salmon Street pots never boiled over while the baby cried and a thunderstorm loomed over the wash drying on the line. Order reigned, and everything was under control.

The Beards also ate better than most comparable families. Mary knew where to shop, how to cook, and had catholic tastes based on travel and experience. Like most Portlanders of their class, they ate salmon, Dungeness crab, and Olympia oysters as daily staples, but menus for guests and holidays could be more ambitious and exotic with foie gras, white asparagus, and Jue-Let's roast boned shoulder of lamb with soy and garlic. In the autumn there was game—duck or pheasant roasted and served with grilled polenta squares—and winter brought a lengthy cycle of roast-beef-and-Yorkshire-pudding dinners, commencing with tomato soup and accompanied by puréed parsnips and home-canned-asparagus salad. Lunches for Mary's friends could be simpler and more conventionally ladylike fare, such as cold salmon or chicken, or, on a whim, turn substantial with a hearty pot-au-feu. Mary also had a penchant for startling juxtapositions. There was a Thanksgiving dinner that began with foie gras and smoked salmon, paused for turkey, and moved on to mince and pumpkin pies, running—rather like Mary herself—the gamut from Oscar Wilde to Laura Ingalls Wilder.

Christmas saw twenty guests—including Owen Summers in a Santa Claus suit—arrive for a midnight buffet of roast turkey, chicken, and Olympia oyster stew. On Christmas morning John fried porterhouse steaks and concocted hot buttered rum and Tom and Jerrys for an afternoon's drinking with friends from the wharves. The day ended with another roast turkey with giblet gravy, followed by fruitcake and Christmas puddings, which together with leftovers stretched through the short, dark, rainy days until New Year's dinner, held at House's Restaurant downtown. The chef, a friend of Jue-Let's named Billy, prepared a roast goose with apple-and-chestnut stuffing, and there was a box of anise-flavored springerle cookies for James, who was inevitably the only child present, entertaining the grown-ups with his precocity, worldliness, and infant wit.

Despite his early absorption into the adult universe, and the rarefied gastronomic air he breathed there and in Mary's kitchen, the food that genuinely moved James was in large part children's food—sweets and baked goods—though he had a number of idiosyncratic personal cravings that could only be filled by total immersion. Young James could eat chicken gizzards and hearts by the bucket and, more conventionally, Parker House rolls, cinnamon rolls, currant teacakes, crumpets awash with butter and strawberry jam; scones from Mrs. Stewart next door, which Mary drenched in 40 percent butterfat Tillamook cream; and Mary's trademark, thinly sliced rounds of onion on buttered fine white bread. Then there were visits to Swetland's downtown—"the first sanitary iceless soda fountain to be installed on the Pacific coast"—for clear and striped stick candy; candied violets; pineapple Melba; hot cherry punch; fig Celeste; crushed lemon sundaes, malts, and sodas; and ice cream upon ice cream.

By age five, when James started school at Hawthorne Elementary, he was already a head taller than most of his classmates, a round-faced, petulant child whose pouting expression even at rest seemed to foreshadow a stuck-out tongue. His frequent illnesses and girth meant he was incapable of playing hide and seek, cowboys and Indians, or any other game that involved running, jumping, or racing. He lived in a world apart: He had few friends among other children but avoided being bullied and teased by virtue of his size and considerable self-possession. For James the stuff and essence of child-hood would lie elsewhere—in the world of adults and the arts.

That same autumn a touring production of *Madama Butterfly* came to town, a not unusual occurrence with Portland figuring on the itineraries of a half dozen nationally and internationally known theater and opera companies. Mary took James, who at five was unlikely to comprehend much of the volcanic sentimentality, imperi-alism, racism, and sexual possession and obsession that were the opera's themes. Other Portland mothers might also have found the plot unsuitable for a small child: in particular the bloody climax, in which Butterfly cuts her own throat and crawls, arms outstretched, to the son she has surrendered to the American officer who married her for his sexual convenience while abroad, only to renounce her for a *"vera sposa americana"*—a "real American wife."

While the opera—and in particular this opera—may have been a questionable place to take a five-year-old, James was by his own account already sophisticated well beyond his years, and *Butterfly* was full of resonance for Mary: the perfect domesticity and perfect sacrifice of the foreigner for an American official; his willful and conscious use of her for short-term gain; her final heroism and redemption through self-sacrifice and a son. But Mary's self-abnega-tion was, unlike Butterfly's, only partial: Her son was not an inno-cent bystander in the drama of her life, but from far too early an age was compelled to be an actor in it. He sensed, if he did not under-stand, its dynamics, its irony, and its denouement, in which son dis-places husband. Though both too small and too enmeshed in adult affairs beyond his devising or ken to understand what he himself might feel, James knew his role. Recalling that first performance of *Madama Butterfly* years later, he said, "I cried. I suppose that was the appropriate response."

By the first decade of the century, Portland had become a radi-cally different city from the wooden-sidewalked, end-of-the-trail town in which Mary arrived in the 1880s. The population was reaching one hundred thousand, and the backroom coalition of Republican party regulars and business interests that had run the city for the past twenty years began to unravel. Scandal followed scan-dal—chiefly the fraudulent acquisition of federal timberlands and the hidden ownership of Portland's bridges, transport, and—not least—

vice operations by the city's leading business and social figures.

In June 1905 Portland elected Harry Lane, a Democrat from the east side of the Willamette, the middle-class stronghold of John and Mary Beard, as mayor. As in the New England from which the city claimed so much of its ancestry, in Portland hypocrisy and high principles had always worked in tandem, just as the Pacific Northwest as a whole thrived by simultaneously sanctifying and heedlessly squandering its environmental resources. With Lane's election, Portlanders asserted the need for their city's reform even as they celebrated its virtues with the Lewis and Clark Exposition of that same month. Two and a half million visitors, the Beards among them, took in the world's largest log cabin and other exhibits designed to put Portland on the map. By summer's end all save the log cabin were dismantled, and the fairgrounds in northwest Portland were converted by real estate speculators to freight yards, factory lands, and river-bottom warehouse districts.

As it had with the remnants of the Lewis and Clark Exposition, business was able to squeeze a buck from the public's high-mindedness—even varieties of reformist high-mindedness that appeared unmistakably antibusiness. One example was the public concern over the safety and purity of processed foods and meat, which had been mounting for years and reached a flash point with the publication of Upton Sinclair's *The Jungle,* a hair-raisingly melodramatic account of the Chicago stockyards and meat-packers. The result was the Pure Food and Drug Act of 1906, a landmark law—in part written by the giant processors whom the act was intended to police—that proscribed the food industry's worst abuses while reinforcing the dominance of its largest members, who enjoyed both close relations with government officials and economies of scale unavailable to their smaller competitors.

Nevertheless the act was a genuine boon to the consumer, bringing an end to bread whitened with alum, canned goods preserved with noxious chemicals, and adulterated and contaminated milk and meat products that were a fact of nineteenth-century life. But while the act and its sponsors assured consumers that what they ate met certain standards, those same consumers would find their choices in the marketplace increasingly defined by fewer and fewer but ever-larger food corporations. In addition to government-regulatory programs, other trends evident at the turn of the century favored the concentration of food processing in a few hands. Brand-name products, marketed with the kind of national advertising and distribution programs that only corporate capital could afford, began to overwhelm the grocery shelves, bolstered by the glamour that the era's cult of progress and modernity attached to anything produced in a factory under "scientific" controls. By 1913 Nabisco controlled 70 percent of the nation's biscuit trade; Swift had six processing plants and three hundred branch distributors; Jell-O was distributing fifteen million recipe books a year; and the use of canned goods from Heinz and others had increased fifteenfold from its level in 1900. Other factors would also change the way the nation cooked: the introduction of aluminum pots and pans and, in 1915, Pyrex; in 1912 the creation and rapid acceptance of Crisco, an industrially manufactured cooking fat; the rise of commercial bakeries; and the appearance and national spread of chain grocery stores, led by A&P. Companies like Heinz were already practicing what would come to be called "vertical integration," owning not only their own factories, but farms, jar and can manufacturing plants, railway cars, and distribution networks.

The results affected more than shopping and eating habits. The major cost factor in a family market basket was now not the food itself but its processing, packaging, marketing, and distribution—in effect, reflecting a massive transfer of income from farmers, bakers, fishermen, and other producers as well as small grocers and market stall holders to food processors and distributors. In all this the consumer was told she was both the chief beneficiary and ruler of the marketplace, with home economists quick to describe her role as an exalted and serious duty akin to citizenship itself. In reality the only power the consumer held was to choose from among the range of options dictated by the corporate food industry, options that increasingly excluded not only small producers, but also local and regional foodstuffs, in turn threatening both the diversity of foods and flavors available and the continued existence of local cooking and eating traditions.

By the time James entered elementary school in 1908, the domestic economy practiced by Mary—a household that consumed but also produced much of its food supply—was already something of an anachronism. More unusual still were Mary's direct contact and frequent friendships with those who supplied her in a time when the relationship between producer and consumer was increasingly mediated by processor and retailer. Mary not only knew most of the farmers and dairy people she bought from, but invited them home for lunch and to parties, often trading her own jams, baked goods, tea blends, and fruit for their produce.

Just before James's fifth birthday, the Beards' involvement with the producers of their food became still more direct. In partnership with colleagues from the Customs House, John purchased a large tract of land in Washington County west of Portland and, after selling off several small pieces to recoup his investment, installed a family named Ruley as tenant farmers. The Ruleys supplied the Beards with pork that was then cured in a smokehouse constructed in the backyard at Salmon Street. In turn Lucille, now a certified teacher, was shipped out to board with the Ruleys and teach in nearby Aloha.

Even as Mary strengthened the links between her food and the land, in most of the country they were gradually but inexorably being severed. The small family farm, such as that worked by the Ruleys, was already endangered, suffering a series of depressions and price collapses exacerbated by pressures from the food industry as well as growing indifference on the part of consumers to its fate. The home economics movement had made the domestic kitchen as valid an arena for women as the modern office or factory was for men even as it proceeded to strip cooking of much of its flavor and cultural and aesthetic meaning and pleasure. But part of that task depended on rendering food itself as sterile and tidy as chemical reagents in laboratory jars—to sever the messy, grubby, and, to the modern woman consumer, unappetizing links to the slaughterhouse, the dairy barn, the chicken coop, and the humus of the field. It meant preparing it in ways that tended to disguise its origins, and often its taste and aroma, whether by sculpting, decorating, or sealing beneath a carapace of white sauce, the universal glue—too often literally—that bound turn-of-the-century American cooking.

Still, flavor sometimes found a way of intruding its presence, and not everyone in the home economics movement was oblivious to it. In *The Boston Cooking School Cook Book*—the nation's most influential and bestselling cookbook until it was overtaken by *The Joy of Cooking* in the 1940s—Fannie Farmer offered recipes that, if not frankly sensuous, nevertheless showed an appreciation of contrasting flavors, surprising and amusing garnishes, and, most of all, sweetness. The mother of fruit salads, she combined whipped cream and chicken, mayonnaise and fruit, and bananas, potatoes, and Parmesan even as she furthered her milieu's penchant for molding, stuffing, and generally structuring and restricting food. At the turn of the century, food was allowed to taste of something and even to appeal directly to the senses, provided it did not get out of hand. The signature dish of the day, the molded sweet gelatin salad, was nothing so much as fruit cocktail and marshmallows in a corset.

If the domestic science agenda meant the distancing of the kitchen from the farm, it also meant minimizing the time spent in the kitchen itself—that smoky, hot, and forever messy sweatshop that was the workplace of American women—through the use of labor-saving appliances, ingredients, and cooking techniques. Following closely on the molding, salad, and white sauce crazes of the era was the chafing dish. Ingredients were assembled and prepared in the kitchen, brought to the dining room in a largely denatured state, and cooked in the chafing dish over a flame at the table, simultaneously taking the cook or hostess out of the kitchen and making her the star of a show of culinary artistry, a display of competence and craft at once domestic, glamorous, and—in the ubiquitous term of the period—"dainty." "Dainty" was the watchcry of turn-of-the-century domestic science, and "daintiness" the quality for which every woman strove, the polar opposite of the kitchen drudge, the household grind, and the dirty, unremitting thanklessness of women's previous lives. "Dainty" was feminine, ladylike, refined, light, and white or perhaps spring green in color. It did not boil or scrub or haul and carry: It floated, not of the earth but of the air.

The chafing dish had arrived in Portland by 1897, with the publication of Oregon's first commercial (rather than fundraising) cookbook, Alice Sansbury's *A Portland Girl at the Chafing Dish*—a slim volume that transported Portland's habitual Olympias in Cream Sauce to the tableside on clouds of fey, breathless prose. Five years later the Ladies Aid of the First Congregational Church issued a fundraising recipe compilation entitled *Dainty Dishes*. A far cry from the pedestrian if moneyed *Web-Foot Cook Book* of seventeen years before, *Dainty Dishes* was interleaved with poetry, uplifting quotations, and coy line drawings with captions in a loop-laden, art

nouveau–influenced backhand script that seems determined to levi-
tate off the page. The food was unremittingly white, with angel food
cakes, creamed fish, and vegetables of every description; salads
bound by mayonnaise and whipped cream, and milk and egg whites
abounding. Cream puffs, macaroons, meringues, and vanilla extract
loomed large in the baking section. Duskier, more ethnically inspired
dishes gained admittance only when they struck the right, ladylike
note, for example incorporating Fannie Farmeresque ingredients like
raisins and walnuts in stuffed chiles. Pie—the sweet, bountiful exemplar of the traditional American kitchen and the bane of domestic
scientists—was for the most part banished.

Dainty Dishes concluded with a remedy for dyspepsia, the ubiquitous nonspecific malady of the nineteenth century that was universally ascribed to overeating and, in particular, the consumption of
gross and unrefined cooking. The symptoms were gastric distress
and, more generally, a sensation of lassitude and heaviness. At the
turn of the century, however, among women dyspepsia was rapidly
replaced by neurasthenia as the condition of fashion. An affliction of
the nerves rather than the gut, it was associated with feelings of
faintness, light-headedness, and overall frailty and was often
described as "the vapors," its rise coinciding with that of another
wasting condition, anorexia nervosa.

Dainty food for neurasthenic bodies was accompanied by a
widespread change in the view of the body itself. Stoutness, once
symbolic of plenty and success, was increasingly viewed as a sign of
excess, ill health, sloth, and a lack of self-control. Regulation of the
body—through Houdini-like stunts, marathon fasts, and bizarre
dietary cults—was a running theme of late Victorian and early-twen-
tieth-century life, but so too was dietary reform based on legitimate
(if frequently misguided in practice) health concerns. It had also been
a tenet of the domestic science movement: As early as 1888 Maria
Parloa, the founder-teacher of the Boston Cooking School, wrote,
"All food . . . should be as light, porous, and free from fat as possible." A year later Sarah T. Rorer instructed that "dainty cooking,
not such as tempt men to gluttony, is what our housewives should
study," and was by 1917 featuring calorie totals for the recipes in
her cookbooks. Dainty food was ultimately not only a style, or even
a reflection of domestic science's aspirations for women, but one of
the first volleys in the incipient battle between Americans and their

appetites; a war that would begin with dainty recipes and "Fletcher-izing" (the slow-chewing regime founded by the fasting-and-bowel-regulation crank Horace Fletcher) and—with the bathroom scale an increasingly indispensable fixture in American homes—continue on through Metrecal, amphetamines, *The Drinking Man's Diet,* and NutriSystem. At the dawn of the twentieth century, fat was about to be abolished, the appetite controlled, the body regulated, and the garden and the kitchen put in their proper places. In food as in all things, modernity would turn the world upside down.

On Salmon Street no one counted calories, and the food remained hearty but refined, if rarely dainty—barring the occasion Lucille prepared a recipe for pineapple-and-grated-cheese salad learned at the YWCA, calculated both to annoy and revolt her step-mother. But the Beards had always been a family apart, if for no other reason that James's parents were on average some twenty years older than those of his contemporaries in the neighborhood—old enough to be the grandparents of the boys who tore up and down the still-semirural streets between James's house and Lone Fir Ceme-tery, while James sat inside and began teaching himself to read. But Mary would never have accepted a definition of herself as anything less than au courant. Portland was still a small place for someone of her experience and sensibility, and she found excuses to disappear to San Francisco for artistic, social, and gastronomic rehabilitation. At home, she continued James's cultural education, and he served as her escort at the opera, the theater, and in restaurants. In many respects James grew up in restaurants to nearly the same extent as he did in Mary's kitchen, and Portland's restaurants in many respects grew up with him: By the time he was eighteen, both they and he would be transformed. The trends that gave birth to daintiness, diets, and the new body were little felt in the restaurant business until Prohibition, and if the foodstuffs, recipes, and tastes that made up Mary's approach to food were slowly washing away in the tide of the con-sumer economy and the reform of the body, Portland's restaurants remained still comfortably familiar. Mary could talk shop, criticize, and give tips like a retired champ, and James could play the role of the boss's son.

House's—where the Beards often went as a family, where John ate lunch virtually every day, and where Mary frequently took James after a matinee—was a German American grill of a kind that was something of a Portland specialty. Founded in 1880 by Ernest House and staffed, inevitably, by Chinese chefs, it fed men like John Beard oysters—fried, stewed, pan roasted, and pepper roasted—steaks and chops accompanied by country fried potatoes in beef fat, cold meats and potato salad, and sandwiches of fried ham, pickled tongue, and roast veal with House's invincible cole slaw. Mary went for chicken, duck, and fried smelts in season. Just down Third Street, Hubers— another German place serving American food prepared by a Chinese chef (this one with enormous jade bracelets encircling his wrists and arms)—was also celebrated for its cole slaw but specialized (as it does to this day) in roast turkey. It, too, was the site of numerous family and pretheater meals, as was Swetland's, the sweet shop and soda fountain, which also had twenty ways with oysters and clams and did a lively trade in ladies' lunches of soup and salads. On other occasions, such as after a matinee with the Chicago, Henry Savage, or San Carlo Opera companies, James and Mary liked to repair to the Royal Bakery for a sandwich and marzipan cake or charlotte russe.

German American grills like House's, Hubers, and the Bohemian (another family favorite) served a kind of cooking that all the Beards could appreciate, but Mary's dining interests and aspirations for herself and for James ran both higher and wider—in particular to the city's more pretentious hotel dining rooms and to foreign restaurants that enjoyed somewhat "fast" reputations. Not easily impressed, she could be dismissive of the food at the city's grand hostelries like the Portland and the Multnomah, sending dishes back to the kitchen accompanied by advice on how the chef might improve his cooking, then moping for the duration of the meal, refusing to touch a bite of food.

More to Mary's taste were pseudo-French places like Falt's Quelle, a "gay" joint with music, a bar, hors d'oeuvres, and a menu of simple but dignified fish and meat dishes. Patronized by "travelling men" and their escorts, it offered a taste of sophisticated bohemian nightlife rarely available in Portland. By Mary's well-traveled and worldly standards, it was both tame and faintly seedy, but it revivified a part of her that Oregon life with John on Salmon Street starved. She became close friends with the proprietress, Mrs. Falt, and with James frequently visited her home.

Neighbors would have found Mary's patronage of Falt's Quelle of questionable propriety: Like most Americans they tended to view the mere consumption of fancy European food with suspicion, an attitude reflected in the then-common usage of the term *French restaurant* to denote a bordello. Her visit to the Louvre—Portland's most notorious drinking and dining establishment—with five-year-old James in tow would have outraged them. Like the turn-of-the-century "lobster palaces" on New York's Broadway, the Louvre provided dancing, oysters, champagne, and private dining rooms where men could entertain (and sometimes be sexually serviced by) showgirls and pedigreed call girls. James later recalled, "Mother was out of her mind to take me there."

Such experiences provided James with a kind of excitement unavailable, and probably unimaginable, to other children. However, they also took a toll, not only making James more Mary's child and less John's but also making it increasingly difficult for him to be a child at all. Mary's early life had been one of countless moves from place to place and removal from her parents and siblings, engendering both a pressure and an inclination to grow up fast. James's outward circumstances were vastly different—childhood on Salmon Street with its nice families and nice schools could and should have been an Oregonian idyll—but Mary seemed determined to plunge James straight into her vision of adulthood. Portlanders and other Americans would have disapproved of James's diet and the places he partook of it: It and James's general upbringing were clearly an unseemly and unhealthy immersion in the most disreputable corners of the public world and its excesses. James's ever-mounting girth was an outward sign of a spoiled and worldly child whose parents ought to have known better. By the time he was six, James was by his own later estimation petulant, rude, impossibly precocious, lonely, and insecure. Despite his weight and height his sense of his own self seemed diminished to the point of weightlessness, drifting and detached from any person, affection, or place.

As it happened there would be a refuge at the edge of the world, a beach below the mouth of the Columbia River on the Pacific Coast where one hundred years earlier Lewis and Clark had ended their two-year-long journey to the Pacific; a place of wrenching tides, icy winds, towering rocks, and stinging fogs that Clark described as "tempestuous and horiable." From the site of present-day Astoria, Lewis and Clark had followed the Necanicum River south past a strand of dunes and meadow on which an Iowa farmer named Philip Gearhart would establish a claim in 1845. But sandy soil and an almost totally inaccessible location made profitable farming impossible, and in 1888 the land was sold and renamed Gearhart Park. But two miles to the south, Portland hustler and tycoon-vulgarian Ben Holladay had built a hotel at Seaside, a town destined to become Oregon's Coney Island, and soon a railway connecting it—and Gearhart—to Astoria followed.

Gearhart was conceived from the start as a summer resort for Portland's better families, with a hotel, "Natorium" (an indoor salt-water swimming pool), golf course, and cottages along the ridge overlooking the beach following in quick succession. By the end of the century, Gearhart was well established as the retreat of choice for fashionable Portlanders, its sedate good taste in striking contrast to the relentless salt-water taffy honky-tonk of Seaside.

Around the time of James's birth in 1903, Mary had struck up a friendship with Polly Hamblet, an Englishwoman who shared her interest in food and in setting a good table. Polly's husband, Harry, was an entrepreneur whose schemes had a habit of going sour, the result of an innate generosity at odds with the ruthless character the times seem to have required as well as of plain bad luck: A lucrative oyster-raising business faltered, for example, when thirty thousand dollars' worth of stock froze on an eastbound train. By 1906 Hamblet began building capacious, shingled houses in Gearhart directly on the beachfront in a strip whose cachet among the cocktail party set eventually earned it the name Gin Ridge. The Hamblets—Harry, Polly, and an angelic-faced daughter, Mary, born in 1906—built, occupied, and moved from one house to the next down the ridge as each was sold. By 1909 the Beards had joined the Hamblets at the beach for the summer, and in 1910 Mary purchased land and built a tiny cottage in a meadow well back from the beach. As was the case with Salmon Street, title was solely in her name, and even more than in Portland, the house was to all intents and purposes hers alone. As if in tacit acknowledgment of this, John claimed to dislike Gearhart and rarely rode the Friday afternoon "Daddy Train" down from Portland, by which other fathers joined their summering wives and children each weekend.

Gearhart would have been the stuff of dreams for any child—its dunes full of spots for hiding and for forts, its tidal flats and pools teeming with clams and crabs, and the Necanicum perfect for toy boats, rafts, and catching crayfish—but for James it was more. It was a haven from the loneliness and insecurity of his Portland neighborhood, a haven where he and his mother could be together without the distraction of other claims on her attention, a place apart from her worldly ambitions for herself and for him. Moreover, in Gearhart James could choose to do the things he liked to do and excelled in—walking, swimming, and catching sea creatures—rather than attempt to meet and inevitably fail the expectations of the children on and around Salmon Street. He could also choose his own friends, and he chose Mary Hamblet.

Mary was three years younger than James, a girl, and had been slightly crippled by polio as a toddler. In these respects friendship with her was unthreatening, and for perhaps the first time in his life James could set the pace in a relationship. But Mary refused to be dominated: She was and remained fiercely independent and strong-willed, and her first response to James was to inform her parents that she didn't wish to play with "that fat little boy" again. But Mary brought out in James—and he in her—a happier, stronger self; one that was funny in a dry, faintly mocking tone and one gripped by an imagination and energy that could construct games, plans, and projects amid the magical dunes and looming rocks of Gearhart.

Mary's parents also provided James with the kind of family life he craved. Polly—known to all the children as "Grammie" despite never having had grandchildren—was steady and affectionate, and her company tempered James's mother's habitual aloofness and impatience. Harry was a hearty, handsome, gentle Santa Claus of a man; the kind of man who, like Owen Summers, James wished his father was; the kind of man he was to spend his life searching for. For the rest of his childhood, life for James was Gearhart: Mary Hambler and her pony on the beach, dawn plunges into the treacherous Pacific surf, dives from the rafters of the Natorium, pulling crayfish from the Necanicum on strings, and countless picnics and cookouts on the beach with the Hamblets.

If Mary Beard necessarily left her bohemian and cultural preoccupations behind in Portland, she nevertheless transported her usual domestic and gastronomic arrangements to Gearhart with her cus-

tomary thoroughness and fastidiousness. Food and household supplies were planned as though she were launching a military campaign—a summer's worth of wax paper and toilet tissue was packed
along with trunks of clothing, books, and miscellany—and regular
food shipments from reliable Portland merchants arranged. Each
June all this, together with lunch, was hauled down to the station,
where the four-hour journey up the Columbia to Astoria and thence
southward to Gearhart began. For James, perched in his proprietary
seat on the smoke- and cinder-blasted open observation car, the trip
had features of both an imperial progress and a jungle expedition. By
the age of six, James had discovered that people (or at least some
people) wanted to do things for him—that his sassy, spoiled, and
imperious demeanor drew favor as sweet Tillamook cream drew
bees—and although the train in theory had no food on board, the
train's longtime porter, Jimmy, supplied him from a cache of snacks
and sweets.

At Gearhart the train stopped deep in the woods, and Mary and
James would be met by William Badger, who had already opened the
house and now hauled the bags alongside the boardwalk that passed
through the trees and into the meadows and dunes toward the sea.
Perhaps twenty feet square, and about three blocks back from Gin
Ridge in a place known simply as "the meadow," the house was a
one-story, peak-roofed gnome's cottage on stilts with a porch.
Socially and economically it stood in relation to Gin Ridge as
Salmon Street did to the Summerses Madison Street manse, but as
she had done in Portland, Mary was equal to the task of making
both modesty and necessity a virtue—specifically, by becoming a specialist at cooking, eating, and entertaining out-of-doors.

Gearhart food—the food that would blanket James's memory
and consciousness like a warm, slightly frayed but freshly laundered
quilt for the rest of his life—lent itself to such treatment. On the
Pacific Coast at the mouth of the Columbia, it rained salmon, halibut, sturgeon, and Dungeness crab all summer; berries—fraises des
bois, salmonberries, thimbleberries, blackberries, and huckleberries—grew like weeds; and the rivers, bars, and beds were fat with
razor clams, crayfish, and oysters. It was all food best left alone,
either eaten raw, grilled, or steamed, and accompanied by peas from
Seaside and a piece of Cheddar from the Waterhouse farm down the
coast. So there were picnics amid the dune grass and on the beach

and, more daringly, outdoor cooking in and under the sand with driftwood coals—a proposition a little disconcerting for Oregonians whose families had given up the wagon trail and the campfire only forty or fifty years before.

Mary's picnics were a world away from sandwiches consumed on top of a blanket. Although picnic standbys like hard-boiled eggs figured in the menu, they came wrapped in decorated papers, together with napkins folded origami-style and individual baskets with a name tag fastened to each one. Within a short while it was fashionable for visitors to Gearhart to have Mrs. Beard cater such meals, a service she performed for a small and select clientele. For the lucky few and herself, James, and friends like the Hamblets, there were clam chowder, clam broth, clam fritters, clam-and-corn soufflé, and scalloped clams with cracker crumbs; deviled crab, cracked crab, or crab salad served in Chinese peach-blossom bowls; stuffed salmon, pickled cold salmon, and grilled salmon cheeks; fricassee of chicken; hash browns in cream; and popovers and huckleberry preserves. Simpler daily fare began with sour-milk pancakes and bacon for breakfast; sandwiches of roast beef, tongue, and chicken with Grammie Hamblet's egg, mayonnaise, and potato salad plus berry tarts and pies for lunch; and for dinner perhaps wild mushrooms sautéed in butter with ham, scrambled eggs, a salad of dandelion greens with sprigs of wild mint, and a piece of cheese.

For James, as for any child, cooking on the beach itself was possessed of a kind of magic: The outdoors and indoors unexpectedly mingled and harmonized in sizzle and smoke; the sear of the fire on legs, arms, and cheeks; the granular cool of the sand; and the low, incessant simmer of the surf. Steaks and salmon were grilled for the adults and frankfurters and hamburgers—sometimes with onion, garlic, and herbs—for the children. Whole potatoes wrapped in wet newspaper nestled in the coals, and afterward there were popcorn and marshmallows. The evenings—June and July's fog giving way to August's starry, moonlit indigo—passed deliciously and slowly into sleep in the smell of summerhouse blankets and faintly damp sheets.

Mary and James were habitually early risers, generally up by six to dig clams, catch crabs, or walk on the beach. James, a proficient and fearless swimmer with no other athletic inclinations, swam every morning and generally later in the day as well. After breakfast Mary packed James a few sandwiches, and he collected a friend or two for play in the woods or on the beach. Much of that play revolved around food, as when James constructed a mold of sand, seawater, and pink marshmallows that he compelled Mary Hamblet to taste. But some efforts were more serious, and amid the fort building and imaginary South Seas expeditions that were staples on the beach and in the dunes, at age ten James began to conduct his own experiments in outdoor cooking. At first, tiny fish from the Necanicum were incinerated over hastily gathered piles of bark, dried beach grass, and twigs, but as the weeks went on, James came to understand the principle of cooking slowly over coals rather than quickly over flames. He also began to raid the larder at home and eventually turned out a credible seaside meal of ham grilled on a toasting rack, roast potatoes, and coffee.

Over and above such days on the beach, or in the Natorium, or racing around the hotel, Mary or the Hamblets organized day trips, generally in the Hamblets' carriage or, slightly later, in Harry's car— one of the first in Gearhart. They made quick forays into the otherwise beyond-the-pale Seaside for a milkshake in one of twenty-eight flavors at West's Dairy, but most expeditions were more bucolic: down the coast to the high bluffs and towering rocks of Ecola or Cannon Beach, or northward to the wreck of the *Peter Iredale,* a British bark consumed by the coastal tide in 1906, at Clatsop Beach. At the cottage, friends of Mary's and visitors from Portland came and went, as did neighbors who shared the Beards' devotion to food—the Marias, the Antiches, and the people next door, whose French cook raised Mary's competitive hackles.

When John turned up, as he did on occasional weekends, the family went swimming, three egg-shaped figures identical in basic form but varied in size, whose arrival on the beach Gearhart regulars awaited with barely concealed amusement. But, as he did from time to time at home, John also made sporadic attempts to do the things a father ought to do with and for his son. Naturally enough he gravitated away from Mary's Gearhart axis north to Astoria on the Columbia, where he had connections and acquaintances on the wharves and—as was his wont—in the Chinese community. He showed James what he loved—boats, docks, bridges, and, above all, things that came from China—and told him of life on the Oregon Trail when he was five; of wagons, hunting, and the stomach-churning threat of Indian attack; and of the last few miles of passage along this river, the Columbia, to the head of the Willamette, the gate of the damp, green, God-blessed paradise that was Oregon.

James tried to love what John loved, but, save for the drama of pioneer life and the Oregon Trail, without much conviction. Even had John been so inclined, there was no chance of his entering James's affections on an equal basis with Mary, and no way for James to entertain—or comprehend—his doing so. So John made an effort with James as blood ties and duty dictated, but with the feigned enthusiasm and stilted energy of one who knows he has lost before he has begun. He accepted his separate life from Mary and, in James's memory, at times relished it: Barred from the Salmon Street kitchen for most of the year except for his weekly ritual preparation of Sunday breakfast, during Mary's summer absences he was free to roast meat and game to blackness and fry smoked fish in bacon fat, filling the kitchen with aromas from the Oregon Trail that clashed head-on with the haze of incense burning among the heaps of good and awful Chinese bric-a-brac in the front parlor.

Summer's end was hard for James, and with each season in Gearhart his disenchantment with life on Salmon Street grew, the company of Jue-Let being one of the few consolations of returning from the beach. He read and knitted while other children played and roamed the streets and parks, and although he was rarely teased—given his imposing size, it might not have seemed worth the risk—his sense of his separateness from that community became more acute, as did a conviction that he was disliked and disapproved of. But in other respects life grew easier, particularly as his native charm, good humor, energy, and generosity began to emerge. In any event Mary brought home some of the spirit of Gearhart, and by the time he was eight, James's birthday parties were the stuff of legend. Mary knew how to entertain children with the same skills she brought to bear on adults.

Each May Mary transported twenty or so of the neighborhood children, together with vast quantities of sugar and coconut-laden food, to Washington Park in Portland's western hills or to the Oaks, a privately owned amusement park and pleasure ground reachable by streetcar. The Oaks, opened in 1907 and chockablock with rides and concessions of a reasonably decorous sort, was an immediate hit with middle-class Portlanders and their children. Birthday parties there were an opportunity for Mary and, increasingly, James to play host with food from midday until seven in the evening; with sweets, sandwiches, cakes, and pies that made a much stronger impression on guests than did the still diffident and somewhat distant James himself. James was remembered as bookish and as a boy more interested in people and conversation than in games or in attending dancing school, a rite of passage required of the rest of neighborhood children. Always bigger than anyone else, James was also on the surface considerably more grown-up in his interests and attitudes, less a child than an adult-in-waiting.

James busied himself more and more in the kitchen—burning but then mastering bread by age eight—and continued his cultural education under Mary. By the time he was nine, he showed a talent for singing and participated in the choir at Trinity Church. The Beards had little appetite for religion but appreciated the blue-blooded cachet of the congregation. John in any case felt by virtue of his background that he did indeed belong among them, noisily striding up the aisle to his accustomed pew at Trinity each Sunday and joining Auld Lang Syne, a club for men whose families had arrived in Oregon in the pioneer era. However, when the twenty-eight-year-old Lucille married a real estate salesman named Clarence Ruff later that year, economics dictated that the ceremony be held at home on Salmon Street.

Conditions became both crowded and tense as the newlyweds took up residence for the next few years in what had always been more a cottage than a house. But James was now old enough to accompany Mary on some of her trips away from Portland, absences for James previously shrouded in mystery and a sense of abandonment. Now at least once a year Mary and James would go by train or ship to San Francisco to gorge themselves on the arts, food, and the fascinating people Mary knew there: actors, decorators, singers, and strong women like herself in the hospitality business. They shopped—Mary purchasing the best outsize underwear for James—and attended plays and operas, seeing Tetrazzini sing *Lucia* and Pavlova dance. But above all there was food in sophisticated company at Solari's, sumptuous buffet lunches at Marquand's, tea under the glass-covered central court of the Palace Hotel, crab, sand dabs, and abalone at Jack's, and dinner among the city's glamour brigade at Tait's.

At home James consolidated his friendship with Mary Hamblet, as their mothers spent each Saturday together. Sometimes John would take both children downtown, either to the Customs House, where Mary and James played in John's paneled office or, more likely, to Chinatown. Headily exotic on any day, during Chinese New Year the streets pulsed with costumes and noise. Every year at this time, John made formal calls at the homes of virtually everyone he knew in Chinatown, usually with the children in tow. At each stop tea was served and the children given sweets of ginger and mandarin orange. The day ended with dinner, usually at the home of a merchant named Jue-Su, from whose lofty balcony above Second Avenue the festivities could be observed.

At about this time in 1913, when James was ten, Jue-Let left Portland on a ship bound for China, from which he was never to return. He had been a steady if sometimes elusive presence, and his departure devastated James. James had adored Jue-Let, not least for his capacity to stand up to Mary's steam-driven single-mindedness and intransigence, frequently on James's behalf. Now he was in many ways alone, although the spirit of China still lay heavy on Salmon Street as a result of his father's growing collection of orientalia, which had collided with and finally overwhelmed Mary's perfectly polished English brasses in their parlor nook. At home John had taken to wearing Chinese tunics and slippers, shuffling through the fogbank of incense in the front parlor with a cigar wedged in his hand, a sight neighborhood children found both intriguing and bizarre.

John had always engaged the services of prostitutes and often kept mistresses, a practice his generation tacitly accepted as the only way of accommodating men's sexual needs and those of society for upright, chaste wives and stable families. By the turn of the century, however, feminism, a reformist sense of public interest in private morality, and a belief that marriage ought to be more for love than convenience combined to make such arrangements increasingly less acceptable. But Mary and John's marriage was scarcely even convenient, and each had the other's unspoken consent to go his or her own way. John had become more at home in Chinatown than on Salmon Street, shrouding himself in the Orient as the happy family, compliant wife, and pioneer privilege of his own Oregon dream receded before the reality of his willful, haughty spouse and her spoiled and distant son. Sometime before 1910 he took (and kept for many years to come) a Chinese mistress—a Chinese wife, in reality— and together they had at least one son. In an ironic variation on *Madama Butterfly,* John played a Pinkerton for whom the Asian wife was the *"vera sposa."*

In later years James claimed to have met his half brother and other members of his father's second household, presumably during John's weekend walkabouts through Chinatown. If the occasion caused him any stress, he seemed unaware of it and, in any case, by age ten, James was largely inured to his emotional circumstances; to a father who, in the words of a Salmon Street neighbor, "simply didn't exist" and a mother for whom he was less the object of unequivocal love than a "project" through which vicariously to explore her own frustrated needs. As an adult in New York, James would relate all this as a strand of exotic, faintly amusing lore about bygone times on the nation's nether shore, but the tone was defensive—an attempt to transform the sad and bitter facts of his boyhood through the sophisticate's habitual pose of ironic insouciance.

He also claimed to have discovered his homosexuality at this time, and to have explored it deep in the woods and behind the dunes at Gearhart with other boys—and probably with men as well—over subsequent summers. Mary had openly discussed sex of all persuasions and types with James and cautioned him not to believe whatever dreadful things he might hear about masturbation. Then as later he was drawn to boys who were handsome and who either were for the most part heterosexual or could pass for it: generous, kind, attentive, and patient men who were or would become husbands to mothers and fathers to sons in the kind of happy family that lay just out of James's reach but was evident to his eyes everywhere in Portland. But James himself was not handsome anymore than John was the father he would have wished, and in his early sexual experiences it seems likely that he both exploited younger boys and was himself exploited by those older than him.

By the time James was twelve, he had begun to participate in amateur dramatic productions in Portland, and in these as in singing he showed some talent and promise, enough so that Mary enrolled him in acting classes. Initially he was everything in these endeavors that Mary might hope for, but he also displayed fits of rebelliousness that she found intolerable: For the first time James's long-standing insecurity and flimsy conviction that he was also someone special— self-esteem founded on a thin, brittle crust of self-loathing—fused to produce the stung resentment that is the adolescent's incurable and perennial stock-in-trade. When James was thirteen, Mary seems to have decided that he needed the experience of a proper English school—or at least an approximation of one.

Canada was as close to England as Mary's budget could manage, and so James was sent north to Vancouver, British Columbia, to board at a boys' school staffed by English and Scottish masters. James was habituated to his parents' prolonged and sometimes unexplained absences, and in that respect boarding school life was not so different from life on Salmon Street. But it was his first encounter with a society consisting wholly of other children, with a highly regimented daily routine, and, perhaps not least, with the starch, stodge, and boiling of institutional food. It did not go well, and James left— or was asked to leave—before the year was out.

He bided his time at home until admission to Washington High School, the public school a few blocks away and next door to Hawthorne Elementary, could be arranged. He read novels and history and walked great distances, sometimes all the way down Hawthorne Boulevard to the bridge over the Willamette, just across the river from the Customs House and the restaurants and theaters of downtown Portland. Walking what he was to call "that lonely road" and pacing the bridge, he constructed dialogues with the people in his life and with Portland in general, conversations with those who disapproved of him, who criticized him, and who said cruel things about him; conversations to be held once he was famous and lived in New York, far away from the rosebushes and neatly stacked sidewalk woodpiles of this small-minded, hypocritical timber town. He would return here someday, and his celebrated voice, his clothes, his bearing, the sparkle in his eye, and the very fact of his name would mock them. He would cultivate the world and harvest fame and serve it forth.

THREE

1916–1923

By the spring of 1917, when he turned fourteen, James's life was on a surer, happier course, albeit in directions set by Mary. He continued to appear in local amateur and community theater productions, sometimes receiving a token payment for his work, and for the first time he began to participate in the community of his contemporaries in the neighborhood and at Washington High School. Still bookish by nature, he impressed his teachers by plowing through Turgenev, Tolstoy, and biographies by the dozen on his own while completing his class reading list well in advance of his cohorts. He signed on to the school library committee in his sophomore year, organizing displays on subjects that interested him and writing up library activities for the student monthly, *The Lens*. In what was to be his first appearance in print—and to foreshadow the stilted prose that would afflict him all his life—he wrote:

All Portland was enthusiastic over the coming opera season, and our bulletins showed pictures from the operas to be presented. Stories of different operas, and biographies of various composers were shelved below the pictures. . . . Of special interest to the boys is the present group of prints, portraying all the different forms of aeroplanes and air-ships. . . . All boys are more or less interested in the great machines of the air, and should surely find absorbing reading here.

It is unlikely that James was any more intrigued by aircraft than "all Portland" was by the opera, however much James might wish it were. Portland had cultural pretensions and was not without gastronomic interest, but to James's mind it remained a backwater oblivious to its own considerable shortcomings. Indeed, other people—chiefly outsiders—had begun to take James's view of his hometown. An article entitled "Portland the Spinster," which appeared a year before in *Collier's Weekly*, contrasted the city's smug pride in its clean downtown sidewalks with the urban squalor that reigned a few blocks to the north, and a reporter from England remarked: "Portland's biggest vice is her exaggerated virtue." He also noted that "Women are probably slaves all over the world, but it seems worse in Oregon." That same year John Reed, journalist/enfant terrible and socialist son of one of the city's most eminent and wealthy families, persuaded Margaret Sanger, America's pioneer birth control crusader and a friend of his from Greenwich Village, to lecture in Portland. Like Emma Goldman—another radical comrade of Reed's, who had been prosecuted in Portland the previous year for violation of a city ordinance proscribing the distribution of obscene literature—Sanger was promptly arrested on the same charge, an adjunct to Portland's two-year-old movie censorship program. A jury convicted and fined her.

Ironically, Oregon's newly enfranchised women were coconspirators in creating such an atmosphere, and electoral records reveal their penchant for conservative candidates during this period. From the standpoint of Portland women—too often the victims of the violence and domestic instability fostered by a milieu that boasted the world's longest bar at Erickson's Saloon on Burnside Street—the civic enforcement of morality seemed more progressive than repressive. That was particularly true of alcohol abuse, and Oregon declared its own Prohibition in January 1916, three years ahead of the rest of the nation. As was Portland's wont, however, once the principle was established, it was loosely enforced and had little impact on the city's appetite for discreetly managed vice. At least one middle-class lady commented that Prohibition's chief effect was that "now our husbands come home for lunch."

If Prohibition meant Portlanders were eating at home more frequently, it also meant that they—and Americans generally—were eating in restaurants less. No single event altered the course of gastronomy in America more radically than the fourteen years of national Prohibition that began in 1919. As a practical matter, restaurants then as now depended on alcohol sales for a crucial portion of their revenue and without them many were ill equipped to survive. Prohibition effectively halted in its cradle the development of the serious, cooking-conscious restaurant which only recently had begun to evolve from the plutocratic trough feeding of Delmonico's and the lobster palaces to the nascent but well-intentioned European-inspired, quality-conscious places Mary liked to patronize.

It also assured the triumph of the dainty, dull, and denatured food advocated by the domestic science movement, consolidated the increasingly dominant position of corporate agriculture and food processing in the nation's diet, and further promoted the desirability of a race of healthy and lean Americans wary both of their cooking's caloric content and of its aesthetic appeal. The intemperate use of alcohol and the intemperate consumption of dyspepsia-promoting food—whether gourmet or simply hearty American-style—were by now firmly linked in the public imagination.

Prohibition helped snuff out what in retrospect seemed to be a brief golden age of food in Portland's markets, hotels, restaurants, and homes during James's early adolescence—a last gasp of appetite before the dry, lean days ahead. In 1913 the city had seen the publication of its most ambitious charitable food compendium yet, *The Portland Woman's Exchange Cook Book*. The names and families of most of the contributors were familiar from *Dainty Dishes* (and even from *The Web-Foot Cook Book* of nearly thirty years before), and it was clear that egg-based entrées, chicken dishes in cream and white sauces, and molded salads and puddings had not lost their grip on Portland ladies of refinement and style. But such recipes no longer dominated the collection, and there was a new diversity and robustness to much of the food; a fusion of the covered wagon, Fannie Farmer, and the city's better hotel cooking founded on a sophisticated openness to new things—including ethnic and foreign food—from chicken Escoffier to tamales.

There were more than a dozen recipes for curries—a trend that reached America via Imperial Britain—as well as for pasta and polenta, followed by gutsy stews of beef, mutton, and terrapin; sausages, brawn, and soon-to-be-despised organ meats; and a cornucopia of pies and cakes. Manifold tastes and influences crowded each page: Halibut cheek salad, pâté de foie gras, and fruit salad appeared on one, while haute-cuisine béarnaise and hollandaise joined domestic science's universal white sauce on another. Oranges, lemons, and grapefruit were ubiquitous, as they had been for years, but new ingredients like pineapples, avocados, and Roquefort cheese were making their way into Portland's kitchens. Other, sometimes less benign trends were also apparent: Recipes for baked goods invariably featured baking powder—a chemical substitute for natural leavening—and bread doughs incorporated sugar, a practice encouraged both by the burgeoning sugar industry and the flour milling industry's overrefined product.

If food begins with the farm and ends in the kitchen, it does so by way of the market, and the diversity and interest of the food in *The Portland Woman's Exchange Cook Book* reflected the variety and richness of Portland's food suppliers. Although the city was well-provisioned by virtue of its bountiful local foodstuffs and its position as a center of Pacific Coast and international trade, Portland had never possessed a genuine farmer's market. Indeed, the city fathers prided themselves not only on their clean sidewalks but on the absence of street vendors and stalls, a view in which they were encouraged by food retailers and those who held one of the limited number of concessions available in the Metropolitan Public Market on Third Street. But in 1914 an open public market was created on Yamhill Street, where farmers and producers could deal directly with the public. Food prices fell, choice increased, and other less tangible benefits ensued, not least a vibrant civic mix of diverse people and classes that Portland had rarely experienced before. For James it was, together with Gearhart and the stage, one of the magical settings in his life, a place where food was given its due.

Restaurants, too, remained a favorite haven during James's adolescence, but as Prohibition took its toll, good ones were becoming more difficult to find, although there were noteworthy exceptions. During his first year at Washington High School in 1917, James was befriended by a boy named Chester Benson, the son of lumber tycoon Simon Benson. Chester's parents were divorced, and he and his mother lived not far from Salmon Street. James and Mary—a divorced family themselves in all but name—quickly hit it off with the Bensons, Mary and Chester's mother baking and taking tea together while Chester and James talked theater and ran up bills at Chester's father's hotel downtown. The hotel, formerly the Oregon, which Simon Benson had bought four years earlier and rechristened the Benson, was a deluxe establishment that quickly rivaled the Portland in its cachet and in the quality of its food and accommodations. Its Franco-Swiss chef, Henri Thiele, was arguably the best in Portland, and their friendship with the Bensons gave Mary and James access to the city's most exacting food and the people who cooked and consumed it.

In his heyday at the Benson, Thiele prepared a cuisine—part French, part Swiss, part Anglo-Oregonian—that was to linger in James's memory for the rest of his life: paupiettes of sole garnished with Olympia oysters; crabmeat Newburg on muffins or brioche; poached fillets of salmon stuffed with salmon mousse; crayfish meat blended with avocado, mayonnaise, and cream; and a Princess Charlotte pudding of thick praline-studded cream with cassis sauce—a dish James would later try repeatedly to re-create, but without success. Thiele was by all accounts brilliant, and he introduced Portland to genuine French haute cuisine, prepared according to the standards established by Georges Auguste Escoffier and served with European self-assurance. America, and particularly America's rich and those who catered to them, had toyed rather nervously with French cuisine since Jefferson occupied the White House, and French—or a sort of Franglais—was the official language of the best people's menus, even if the food itself was the usual oysters, game, and roasts.

But events in the late nineteenth century in France itself, and particularly in the kitchens of hotels such as the London Ritz, produced a systematized and codified version of French cooking that lent itself to importation into the world's high-class hotel dining rooms—including the Benson. As in music and the theater, a standard repertoire of "classic" dishes—sometimes but a few years old—now appeared and could play from Paris to Portland, usually featuring meat, fish, and an emulsified sauce and lent structure and decorum by sculpted garnishes, carapaces of aspic, and the baroque heaping up of deluxe ingredients like foie gras. The difference between a molded dish by Fannie Farmer and one by Escoffier—both of whom were prime examples of the emerging phenomenon of the chef/food writer as star—had to do less with aesthetic form than with sheer social, economic, and ideological content: The food itself was highly structured and denatured and aimed to celebrate the aspirations— whether to daintiness and propriety, style and sophistication, or imperial and financial power—of its consumers. Moreover, however much they were the inheritors of traditions going back hundreds of years, Escoffier and Farmer were innovators: Whether described as reform or novelty, what they offered was new, and innovation was the driving engine of consumerism and its heralds in the media.

French haute cuisine thus swept the world's moneyed precincts, even if only fitfully in the United States, where public mores and Prohibition caused its commercial disappearance, eventually driving it into an underground peopled by "gourmets" and the well-to-do that paralleled the speakeasy of the 1920s. The career of Henri Thiele was to follow the general course taken by cooking in the United States, whose tastes were moving increasingly toward the soda fountain, the coffee shop, and the cafeteria. By the 1920s, having left the Benson, he launched a business that sent packed lunches out to office workers and then established a popular family-style restaurant, open from dawn to midnight, a mile west of downtown Portland, which was to survive both his and James's deaths.

All these developments served to cap the end of a childhood whose milestones and memories were etched in marketing, cooking, and meals. But, like James's childhood, the efflorescence of good food evident in the market, the Benson, and *The Portland Woman's Exchange Cook Book* was brief and, however vivid in the sudden and uncanny déjà vu of a smell or a taste experienced years later, seemingly irrecoverable. In a culture simultaneously intoxicated with the vision of a future based on technology and unsure of its own worth, there was little sense that anything was being lost in the dietary and food production and distribution changes then under way. But there were dissenting voices, from which Mary and James might have taken some solace. One of them was that of Henry Finck, a widely traveled New York journalist born just south of Portland. In 1913, while the ladies of Portland produced their cookbook and the Yamhill Market was being planned, he published *Food and Flavor,* a book whose fundamental premise was that, despite the slight regard paid to flavor by home economists, dieticians, and food processors, it was actually paramount.

In some respects cranky and overblown—the word *flavor* is capitalized throughout—the book is no more so than most works on health and diet of the day, whose devotion to progress and science Finck somehow melds with his own views on gastronomy. Chief among these is that flavor depends less on cooking techniques than on superior ingredients—preferably fresh from local sources. Finck connects America's romance with refrigeration, the railway boxcar, and processed national brands to food adulteration, still common despite government action taken in the previous decade and recounted here in a grisly litany of food tainted by corrosive acids, formaldehyde, borax, and coal-tar dyes. If such associations are reminiscent of public concern over pesticides and additives nearly eighty years later, so too are Finck's complaints about bland chickens, flavorless corn and cornmeal, tired fish, and cosmetically perfect but tasteless fruit and vegetables. Finck also laments the impact on the food supply of what today would be called environmental degradation: the effect of pollution on the nation's renowned oyster beds, topsoil erosion and the loss of farmland to urban development, and the extinction of native crayfish—which Finck, like James, caught as a child with a piece of liver tied to a string—in the streams of his native Oregon. Finck's other prejudices—sweet rather than salted butter, crusty bread, and ripe, distinctively flavored cheeses—are familiar as well, and he concludes his book with a vision of American cities provisioned with superb, fresh foodstuffs, equal to the best of Europe, by small family farms on their outskirts.

Finck was a gastronome—someone whose interest in food was both gustatory and intellectual—and cared passionately about preserving America's gastronomic bounty so that it might realize its potential to match the cooking and ingredients of any nation in the world. But he was also a gourmet—and therefore to ordinary citizens the unacceptable face of capitalist wining and dining. The only cookbook Finck cites in *Food and Flavor* is Mary Ronald's *The Century Cook Book,* an 1896 volume heavily weighted toward French cuisine (and printed, in a perhaps mitigating circumstance, by his own publisher). In that preference as well as in fact, he was clearly well-to-do and well-traveled, accustomed to the company of wealthy and powerful men with whom he shared exquisite wine and food in the best restaurants and hotels of New York, London, and Paris. Such a life, such companions, and such places were in a very real sense contingent on the destruction of the very things that Finck loved and celebrated. The wealth and privilege that demanded the kind of food created by small, local, traditional producers was the product of an economy that tended—through colonial exploitation, corporate ownership, mass production, marketing, and distribution—to destroy the livelihoods of such producers.

Such contradictions were and remain inherent in the very nature of the food lover, and form the central dilemma of gastronomy. The gastronome is nearly always also a gourmet, alternating, as in Finck's case, between the role of solipsistic fop who epitomizes the triumph of style over substance and that of crusader pursuing issues of genuine interest to the public good. In their criticism of cooking and restaurants, their interest in the quality of foodstuffs, and their influence on the wider public's eating habits, gastronomes were as sincere a force for the education and the betterment of the nation's diet as were home economists. But the domestic science movement's approach to food production and consumption was free from the gastronomes' conviction that food might not only be a means to a nutritional end but an aesthetic and cultural end in itself. By contrast, domestic science reflected nothing so much as an interest in food untainted by appetite.

Ironically, by 1917 it was corporate agriculture and food processors who, with the support of government and domestic science, were able to claim—by virtue of their emphasis on uniform quality, purity, abundance, and low prices—to be the ally of average American working families even as farmers, small processors, and retailers together with regional tradition, flavor, and diversity withered and died. Moreover, with U.S. entry into World War I, Americans were urged both to eat less and to eat less well in the interests of feeding the troops overseas and relieving hunger in Europe. Dining out and taking pleasure in food and cooking had become not only more difficult and unfashionable but unpatriotic. The perennial notion that too much interest in eating—manifested in one's waistline or in one's aesthetic sensibility—was a sign of self-indulgence and of indifference to the hungry acquired a new life. Concerned gourmet-gastronomes like Finck might well have been the inheritors of Jefferson's vision of an agrarian democracy—and Jefferson himself was the nation's first prominent gastronome—but for reasons both within and beyond their control, their voices had little influence or rang hollow, as they would for decades to come.

Neither Prohibition nor the war in Europe seems much to have preoccupied James, who continued to develop his capacity to charm and please other people, even while pressing his own interests to the fore. By his junior year at Washington High School he was writing full-fledged book and theater reviews for *The Lens*, performing and doing production chores in school plays, and was sufficiently well known and popular on campus to consider running for student office. In one particularly heartfelt review, in *The Lens* of March 1918, James wrote of "the value of the drama—its great relation to humanity and its great message of life."

For James the drama, together with opera, was life itself and the basis of his identity. He was known to others as well as to himself as someone obsessed with theater and as someone determined to make a career on the stage. But publicly he wore his ambition lightly and fell into the role of the genial class wit with a sharp ear for gossip and an eye for detecting the interpersonal politics of any situation. Although the sophistication he cultivated so intently, and his open enthusiasm for a world most Portlanders regarded as alien and pretentious, had the potential to render him a figure of fun, his full-grown height of six foot two and his bulk made him formidable and he was careful to mock himself before others had the chance. He now made friends with ease and kept his resentments, doubts, and chronic sense of loneliness to himself. He and Mary remained, in their fashion, as close as mother and son could be, spending winter weekends and holidays together at a deserted Gearhart, walking the beach amid the shrieking winds.

By his final year at Washington High in 1919, James was not only popular—though more so among the girls than the boys—but a student of some consequence. In the senior class elections, "Jimmy," now a baby-faced giant with slicked-back hair, was elected sergeant at arms (or, as the yearbook quipped, "chief of police: Reasons for his election are self-evident"). In the class play, *Pomander Walk,* he played Admiral Sir Peter Antrobus, an absurd, buffoonish character who swaggers across the stage uttering such lines as "Intoxicated! Me? Bless my soul!" while his friend Chester Benson oversaw the stage crew. Mary Hamblet joined James at Washington High that same year as a freshman; and he made other friends, among them Edith Anderson, a vampish, voguish girl whose nickname was Theodora, and James's female counterpart in worldliness and wit. In the class will James bequeathed her "his genius-born soul."

He earned good grades, learned Spanish, polished his now-considerable knowledge of stagecraft and costume, and joined Hi-Y, the leading student social club. But, as his high school yearbook attests, theater and food were the centers of James's life: A mock playbill announces "James Beard's Playhouse" featuring "Miss Edith Anderson" as "the mystery act" and suggests after-theater dining and dancing at "Beard's Roof Garden." The class profile and horoscope, cowritten by James, present him enthusing on the possibility of becoming a leading man at the Alcazar, a downtown repertory theater at Twelfth and Morrison, and predict that he will appear in films with Fatty Arbuckle. The motto beneath his graduation photo, an oval set against a background of Portland's signature roses, has a perhaps-unintended resonance: "Actors are born in the best of regulated families."

January 1920 was a busy month for the Beards. Shortly after the round of holiday dinners and parties ended, James's high school graduation took place, followed by the Auld Lang Syne society's annual dinner, the highlight of John's calendar. It was held at the Benson, with Portland Mayor George Baker and State Supreme Court Justice Thomas McBride in attendance, and its menu—Benson special relish tray with Thousand Island dressing, mock turtle soup, broiled salmon, roast turkey, and "tuitti fruitti" ice cream—was more calculated to please men like John than to exhibit the talents of Henri Thiele.

Such events should have marked Portland's entry into a new era of good feeling: The war was over, the economy prospered, and Mayor Baker's administration was both popular and effective. But the good times were tempered by an unease, a fear that, even if the Hun had been dealt with, other enemies were at the gates and there were not enough provisions to go around within. Anti-German sentiment generated during the war had metastasized into often-virulent hostility to Asians, blacks, Catholics, and Jews, and bills to limit the presence or activities of one group or another crowded the legislative calendar in Salem. In an attempt to thwart left-wing unions, the state passed one blatantly unconstitutional "anti-syndicalist" law after another, and the public appearance of socialist journalist Lincoln Steffens caused civic outcry verging on riot. The head of the city library, a pacifist who had refused to buy war bonds, was hounded from office.

Cultural and educational institutions found themselves victims of the same atmosphere. In 1911 Portland's eminent Reed family had founded Reed College with the enthusiastic backing of the city establishment and had hired William Trufant Foster as its first president. Foster hired a stellar faculty in both arts and sciences, setting a standard for excellence in a small undergraduate liberal arts college that Reed enjoys to this day. But during and immediately after the war, Foster—progressive rather than socialist—was nevertheless increasingly regarded as too left-leaning by the college trustees. In 1919 he was forced out.

Reed had apparently recovered its equilibrium by the fall of 1920, when James matriculated as one of 85 freshman in a total enrollment of 247 students, each paying $125 annual tuition. James had spent the eight months between his high school graduation and the autumn term at Reed in his habitual pastimes, summering at Gearhart, polishing his now-impressive borderline tenor-baritone voice, and acting or doing production chores in local theater. Among the groups he involved himself with was the Red Lantern Players, a professional troupe headed by Earl Larrimore, an actor-director who would give Clark Gable one of his first stage roles and later attain some fame on Broadway. The Red Lantern Players was essentially a traveling company, bringing a repertoire of stock plays to smaller towns in the Willamette Valley and along the Columbia. For James it was an extraordinary opportunity to work and be counted among professionals and to enjoy a genuinely adult life free from the constraints of home in the company of sophisticated, free-spirited, and like-minded people.

James therefore arrived at Reed in the full bloom of his burgeoning and now somewhat reckless self-confidence, and quickly established himself as a man to watch on campus. He ran for and was elected treasurer of the freshman class, serving with Alice Abbott, a neighbor in Hawthorne Park and fellow Washington High graduate, who was elected president. Within weeks his name was a constant feature of the college weekly, *The Quest,* whose arch, satirical style was a perfect match for James's increasingly wry and brittle wit. When Warren G. Harding was declared the victor in a student mock-presidential election in October, *The Quest* reported, "James 'Jimmy' Beard was highly elated over the outcome. 'Immense,' he ejaculated. 'With Mr. Harding as president there need be no fear of lean years.'"

The Quest also heaped approval on James as "super of supers" among a group of Reed students who worked as extras in the Scotti Grand Opera Company's touring production of *Tosca* in Portland that month. In a scene set in a church, as the secret policeman Scarpia sings an aria of lust and villainy and a procession of choristers and priests chants the Te Deum in counterpoint, an enrobed and mitered James, in the role of the cardinal, bestowed his blessing on the crowd. Although the paper treated the event with its usual satirical detachment, it was a watershed for James and confirmed his growing determination to pursue an operatic rather than a theatrical career.

A later article in *The Quest* describes a fictional meeting between James and concert singer Cecil Fanning, who had appeared in Portland that winter. Gaining entrance to Fanning's hotel room through a window, the "modest but well grown and comely youth" is questioned by the singer—"'Are you engaged?' 'Not very much,' was the timid answer."—and is finally persuaded to lift "his sweet tenor in melody, and it was as [if] the spirit of springtime, the verdant, laughing waters and sunshiney woods filled the air." Impressed, Fanning counsels training with the celebrated Herbert Witherspoon. "'Shall I cut college?,' queried the youthful Caruso. 'Yes, after three years,' was the answer. 'But while you're gittin', git a plenty.'" The article concludes by proclaiming: "This is the true story of our own Jimmy Beard's visit to Mr. Cecil Fanning . . . and serves to break the unhappy news that our budding Caruso will leave his native haunts within three years and journey to New York for special instruction under Mr. Herbert Witherspoon."

Given the student paper's penchant for proto–Jazz Age drollery, it is difficult to say how much—if any—of this was true, but it was nevertheless to be prophetic and increased James's celebrity—and perhaps notoriety—on campus. His witticisms appeared with growing regularity ("History Prof—What made the tower of Pisa lean? James Beard—I don't know. If I did I might try it.") and he attended the freshman Halloween party in full drag, making, according to *The Quest*, "a perfect lady" and winning a prize for his costume. ("Honorable mention was given to that adorable child, James Beard.") None of this was especially untoward, but James's flamboyant, self-advertising style seems to have begun to attract the notice of college officials. A widely publicized rash of student cheating on January's examinations exacerbated tensions among Reed's carefree, gilded youth, its hapless administration, and the civic establishment up and across the river from the college's halcyon suburban campus.

Meanwhile James continued his daily commute southward from
Salmon Street to Reed, worked in the campus theater, and at some
point became lovers with one or more male students and a professor.
Given James's high profile, this was too much for the administration
to ignore. In mid-March, shortly after finishing production chores on
a play called *The Yellow Jacket*, he was expelled. The matter was
accomplished quickly, quietly, and with no formal explanation, and
every trace of his name was expunged from the college yearbook
only a few weeks away from publication. James, the celebrated wit
and rococo Gargantua of the class of '24, was excised and forgotten.

Although Reed had seemed a refuge during his six months there,
James's experience was consistent with that of other gay men at the
time, who, together with racial minorities and foreigners, were the
targets of a rising mood of intolerance among the public. By early
1921 Portland's once well-hidden bigotry was on public and often
prideful display. Formerly moderate state and city leaders competed
with one another in advocating the restriction or exclusion of Asians
and blacks. The Ku Klux Klan—dedicated to the elimination of
"Koons, Kikes, and Katholics" from American life—was becoming a
serious force in Oregon politics, claiming to have at least 150 members in the ranks of the Portland Police Department. Klan leaders in
sheets and hoods posed for photos with the mayor, the district attor-
ney, and other public officials.

The Portland police began a series of generalized crackdowns on
vice activities of all kinds that spring and summer, arresting hundreds of gamblers, prostitutes, and male homosexuals. That same
summer Congress examined a report by Secretary of the Navy
Franklin D. Roosevelt on a federal operation designed to entrap gay
sailors and shipyard workers in Newport, Rhode Island. Public opinion had been outraged to learn that not only had bribes been offered
to obtain testimony, but that government agents had engaged in sexual relations with potential suspects in order to secure arrests.

If the actual sexual practices of the heterosexual majority
reflected some ambivalence about homosexuality, so too did its
social attitudes toward homosexuals themselves. Until the early part
of the century, homosexual acts were viewed simply as undesirable
forms of behavior—lumped together with adultery, masturbation,
and other forms of sexual vice rather than seen as the expression of a

particular psychological identity or inherent preference. But by 1900 the medical and nascent psychiatric establishment had launched the notion of the homosexual as a full-fledged type of personality and one in the grip of a pathology deeply rooted in his or her character. Much as turn-of-the-century culture took control of the body through diet and health regimes, notions of genetic superiority and inferiority, and classifications of desirable and undesirable types—for example, categorizing individuals as dyspeptic or neurasthenic—it sought to control sexuality by locating it in the individual body and psyche rather than in sex acts themselves. Thus did science create the homosexual and his or her "illness"—homosexuality—a diagnosable and presumably treatable personality disorder.

For mainstream society the creation of the homosexual made gay people at once more repellent—and thus more convenient targets for intolerance and repression—and more mysterious and therefore fascinating. Homosexual themes, fashions, and personalities increasingly intrigued affluent, educated heterosexuals in the 1920s. In 1895, the world had been gripped by the trial and jailing of Oscar Wilde, who provided an archetype for the homosexual as acid social commentator and arbiter of art, fashion, and taste. Other such figures would come onto the scene as the celebrity "personality" came to occupy a crucial role in the rise of public culture and the media. Lesbianism became a subject of some fascination to heterosexuals with the emergence of the writing of Djuna Barnes and other works in a similar vein. Gertrude Stein became as much a star of the Jazz Age as Scott and Zelda Fitzgerald.

The flapper—whose clothes and body celebrated androgyny and dieting—represented not only a considerably more socially and sexually liberated model of womanhood than the recent past had afforded, but a discernible blurring of sex roles and, presumably, sexual preferences. By 1921 young people and sophisticates of every stripe toured Greenwich Village, not only in pursuit of the area's bohemian culture and nightlife—but in the hope of observing gays and lesbians in their aboriginal habitat; a locale that not incidentally was one of the last in the nation where interesting food could be found. Although homosexuals still found residence in such enclaves as Greenwich Village, the only means of leading their lives in an atmosphere relatively free of oppression, the vanguard of the straight world was in hot pursuit, eager to avail itself of the ideas, tastes, and vogues of the incontestably more avant-garde denizens of the gay world. In a variation on the same theme, fashionable New Yorkers as well as tourists flocked uptown to Harlem to soak up the black jazz subculture in clubs presided over by figures such as Gladys Bentley, an openly lesbian transvestite entertainer.

Although the repression of some of these newly emergent forms of public leisure and sexuality was on many civic and political agendas, it was not necessarily good business, and in the 1920s, as President Coolidge reminded Americans, "The business of America [was] business." Sophistication, whether in literature, fashion, theater, music, film, decoration, or, eventually, food, was a marketable commodity, and consumer capitalism had never been scrupulous about the provenance of the goods with which it stocked its shelves. In the 1920s, despite the eruption of conservative reaction in susceptible places like Portland, the one-time demimonde was joining the larger world at the world's fervent, if inarticulate, request.

As ever, Mary had a plan and the means to effect it. Outraged by Portland's rejection of her son, yet mindful of the real reasons for his expulsion and her own position in the community, she calculated to send James not merely to New York but to London for voice training. Letters were sent, references culled, and departure arranged for early the following year. In the meanwhile there was more local theater, the consolation of friends like Mary Hamblet and Chester Benson, still at Reed, and one last childhood summer at Gearhart before James boarded his ship and retraced his mother's passage of forty years before; down the Pacific shore, across Panama and the Caribbean, and then three thousand miles across the Atlantic to the rain-shimmered streets of London.

James's shock at his expulsion was mitigated by the fact that, despite the education and popularity he had enjoyed at Reed, he was now on his way to pursuing his real career with a three-year head start. But that summer in Gearhart, James paced the beaches and watched the construction of a new hotel next to the golf course, still unable to comprehend wholly the fact of his humiliation. Despite the self-evident success reflected in his impending trip to London, there had been talk around town of the real reasons for his departure, and James's adolescent fantasies of Portland's disapproval crystallized into fact, into what he would later call "a bitter, biting thing." By contrast, his father enjoyed continued success at the Customs House. That same year John—whose expertise in Orientalia was now legendary—was charged with examining the accuracy of valuations placed on cargo from China and Japan for the whole Pacific Coast. He traveled down to San Diego and northward again at the head of a delegation of federal bureaucrats, a pioneer boy from Linn County who had made good by hard work, apple-polishing, and Asia.

James had his portrait taken—dressed in an unbuttoned coat with tall, straight-sided hat atop his still childish if bemused face—in the new year of 1922, and boarded his ship, the *Highland Heather*, a second-rate hulk bound for Southampton with a half dozen stops along the way. It ambled up the Willamette and down the Columbia before entering the Pacific at the Columbia Bar just west of Astoria—a place, his father had told him years before, whose shallows, rips, and surf had forever torn ships apart and drowned their sailors—both Oregon's bulwark against invaders and its deterrent to escapees. But the voyage went calmly, and James lost weight on a diet of cheese, biscuits, and the galley's fiery canned-fish curry. The first stop of consequence was Saint Thomas in the Virgin Islands, where James was stunned by the color, variety, and sheer strangeness of the food in the market. After downing lunch at a port hotel, he filled a basket with greens, limes, pineapples, melons, and tomatoes, which lasted until the *Highland Heather* reached the Canary Islands.

On arrival in Southampton, James gorged himself on pea soup, lamb cutlets, and potatoes in their skins at the station restaurant while waiting for the train to London. He was met at Waterloo Station by his uncle Fred, the only one of her many siblings Mary had kept in touch with over the years. He moved into Fred's flat for at least awhile and let London—seventy times the size of Portland and still able to call itself the most important city in the world—blow over him, a hurricane of theater, opera, personalities, and food. Despite his youth and ignorance of the city, James already possessed an innate capacity to track down, cultivate, and charm the best, most interesting people or those who knew them. Among his first acquaintances was Helen Dircks, publicist for the Palladium Theatre and a formidable woman with formidable connections who acted as his London mentor, showing him where, how, and with whom to eat, drink, and socialize. Although James had come to London with the specific goal of studying voice, he had not made any formal arrangements for a coach or conservatory. But by the autumn Dircks had arranged an audition, and James found himself taking what he imagined were the first steps to stardom.

James's voice teacher in London was Gaetano Loria, a Neapolitan and a former assistant to the legendary Caruso whose expertise in diction was such that he was retained by the royal family to correct the stuttering problem of the future George VI. His plans for his new student were to transform a promising but largely untrained high baritone voice into that of a Wagnerian tenor, playing the outsize roles suited to James's immense size. In Loria's studio above Wigmore Hall, James learned sixteen roles and performed at dozens of private concerts and musicales. The following summer, on July 13, 1923, he made his formal debut at Wigmore Hall with eleven other students, singing four pieces and closing with a song entitled "When I Was Twenty"—which he had in fact turned two months earlier.

Mary and James—his instinct for publicity (and perhaps revenge) already sharp—made certain that Portland heard about his emergence on the international concert stage. An account of the concert together with a report from James on the London stage and musical scene was telegraphed to the *Oregon Journal*. On July 22 a photo of James, every inch the musical artist in an open-necked shirt and herringbone tweed jacket, appeared together with his "Letter from London." James reported the success of other Oregonians on the English concert circuit, noting that American music, bands, and cocktails were in vogue in London, and Americans enjoyed easy access to the normally complex and impenetrable strata of British society. By virtue of his English ancestry, James himself was doubly welcomed, gaining entry to dinner parties and restaurants by virtue of his skill at flattering hostesses and his status as a presentable, conversationally fluent bachelor. His capacity to please other people and be sensitive to their needs—developed in the face of Mary's inconstant affection and incessant demands for achievement during his childhood—had become a formidable asset.

However inwardly fragile his self-confidence, James at twenty was not averse to expressing himself. In his letter to the *Oregon Journal*, of the English National Opera he wrote: "As for the . . . repertoire and the company, little can be said in the way of praise. They simply prove that Italian and French operas are not suited to the English tongue." He was kinder, though restrained, in his treatment of the theater season, but ecstatic over concerts by the pianist Paderewski and soprano Nellie Melba (memorialized by Escoffier in a concoction of ice cream, peaches, and raspberries known as peach melba). James was now a man of the world, with ideas and opinions to match.

While the United States had to struggle in the early 1920s to throw off cultural and gastronomic repression and propriety, London between the wars was entering its final imperial heyday on a flood tide of food, parties, and artistic endeavor. Gaetano Loria knew and loved food and was acquainted with many of the leading musical and theatrical celebrities of the day, introducing James to the backstage life of Soho and Covent Garden, and in particular their Italian restaurants. Despite England's reputation for brown Windsor soup, gray beef and mutton, and sodden greens and vegetables, London was hardly negligible in gastronomic terms. Escoffier had retired from the London Ritz only a year before James's arrival, and the city's better hotels and French restaurants probably served the best haute cuisine in the world outside France itself.

But despite the quality of the practitioners London engaged in its best dining rooms, England and France were neighbors as uneasy in the kitchen as at Waterloo. In the seventeenth century English cooking had apparently been of much the same quality as that of the French. But by the end of the nineteenth century, England's own culinary traditions had been overshadowed by the global ascendancy of French cuisine, and its diffident cooks found themselves in a state of creative torpor. They subsequently absorbed the worst aspects of the domestic science movement and incorporated them into the menus of its restaurants and hotels and what became notorious as perhaps the world's most institutional cooking.

Still, what little aid and comfort cooking in England received during the 1920s and 1930s tended to come from France or from English Francophiles. While British publishers printed multiple editions of such works as N. Newnham-Davis's *The Gourmet's Guide to Europe,* an intelligent and thorough guide to eating well on the Continent, few if any of the food conscious were in a position to help English cooks prepare better English food. A column in *The Times* published a few days after James's concert at Wigmore Hall begins with a lament for the English country breakfasts of fifty years before, only to end by commending *Simple French Cooking for*

English Homes by Marcel Boulestin, a celebrated French restaurateur in London. In 1933 English gastronomes would organize themselves into what would become the world's most influential food club, the Wine and Food Society, but both its leader, André Simon, and its ideals would be French.

For less pretentious dining, London turned—as it would until at least the early 1970s—to Italy, which was everything in personality and in eating that France was not. Restaurants like Gennaro's (whose owner was a close friend of Gaetano Loria), Pagani's, Ristorante del Commercio, and Bertorelli's provided lusty feeding amid good company that sated James's appetites for bountiful food, beautiful people, and gossip. At the Commercio, a humble carafe-wine place, full of family feeling, off Soho Square, James learned to eat raw artichoke leaves in a garlic dressing, veal scallops with lemon, and salads of dandelion greens—food from a totally alien world whose simplicity and directness were nevertheless reminiscent of meals at Gearhart, six thousand miles away.

However, James had lost none of his appetite for London's opposite gastronomic pole. His allowance from Mary would permit him to take tea at the Ritz, though not lunch or dinner in the dining room over which Escoffier had so recently presided. Still, James remained adept at cadging lunches and dinners at the best places, as well as invitations for a day at the races at Epsom, complete with picnic hampers from Fortnum's. He drank cocktails at Verrey's, a fashionable bar, and coffee and tea at the bohemian-flavored Good Intent in Chelsea. Meanwhile Helen Dircks continued to tout James among London's social and theatrical networks. It was something she—and a succession of otherwise strong, no-nonsense women to follow—somehow felt they needed to do for James, despite getting little back in return save his humor, his gossip, and his easy, undemanding, enormous but boylike presence.

Despite the efforts of both Dircks and Gaetano Loria, the future of James's singing career was uncertain. His vocal cords developed nodes as a result of what he claimed was overuse of his voice, although whether he genuinely possessed the talent to succeed is open to question. He was ambitious but also aimless, possessed of a short attention span and an inability to sustain his enthusiasm if success did not come easily. Genuinely fond of James, Loria may have steered him gently in directions other than opera.

In any case, not long after his debut, James took the boat train to Paris, and moved into a pension on the Rue Jacob near the Boulevard Saint-Germain on the Left Bank. If London was the world capital of music and theater, Paris was the holy of holies of food, and James arrived there as if he were a pilgrim at long last in sight of Mecca. Ostensibly he had arranged for further vocal training there, but in practice life in Paris was for James, as for the many expatriate Americans sheltering there, an exercise in high-style bohemian living. In the 1920s Americans went to Paris to escape repression at home, to submerge themselves in culture, and to paint, write, and take on lovers without regard to convention and propriety. They also went to eat and drink: It was no accident that Hemingway referred to Paris as a "feast," a place in which life could be lived with abandon; a liberation of body, mind, and appetite whose setting was inevitably the café, the bistro, or the brasserie. While the gourmandizing of the well-to-do might be a sign of their indifference to anything other than their own comfort, the epicurianism of bohemians was yet another aspect of their moral and artistic virtue.

Paris in the twenties was a feast for journalists, too, a tableau vivant of characters and compelling scenes. It was the era of the foreign correspondent, typified by Hemingway, who would park himself for hours with a tray of oysters and a bottle of icy, tart Loire wine at cafés along the Boulevard Montparnasse. Two American journalists who settled in Paris at about the time of James's visit also became more than a little preoccupied with food: Waverley Root, who became America's first popular food historian, and future *New Yorker* writer A. J. Liebling, who settled into a comfortable daily routine built around bistro dishes and Tavel rosé at the Restaurant Beaux-Arts on the Rue Bonaparte, a few blocks north of James's lodging; a place James—on a limited budget and therefore appreciative of its student prices—certainly knew. He himself took most of his meals at his pension, or at another boardinghouse also in the Rue Bonaparte, whose simple stews and braises, redolent of thyme, bay, and garlic, were tinged with the flavors of Provence. But for an insatiable walker like James, the Rue Bonaparte was the start of a path to other pleasures. He would stride along its narrow pavements fronted by picture framers, booksellers, and antique dealers, and cross the Seine on the Pont des Arts, drawn inexorably northward by Les Halles, the central market of Paris and, therefore, the world.

James had been delighted by Yamhill Street in Portland and stunned by Covent Garden in London, but for him as for Liebling, Les Halles was of a magnitude he could scarcely begin to fathom, an apparently bottomless cauldron of smells, sounds, colors, and flavors churning as though it were the gut of the universe itself. His experience there led James to a lifetime of market prowling and the conviction that the way to learn a city's heart was to examine the contents of its stomach.

Part of the wonder of Les Halles was the sense that it was less a collection of vendors than a full-blown organism whose life came not from any conscious effort but through the transcendent totality of its constituents. In a sense this was true of food in France generally and was a major part of its magic: Its excellence seemed effortless, art subsumed into daily routine. But, as Boulestin had written to his English readers, "Food which is worth eating is worth discussing," a notion at the center of the gastronomy to which France had given birth. French gastronomes thought that while their compatriots certainly enjoyed food, serious discussion about it was at best nascent, and they launched a number of efforts and organizations dedicated to its exploration. The goal was less to create or recover a culinary identity—something in which France needed little help—but to foster an understanding and appreciation of French cuisine by consolidating and codifying its disparate parts.

During James's time in Paris, the prime mover in this arena was Maurice-Edmond Sailland, a ebullient journalist with a zany, bohemian edge, who wrote under the name "Curnonsky" (Latin for "Whynotski"). Sailland moved in the usual gourmet circles—the clubs and eating societies largely founded in the previous century—but he had more serious goals as well: for example, the creation of a thirty-two-volume encyclopedia on the regional food of France, entitled *La France Gastronomique*. He argued endlessly for simpler preparations based on carefully husbanded ingredients and promoted the link between good eating and tourism that resulted in the *Guide Michelin* and the rise of the three-star restaurant strategically situated near major auto routes. All these efforts, and in particular his foundation of the Académie des Gastronomes in 1928, were models for British and American gastronomes in subsequent years, as was the infusion of Left Bank avant-garde with which he tempered the stuffy, status-conscious swank of the mainstream gourmet.

James's budget meant that he ate like a bohemian whether he liked it or not and took swank when and where he could. He spent his own money on a dinner at the legendary Maxim's and was sorely disappointed, finding pastry, tea, tarts, and cakes at Rumpelmayer's, Colombin, and Louis Sherry at the end of the Champs-Elysées both cheaper and more satisfying. But when Gaetano Loria came to town he took James to Tour d'Argent, famous for its pressed duck, its wine cellar, and its fawning treatment of celebrities and the international rich—an experience that impressed James greatly and confirmed him in his aspiration to make himself a regular at such places. Determined to create a similar impression on a visiting Portlander, he collected her in a carriage and took her to Le Caneton, a restaurant specializing in champagne and caviar and run by refugees from the Russian revolution. The check came to one hundred francs, about four dollars, a hair-raising bill in a city among whose attraction for expatriates was its cheapness. James returned to the Rue Jacob feeling chastened.

But there were other compensations and, in particular, opportunities to explore his sexuality without constraint. He met a young Dutchman named Hans, whom James would remember as one of the loves of his life—handsome, willing, and utterly accepting of both James's body and the fragile psyche that he revealed to so few. Together they went to Berlin, itself enjoying a bohemian and arts renaissance on the scale of Paris's. It was especially hospitable to gays and lesbians from less tolerant places such as England, and there and in Paris James found for perhaps the first time a pleasurable and easy equilibrium between his cultural, psychological, gustatory, and sexual appetites.

But late that year, as though on cue, Mary appeared in London and announced that it was time to come home. Despite a few more sessions with Loria, James's operatic career appeared unlikely to prosper, and Mary's financial resources and patience were wearing thin. But before her departure for home James was able to persuade her that their dreams for his future were still worth pursuing—if not in the opera then perhaps on the stage—and that her lifelong belief in the beneficence of constant travel was as valid for him as it had been for her. A ticket was issued—not to Portland but to New York—and James sailed westward alone on a cold and bitter sea in the early winter months of 1924.

espite his adolescent dream to live, and become famous, in New York, James, having been torn from Europe's—and Hans's—bosom, was at first a reluctant Manhattanite. But the city won him over quickly. It was by his own description "more European" then than it is today, and by 1924 possessed some of the avant-garde, liberated spirit of the Left Bank. New York, leading the rest of the country, had established a way of living with Prohibition, consisting chiefly of ignoring it. New York State had repealed its own Prohibition enforcement law that year, leaving the pursuit of bootleggers and liquor dealers mainly in the hands of the FBI and its newly appointed director, J. Edgar Hoover.

Opportunities to drink alcohol were limited only by the public's ingenuity, and the speakeasy was ubiquitous, throwing together diverse individuals and groups initially united only by their desire to have a drink. One of Prohibition's unanticipated effects was to make the majority of Americans—among them the nation's social, economic, and political leaders—members of a vast underground that openly flouted both the law and many of the traditional conventions of law-abiding citizens. Having grown accustomed to rebellion and to illicit pleasure, and with well-developed appetites for cultural novelty and fashion, the middle and upper classes were increasingly open to the intellectual and artistic passions of the bohemian fringe: In the 1920s nearly everyone, at least in New York, wanted to be part of the avant-garde. Prohibition, a repressive measure designed to enforce conformity, had brought nonconformist notions of personal and cultural liberation into the mainstream of American life.

Perhaps nowhere was this so apparent as on the stage, and twenty-one-year-old James soaked up the 1924–25 season with enthusiasm, if not necessarily understanding the momentous ferment under way. The theater business in which James now began to seek auditions had once been dominated by producers and theater owners intent on drawing mass audiences through a hackneyed mix of spectacle, sentimentality, and titillation, the kind of wares James had grown up among during his youth in Portland. But the American theater of the mid-twenties had become increasingly thoughtful and adventurous. Playwrights like Eugene O'Neill (three of whose plays opened that season), critics like Alexander Woollcott, and production companies like the Theatre Guild (which would spawn the Group Theatre and ultimately the Actor's Studio) created a drama that was literate and anxious to explore social, political, and psychological concerns that had previously been ignored or suppressed.

The new mood in the theater extended to sexuality as well as the examination of politics, social issues, and the national character. That same season the Provincetown Players opened O'Neill's *Desire Under the Elms,* a drama of sexual passion and obsession set on a New England farm, at the Greenwich Village Theatre. The previous season the same theater had presented *The God of Vengeance,* which featured a frank depiction of lesbianism and was moved uptown to Broadway by popular demand, despite persistent harassment by police and public officials. Driven by a genuine artistic urge to explore the sexual underground in a sympathetic manner, as well as a commercial desire to exploit the box office potential of a sensational subject, homosexuality was a staple theme of the new American theater over the next decade. Such theater also implicitly communicated the fact that to an extraordinary but still unacknowledged extent, America's cultural establishment—beginning with "America's first lady of theater," Katharine Cornell, and dozens of important actors, writers, directors, designers, and artists—was also its homosexual establishment. Commenting on the gay elite, consisting of figures like lyricist Lorenz Hart, songwriter Cole Porter, and director George Cukor, one playwright said, "It was the most exclusive club in New York."

James's goal was to move in such circles and to secure acting work, accomplishments he felt his talent, personality, and experience should put within relatively easy reach. As it was, he spent much of his time in his furnished room in Chelsea and in prowling Greenwich Village and the markets to its west, supported by a stipend from Mary. But he found friends, and as ever secured dinner and party invitations by cultivating hostesses and and wearing his genial bachelor wit like a boutonniere. He ate surprisingly well, both in speakeasies—which in the case of the Eugenie on West Forty-ninth Street boasted a credible French restaurant—and in hotel dining rooms like that of the Waldorf-Astoria, then on the present site of the Empire State Building. Unless they had the financial support of either illicit booze sales or the shelter of a hotel, however, restaurants of any seriousness—and those offering high-end French cooking in particular—were unsustainable in the 1920s. In response, their most devoted former customers resorted to the anachronism of private—and now underground—dining clubs, hiring once-celebrated-but-now-jobless chefs to prepare menus accompanied by wines smuggled down from Montreal.

Despite the moribund condition of fine dining in the United States, the number of restaurants in the nation tripled in the 1920s—albeit chiefly at the opposite end of the spectrum, in the form of coffee shops, luncheonettes, cafeterias, automats, and tearooms. Often set up as regional or national chains, these new middle-brow restaurants thrived on the absence of liquor and promoted the virtues of cleanliness, consistency, and economy as well as their unstinting use of national brands such as Heinz Ketchup. On his limited budget, James was not averse to patronizing their New York incarnations, such as Schrafft's, Horn & Hardart, and Child's, a chain of coffee shops whose impeccable white-tiled rooms and pancakes—fried on a griddle set just inside the front window—were an improbable but long-standing staple of the less well off members of Manhattan's arts community. As James recalled fifty years later, "In the 'twenties in New York, you'd have a good cup of Maillard hot chocolate and a chicken sandwich for 75 cents and you thought you were whirling through the world."

James also made himself at home at the Algonquin Hotel on Forty-fourth Street, whose dining room was more than acceptable and whose bars and lobby were frequented by people in the theater, whether in fact or—as in James's case—only in aspiration. To support himself he took odd jobs while writing letters, scheduling interviews and auditions, and pursuing connections from Portland who had made good in Manhattan, such as Earl Larrimore—all to little avail. But at the end of August he received a letter from Walter Hampden requesting that he audition. One of the leading actors of his day,

Hampden had bought a theater north of Broadway and established a company dedicated to producing the classic repertory, usually with himself in the leading role. In 1923 he had mounted a revival of *Cyrano de Bergerac,* which he was now set to take on the road. Hampden was in a hurry to cast the touring company and liked big men—James's chief liability in the eyes of most directors. He offered James a small part, with rehearsals to begin immediately.

The Hampden Company's tour in the autumn of 1924 was on a scale undreamed of by the Red Lantern Players, accompanied by scenery, horses, and stage mothers and filling the better part of a train that headed west and south through the fall and returned to New York to open in December at the Broad Street Theater. Within weeks of its return Hampden had gone into rehearsals for a new production of *Othello,* and another walk-on role was found for James. Despite good reviews the play closed quickly, and with no other prospects with Hampden or elsewhere in sight, James returned home.

James rode the train westward, his mood alternating between trepidation and anticipation. He had been to London, Paris, and New York; he had performed; he had moved among celebrities; and his native sophistication now shone with the polished credibility of genuine experience in the world. But he was hardly a star and was not likely to become one anytime soon. By that crucial measure, Portland was no more likely now to appreciate and approve of him than it had been three years before.

The transcontinental train journey—James's first—followed in large part the old Oregon Trail, which John Beard had ridden and walked sixty years before as a five-year-old. It was no longer dangerous, but the sheer emptiness of it all—a desolate, arid ocean from Omaha to the fringe of the Cascades—astonished the urban creature James had become. But the food along the route, whether inside the train or in towns along the way, was increasingly of a piece. On the fourth day the train entered Oregon and made its first stop at La Grande, a town in the state's northeastern corner. The ladies of La Grande had published *The St. Peter's Guild Cook Book* that year, a recipe collection every bit as ambitious as *The Portland Woman's Exchange Cook Book,* in a city one-tenth the size. But the book had its feet not in the high-desert and mountain soil of La Grande but in an increasingly nationalized and commercialized culinary sensibility that now extended even to small and comparatively isolated towns. Like so many community cookbooks of the day, printing was underwritten by Royal Baking Powder and Knox Gelatine, and recipes specified these products as well as Swans Down flour, Fleischmann's Yeast, and Borden's Sweetened Milk. Dishes like "Salad of the Gods" and "Little Pigs in Jackets" reflected the now-total dominance of the powdered sugar, marshmallow, and toothpick school of domestic science cookery. The women of La Grande no longer learned to cook from their pioneer mothers but from figures such as Ida Bailey Allen, once a starchy home economist who had engaged chemists to write the prefaces of her cookbooks, but who had now bobbed her hair and broadcast a radio cooking program from New York.

Despite the onslaughts of domestic science, the food industry, and the commercial media, however, American regional cookery survived. In a sense it, too, had gone underground, practiced in places and by persons ignorant of or oblivious to the dictates and fashions of corporate consumerism. More public expressions of concern and support came not from America's unshakably Francophile gourmets but from the nation's cultural vanguard—artists, intellectuals, writers, and political radicals—who shared not only the 1920s avantgarde's appreciation of the table but an increasing interest in their own country's social and artistic traditions. In 1923 *The Nation*—decrying an "American" dinner, consisting of dishes like mousse of sole, prepared by Oscar of the Waldorf for former British Prime Minister David Lloyd George—organized a roundtable discussion on the definition of American food and came up with eight thoughtfully written responses from eight regions of the country.

In 1925 H. L. Mencken's *American Mercury* began a food column devoted not to recipes but to analysis of the state of the nation's cooking and the loss of its character, one writer opining: "Our cooking reflects our mores, its formation is bound up with the characteristic philistinism of our people. A nation capable of supporting the Fundamentalists, the American Legion, the Ku Klux Klan, John Roach Straton and Billy Sunday is not likely to possess a temperament and palate that rise higher." Mencken himself weighed in a year later in his column in the *Chicago Tribune,* damning the loss of Maryland terrapin and the rise of "the cooking school marm" and urging Americans to put aside the hot dog in favor of the food of the nation's regions and immigrants: "The Sicilian in the ditch, though he can never be President, knows better: he puts a slice of onion between his slabs of bread, not a cartridge filled with the sweepings of the abattoirs." Citing "the depressing standardization that ails everything American," he ended with a condemnation of Pullman car cooking, in which the traveling American "gets used to dishes that all taste alike, whatever their ostensible contents, and ends by being unable to distinguish one from another."

James's train brought him home to Portland not in triumph but to a job in the decorating department of Meier and Frank, Portland's leading department store, whose chief consolation for James was its restaurant, which featured a special dessert of frozen whipped heavy cream. But if times were bad for regional food, they were growing brighter for regional theater, and James plunged into Portland's increasingly sophisticated and varied dramatic scene.

At its core was a tough-minded, dynamic woman named Bess Whitcomb, who had never married but was rumored to be the mistress of the husband of the headmistress of one of Portland's tonier private schools. Sixteen years James's senior, Whitcomb, like Helen Dircks, immediately liked him and took it on herself to nurture his career. That August he joined her theater company, the Bess Whitcomb Players, with a role in *Captain Applejack* as Ambrose Applejohn, one of whose lines—"Hell, said the queen, not thinking"—James adopted as his own.

That autumn he left Meier and Frank for a teaching position at the Gabel Country Day School, filling his evenings with scenery painting and the company of Chester Benson and David Piper, whose father—editor of *The Oregonian*—was as important a figure in Portland society as Chester's. As in New York, there were ample opportunities to drink in Portland's two hundred or so speakeasies, and John Beard had access to copious supplies of high-grade booze on the waterfront. James himself turned his culinary skills to producing wines and liqueurs based on grain alcohol and whatever flavorings were to hand.

During 1926 James found work in radio, chiefly as a continuity announcer and pitchman for local businesses on KGW, which was owned, not inconveniently, by *The Oregonian*. But acting opportunities also increased with the founding of the Art Theatre Players, a group formed in part by refugees from Bess Whitcomb's often high-handed and prickly management of her own company. When James was offered and accepted the part of Father Hyacinth in the new company's production of Ferenc Molnar's *The Swan* that November, Whitcomb was apoplectic with rage, not least because of the excellent reviews her fledgling rival garnered. Newly confident with his success, and eager to escape Whitcomb's ire, after the New Year James went south to Hollywood.

Hollywood in 1927 was in many respects closer to Paris than to Portland: A desert island only tenuously anchored to the rest of the country, it was inexpensive, tolerant, and filled with people from the nation's arts community drawn by studio salaries or the simple desire for fame. Despite the Fatty Arbuckle–starlet murder scandal of a few years before, Hollywood remained an erotic free port, abuzz with the pansexual exploits of Ramon Navarro and Rudolph Valentino. Shortly after his arrival James was befriended by Paul Fielding, an aspiring actor who would achieve no more success in the movies than did James himself, but whose connections were nonetheless impressive. Among them were William De Mille, a director and playwright whose brother Cecil was arguably the most powerful producer-director in Hollywood. James attended dinner parties and developed what was to be a lifelong friendship with William's daughter Agnes, who later became Broadway's most eminent choreographer. James cooked for the family, as increasingly he cooked for anyone who would give him the chance, and finally connected with Cecil B. De Mille. A role as an extra was found for him in the crucifixion scene of De Mille's *King of Kings,* which James parlayed into another extra's job as a German soldier in Erich von Stroheim's notorious *Queen Kelly,* with Gloria Swanson. Other work turned up with sufficient frequency to keep James in rent and groceries—in particular, jobs in live stage prologues presented before the main film feature at Grauman's Chinese Theater, in which he occasionally had the chance to sing.

But as in the opera and in the New York theater, James felt himself held back by his own physical and creative limitations—or at least other people's assessment of them. In truth, he had little tolerance for frustration—for James success was not a task but a psychological and existential imperative—and he was unwilling to spend much time struggling to build a career that might at best assure him of nothing more than steady work as a character actor. James headed north again.

By the end of January 1928, James was in rehearsals with Art Theatre Players for *He Who Gets Slapped,* which opened in February to restrained critical praise. While lauding James's performance, *The Oregonian*'s reviewer implied that anatomy might be destiny: "Some of the character types were excellent: Mr. Beard as the all-but-bursting baron. . . ." But similarly suitable roles failed to appear as the year progressed, and James made and painted scenery for the company's productions and cooked backstage dinners for the casts.

Ingredients for these and other meals that James catered for acquaintances on an informal barter basis came, of course, from the Yamhill Market, which by now possessed something close to a national reputation for its variety, character, and the excellence of its vendors. But even as social and cultural critic Lewis Mumford argued that summer in the pages of the *New Republic* for a rural economy based on food and its provision to local urban markets, Portland's business elite began to plan the Yamhill Market's demise. It would be replaced by an indoor market to be built on the riverfront on vacant land owned, not uncoincidentally, by members of the city's financial and political establishment.

Like most Portlanders, James was unaware that these plans, negotiated largely in secret, were moving forward. But he did know of, and undoubtedly protested, Mary's decision that autumn to sell the house at Gearhart for four hundred dollars. James's childhood was over, but he already had formed the habit of endlessly reenacting and recovering it in his memory as though it were not quite finished—as though essential parts were missing. Now the places that were its touchstones were disappearing beneath the tides of money and progress, sweeping away what James possessed of his past with them.

What Americans would initially call "the slump" hit the nation's economy in the autumn of 1929. As elsewhere, banks and businesses failed in Portland, and the depression that followed resulted in smaller audiences and fewer opportunities in the theater. For the next two years James drifted, south to San Francisco, where he found radio work and some small stage jobs, and, when money ran low, back to Salmon Street. But none of this shook his conviction that he belonged in the theater, although he began to accept the idea that his career might hold more promise in backstage positions than as an actor. Among other options, he considered costume and scenic design as well as teaching drama and voice, and to that end worked toward building a résumé that would incorporate not only stage experience but professional credentials.

In early 1931 he moved to Seattle, where he took a room in the Wallingford district, not far from the University of Washington. B. Iden Payne, an English actor and director of international reputation, was serving as visiting professor of drama in the university's theater department, and although James never formally registered as a student, he was able to attend classes on the strength of his connection to Walter Hampden, with whom Payne had worked. Beyond strengthening his knowledge of classical acting, James took in what was a fairly bohemian atmosphere—for the Pacific Northwest—around the campus, and shopped in the city's waterfront market and ethnic food stores.

But whether because of his habitual impatience or because he could not secure entry into the university's drama program, James decided to leave Seattle and applied to study at Carnegie Tech in Pittsburgh, where he was accepted for the fall 1931 term. Between September and February, he took nine classes, mostly in scenic and costume design. He did not reenroll for the second semester.

On his return to Portland in the spring of 1932, James moved back into the house on Salmon Street and entered what was to be his heyday as a performer and theatrical jack-of-all-trades. He found fairly steady work in radio, on KGW, where he played dramatic roles at two dollars a show in such local serials as "Covered Wagon Days." He performed in similar vehicles, like "Homicide Squad," on KOIN, where each Sunday morning he also dramatized characters from the funnies for a studio audience of children, who were then taken around the corner for ice cream at the Heathman Hotel by James and other cast members, as often as not tired and hung over from the previous night.

In partnership with David Piper, he set up "Midnight Movies," projecting European films in rented space during the weekend late hours to appreciative members of Portland's arts community. As ever, he did production work for a number of theaters and by the spring of 1933 was billed as one half of the Taylor Street Theatre's

Comedy Team in light items and farces like *Kempy*. But his main work in this period was with the Portland Civic Theatre, the result of an amicable merger in 1929 between the Bess Whitcomb and Art Theatre companies. Whitcomb was in charge, and the breach between her and James had apparently healed. His first role was as "Mr. One" in a production of Elmer Rice's *The Adding Machine*, an examination of the dehumanizing, conformist, and homogenizing tendency of modern economic life, which had been a hit in New York in 1923.

Plays like *The Adding Machine* were a break from the more conventional fare Portland theater tended to specialize in and appealed to the emerging political radicalism of James and his friends. Despite a growing mood of tolerance both locally and nationally, Oregon political and labor activists could be, and were, sentenced under the state's antisyndicalism law for espousing what might be considered communist views. The conviction of Dirk DeJonge, a labor radical active in the Portland dock strike of 1934, was a cause célèbre among the city's left-wing community until it was reversed by the Supreme Court in 1937. As self-styled heirs to native son and radical playwright-journalist John Reed, James and his friends took an active interest in the case even as it confirmed their professional, personal, and political desires to leave Portland and its reactionary parochialism behind in favor of New York.

One by one they did just that. Harvey Welch, an actor James met and befriended at the Taylor Street Theatre, left for New York early in 1933, and Harriet Hawkins, another local actress, followed in the summer, accompanied by Fred Patterson, a Portlander who had recently returned from the Royal Academy of Dramatic Art in London. All of them knew James as a fixture on the Portland theater scene, and in particular from a series of outdoor productions of *Alice in Wonderland* that James began to stage on Portland's Park Blocks in 1932 and that continued until 1937, James himself playing an effortlessly rotund Tweedledum.

As his friends drifted eastward—James supplying each with tips on the best people and places in New York—the Portland Civic Theatre came to occupy more and more of his time. In December 1933 he played "a Benevolent Gentleman" in *A Christmas Carol*, and in 1934 created costumes for two more productions, closing the year with another appearance—this time as Mr. Fezziwig—in that year's production of *A Christmas Carol.* For the next three years, James busied himself with costumes and scenery for plays ranging from *Once in a Lifetime* to *Ah, Wilderness!* but he was also getting the chance to play more substantial acting roles. Bess Whitcomb cast him as Andrei Prosorov in *The Three Sisters,* and his March 1935 performance as Burbage in *Elizabeth the Queen* was cited by *The Oregonian*'s drama editor as "outstanding."

But it was in April 1936 that James attained what was to be his greatest—and, for all intents and purposes, final—moment on the stage in a lightweight comedy-mystery entitled *The Bishop Misbehaves. The Oregonian* wrote:

> James Beard gave a demonstration of how it should be done when he played the leading role in "The Bishop Misbehaves." . . . Mr. Beard plays the part of the detective born bishop as though he had been reading mystery thrillers all his life and spent his spare time in a bishop's palace. A veteran of the Civic Theater stage who made a tardy return last night, Mr. Beard gave every indication of just being poured into the part of the Bishop of Broadminster. He lost none of the opportunities to squeeze without effort every last drop of comedy from the delightfully humorous characterization. He reveled in the chance to solve a crime, got into very deep water and came out still smiling.

Despite such winning reviews—based, no doubt, on his relish of one of those rare roles that suited both his physique and character—James found himself backstage again, as well as offering his services as a drama coach without much success. His work in costume and scenic design had long before this led him naturally enough to contacts in the world of design generally, and to interior design in particular—and ultimately to food and cooking. Just off the Park Blocks in downtown Portland, a woman named Agnes Crowther had set up a business making and selling lampshades that had gradually expanded to a full interior design service catering to the better class of Portlanders. Crowther had known James casually since childhood and, like James, had grown up to be talented, ambitious, and a sophisticate by Portland's lights.

The people Crowther decorated for were keen not only to live but to eat in style, and she and James devised an arrangement whereby James could do for their dining tables what Crowther was doing for their upholstery and drapes. Cooking came instinctively to James; so, too, did teaching, and by late 1932 he was supplying cooking lessons to Crowther's clients on a regular basis. However delicious the oysters, salmon, and roasts of traditional Anglo-Oregonian cooking may have been or how nutritious and right-minded the creations of the domestic scientists, neither possessed the qualities of novelty and style sought by Portland's well-to-do and emergent middle classes. By contrast, James taught "international" cooking, an amalgam of French, English, and Italian dishes capable of simultaneously supplying allure and conferring status on those who offered them.

Foreign food was of increasing interest to Portlanders generally, who on the eve of the repeal of Prohibition were beginning to recover some of the variety that had characterized the city's cooking fifteen years before. A writer in *The Oregonian* in January 1932 admitted that while the effects of Prohibition has meant that a request "for pate de foie gras will cause all members of a dining room staff to raise their eye-lids," the city nevertheless contained a number of worthwhile Chinese, Italian, Russian, and German restaurants that formed a real alternative to tearooms and cafeterias. In the mid-thirties the Town Tavern, a hangout of James and his acting friends around the corner from the Taylor Street Theatre, offered a menu in an English horse-and-hounds atmosphere that was nothing if not eclectic: steaks, chops, hamburgers, and fish joined by chili, tamales, ravioli, pigs in blankets, sukiyaki, chop suey, châteaubriand, toad-in-the-hole, and a dessert called "Arabian Iudabah."

Despite the public's growing enthusiasm for more diverse food— however scattershot and unformed—the foundations of cooking continued to be steadily undermined. The Dust Bowl and the depression destroyed what little was left of the dream of the family farm as the backbone of Jeffersonian agrarian society and assured the dominance of factory farming in the future. In Portland city power brokers had finally triumphed, with the closing of the Yamhill Market at the end of 1933 and the opening of the new Public Market Building on the waterfront. Within months the new market was embroiled in litigation and both vendor and consumer dissatisfaction, and by

1943 the building was scheduled to be torn down. Thereafter Portland, whose bounty had once stunned visitors from around the nation and the world, had no market at all.

Not all the displaced Yamhill Market stall holders were discomfited by this turn of events, which would repeat itself in city after city during the next two decades: One, a coffee and tea vendor named Fred Meyer, would become the principal supermarket operator in the Pacific Northwest. The rise and eventual dominance of the supermarket, processed foods, and national brands continued unabated through the 1930s, thriving on rather than encumbered by the depression, which steadily drove small farmers, producers, and retailers out of business. From dining cars to coffee shops to home kitchens, the nation fried in Crisco and increasingly served Chase and Sanborn Coffee and Postum. Chase and Sanborn was controlled by J. P. Morgan, who also owned Royal Baking Powder, among other products; Postum was part of mammoth General Foods, who had by then acquired Jell-O, Baker's Chocolate, Post cereals, Log Cabin syrup, Minute Tapioca, and Maxwell House Coffee, and was on the verge of launching Birds Eye frozen foods to fill the increasingly common electric refrigerator-freezers of the nation's homes.

In a sense, however, a corporate, nationally marketed food supply promoted by national magazines and radio appealed to an economically ravaged America's sense of itself as a unified people with a common identity, even as it eroded the identities of the diverse and distinctive constituents that made up that whole. Since the 1920s Americans had expressed to researchers a desire for simpler, more "American" food—although such food might easily include spaghetti and chop suey, albeit nothing from France—to which restaurateurs responded by changing their menus and firing their European chefs. Another study found that merely listing a standard menu item in French rather than English caused sales to fall. In the early thirties, a survey conducted by *American Restaurant* magazine found that 91 percent of restaurateurs believed this trend toward a vernacular cuisine was on the increase.

Although undoubtedly driven by Prohibition, concern about diet and health, and the success of domestic science's culinary agenda, the preference for American food during the thirties also reflected a more general cultural nationalism. Interest in American places and peoples was evidenced in the collection of folk songs, the compilation of regional lore by the WPA Federal Writer's Project, and the celebration of local rural life—often melded with a politically conscious social realism—in the paintings of Thomas Hart Benton, the novels of John Steinbeck, and the public's bottomless appetite for anything southern, from *The Sound and the Fury* to *Tobacco Road* to *Gone With the Wind.* The South was perhaps the closest approximation within U.S. boundaries to a distinct and nearly foreign culture, and in the thirties stylish Northerners and Midwesterners dug into Southern fried chicken with the kind of relish they would lavish in coming decades on fondue, boeuf bourguignon, quiche, sushi, and—in a convincing demonstration that what goes around, comes around—blackened redfish from Louisiana.

In 1930 this fashion was in its infancy but already of sufficient import that the *Saturday Evening Post,* then one of the largest and most influential magazines in the country, allowed screenwriter Nunnally Johnson to declaim at length against the practice in kitchens outside his native South of putting sugar in corn bread, among other insults to regional culinary traditions. In 1932 Sheila Hibben, a journalist of radical sympathies, whose late husband had been honored in Moscow for his support of the Soviet regime, noted in the pages of the *New Republic* that American cookery had become sufficiently au courant that the venerable Waldorf-Astoria, once home to Oscar and the pseudo-Parisian Peacock Alley, had instituted new menus featuring Wisconsin chicken cake, apple pan dowdy, and corned beef hash. The article attracted amused and approving comment on the editorial page of the *New York Times,* although both the *Times* and the *New Republic* may have been unaware that Hibben, who in fact had a cookbook on American regional food in the pipeline, was pioneering the perennial food writer's gambit of announcing that one's current project just happens to be the next hot trend.

Hibben was a bright and thoughtful journalist possessed of a genuine affection for American food and sufficient irony and perspective to avoid either jingoism or sentiment. In the introduction to her *The National Cookbook: A Kitchen Americana* she wrote:

We have been off our base in more ways than one, and this book is aimed to call people home, not only to take stock of the vast variety of our native materials, but to learn from the experience of our fathers the best and simplest way of eating. For it is in over-ornate-

ness as well as in carelessness that we have made our victuals vulgar
and commercial. Some of the women's magazines may have given a
press to dressed-up food as well as dietetics—the marshmallow
owes as much to them as does the spinach—and have thus encouraged a lot of show-off, which has helped to obscure what they never
really learned, that honest, savory cooking is the basis of happy
family life. . . . If the American housekeeper would only pay attention to how things taste, would study the materials of her own district, would become a virago about fresh materials, how much happier everybody in her family would be!

But Hibben was careful, as a Manhattanite in the self-consciously sophisticated 1930s, to base her appeal on more than simply
flavor, patriotism, and domestic harmony: "Efficiency aside, American women are overlooking a great opportunity if they do not see to
it that good food becomes *the style*. Mink coats and period furniture
are not always possible, but at least we can have omelets that are
soft and melting and even beans that are succulent and satisfying."
Moreover, as much as any food writer before and perhaps since, she
was aware of food's social and historical contexts: "Lobster Newburgh . . . is not an ancient gastronomic landmark, but landmark it
certainly is, and when the full history of the Mauve Decade comes to
be written, lobster Newburgh will be as much a part of the picture as
hansom cabs and feather boas."

In so forthrightly and audaciously commending corn pone,
baked beans, and buckwheat to her largely elite readers, Hibben may
have risked creating not a newfound appreciation of the nation's
culinary heritage but one more breathlessly promoted and quickly
forgotten fashion. In any case Hibben's curiosity about American
food was both intelligent and heartfelt, and her culinary instincts
were applicable to good cooking at any time in any place. However,
the book that would prove to be of greatest moment for American
cooking—and for cooking generally in the United States until the
present day—gestated not in Manhattan but in Saint Louis as a privately printed recipe collection hastily produced by a fifty-three-year-
old German American woman in order to distract herself after her
husband's recent suicide.

In 1931 Irma Rombauer had gathered her own and her friends'
recipes into a sort of one-woman community cookbook, named *The*

Joy of Cooking, and paid a local printer to produce three thousand copies, which she hoped she might sell locally. The book sold surprisingly well, and after being rejected by dozens of publishers, Rombauer persuaded Bobbs-Merrill to produce a trade edition in May 1936. Approximately seven thousand copies were purchased each year until Rombauer revised and enlarged the book in 1943. Sales of this new edition leapt to 167,000 in 1944, and by 1956 1.25 million volumes were in print, with something approaching one in twenty households in the country owning a copy. The success of *The Joy of Cooking* owed much to the shrewdness of its publisher, but more to the ability of Rombauer—the status-conscious child of an immigrant family who wanted more than anything to be genuinely American—to create an approach to food that straddled the social and technical distance between béarnaise sauce and pancakes in a manner whose comprehensiveness, efficiency, and cheerful egalitarianism rendered food of any stripe at once safely middlebrow, intriguing, and, as the title had it, joyful. Although Rombauer was an admirer of Fannie Farmer, whose food she understood to be authentically American, *The Joy of Cooking* represented a movement away from the rigorous scientism and dietary reform of domestic science toward flavor. It fostered, perhaps more than any other cookbook in history, the creation of a genuinely American cookery, diverse in substance but one in spirit, that avoids both the class-laden predilections of the gourmet and the leaden contrivances of the "cooking school marm."

By the beginning of 1937, James felt alone and frustrated in Portland. He had been living there off and on for the last ten years; many of his closest friends and colleagues had moved away; and his career—whether as actor, designer, or teacher—remained as shapeless and piecemeal as ever. Three years of letters about life in New York from Harriet Hawkins (and now from Agnes Crowther, who was rapidly establishing herself as an interior designer there) only increased his sense of isolation and failure. He became determined to go to New York himself, a move that Mary might applaud but one that she was unwilling or—with John's recent retirement from a career in which he had amassed virtually no savings—unable to finance.

But James had earned enough from cooking lessons and design work to pay his own way and propelled himself onward with fantasies of winning in what he was to call "the great and wonderful game" that is success in New York. By the autumn he was ready, and at 9:35 on Tuesday evening, September 7, 1937, he boarded a train to have one last try at a career in the New York theater. At about 10:20 on the clear, windless, warm morning of September 10, Beard pulled his suitcase and his six-foot-three, three-hundred-pound, thirty-four-year-old frame up along the brass handrail and into the filtered shadow and light of Pennsylvania Station.

He was met by Harriet Hawkins and Jack Stipe, a Portlander who had come to New York to study social welfare at Columbia and would later become a priest, first as an Episcopalian and later as a Roman Catholic. Harriet, now a stylish and sophisticated young woman, had taken to calling James "Baron" on account of his penchant for tweeds and plaid sport coats; he in turn called her "Duchess." Since her arrival in New York, she had worked variously in summer stock, for B. Altman, and for the *New York Times*. Together, Hattie and Jack took Beard to the recently vacated apartment of Agnes Crowther, whose own success was now such that she had moved on to more palatial quarters.

The apartment, at 126 West Forty-ninth Street, was halfway between Sixth and Seventh avenues. One end of the block housed a shabby corner grocery store (whose produce formed the basis of a succession of beggar's banquets Beard would cook in the apartment) and gave onto the still-glamorous Broadway theater district; the other faced the newly constructed Rockefeller Center and the RCA Building, with its four-year-old Rainbow Room ("New York's unique, gay skyscraper supper club," according to an ad in that week's *New Yorker*).

Inside the apartment James, Harriet, and Jack talked and smoked and made plans to dine that evening at the Lafayette on Eleventh Street in Greenwich Village, a place James had haunted in the twenties. Hattie knew the restaurant from a set of instructions for surviving in New York that Beard had written carefully on the back cover of a blank book he had given her the morning she had left Portland four years earlier. What made the Lafayette so desirable for the budgets of out-of-work actors in the twilight of the depression was its two-dollar dinner, instituted in 1912 and still intact, together with its unrepentantly French menu, twenty-five years later. James, Harriet, and Jack would dine that night on consommé and cherrystone clams; cassoulette of lobster, sweetbreads, suprême of chicken, pâté de la maison or steak marchand du vin; and Camembert. On Monday James might begin looking for work in the theater, but that—amid food and wine unimaginable three days earlier in Portland and friends unseen for three and four years—could wait, and dinner, as it so often would, went on till dawn.

The front page of the *New York Herald Tribune* that sunny morning of September 10, 1937, revealed a world in which Europe squabbled over a treaty on Mediterranean shipping; Japan warned travelers to stay out of its war zone around Shanghai; a former singer with Rudy Vallee's band secured her Loyalist husband's release from a Spanish jail through the personal intervention of General Franco; and—proving that while Europe prepared for war, America was still America—a twenty-seven-year-old who had worked at the New York Stock Exchange as a page since he was a teenager was elected to a seat on the exchange in recognition of his hard work. Elsewhere *The New Yorker* launched a three-part profile of celebrity G-man J. Edgar Hoover; *The Prisoner of Zenda,* with Ronald Colman, began its second week at Radio City Music Hall; and *Tobacco Road* continued into its fourth year at the Forrest Theatre.

In 1937, shaking off the depression like a tattered winter coat, New York was less a world capital than a cluster of highly sophisticated island hamlets ranging from the Greenwich Village avant-garde to the East Side aeries of the rich to Harlem, still hospitable to tolerant and adventurous whites. New Yorkers were relatively unworried about street crime and prowled the streets until late at night. The subway was clean and safe and relatively efficient. Considering the richness of culture and experience the city afforded, life was cheap and because deflated depression prices still prevailed, life for James was good. His savings, bolstered by intermittent donations from Mary, would stretch for many months. He paid perhaps sixty dollars a month in rent and food, and decent restaurant meals were within his reach—or within that of friends and acquaintances who were happy to take him out.

Basking in what he always believed was his true element, James was good company: His eyes sparkled with a faintly mischievous twinkle or rolled upward in mock disbelief, and his voice was low, rounded, and droll. He told wonderful stories about the famous people he claimed to know, about his travels, and about Mary. He blandished hostesses with the delivery of a single rose and a card—a strategy he had pioneered in London—and found himself once again in demand as an "available bachelor" at dinner parties. To sit next to James, dressed in the bow tie, tweeds, and scarves that rendered him at once professorial, eccentric, worldly, and yet cozy, was to feel that this amusing, skeptical, gossipy, benevolent bear of a man was wholly yours: "He was the most charming man I ever met," recalled more than one acquaintance. To know him was to want to do things for him. And so people did.

James, however, appeared more than capable of doing for himself. He possessed the eternal qualities that those who aspire to success in Manhattan have always possessed: ambition and drive, to be sure, but also an enormous capacity for self-salesmanship and the aura of being someone who made things happen and around whom people and money spontaneously whirled like planets and moons. As time went on, there were separate orbits of friends utterly unaware of one another's existence. In the course of a day James might travel from the theater district to midtown and the Upper East Side to the apartments and boarding hotels of Oregonian friends to the bars and baths of Greenwich Village. There were, in a sense, as many Beards as there were people who knew him.

James was a voracious reader of biography and newspapers, and in particular the theater, social, and cooking sections. The harvest of 1937 had been good, and on the day of Beard's return to New York, Clementine Paddleford, the *Herald Tribune*'s six-day-a-week food columnist, was urging her readers to put up applesauce, just as earlier in the week she had been extolling the virtues of grape, bayberry, and quince preserves and celebrated bumper crops of McIntosh, Gravenstein, and Dutchess apples, Seckel pears, and peaches. The day before, she had reported the arrival in New York of something new called "print butter," which came in wrapped quarter-pound sticks and packed in a box rather than in the traditional tub. There were other sorts of progress: "Canned and frozen foods [are] in many instances proving cheaper than fresh," Paddleford wrote, "for there is no waste and the product is preserved at the peak of its perfection as it comes from [the] field."

That same week Paddleford reported that food producers and processors would occupy twenty-five acres at the upcoming 1939

World's Fair in Flushing Meadows. The theme of the fair was progress—progress as a symbol of a renewed national well-being, as a sign of destiny for the entire American community tying the American people's past to a bountiful and thrilling future. There was little concern that progress and consumerism might be deleterious to community and tradition; and few found anything sinister in the relation of processed, canned, and frozen food to the survival of regional products and cookery. Progress had its price, but it was a positive price: "Once homely ladies could rest on their kitchen talents and face the world without apology," Paddleford wrote. "Today every wife is expected to be attractive, a charming hostess, and a good cook all in one breath. These new requirements make life almost as hard for Jennie Wrens as for the work-bent matrons of the Middle Ages. But there is no turning back, so learn your groceries and rejoice."

Self-improvement indeed became the watchword of the era, accompanied by the fad for "how-to" books and radio shows, in which experts—frequently self-styled celebrities who not only taught a given skill but whose very lives embodied its successful application—taught manners, bridge, golf, or, in the case of Dale Carnegie, how to be "well liked." The world of food participated in this development, too, albeit through figures literally synthesized from older traditions: "Betty Crocker"—an invention of General Mills's advertising department who combined the domestic wisdom of a Fannie Farmer with the compassion and concern of a favorite aunt—dispensed household advice on a popular radio program and in print, while Pillsbury responded with its own "Mary Ellis Ames." Newspaper and magazine publishers attempted to market the expertise of real persons like Paddleford and *Ladies Home Journal* food editor Ann Batchelder with less success, and the role of such food writers remained essentially that of journalist—and women's page journalist at that—rather than full-fledged celebrity personality. Cookbooks were still marketed less through the writer's real or apparent status than as manuals or encyclopedias, which frequently had no credited authors at all, as was the case with the *Herald Tribune*'s own *Home Institute Cookbook*.

But however anonymous its popularizers and however invisible their audience of housewives, interest in food and cooking was on an ascendent of sorts, and the interest in American food Sheila Hibben reported in 1932 was still evident at the end of the decade. In 1939 a Fifth Avenue department store opened a shop selling food products from every American state (with honey from thirty-two of the forty-eight) while *The New Yorker*'s "Markets and Menus" column ran a four-page list of regional American foods available by mail order, and Paddleford reported on efforts to produce goat cheese and truffles on Long Island. Even grandstanding politicians accorded culinary regionalism a measure of respect: A state legislator in Maine introduced a bill making the addition of tomatoes to clam chowder (as in Manhattan rather than New England chowder) illegal, a move that attracted considerable press coverage, including an editorial (against) in the *New York Times*. At the same time awareness of ethnic foods—at least in New York—was spreading beyond its indigenous neighborhood bases: A few weeks before James's arrival in New York, *The New Yorker* featured a "Talk of the Town" report on squid and the markets and Italian restaurants where one could find it; Paddleford, whose tastes were broad and whose enthusiasm for flavor and color could not be restrained despite her domestic science–like gravitas, frequently brought ethnic shops and products to the attention of her readers.

When James returned with his *Herald Tribune* from the corner grocery at Forty-ninth Street and Seventh Avenue on his first Saturday morning in New York, he found a mix of what was new and efficient, what was fresh and cheap, and a daily recipe for a one-dollar meal for four. (That day it was corned-beef-hash casserole with lima beans: "Place one can of corned beef in a casserole. Cover with one can baby lima beans and add one-half cup condensed tomato soup. Place in a moderate oven and bake for thirty minutes.") For further recipes readers were urged to write or phone the *Herald Tribune* "Home Institute," a name designed to evoke the authority and status of domestic science and its legion of experts. Despite the movement's lessening grip on the nation's eating habits, it still exerted considerable influence through magazines like The Boston Cooking School's *American Cookery*, which continued imperturbably to crank out recipes like "Jellied Bananas," in which scooped-out bananas were glazed with raspberry-colored gelatine, filled with melted marshmallows, and encrusted with pecans. But for the majority of women, the ideals and models established by domestic science remained perhaps the only vehicle through which their involvement with food would be taken seriously.

If the right-hand column of page 8 of James's Saturday *Herald Tribune* reported on food and drink as domestic science and women's work, the left-hand side, in the form of Lucius Beebe's "This New York," approached it as male-centered, plutocratic gourmandise. Beebe, a flamboyant homosexual dandy with an astonishing deep voice, who favored top hats, ascots, and mink-lined topcoats, wrote about New York society and its orgies of clubs, haute cuisine, and rare wines in a style at once smart-aleck and baroque:

> The urban theater season opened with a tremendous crush of linen dinner jackets last week when the astute Rockefellers, who are always aware of the uses of timing, tossed a musical spectacle called "Virginia" at a public virtually panting to spend its money on almost anything that's new. . . . There was a concerted rush to Jack and Charlie's [the "21" Club] afterward and by 11:30 you couldn't get standing room at the bar there. The Stork was a shambles of chi-chi a few minutes later, and by breakfast the entire town knew the summer's dirt on every one. It was a night of reunion and dishing it.

Beebe might mock the club scene, but food and wine—at least as understood and interpreted by French chefs and British aristocrats—were a different matter: "Lunched [at the Ritz-Carlton] magnificently off an English sole Chambord, which is with a magnificent claret sauce; a breast of chicken Eugenie, a green salad and chilled fruits in kirsch, the whole accompanied by a bottle of [Gruaud-] LaRose '26, and as comfortable a summer meal as one could wish." The distance from Paddleford's corned-beef-hash-lima-bean casserole and instant butterscotch pudding to Beebe's claret and sole and Escoffier-trained chefs was more than a few columns and more than a matter of mere attitude, income, or class. Few readers would have read both features, and fewer still would grasp that the articles might in fact be in some way about the same things.

But all these movements—Finck, Mencken, and Hibben's neo-agrarian culinary nationalism, Paddleford's enthusiasms on behalf of regional and ethnic foodstuffs, and Beebe's gourmet dining—did occasionally converge, albeit not entirely comfortably. With the end of Prohibition, gourmets returned to business as usual, dining out as

New York's restaurants recovered, but still more typically at meals arranged by Les Chevaliers du Tastevin, the Lucullus Club, Les Amis d'Escoffier, and other wine and food societies established locally or imported from abroad. Their menus, frequently written up in all their stuffy, arteriosclerotic glory by jowly, cigar-smoking, wine and society writer Selmer Fougner of the *New York Sun*, were top-heavy with foie gras, lobster, baron of lamb, soufflés, and ancient champagnes, Burgundies and Bordeaux, and ports. But gourmet societies also made fitful attempts to go native, producing one Manhattan dinner featuring mignon of beef Henri IV accompanied by corn bread, Minnesota wild rice, Maryland terrapin, and "Le Gombo Clair." Another meal in the winter of 1938 at the Waldorf-Astoria, whose touch in American cookery was surer, featured a menu entirely based on the food and produce of Idaho.

The gourmet's emphasis on rare ingredients, the classic repertory of French haute cuisine, and on cooking as the alchemical refinement of base metal did not, however, marry well with the more direct pleasures at the heart of American traditions. Domestic science, which disapproved of excess, flavor, and anything too redolent of the farm, did not have much good to say to either tendency. A synthesis of native and gourmet tendencies instead emerged from an unlikely source: the cultural avant-garde and artistic and intellectual elite. Sympathetic to American regional dishes and ingredients, and familiarized by the cafés and bistros of Europe with the possibilities of fare that was simple but delicious, the avant-garde saw the potential for food to be an aesthetic, psychological, and—its capacity to reinforce the economic and social strength of communities—political good.

The most tangible evidence of this development was the publication in 1939 of *Fit for a King*, produced by a highbrow music impresario and book and set designer named Merle Armitage. Never a bestseller, the book was nonetheless a landmark and certainly one of the most striking cookbooks ever produced in the United States, with stunning late-thirties streamline graphics and typography, an oversize format, photos by Edward Weston, and recipes and comments contributed by artists and social critics like Lewis Mumford, Alfred Lunt, Edgard Varèse, Rockwell Kent, Louis Untermeyer, and Gertrude Stein. The recipes comfortably encompassed tastes ranging from truffles in champagne to vegetarian enchiladas, blinis, risottos, and various Chinese, Indian, and Middle Eastern dishes, but the book's message was as much intellectual as practical. In his introduction Armitage took pains to establish the legitimacy of cooking as an art on a par with music or painting ("The esthetic pleasure induced by food can be so closely related to that produced by certain music and other arts, as to defy separation or separate identification."); to promote the virtues of traditional American food and ingredients as well as ethnic cuisines; to decry not only food processing but the "canned" music and drama he saw as related developments; and to urge a kind of personal gastronomic liberation free from worry about "diet platitudes."

Perhaps most important, he suggested that the appreciation of food, as with other arts, depended upon an educated public with sufficient leisure time to cultivate an interest in it: "Cooking is a thing women *have* to do. Remove the daily necessity, and you would, undoubtedly, remove most of the indifference, making room thereby, for lively interest. Perhaps additional leisure will, in time, have a wholesome effect." Attempting to wrest food away from both the gourmets and the domestic scientists, Armitage and his contributors proclaimed that cooking was neither a luxury nor a science, but an art whose role was crucial in the "art of living"; in what—as consumerism eroded the distinctions between art, fashion, and leisure— would later be called life-style. Although they raised their voices in concern over the increasingly "canned" nature of American life, the culinary-cultural avant-garde was convinced that social and economic progress could mean good things for food.

During his first year in New York, James made little headway in either costume and set design or as an actor. Some of his friends, like Harvey Welch, another member of the Portland *Alice in Wonderland* cast, were already steadily employed in New York theater; others, like Bob Hanes, also from Portland, who shared James's West Forty-ninth Street apartment, struggled unsuccessfully as singers, or, like Hattie Hawkins, had of necessity drifted into other kinds of work. James was at least outwardly an optimist by nature, but through the fall and winter of 1937 and into the spring of 1938, he became more and more privately disheartened as not a single stage job came his way and his funds dwindled. He continued to cultivate various theater figures who might help his career. Through Agnes De Mille, now launched as a choreographer, and Harriet Hawkins, James met

Cheryl Crawford, a critical figure in the new American theater who had produced plays for the Theatre Guild and had founded the Group Theatre with Lee Strasberg a few years before. But even Crawford—who had produced at least one play on Broadway every year for the previous decade and routinely worked with Clifford Odets, Kurt Weill, Judith Anderson, and Tallulah Bankhead—could find no work for James, although she did arrange a paid job for him catering a party.

Meanwhile James and the other Oregonians—Hattie Hawkins, Jack Stipe, Harvey Welch, Fred Patterson, and Bob Hanes—established a way of life in Manhattan that was comfortable if hardly lush. There were ritual Sunday dinners at Longchamps on Fifty-ninth Street, one of a chain of six French-inspired restaurants, at which the group recounted the week's news over deviled stuffed lobster, broccoli hollandaise, and oversize cocktails for around two dollars a head. The group also frequented Child's, at whose twenty-five locations you could get a fried oyster sandwich with cole slaw for thirty-five cents or a meal of clam chowder, salad with Russian dressing, roast leg of lamb, fresh spinach, hash browns, and the dessert of your choice for seventy-five cents. James, however, also led forays into Greenwich Village for pizza—an utterly alien substance to the other Oregonians—or spaghetti, served by singing waiters at Asti on East Twelfth Street. They shared Greek meals at the Athena (on Sixth Avenue at Twenty-ninth Street) and Martinis, onion soup, and tête de veau at Charles, a fashionable place near Sheridan Square amid the otherwise resolutely bohemian-ethnic restaurants and cafés of the rest of the Village.

James himself cooked for some or all of the group at least once a week, either informally—as when mushrooms from the corner grocery would surface grilled on toast—or in a mutually beneficial arrangement whereby a friend would supply the kitchen and the groceries (usually a chicken) and the habitually impoverished James would cook in return for a seat at the table. "Jim could produce miracles with a chicken and a few sad looking vegetables," Harvey Welch remembered. And there were parties—parties at which trays of Manhattans and Martinis arrived and disappeared in wave after wave. Drunkenness and monumental hangovers were the rule, although James himself could metabolize alcohol at a prodigious rate with no effect on his charm or conversation.

Many of these parties were given by Jim Cullum, a bland, round-faced, independently wealthy ex–West Pointer, at his apartment at 14 East Washington Square Place in Greenwich Village. His "girl-friend," a fashionably dressed woman named Peggy Martin—whose pretensions James mocked as "piss elegant"—lived in the same women's residential hotel as Harriet Hawkins, on West Eleventh Street. Hawkins also knew another of Cullum's girlfriends, Ruth Norman, who had become Cheryl Crawford's lover. Cullum's father, a major Pennsylvania industrialist, had died four years earlier, shortly after being indicted on charges of evading more than one hundred thousand dollars in income taxes. Aimless but armed with a fortune, Cullum now aspired—unsuccessfully, in the eyes of most—to the sophistication and panache of a Lucius Beebe: a man-about-town complete with Rolls-Royce, a cellar of good wine, and a group of friends drawn from New York café society and the arts commu-nity, whose tastes were fashionable and diverse and whose sexual preferences were ambiguous. By the end of spring 1938, James was a full-fledged member of the Cullum circle.

That summer James's professional and financial situation became impossible. Bob Hanes, who shared and paid half the rent of the apartment on West Forty-ninth Street (and instituted hilarious vocal duets with James at dinners there), decided to return to Portland, leaving James with a home he could no longer afford. At the same time, despite the solace of occasional meals at "21" with Cheryl Crawford, James was coming to realize that there was no future for him in the theater. After a dinner party at the apartment, he and Hattie Hawkins talked through the night about what he ought to do. "It was an extraordinary evening," Hawkins recalled. "No one was a better conversationalist than Jim, but he never really talked about himself—about what he was really thinking or worrying about." Again and again James despaired of ever becoming an actor, and Hawkins responded by bringing up his obvious and extraordinary gift for cookery and food. Both with friends and on his own over the coming months, James pondered the idea of forgetting the theater and trying to make a career in food. But beyond the idea of giving cooking lessons as he had in Portland, he had little idea what direc-tion such a career might take.

In late summer Jim Cullum suggested that James move into his apartment in the Village, commencing what would be a mercurial relationship over the next few years. The sexual component of their friendship was unclear to James's friends, but in any case Cullum suited James's lifetime attraction to well-bred men who either were— or could pass for—straight. One friend suggested, "Jim didn't like being gay, and he didn't like anyone else liking being gay." Although Cullum lacked James's sophistication and polished, genial style, his money made Beard's life in New York possible for the next few years, and through weekend visits to the Cullum family farm in Pennsylvania, James became a kind of adopted son to Cullum's mother, Anne. If Cullum did not satisfy Beard, he nevertheless sustained him.

At the same time James moved in with Cullum, Mary Houston Davis, a Scotswoman and teacher at Columbia whom he and Harriet Hawkins knew through a mutual friend in Portland, arranged a job for him teaching social studies, English, and French at a private school in New Jersey, whose socialist politics went some way to ameliorate James's frustration at being stuck in yet another pointless, dead-end job. As James led his students through irregular verbs that autumn, Neville Chamberlain returned from Munich, and German tanks crossed into Czechoslovakia. At Flushing Meadows construction meanwhile continued on the "Court of Peace" and other pavilions for the 1939 World's Fair, the national ode to progress and possibility now officially subtitled "The World of Tomorrow." But, as for James, the shape that future might take was more and more a mystery whose imminent resolution begot as much apprehension as hope.

FIVE

1939 – 1949

He was, Beard would recall still a little breathlessly thirty years later, "handsome as hell." In November 1938 Jim Cullum had held yet another cocktail party that Beard, as permanent houseguest, was compelled to attend, despite his dislike of crowded, boozy gatherings accompanied by the hackneyed canapés and finger foods he had christened "doots." But all the smoke, din, and inane chitchat were forgotten when James spotted a thirty-four-year-old named Bill Rhode. A minister's son born in Berlin, Rhode had what at the time might have been called "Continental charm," claimed connections with European aristocrats, and cultivated useful figures like Lucius Beebe (Beebe would offer thanks in his New Year's Eve column that year "to Bill Rhode for two flagons of hock"). Moreover, he was erudite and witty, he had published a cookbook called *Of Cabbages and Kings* just that year, his face and slicked back hair were beautiful to behold, and he was married with two sons. James gravitated toward him with a ferocious, nearly mindless resolve.

He was everything Cullum wanted to be and was not, and possessed in effortless superfluity all the qualities that James sought in others and wished to cultivate in himself. By the party's end, Beard and Rhode had fallen into rapt conversation, went back to Rhode's apartment, and, together with Rhode's sister Irma, talked late into the night about food. By the end of the evening they had convinced themselves that—with well-to-do New Yorkers still scrambling to make up for drinking time lost during Prohibition and some 250 cocktail parties being held each day on the Upper East Side alone—there was money to be made providing food to Manhattan's higher social echelons. In particular, an hors d'oeuvre catering business offering an alternative to "doots" could make a killing.

Beyond any social, psychological, and physical attraction,

James's and Rhode's culinary sensibilities dovetailed well. Rhode played the possibilities of his admittedly murky connections to the European aristocracy to the hilt, all the while insisting that food, society, and entertaining should above all be fun. His *Of Cabbages and Kings*, a compendium of recipes and advice loosely based on the supposed past and present dining habits of European nobles, was another example of the more distinctively personal, intimately scaled food writing that emerged in the later thirties. Rhode's impeccable social credentials and cool savoir faire permitted him—as no mere cooking school or women's page "marm" could—to suggest disarmingly that the only thing socially ambitious Americans intent on emulating their blue-blooded betters needed to do was relax:

> Thank heaven, people pick their teeth again, and burping, the favorite after-dinner pastime of the gourmet, is back in polite society once more, even on the stage and on the screen. . . . Social developments of the past decade have made possible a leisurely outlook toward life on the part of many people who were formerly caught up in the whirl of big business and nervous profit-taking. . . . Eating is fun, and cooking is fun, and to hell with all the calories and balanced meals! Let us again sit around big, comfortable tables and enjoy our meals. . . . Good food is best at home, and bad food is bad everywhere. Good food is fun, and bad food is a menace.

Rhode's food preferences, presented with equal self-assurance, were also faintly outrageous. He exalted foie gras and caviar, Escoffier's now-hallowed battery of emulsified sauces, and canard Tour d'Argent but was equally enthusiastic about ham-and-potato casserole, tamale pie, jambalaya, hominy squares, and nine varieties of hash. Like James, Rhode cared desperately about status and style, but he disdained the stuffed-shirt cookery of gourmets and "the condescending lectures of these self-appointed epicurean masters" in favor of a free-spirited eclecticism whose earnest yet ironic embrace of apparently low-brow food was distinctly "camp" in spirit. That same sensibility was apparent in Rhode's mastery of publicity and self-advertisement, which was based on an understanding that stardom, properly managed, can be less an achievement than a self-fulfilling prophecy.

Beard finished out the fall school term in New Jersey, and, with

financial backing from Jim Cullum, he and the Rhodes rented a
tastefully decorated front parlor, with a large marshaling area behind
it and a basement kitchen, at 128 East Sixty-sixth Street, off Lexington Avenue, just opposite the New York Armory. Beard and Irma
Rhode were joined in the kitchen by Mack Shinn, a would-be-actor
friend of Beard's from Seattle who had excelled in discovering inexpensive restaurants for the Oregonians' weekly meals. Bill Rhode,
meanwhile, exploited his considerable social and press connections,
and within weeks of opening in January 1939, Hors d'Oeuvre, Inc.,
was an obvious success. On April 29, between his customary notes—
"About the last place in town where one can command Moet &
Chandon '21 Dom Perignon Cuvee are the Colony and the Monte
Carlo"—Lucius Beebe praised the new endeavor of "the culinary
scholar, Bill Rhode":

> He has turtle livers flown in from Florida, the finest of Danish hams
> and caviars, anchovies, lobsters and game pastes in every known
> combination. There are also mousses, aspics and en croute arrange-
> ments, sandwich loaves, roast and smoked game, and just about
> anything one can dream up in the line of cold buffet. The special
> merit of Mr. Rhode's service is that everything is prepared to order
> and there are no ice box confections that have been sitting around
> since the day before yesterday. It's a brand new sort of gastronomic
> agency and already shows signs of being a minor Klondike.

Danton Walker of the *Daily News* also made frequent mention of
Hors d'Oeuvre, Inc. On June 16 Clementine Paddleford devoted
most of a column to it and to Bill Rhode, in her at once breathless
and congested style:

> Sample the entire collection and it is the brioche onion sandwich
> that gives the palate its great moment. This is concocted of brioche,
> the bread baked into loaves rather than individual breakfast por-
> tions. The loaves are thinly sliced and from each slice three tiny
> rings are cut. These are spread with mayonnaise and a thin ring of
> Bermuda or the Italian red onion laid on, with a second ring of
> brioche for a cap. Now each small sandwich gets a tight little
> squeeze until it oozes dressing. Then the side of [the] ring is rolled in
> minced parsley which coats the mayonnaise and finishes the sand-
> wich in a frosting of green curls.

This sandwich, together with vichyssoise—then still a novelty—at the breathtaking price of two dollars per pint, was Hors d'Oeuvre, Inc.'s most popular item. In a write-up on June 24 in *The New Yorker,* Sheila Hibben noted that "Hors d'Oeuvre, Inc., knows everything there is to know about that soup, except, I noticed, how to spell it."

As did Paddleford, Beebe, and Walker, Hibben described Rhode as the sole chef, creator, and proprietor of Hors d'Oeuvre, Inc., despite the presence of Irma Rhode, Mack Shinn, and James Beard. But success stilled resentment for the moment, and in any event Beard's not-inconsiderable charisma could hardly be confined to the basement kitchen for very long. In the spring of 1939, Hors d'Oeuvre, Inc., catered a reception for the five-year-old New York chapter of the International Wine & Food Society, arguably New York's most sophisticated consumers of fine food and drink, with Richardson Wright, editor of *House & Garden,* as president, and members like gourmet writer Julian Street, wine importer Frank Schoonmaker, and theater producer/epicure Crosby Gaige, an intimate of the society's London-based founder, André Simon. The organization was run, with white-hot efficiency, out of Gaige's Manhattan office by the society's secretary, Jeanne Owen, a Californian raised in Paris. Chicly dressed, energetic, outspoken, and bossy, she flaunted her French background and food training—insisting her name be pronounced "Jaahn"—before what was a hopelessly Francophile group and thereby utterly dominated the society. James had been her contact at Hors d'Oeuvre, Inc., and when the reception was judged a success, she quickly became the latest and perhaps most formidable yet of the stage mother/promoters who had been a constant in his life.

The summer of 1939 was hot and Hors d'Oeuvre, Inc., prospered against the background of a visit to New York by King George VI and Queen Elizabeth in June; the impending European war, which finally broke out on September 3; and, not least, the New York World's Fair. The International Restaurant Conference celebrated Restaurant Day at the fair and was told by Dr. H. B. Meek, director of the Cornell School of Hotel Management: "Eating [will] be done less at home and more in restaurants in the world of tomorrow." In Owen's tow James visited the fair and ate at the restaurant of the French Pavilion, run by a short, serious, and supremely controlled man named Henri Soulé, who would, after the fair, reopen the restaurant as Le Pavillon, the most exalted dining room in America for the next three decades. Other pavilions, notably the Belgian and Swiss, boasted exceptional restaurants that would also be reborn in Manhattan after the fair, and these three and their manifold progeny—founded by managers, waiters, and chefs eager to make their own mark—were largely responsible for the Eurocentrism of serious restaurants in New York, which would last forty years to come. Despite the culinary nationalism of the previous twenty years, the emergent class of "food professionals"—James among them—were stunned by the fair, which suggested that in the "World of Tomorrow" the food would be international everywhere and everywhere international. While it brought foreign culinary talent to the United States on a scale unseen since the turn of the century, the 1939 New York World's Fair, born of America's hard-won cultural self-esteem and belief in its own future, proved to be a significant force in the decline of American cooking and ingredients in their native land.

Beard, Irma Rhode, and Mack Shinn continued to work and develop recipes through the rest of the year. Special items were created for the holidays, and a take-away meal service offered on Thursdays and Sundays, when the domestic staffs of Hors d'Oeuvre, Inc., customers were likely to have the day off. Meanwhile Jeanne Owen—whose constant phone calls and monitoring of his activities made her interest in James almost literally proprietary—began his formal education in food. James's approach to cooking and food, however inherently sure, was largely instinctive: What he had learned from Mary, who disliked company or interference in the kitchen, was not so much taught as picked up through observation and furthered by his own experiments and his colossal memory for both facts and flavors. Although Owen could not extinguish James's reliance on the American flavors of his childhood as the wellspring of his culinary sensibility, she gave him a French sense of theory and system—the principles of cooking technique and the repertoire of ingredients and dishes—that made cooking codifiable and therefore communicable to others. She taught him to write and research recipes, to harmonize flavors and menus, and to cook efficiently and with consistent quality—to make sense of what heretofore had

largely been sentiment. To what would ultimately be her own cha-
grin, she also turned him from a student to someone who was all too
ready to be a teacher.

In early 1940 Owen had obtained a book contract from a publisher called M. Barrows, which specialized in "how-to" books. *A
Wine Lover's Cookbook,* as it was titled, consisted entirely of recipes
that in some way incorporated wine together with an introduction
by Richardson Wright, written in the customarily baroque prose of
the gourmet:

> Amid the spate of cookery books that is pouring from the presses (a
> sure sign of America's gastronomic rebirth) it is a rare pleasure to
> find one that dares to look on wine when it is red or white or trans-
> lated into bland Cognac or toothsome liqueurs. All too many of the
> minor Apicians who pen our kitchen guides necessarily avoid the
> subject of wine in cooking. Daughters of the Dark Ages of Prohibi-
> tion, their ignorance of wines is so profound as to make the angels
> weep. Not so the ebullient Jeanne Owen, gourmette by birth and
> practice. At baptism, having been regenerated by water, her parents
> then assured the salvation of her palate by touching her infant lips
> with rare old brandy.

Surprisingly the "ebullient" Owen's own style was less florid than
choppy and epigrammatic, consisting of disconnected paragraphs of
one or two sentences: "Cooking has been the hobby of kings,
queens, picturesque ladies of the court, and of the great in genius."
"Petty economy in the kitchen shows no results at the end of the
year, except, perhaps, a little more to spend on digestive tablets."
The recipes themselves were more inspired, with one contributed by
James (described as "one of the Brotherhood of Bachelor Cooks")
for a molded "Ham Mousse" of chopped ham, consommé, and
cream. Owen, for her part, brought Beard to Barrows, which signed
him for a book titled *Hors d'Oeuvre and Canapés,* whose recipes
were written and tested in a matter of weeks that spring.

Hors d'Oeuvre and Canapés was, on the surface, of no special
merit, written in a slightly fussy style in a tone that steered a nervous
course between the avuncular and the condescending, as though
both writer and reader were parvenus crashing a party at which they
had had, until recently, little business. In that respect it was as much

about new and shifting social aspirations as it was about food. But James had also produced a book—perhaps one of the first in the field of food—which reflected distinctly contemporary ideas and attitudes about self-improvement, progress, and modernity. It was a volume of recipes but also a kind of social self-improvement course, offering "A Key to the Cocktail Party" in which the reader was trained both practically—"Have plenty of cigarettes and not just your own brand"—and psychologically—"Don't try to force liquor on your guests"—in the theory and practice of entertaining. Its author presented himself not as a domestic scientist but as a genial figure who incorporated the best features of the expert professional and the knowledgeable amateur. However slapdash and awkward, *Hors d'Oeuvre and Canapés* communicated the presence of an engaged and engaging "personality" who lived this kind of life and lived it well, rather than a dispenser of terse gastronomic prescriptions like Owen's.

Beard presented the cocktail party as a post-Prohibition phenomenon, "an institution . . . as democratic as the subway" as well as being the "Twentieth Century salon." Of course, for most Americans emerging from the depression, it was nothing of the kind, but it nevertheless represented another step in the nation's progress: "It is a far cry from the fly-specked and hearty free-lunch table of the American pioneer saloon to the perfectly appointed hors d'oeuvre table of today, but I think America has jumped the gap and is safely on the modern side. It is this modern picture I hope to present in this book." And so it was *modern* food, at least in its social aspect, based on the spirit of the late thirties and the World's Fair, that Beard launched in that flotilla of open-face sandwiches and deviled eggs that would dominate American entertaining for the next two decades. Despite being published as the nation was near to going to war, *Hors d'Oeuvre and Canapés* was in its third printing by 1944 and has remained continuously in print ever since, a longevity matched by few titles among twentieth-century American cookbooks. If only for that reason, it was a much more significant book in its social and cultural impact than has been usually recognized.

Bill Rhode was enraged when he learned that Beard was to write *Hors d'Oeuvre and Canapés*, and so he might have been later, when reading lines like, "I am frequently asked in my shop, 'What is the difference between a canapé and an hors d'oeuvre?'" Beard's relationship with Rhode and the business did not survive the book's publication, and Beard was gone by mid-1940. In the wake of his departure, Rhode renamed the business "Bill Rhode's Hors d'Oeuvre, Inc.'" Irma Rhode and Mack Shinn stayed on until the business was sold in 1941; having moved to 746 Madison Avenue, it disappeared in 1943. To what extent Rhode's public relations savvy and market sense were more crucial to its success than his sister's and Beard's food is difficult to say; and it is more difficult still to say what specific influences on its culinary repertoire were Beard's alone. The Rhodes' lengthy experience among the foie gras and caviar set suggest that their contribution lay on that side of the menu, while trips to ethnic markets and delicatessens were probably inspired by Beard. Some of the most interesting food—tiny artichokes stuffed with pricey fillings, for example, or "cornucopias" of rolled sliced meat with various fillings—seems the product of genuine creative collaboration. Beard's own input most likely came from what remained his principal source of inspiration: his childhood with his mother.

Beard took credit for introducing a number of dishes popularized at Hors d'Oeuvre, Inc.: a potted beef spread called Strathborough paste; a rum-based white fruitcake made for the holidays; and a luxurious corned beef hash. But all of them, without exception, are recipes of Mary Beard's or dishes she served him that he re-created from memory. At about the time *Hors d'Oeuvre and Canapés* was published, in the early summer of 1940, Mary Beard—who had been in poor health for the previous ten years—fell ill with chronic myocarditis, an inflammation of the heart muscle. Beard boarded a train for Portland and was with her when she died on August 16. He remained in Portland for another month, distributing her effects— pieces of English brass, buttonhooks, and thimbles—to friends, selling the rest, and taking an outing to Mount Adams across the Columbia in Washington State. As best his friends could tell, her death did not devastate him, and his grief rendered itself not in tears but in a growing pensiveness.

Years later in his memoir, *Delights and Prejudices,* Beard seems to have coined the term "taste memory." But for him, it existed in a much broader and deeper sense than the mere recollection of particular flavors. *Delights and Prejudices* is as much an essay on memory, in the tradition of Augustine and Proust, as it is a memoir; and the recipes do not simply serve to recall the events to which they relate but to reenact them. Memory was a kind of muse for Beard, and he did not so much create as revivify his past, a past with more imaginative and psychological resonance than simple recollection could ever suggest. For Beard, food and his mother comprised his most intense memories, and they were inseparably intertwined. As a captive of his mother's incessant psychological presence, he was oppressed by them; insofar as food was his singular gift, he was liberated by them. But with Mary's death James was finally free to speak with his own voice—a voice from the past, formed of childhood marketing trips each day on Yamhill Street and the companionship of Jue-Let; the flour and oven heat of the kitchen in Hawthorne Park; and the grilling and salmon and clams of Gearhart Beach. In coming years he would speak of Mary with increasing bitterness, awareness, and a sense that the very chains she had cast around his massive wrists, through her frustration and unfulfilled needs, could at least in part set him free.

He returned to New York few weeks later, age thirty-seven, taking over the guest bedroom in Jeanne Owen's apartment. By autumn, *Hors d'Oeuvre and Canapés* was selling well enough for Barrows to commission another title from Beard, to be called *Cook It Outdoors,* and he spent the winter in Cullum's apartment writing the book. He now had no regular employment, but an advance on the new book as well as a bequest from his mother allowed him to get by, as did a job, arranged by Lucius Beebe and his lover, Jim Clark, managing the Bird and Bottle restaurant in Putnam County, New York, during the summer of 1941. Beard and his publisher seemed to have had a knack for spotting emerging trends and responding to them; more to the point, throughout his career Beard's own experience and interests seem to have coincided with those of the public. Thus, having exploited the cocktail party boom, Beard turned to outdoor cooking, to whose popularity in the early forties and beyond he was a major contributor.

On the surface grilling and barbecuing appear to be a kind of nostalgic throwback rather than another aspect of the rush of the second quarter of the twentieth century toward progress and modernity. But the only thing that the outdoor cookery of the American past and that of the forties and the postwar era had in common was fire: In the first instance it was the product of necessity, in the second of affluence—the contrast a perfect illustration of the difference between a way of life and what has come to be called "life-style." Outdoor cooking was "modern" in the same sense as the cocktail party was modern: It was a leisure and social activity—made possible by increases in income, education, and leisure time—one "learned" to do with the advice of the expert personality.

It was also, significantly, a fashion that allowed men to be cooks again, even if not in the confines of the domestic science–defined kitchen. In fact, appealing to this very audience was one of the principal selling points of *Cook It Outdoors* when it was published in June 1941, as the jacket copy proclaimed:

> No polite cookbook this. It is the answer to the colossal appetites that develop in spring, summer or when active sports and the urge to live in the open air are paramount ideas in every man's head. It is a man's book written by a man who understands not only the healthy outdoor eating and cooking habits, but who is an expert at the subtle nuances of tricky flavoring as well. And it will be invaluable to the woman who aims to please the masculine members of her household. . . . A good workable book that will take a heck of a lot of wear and be a darned good companion to the outdoor cook.

Happily this tone of fastidious machismo was not evident in the book itself. As a piece of writing, it is a far more successful effort than *Hors d'Oeuvre and Canapés,* and the recipes are more attractive and convincing. One senses that Beard simply believed more in this food; in many respects the direct and simple food of his youth and the food he preferred throughout his life. There are extraordinarily vivid descriptions, for example, a hamburger laced with minced garlic in San Francisco, which Beard describes as being served after hours of driving through the fog. There is also a fair amount of amusing personal anecdote: Mary Hamblet is brought onstage to explain how to make a mint julep, and—in a dissertation on campfire cooking—Cheryl Crawford and Ruth Norman appear (first person plural) as "two girls on a camping trip" to the Gaspé Peninsula. There are unlikely recipes for "chippino," chili con carne, and spareribs from Jeanne Owen; Martinis from Jim Cullum's mother (orange rind and onions) and from the Oregonians' bolthole, Longchamps (large and unadorned); and unexpected miscellany like polenta. It is a jolly, hearty, but nevertheless stylish and erudite book written by the Beard "personality" in a more mature and authentic mode.

By 1942 Beard was also beginning to display a rather canny sense of publicity and public relations: The inclusion of recipes in *Cook It Outdoors* from food editors like Nancy Dorris of the *Daily News* and Charlotte Adams of the afternoon newspaper *New York PM* (also a radio personality) both ensured a favorable response from the then–New York food establishment and helped place Beard within it. Moreover, through the good offices of Jeanne Owen, Beard was able to write a piece for *House Beautiful*'s June issue—sandwiched between Owen's wine column (on Ohio's then-still-flourishing vintners) and a home decoration article entitled "Black Out Curtains That Really Black Out"—to coincide with the book's release. (The menu—"A Man's Dinner, Appreciated by Most Women as Well"—was adapted to a nation then seven months at war and included radishes and green onions "Fresh from the Victory Garden" and a "Tray of United States Cheeses," perhaps less from national pride than the fact European cheeses were no longer available. On the other hand, the magazine had published a celebration of American regional foods and recipes titled "The Cult of American Cooking," by the majorette of culinary nationalism, Sheila Hibben, three months earlier.) Beard in turn had parlayed the *House Beautiful* commission into a similar article for the July issue of *Gourmet,* which had begun publication the previous December. It contained the first of what were to be many descriptions of childhood on the beach at Gearhart: "We lived near the Pacific, and were in the habit of setting out early in the morning, to spend the entire day on the beach, which was not only beautifully wide for any sort of game, but also had white sand of the best consistency for building forts. We soon tired of carrying our lunches, and began to experiment with cooking the midday meal ourselves."

All during 1942 Beard had been making a conscientious effort to enlist in one of the services, but he was rejected by all because of his weight. Finally, in August, he was drafted. Sent to Fort Dix, New Jersey, in September, there (despite assurances from influential friends that he would be placed in the Hotel Management Division of the Quartermaster Corps) he remained until he was sent to join the Army Air Corps in Miami in December. In January 1943 Beard was sent to cryptography school—to which, like the Quartermaster Corps and clerical and chaplain's assistant duties, gay men were habitually assigned and in which they could find one another—in Pawling, New York. In the interim a new regulation was enacted permitting draftees over the age of thirty-eight to be voluntarily discharged provided they performed work deemed in the national interest. When Beard learned there was no chance of his going overseas (and clearly no chance of now entering the Quartermaster Corps), he decided to leave the army and was discharged on February 22. Rather than return to New York, where he had no place to live—Jim Cullum having entered the service and given up his apartment— Beard went to Cullum's parents' home, Riveredge Farms, near Reading, Pennsylvania, where he gardened and worked as a dairyman with the Cullum Guernsey herd.

Beard's father, John, died at the age of eighty-two on June 5, 1943, of arteriosclerosis. In contrast to his reaction to the illness and death of his mother, Beard remained with the Cullums until September, when he returned to Portland to settle John Beard's will at the request of his fifty-nine-year-old half sister, Lucille. During the tangle of probating John's meager estate, questions from the authorities had arisen about John's nonpayment of taxes, and the final settlement netted Lucille and James $229.54 each (and gave James the right to sell the incense-scented house on Salmon Street, which Mary, in a final act of defiance and spite against John, had willed to him three years before). But of this last journey back to Hawthorne Park, Beard seems to have remembered only a turkey dinner with Mary Hamblet and her mother, Polly. For that summer at least, as in his childhood, Beard was as indifferent to his father as he was possessed by his mother. John Beard, who had traveled to Oregon by covered wagon in 1865 to end his days on the docks of the Willamette amid the sweet and bitter smells of mandarin oranges and tea crated an ocean away in the Orient, was mourned by his daughter alone, out of his son's mind and memory.

Beard returned to New York later that autumn and rented what was his first apartment in his own name at 36 West Twelfth Street, where he was to live until 1959. It was a small, second-floor apartment, with a tiny kitchen and bath, one large room at the rear of the building in an attractive old brownstone on a pretty block in Greenwich Village between Fifth and Sixth avenues. The neighbors across the hall, the Favershams, quickly became friends. After his summer's sabbatical, Beard was anxious to be busy again, and M. Barrows offered him a contract for a third book, *Fowl and Game Cookery.* The text and recipes were written between October and December and tested in Beard's new kitchen. *Fowl and Game Cookery* was similar in many respects to *Cook It Outdoors:* The book contains many recipes from friends and throughout a conviction that "simple, unadorned dishes are the finest of all." There is also a new streak of opinionatedness: There is too much fried and creamed chicken around (despite this, Beard gives fourteen different recipes for the latter); vichyssoise is overrated; the habitual use of currant jelly with game—something about which, together with lamb and mint sauce, he had always disagreed with Mary—is an abomination. The recipes were often uninspired, although *Fowl and Game Cookery* may well have been one of the last American cookbooks to offer, as a matter of course, recipes for squirrel and muskrat.

As a memoir, however, the book is more rewarding. It opens with a recollection of an illness at age three when Beard was fed pots of chicken jelly by Jue-Let: "I'm sure those little pots of true essence of chicken established a flavor sense for me I've never forgotten." He recalls the abundance of game he enjoyed as a child and, perhaps too tellingly, the fact that neither he nor his mother nor his father could agree to eat the same things prepared in the same way. But the most extraordinary passage of this kind concerns his father, whom Beard describes, with what might be considered faint praise, as having "many ideas and definite ones, about food and life. Not only did he have the ideas but he worked at them with a vengeance.":

> Father felt that he could sauté a chicken better than anyone else in the family, in fact better than anyone else he had ever known. So early on Sunday morning—Father was never a late sleeper—he could be found in the kitchen complete with chicken, utensils, and apron. No one dared set foot in the "domestic offices" till the chicken was in the pan and wafting its glorious aroma throughout the lower floor of the house. He never would keep doors closed.

Continuing for more than another page, Beard describes (in a style perhaps not quite loving but lovingly detailed) his father preparing the bacon fat and the pan, cutting up and flouring the chicken, cooking it, and making pan gravy. "He loved freshly ground pepper and seemed to have a magic touch with it, for no one else I know has ever made it blend and yet retain its individuality the way Father did." And so Beard re-created not the ineffectual, debt-ridden customs appraiser who kept a mistress downtown and was rarely at home, but a father with a "magic touch" in the kitchen, the center of young James's world.

Late that same autumn, a friend who had made it into the army Quartermaster Corps told Beard that he might find similar work with the United Seamen's Service (USS), a sort of USO for the Merchant Marine, which operated clubs and hotel facilities for merchant sailors. The USS was expanding rapidly because of the war, beginning 1943 with only one overseas club but finishing the year with twenty-five and plans for many more. James was hired in early December as a roving manager, who would launch and oversee new clubs and ensure that existing ones remained up to standard. For Beard himself, one of the main attractions of the job was the opportunity to work in France, where an assignment had been promised him. However, he was to arrive there by a circuitous route, being sent first to Puerto Rico (which would prompt a "Caribbean Food" article in House & Garden in April 1948), then to Rio de Janeiro, and finally, in December 1944, to Cristobal in Panama.

The principal job of the USS clubs was to offer food, accommodation, and recreation to Merchant Marine sailors, although their staffs frequently also had to deal with the wounded or shipwrecked who had been torpedoed or attacked by the enemy. As he had done for his younger friends in the theater in Portland and in New York, James played the role of father and older brother to homesick, lonely, and overstressed sailors and oversaw the provision of an American atmosphere abroad and, in particular, of American food: According to a USS report, "Ham and eggs, wheatcakes and bacon, apple pie and steaks and chops are served in overseas units, plus American coffee." For Beard, however, the job also presented an opportunity to explore ethnic materials and cooking, and despite official policy, he introduced local recipes into the clubs he managed. He also seemed to have a knack for locating and cultivating the best local cook in every port; and so there was Manuela in Rio and Margaret in Cristobal and then Eugene in Marseilles, where Beard arrived in May 1945 after a stopover in New York and a stint in Naples.

The Marseilles USS club, housed in the Hotel Continental near the Vieux Port, was an enormous facility, and Beard was able to exploit both American and local suppliers to ensure the quality of the food; American for sailors, French for officers and visiting dignitaries. Beard had not been in France since 1923 and never before in Provence. He explored Cassis, Bandol, and Avignon—bringing back a stash of wines from Châteauneuf-du-Pape for use in the club—and ate and cooked with the iridescent eggplant, fragrant garlic, and deep green olive oil of the Mediterranean. In October he visited a war-ravaged Paris, acquiring a mass of copper pots and pans at bargain prices; and in mid-November, his assignment with the USS over, he boarded a ship for New York, arriving there two days before Christmas 1945.

After his enraptured tour of South America and France under the auspices of the USS, Beard found it difficult to adjust to life in Manhattan. He did not want to write another book, and perhaps, given the comparatively low sales of *Fowl and Game Cookery,* would not in any case have been asked. On the other hand, with the war over, New York was returning to normal, and old friends reappeared along with a new wave of immigrants from Portland like Ron and Isabel Callvert, with whom he had worked at KGW and KOIN radio, and Jerry Alden, another veteran of *Alice in Wonderland.* Beard also became friendly with Sam Aaron, one of the proprietors of Sherry Wine & Spirits on Madison Avenue, whom he had met through Jeanne Owen. Aaron suggested he come to work on the sales floor on a part-time basis, and Beard proved a hit with the customers, particularly society women, to whom he was able to dispense wine advice in an easy, unitimidating manner. In 1947 Sherry opened a specialty grocery and delicatessen called Alan Berry, a few doors away at 676 Madison Avenue. Beard was made manager, overseeing a stock of New England groceries from S. S. Pierce in Boston, puddings and fruitcakes and cheeses from Vermont, and imported sundries ranging from foie gras to caviar to chocolates. Although Alan Berry was short-lived, the Aarons kept Beard afloat through 1946 and 1947, and his presence on the sales floor, on wine-tasting panels, and as the compiler of Sherry's catalog was a constant at the store for years to come.

But in retrospect Beard's most significant activity during this period occurred unexpectedly and in an unexpected field. In mid-January 1946, Charlotte Adams of New York PM met Beard by chance and told him that NBC was planning a new television program for local broadcast on its New York station (WNBT) and that—based on his radio and acting experience and book and magazine credits—he might be a candidate for a regular cooking segment on it. An audition was scheduled; the approval of the sponsor, Borden, obtained; and by spring James was a regular on "For You and Yours," a mix of home hints, reviews, and celebrity interviews. Beard's slot occupied the second half of the show and was introduced by an oversize Elsie the Cow puppet designed by Bil Baird. Within a few months, NBC and Borden found Beard's regular cooking segment sufficiently interesting to merit a separate show of its own, to be broadcast over the entire NBC network (which then consisted of stations in a handful of cities transmitting to a handful of receivers, usually in bars or other public places). On August 30, 1946, at 8:15 P.M., immediately after boxing from Madison Square Garden, the Elsie the Cow puppet announced to the nation's prime-time television audience, "Elsie presents James Beard in 'I Love to Eat!'"

The program lasted fifteen minutes and was the first cooking program in the history of television. In October, it moved to the 8:30–8:45 slot—although it was often delayed or brought forward depending on the results of the fight that preceded it. In April 1947 "I Love to Eat" was expanded to a half hour and acquired a new sponsor, Birds Eye Frozen Foods. The additional air time also allowed, in addition to the regular recipe, appearances by minor celebrities such as Jan Struther (author of the wartime novel Mrs. Miniver and a frequent guest on radio quizzes such as "Information Please"), whose visit coincided with a barbecuing demonstration during which a turkey erupted into flames. But the show was successful enough to rapidly develop competition: By late fall 1946 CBS had countered with a program called "In the Kitchen." On May 11, 1947, Swift and Co. launched an hourlong cooking and homemaking show called, "At Home with Jinx and Ted."

"I Love to Eat" was canceled a week later on May 18, a decision probably less related to Beard or the show itself than to television's inability to deliver an audience to its advertisers. That autumn Borden, for example, withdrew all sponsorship from television, citing a need to "reexamine" the medium's potential, as did General Foods, the parent company of the sponsor of "I Love to Eat." Television was still a medium in search of a message, and programs like "I Love to Eat" and "The World in Your Home"—the roundup of stale travelogues that followed it on Friday evenings—could not compete with radio hits like "Amos 'n' Andy" or Bob Hope and Bing Crosby. Cooking would be absent from prime time for fifteen years, until a friend of Beard's named Julia Child would fulfill the joint possibilities of television and food that Beard had first explored. Beard appeared with regularity on television throughout his career, but only briefly again on a show of his own: Despite his theatrical bent, Beard was never totally at ease on television; his bald head lit badly, and the practiced geniality of his usual demeanor seemed somehow tense and aloof.

Today there is no evidence that "I Love to Eat" ever existed except for an index card in an NBC office at 30 Rockefeller Center, half a block from the apartment where Beard, the would-be actor, had made his home in 1937. There are no kinescopes, scripts, or photos, and no one today recalls much about the program, although James's friends followed it faithfully, and he attained a measure of local celebrity for it at the time. Beard, gifted with astonishing powers of recollection, saved nothing related to it or, for that matter, little from any other aspect of his life. He did not need to and perhaps in some respect could not bear to: He was not, despite—or perhaps because of—the weight of the past in his life, a man who kept souvenirs. But those programs, transmitted from a primitive room far from the grandeur of studio 8-H where Toscanini conducted for radio, were James Beard's only performances in all the time since he had climbed the stairs at Pennsylvania Station ten years before, and they have vanished from memory, into the ether of yesterday's evanescent media.

Through the first few postwar years—more than any lover or friend—there remained Jeanne Owen, who took James to the theater and to dinners, generally panning the performance they had just seen and the food they were eating interchangeably while bullying the waiters. Just as she had taught James to cook in a systematic fashion, she cultivated his inborn talent for pointed gossip and witty, bitchy conversation. But of late her highhanded treatment of others was occasionally extended to him, particularly when he seemed inclined to forget that he was a protégé rather than an equal. Through the rest of 1947 and into the winter of 1948, however—with "I Love to Eat" canceled and scant forward movement on other fronts of James's career—there was little to threaten the established mentor-student pattern of their relationship. But as he had been to his Portland friends and in the USS, James, too, naturally gravitated toward the role of parent or older sibling. James wanted to be to others what Owen was to him, and this, together with his growing reputation in the New York food community—in which he advanced by gentle, persuasive appeal of his personality rather than by bulldozing dynamism of Owen's sort—made her increasingly uneasy. Under Mary's tutelage James had become adept at playing an amalgam of son, girlfriend, and sexless suitor that was irresistible to Owen (as it had been to Helen Dircks and Bess Whitcomb), but in such a relationship possession and control were fundamental, and any movement toward autonomy was tantamount to betrayal. That Owen did everything in her power to advance James's career did not assuage her panic and jealousy when her efforts on his behalf began to bear fruit. Despite her insistence, like Mary's, that he be wiser and wickeder than his years—that he share her lust for status and influence and her contempt for most of those prepared to confer them on her—she could not bear for him to grow up and away from her. Her once-, twice-, or thrice-daily calls to him at ALgonquin 4-1434 grew fewer, while her affection soured through the summer into anger and hurt.

By mid-1948 James's star as a food journalist and writer seemed to be on the rise, even as Owen—still the dragon lady of the New York Wine & Food Society—was reduced to producing twenty-five-cent promotional cooking pamphlets for the National Distillers Products Corporation, her last book having been produced to little response six years before for silk-stocking publisher and gourmet Alfred A. Knopf. Although James would find such promotional work both necessary and lucrative in the future, for the moment he seemed to be moving on an altogether loftier plane—the penthouse offices of *Gourmet* at the Plaza Hotel, where he was now a regular contributor hoping for a full-time editorial job. Despite his natural affinity for the magazine, its contributors, and audience, Beard had managed only one appearance in its pages back in the summer of 1942. It was not for want of trying but for the presence of Bill Rhode, who after a stint at *Look,* had joined *Gourmet* as associate editor in 1943, and remained until shortly before his death at the end of 1946 at the age of forty-two.

Without enemies on the staff, James proved an irresistible force to Earle MacAusland, *Gourmet*'s fifty-eight-year-old founder and publisher. A New Englander who had worked in the magazine business most of his life, it was said that MacAusland had begun *Gourmet* less on the basis of market research or his expertise in food than to create a vehicle through which to satisfy his own curiosity about what he called "the summum bonum of living." In any case, the magazine was a genuine innovation in December 1941, when food journalism consisted mostly of newspaper women's pages, cookery school organs like *American Cookery,* and amateur newsletters and privately distributed quarterlies published by gourmet societies. Moreover, in the quality of its writing and design and the catholicity of its interests, *Gourmet* embodied not just the Eurocentric taste of the gastronomic elite, but some of the influence of the culinary nationalists and the avant-garde eclecticism of a Merle Armitage. Still, at its core, the magazine reflected MacAusland's penchant for Martinis, English suits, good china, and French food. France may have been "the summum bonum," but it was to be attained via England, or rather through the American Anglophilia in which Britain represented a society untainted by vulgarity and consumerism, consisting entirely of honest peasants, genial aristocrats, Noel Coward–like sophisticates, and spaniels and port by the manor fireside.

James was well equipped by ancestry, experience, and wardrobe to service *Gourmet*'s readers' romance with England, but his first contributions were in his familiar domestic mode, a two-part series on outdoor cooking appearing in the summer of 1948, followed by a piece on carving in November. By the spring of 1949, Beard had become *Gourmet*'s restaurant critic—joining Lucius Beebe, Clementine Paddleford, and M. F. K. Fisher as regular contributors—and by April was named associate editor, Rhode's old post. In his first review, Beard laid down his critical manifesto:

Food and wines are first on the list, service is second, and surroundings third. I am not at all impressed by who the person at the next table may be, nor does the presence of the entire social register and half of Who's Who do anything to add to my luncheon or dinner. I can appreciate a restaurant where the food and wines are above reproach and the service a little faltering, but I cannot abide a place where the service and appointments are perfect and the food mediocre or, what is worse, indifferent. Neither the lowest of bows from the waist nor the finest of damask cloths has ever made a poorly cooked dinner taste any better.

The style was not far from pompous and the sentiments expressed somewhat disingenuous, given James's fascination with society and celebrity, but the proposition that food comes first was novel and even radical given Manhattanites' continuing urge to use restaurants first and foremost as social goldfish bowls. Despite the diversity of his own tastes, however, James's unsureness as a writer and penchant for high style and snobbery could all too easily push him into the epicurean windbag school of prose. His first outing for *Gourmet* covered the Brussels (an offshoot of the 1939 fair) where, in a stuffy marriage of belles-lettres and the banal, he praised an omelet "substantial enough to appease the pangs of hunger and light enough to excite the taste buds in anticipation of the dishes to follow," among them a gâteau St.-Honoré whose "cream was diaphanous in its lightness and the pastry as tender as a maiden's glance." An Indian restaurant reviewed in the same article was commended for its loochie, "diaphanous puffs of bread . . . resembling small balloons [that] deflate as quickly as daydreams fade when you bite into them."

In later issues he would write up the other World's Fair transplants, the Swiss Pavilion and Soulé's Le Pavillon, whose food would be found consistently "perfect" and "correct," the benchmark of restaurant cooking in America for years to come. But James also dispensed pointed and useful advice on badly prepared vegetables, condemned overelaborate dishes and presentations, lamented the ubiquity of vichyssoise (which he and the Rhodes had been instrumental in popularizing only eight years before), and brought ethnic and inexpensive restaurants to his readers' attention, among them many of the standbys patronized by him and his Oregonian friends ten years before. Perhaps James's finest hour as *Gourmet*'s reviewer was in a piece on New York Italian restaurants, ranging from uptown chic to Little Italy funk, in which he enthused about salads of field greens, rustic pastas, risotto, and Greenwich Village house specials ("It's not always on the menu, but no one can blame you for asking") in an unfussy and direct style.

Beard's own style was varied and amorphous, favoring tweed jackets and straw hats; rococo furnishings just this side of kitsch; stacks of *Country Life* magazine, the antiques, real estate, and fox-and-hounds bible of the English gentry; and meals—prepared in his closet-size kitchen with dishes washed in the shower—running the gamut from white truffles to corn bread. Much of this mix was the result of James's personal eclecticism and vast curiosity, but he had also been inclined since childhood to play whatever role would please the audience whose favor he was at that moment attempting to win. At *Gourmet*—which MacAusland was selling with increasing success to advertisers as the inside track to the nation's most affluent consumers of travel and luxury goods—James cultivated a persona of British bonhomie. But however much *Gourmet* might propound and refine its cravat-and-claret vision of cruise ship gourmandise for the upper middle classes, the audience for it was necessarily limited. Genuine journalistic power and influence, and their rewards, lay in addressing the needs of mainstream, middle-class Americans, whose incomes and appetite for good living and leisure were being fueled by the booming postwar economy.

Despite the opportunities afforded by a nation at last free of economic depression, rationing, and war, none of the visible trends of the past twenty years was clearly triumphant at the end of the forties. Culinary nationalism and eclecticism, fed by the political radicalism and avant-garde culture of the twenties and thirties, seemed a relic of a more innocent and poorer time unsuited to a society in a triumphant, expansive, and increasingly conformist mood. Nor did domestic science or gourmet dining, which in many respects represented the opposite pole of the American social and economic spectrum, fare particularly well in the postwar years. The earnest, often leaden, seriousness of both approaches seemed increasingly irrelevant to a nation interested in cooking either as a means of eating quickly and conveniently or as a form of recreation.

The forties remained an age of the thousand-page compendium, with *The Joy of Cooking* enjoying sales of 1.1 million by decade's end and *The Good Housekeeping Cook Book* and *The Better Homes and Gardens Cook Book* achieving similarly spectacular results. Through successive revisions, most moved away from the domestic encyclopedia whose mix of cookery, health, and household management advice had dominated cookbook publishing for the past century toward an emphasis weighted less to daily family meals and more to entertaining. Despite their awareness of cooking, eating, and entertaining as an emergent leisure activity, however, such books for the most part remained relentlessly practical and utilitarian—their heft and format suggestive less of stylish fun than of bibles and textbooks—and were intended exclusively for use by women. They were also single-mindedly American, though not through a conscious appreciation of American traditions and materials, but by default, promoting a now-universal national diet of steak, hamburger, chicken, casseroles, and cakes.

Although Europeans had captured and held the high ground of New York's postdepression restaurant scene, foreign food remained a curiosity for most of the nation beyond such now-assimilated standbys as macaroni, spaghetti, and, on the verge of the fifties, chow mein and pizza. *The Gold Cook Book,* by chef and *Gourmet* contributor Louis P. De Gouy, aimed to integrate American and European food in a compendium-style tome and managed thirteen printings between its publication in 1947 and 1960. But, as ever, what the nation was really eating at this time was more apparent from the magazine and institutional cookbooks like that of *Better Homes and Gardens,* from newspaper women's pages, and from homegrown community and charitable cookbooks published in cities and towns like Portland.

Around 1946—the book is undated—*The Trinity Cook Book* was published by the ladies of Trinity Church in Portland. It lacks indignities like advertisements for baking powder—unnecessary given the wealth of Portland's preeminent parish—which peppered the community cookbooks of most towns (such as that of La Grande twenty years before) and suggests a certain Junior League tasteful self-assurance, embodied in its wedding-invitation, sans-serif cover type and brass spiral binding. What is missing is Portland itself: game, oysters, clams, salmon, and crabs followed by wild berry pies

and three dozen ways with orchard fruit. Instead, the recipes of the
city's leading women specified can joined to can of mushroom soup,
creamed corn, and condensed milk, salads cemented with Best Foods
mayonnaise, and gelatine desserts.

Portland's leading food journalist, Catherine Laughton of the
Oregon Journal and proprietor of "Mary Cullen's Cottage," the
Journal's cozier equivalent of Paddleford's Home Institute, also published a book in 1946. *Mary Cullen's Northwest Cookbook* was
not—in its salad rings, stuffed peppers, and variations on meat, fish,
and poultry à la king—much more specifically northwestern than
The Trinity Cook Book. But Laughton was unafraid to commingle
Basque, German, and Polish ethnic specialties, maple bars, and
dishes like fried crab legs and clams ("one of those foods you want
plenty of"), whose origins were clearly more Seaside than Gearhart.
Northwest bouillabaisse and clams à la Cannon Beach (another Portland second-home coastal town) were not traditional preparations
but sincere if contrived efforts to create a regional cuisine from the
contributions of well-meaning *Journal* readers. Some recipes—
notably "Goop," a chicken, olive, mushroom, and noodle casserole
surmounted by a crown of melted cheese for "after skiing, or to
make, chill and take along to the beach or mountains to be
reheated"—are so beyond the pale of culinary propriety as to take
on an innocently raunchy vitality that is disarming if not delightful.
In this, despite its fundamental immersion in ethos of the women's
page, Laughton's book had character, and, in its guiltless, guileless
vulgarity, Northwest character at that.

Concoctions like "Goop" probably owed some of their ancestry
not only to the experiments of home cooks and newspaper food
editors but to the commercial recipe books pioneered by early food
processors such as Jell-O and designed to show the infinite dining
possibilities afforded by their products. The paramount position of
gelatine salads and desserts in American cooking during the first half
of the twentieth century owed much to Jell-O's courtship of prominent domestic scientists and to the product's ability to bring the
dainty, molded constructions they favored to the masses. But the
widespread dissemination of Jell-O recipe books and "serving suggestions" on the package was perhaps even more fundamental to its
success.

Jell-O and its ilk were sui generis, and the consumer needed to be told what to do with them, but the producers of staples like Tilla-mook cheese could expand their traditional market share only by creating new and often outlandish uses for their products or by encouraging their substitution for traditional ingredients. At the same time that "Mary Cullen's Cottage" and Trinity Church pub-lished their cookbooks in Portland, Tillamook cheese was unleashing a series of recipe booklets on Oregonians designed to persuade the housewife to treat her family to corn and clam croquettes with Tillamook pepper slices, Tillamook cutlets with cabbage puffs, and asparagus on toast and new Tillamook chops. To cooks acquainted with these and such recipes as peanut-stuffed cabbage rolls with Tillamook shrimp salad—the offspring of writers, cooks, and home economists who understood the needs of food processors for innova-tion and of consumers for convenience but neither tradition or style—"Goop" was positively tame.

In 1948 James attended a cocktail party in Palm Beach, Florida, whose host's elaborate outdoor grill he would write up for *Gourmet*. He fell into conversation with a woman whose husband was an edi-tor for Fireside Books, a division of Simon & Schuster set up to pro-duce lavishly illustrated, oversize format compendiums on big sub-jects (and modest budgets) in the "Golden Treasury of" mold. By the end of the year, James had contracted to write a volume titled *The Fireside Cook Book* for a flat fee of five thousand dollars. Despite the fact he would earn no royalties, the money seemed impressive given the scattershot livelihood he eked out working for Sherry and as an ingenue contributor to *Gourmet*. It was James's first experience at what would today be called book packaging, and through the fall and winter he collaborated closely with editors who polished and rewrote his prose and with illustrators Alice and Martin Provensen, whose fey, whimsical line drawings filled every page, usually in full color. James found the work exhausting and daunting but congenial: In many respects, such editorial constrictions produced an authorial voice that was surer and more personable than James could produce on his own—in short, more like James himself.

On publication in September 1949, *The Fireside Cook Book* was quickly recognized as an event. Culinary compendiums were the rule rather than the exception, but in its color, illustrations, and relaxed yet authoritative personal tone, this one had style and was less a textbook or an instruction manual than something akin to a handsomely produced mail-order catalog from which one could order painlessly and at whim. It was offered as "a basic cook book" and yet dealt with sophisticated subjects like hors d'oeuvres and wine, recognizing that readers—assumed to be of both sexes and pointedly described as "the man [and] woman of today"—wanted to be treated as intelligent, thoughtful consumers. And while the book understood that its readers' tastes in entertaining and in food might be unformed, it also understood that the display of those tastes to friends and colleagues was serious business, announcing to the world who—in leisure, in aspiration, and in status—their possessors were. Food and the knowledge of it were a full-fledged lifestyle accessory.

While *The Fireside Cook Book* may have taken great pains to assure its readers that food was accessible—at least to au courant, affluent Middle Americans—and stylish fun, it also presented cooking as an entrée to high culture. To a nation ready to lap up the sententious pop history of Will and Ariel Durant and the Kodachrome anthropology of the *National Geographic,* James briefly recounted the history of agriculture, the spice trade, and cooking and proclaimed: "That such developments and discoveries were as important to civilization as the invention of the wheel or the discovery of atomic energy there is not the slightest doubt."

From Eliza Leslie's *Seventy-five Receipts* a hundred years before, and onward through the ranks of domestic scientists and gourmets, food had of course been treated as an important matter; as a practical necessity and vehicle for the attainment of dignity for women by the former and as aesthetic appreciation and an expression of social identity by the latter. But *The Fireside Cook Book* insisted that food, though fundamental to human survival, was nevertheless art—the sine qua non that lay at the crux of not only the good life but of civilization and life itself. James was right in believing this sincerely, and such pronouncements were part of the Fireside Books formula of pretentious cultural window-shopping. But however much they promoted the reader's self-satisfaction, they also served to undermine the credibility of what was, after all, on close examination not a gastronomic encyclopedia but a digest of what James Beard, age forty-six, liked to cook and eat.

Despite the global reach of James's introductory material, *The*

Fireside Cook Book is at bottom as American as *The Joy of Cooking*. The recipes are largely domestic in origin—or, by assimilation into the nation's culinary canon, domesticated—and the lore and advice on selecting and cooking ingredients is conventional and correct. Each recipe follows the next in a seamless fashion that suggests that none is better than another, only different. There are roasts, spoon bread, hamburgers, blueberry muffins, and hash browns as well as crepes, consommé, mulligatawny, and eggs Benedict. Few middle-class Americans would recognize the latter foreign dishes in 1949, but most would within thirty years, whether through experiences in restaurants or in their own homes. At a time when cakes, pies, and desserts occupied formidable portions of most cookbooks, Beard spent more pages on vegetables, salads, spices, and wine than on sweets. In all this, *The Fireside Cook Book* is a triumph of the currency and prescience of James's good taste.

"It's easy to discover James Beard's personal food preferences from his new 'Fireside Cook Book,'" wrote Jane Nickerson of the *New York Times* in an interview with James on October 28. "He has scrupulously avoided turning his book into what he refers to as a 'laboratory manual,'" she continued, and went on to commend the variety and stylishness of the recipes, as would almost all food editors, who found in the novelty of James's book and the easy, old-fashioned charm of his person an irresistible story. By the eighth printing a few years later, the jacket copy would refer to Beard as "America's foremost culinary authority."

A few, however, disagreed. In an unsigned review, *The New Yorker* commented:

> As beautiful and elaborate a picture book (over four hundred color illustrations) as the season is likely to provide, accompanied by 1,217 recipes. The author is obviously a fine cook, and he could have unquestionably produced a useful, workable cookbook if he had not undertaken to write a world-beater. Enormously pretentious, repetitious, padded with bits of women's-magazine anthropology, exotic menus, meals planned for hot and cold weather (hot buttered rum for warm weather, jellied chicken broth for cold [sic]), and pompous generalities about wine, the work attempts an inclusiveness at which Brillat-Savarin, Montagné, and Escoffier in collaboration might well have boggled. The truth is Mr. Beard simply doesn't know enough.

The author of the review was Sheila Hibben, whom James suspected of having been put up to the task by Jeanne Owen, despite his citation of three of Owen's recipes in the book (more than any other acquaintance). The review stung James badly, not only in its attribution of Simon & Schuster's marketing strategy to James's own ego, but in its intended and unintended attacks both on the person he had striven so hard to become and—in its offhand (and erroneous) reference to John Beard's Christmas toddy and Jue-Let's jellied broth— the boy he remained at his core. Beyond speculating on the possibility of Owen's intervention, James could not understand the source of Hibben's ferocity. She had been among the first supporters of Hors d'Oeuvre, Inc., ten years before, but he seemed unaware of her conviction, born of politics and personal need, that cooking should not be exploited and transformed by capitalism from the fundamental sustenance of communities it had been from time immemorial into a consumer commodity. But in that respect, however excessively, Hibben understood the import of *The Fireside Cook Book* better than most.

James remained, however, an actor at heart, and a trouper at that. A few years later, he nonchalantly mentioned to a friend in a letter that Hibben had "panned" the book. By then—and for all intents and purposes by the end of 1949—he was a star in the dwarf constellation of food writing, which—viewed between the brownstone rooftops of West Twelfth Street—looked as brilliant, expansive, and blue as an August night on Gearhart Beach.

Oh, those lovely days when it was all so small, and we were all so very important," Cecily Brownstone would say forty years later. As food editor for the Associated Press from the late 1940s on, Brownstone was one of the half-dozen journalists most assiduously hustled by food industry producers, processors, and their public relations flacks representing various "boards," "councils," and "institutes" for the advancement of commodities ranging from California pimientos to Roquefort cheese. Together with Clementine Paddleford of the *Herald Tribune,* Jane Nickerson of the *Times,* and the editors of "service" magazines like *McCall's, Ladies Home Journal,* and *Woman's Day,* Brownstone was the recipient of a boundless largesse of pretested recipes, product samples, lunches, dinners, and junkets, with the use of a fleet of cars, boats, and planes to ferry her and her cohorts among them. In addition, she enjoyed "a huge expense account, which probably accounted for my popularity."

By the eve of 1950, if James was not quite in that league—in one day's column, Paddleford could reach as many readers as *The Fireside Cook Book* would over its lifetime—he was a rising star who gave every impression of belonging in it. Brownstone, who spent her youth on the gelid frontier of Manitoba writing stories and dreamed all the while of fleeing to New York, had met James through Jeanne Owen a few years before. Beyond childhoods that seemed in some ways parallel, they shared a capacity for mordant wit, a bottomless appetite for gossip, and a genuine interest in the history of food and cookbooks that was rare among their fellow editors and writers. Meant to be friends, they remained so until the end of their lives.

But with or without the aid of Brownstone and her ilk, James had already become adept at taking advantage of his incipient celebrity and had, even before the publication of *Fireside,* secured a place on his first grand-luxe junket, a government-sponsored tour of the wine regions of France to coincide with the harvest of the 1949 vintage. That September James found himself on a circuit of France's vineyards that began in the Loire Valley and transited Bordeaux, the Rhône Valley, Burgundy, and Champagne—each stop punctuated by antique wines and elaborate meals—before returning to Paris, a dinner at Maxim's, and a capacious, first-class seat on Air France back to New York.

James joined the tour in at least three capacities: as correspondent for *Gourmet;* functionary and house aesthete for Sherry Wine & Spirits; and as editor of the quarterly of the "Société des Gentilshommes Chefs de Cuisine," a ten-thousand-member men's gourmet club founded as a promotional device by National Premium Beer of Baltimore, which James served under the title "Chief Potato Peeler." On his return, James wrote up his trip for *Gourmet* in a two-part report that appeared in the January and February issues of 1950. Under the best of circumstances, the sumptuous but unvarying daily round of the wine tour makes for inconsequential and dull reading, and in this case it fostered the worst prose James ever produced. Stilted constructions—"This was to be one of our greatest tasting days, for after our Cruse luncheon we proceeded through a trail of other vineyards"— trip over each other in prissy school–book report style as one "rounded" or "balanced" wine tediously succeeds another.

Gourmet's Earle MacAusland may have found James's account of his French holiday consonant with the largely unformed and unfulfilled travel aspirations of the magazine's audience. But he was livid at the appearance of a scarcely modified version of the same piece in a Sherry Wine & Spirits catalog. In the words of a *Gourmet* editor who knew "Mac" as well as anyone might, "He was dictatorial and possessive. He didn't like anyone to write for anyone else and he didn't like Jim's growing fame." At the New Year, James found himself sacked, though he took some comfort from what he perceived as the unstoppable upward arc of his career and MacAusland's regret at no longer being a part of it: "I found myself out on my can, but I know for a fact that he wept after he fired me," he told an interviewer some years later.

Within days, James's confidence—bolstered by the burgeoning sales of *Fireside*—was reinforced not once but twice. Sam Aaron's brother Jack invited him to retake his old floor job at Sherry over a lunch at "21," at which James was introduced to Jerry Mason, a thirty-seven-year-old Phi Beta Kappa Johns Hopkins and Columbia graduate who had worked in various editorial jobs at *This Week* in the late forties and succeeded to the helm of *Argosy* in 1949. Mason's present task was to transform the twelve-gauge, Mike Hammer ethos of *Argosy* into something approaching what would eventually be recognized as the *Playboy* philosophy; from a downmarket "pulp" into an upmarket "slick," promulgating a male life-style that might include not just sports, firearms, tires, and war but culture and even cooking. As one of the nation's few male food writers, and as an acknowledged authority on the he-manly realm of outdoor cooking, James was a natural for *Argosy*. He left "21" that day with both a job in the wine trade and a column in a national magazine.

That twin coup would mean an even-larger-than-usual barrage of phone calls that evening and the following morning. When James's eyes rolled open at dawn—and certainly by six regardless of the season—he habitually reached for the phone and cleaved to it for the next two hours and throughout the day as work, lunches, and meetings allowed. Among his regular interlocutors were Ann Seranne and Helen McCully, who like Brownstone were Canadian-born editor-journalists of formidable energy and acumen. Seranne—born with the rather plainer name Margaret Smith in Hamilton, Ontario—had been cook, secretary, and mistress to wine and food society czar Crosby Gaige. She moved to *Gourmet* to play a similar role for Earle MacAusland—it was undoubtedly she who reported his tears to James—and eventually became its editor, the author of two dozen cookbooks, and the possessor, like James, of breathtaking quantities of both food lore and dirt about members of the food scene.

Helen McCully was an altogether more reserved figure than Seranne, a demeanor that suited her position as the nation's most powerful and influential magazine food editor at *McCall's*. On her arrival in New York from Canada in the late thirties, she found work as a department store advertising copywriter, first at Lord & Taylor and then at Bloomingdale's. In 1948 she came to *McCall's* with the particular distinction of being the first food editor at a major magazine who was not a home economist. James would later say that McCully brought "elegance" to the magazine's food section, which, like most newspaper women's pages, had remained for the most part mired in "how to" pieces and shopping tips. Although that continued to be *McCall's* basic approach—together with romantic and domestic-tragic genre fiction, dress patterns, decoration, and what would become known as "self-help" psychological advice—McCully succeeded in adding more adventurous elements to the mix, such as ethnic dishes from New Mexico, China, and Indonesia.

But to editors like McCully, how and even where Americans ate was becoming at least as significant as what they ate. In the fifties food became portable, removed from the kitchen and dining room on trays, chafing dishes, and paper plates and consumed in front of the television, standing up in the living room, or even outside on the patio or at poolside, the archetypal leisure spaces of the next two decades. In fifties food portability and outdoor living—or the suggestion of them—dictated techniques and ingredients: Materials were consigned to the flames of the charcoal grill or the broiler; impaled on skewers, fondue forks, and toothpicks; and vivified with the flavors of fruit, tomatoes, smoke, and chiles in a conflation of South Seas tiki-god sacrificial orgy and Old West chuckwagon. And where food—prepared and served either outdoors or in a simulacrum of the outdoors—was not publicly and ostentatiously seared or charred before its consumers, it often appeared in its opposite, raw state in the form of salad. Lettuce sales rose steadily through the decade, even as consumption of virtually all other fresh fruits and vegetables fell—save for orange juice, whose bracing tropical ethos was utterly consonant with the times and which was marketed and advertised as the nation's elixir of health and success. Despite this apparent penchant for visceral, raw food roughly treated, and for a style of cooking and eating seemingly close to the land and to nature, the fifties were also the dawn of the golden age of food processing, epitomized by the launch of the Swanson TV Dinner, the ultimate tray meal, in 1954.

The fifties cult of the outdoors was ultimately less about embracing nature than taming and channeling it, and its food had its origins not so much among food editors and writers as in the home decoration, life-style, and entertaining press. While McCully and her writing staff gently eased their readers away from home economics–based feeding and toward cooking and eating as "dining" and even "entertaining," their stock-in-trade remained the recipe and their fundamental considerations, cost and convenience. By contrast, in June 1950 their counterparts at *House Beautiful* proclaimed "The Station Wagon Way of Life," a mode of living that took place in the suburbs, revolved around the kitchen, and whose summum bonum and quintessence was the outdoor meal.

In the fifties suburban living still seemed an attainable ideal of the best of the country and the city brought together, a land of lanes and parkways with every home its own green-lawned estate connected to shopping and work by the automobile. In that light the embrace of the slower-paced pleasures of country living and the cult of time-saving and convenience did not seem contradictory. In 1950 the consumer could, given enough gasoline and developable land, have it all: the hum of crickets on a moonlit lawn five minutes from a full-service department store; Martinis, steaks, and tossed salad on the patio; or a dinner that cooked itself in half an hour while the family watched television, and that could be plucked from the oven and conveyed to the den or recreation room during a commercial.

The suburb seemed also to represent at long last the perfecting of the domestic sphere sought by women and their advocates since the end of the previous century. And, at least initially, the suburb, like the home, was an extension of women's realm, while the world of work, commerce, and public life continued to be the singular possession of men. The kitchen remained the heart of the home—just as the effortless nexus between the home and the market was the whole point of the suburb—and in many senses became indistinguishable from the home in its entirety: By July 1951 *House Beautiful* trumpeted the merging of indoors and outdoors in building and "the satisfaction of living close to nature." Within six months the same editors announced that "the kitchen [was] merging with the rest of the house" and had regained its ancient role as the social center of the home, juxtaposing these observations with pieces on fresh vegetables and "the staggering truth about the freezer." Architects, designers, and builders removed walls, created pass-through counters, and punched "picture windows" through the once-impenetrable skins of houses whose rooms and their traditional uses flowed into one another. By the first years of the fifties, every boundary or traditional relation—whether between city and country, indoors and outdoors, eating and entertainment, or cooking, the farm, and the kitchen—had seemingly been made indistinct, each one merely another obstacle to be bulldozed by a consumer society convinced of a future of infinite possibility and growth.

The social and economic barriers between men and women remained to be breached, but James continued to chip away at the one between men and cookery. During the first six months of 1950, he worked up story ideas for *Argosy* and threw together the next issue of the *Journal* of the Société des Gentilshommes Chefs de Cuisine. As "Chief Potato Peeler" (a convivial if pointed reference to the chivalric titles and ranks of traditional European-based gourmet societies), James supplied encomiums on veal and parsley—a garnishing sprig of which was beginning to be routinely parked at the side of every lunch-counter plate in the nation—but the bulk of the *Journal* consisted of recipes and correspondence from "members," conducted in a tone of bachelor backslapping one step removed from the golf course locker room or the duck blind. The food was drill-press cuisine, eager and ingenious juxtapositions of ingredients or techniques not so much created out of any culinary tradition as invented on some basement workbench; food that was constructed rather than cooked and that was epitomized by the Dagwood sandwich. For spring 1950, there was "Norwegian Salad" of apples, bananas, and marshmallows; a "Toasted Almond Chocolate Cheese Pie"; "Bagdad Hamburgers," in which a meat patty buffers two slabs of fried eggplant; and a universal seasoning devised by a reader for use at his Canadian hunting camp.

The Société and its *Journal* arguably made a mockery of good food, but they also consciously or unconsciously mocked the stuffy vehicles through which men had traditionally permitted themselves to enjoy and participate in its preparation. The nascent fifties bachelor culture of the Société was one in which men could freely enjoy cooking, especially under certain preconditions: that the cooking be done outdoors, or in settings at least evocative of the outdoors; that the medium be grilling; and that the material be meat, and in particular beef, whose consumption would nearly double over the next decade and a half. The trends being promoted to women in the service magazines—suburban living, outdoor living and entertaining, and cooking and the kitchen as the new American social and family center—also allowed and encouraged men to become involved with food. As a male hobby as opposed to a female domestic concern, food became culturally significant. And as a male conscious of the social uses of food and an expert on outdoor cooking, James was extremely well placed to become significant, too.

Whether by design or good fortune, the better part of James's agenda in 1950 and for the rest of the decade was that of the nation's expanding middle and upper middle class: entertaining outdoors (or at least in outdoor style) with drinks, cocktails, and food. In the chummily macho columns of *Argosy* he might be bylined "Jim" Beard, but he remained devoted to dandified clothes, overstated decoration, opera, and European culture, cuisine, and men. Not, by and large, the kind of men one might meet at the bars and baths near Sheridan Square a few blocks from James's apartment in the Village, but men who were conversant in the arts; who were both physically handsome and socially presentable; and who, like good furniture or a well-made suit, had a burnished luster of quiet refinement that reflected back on their possessor.

In 1950 this role in James's life was assigned to a Dutchman, Ate de Boer, a shadowy presence over the next few years, whom no one remembers much about. According to James's friends, it seems to have been a relationship of little emotional intimacy, if one of some affection and companionship enjoyed in walks, drinks, and the delectation of his lover's body; perhaps not love but nonetheless a quiet and forthright rejoinder to solitude. But even as James gave himself sexually to Ate and his ilk around the Village, he kept his essence for others—for those who by sexual preference, status, or temperament tended to be unavailable. In consequence he was at pains to find a lover and a friend joined in one person. It was not a concern that openly preoccupied him, although by mid-1950 and increasingly thereafter, the sense that he had no one to whom he could really talk would seize him like a sudden shift in the wind and lay him low with depressions that were antithetical to his ambitious professional persona.

Later that year he was given the opportunity to lose himself in travel, a perennial and normally unfailing antidote to his bleaker moods. The Aaron brothers were interested in opening a branch office in Paris and decided that James should be sent to lay the groundwork. He arrived in Paris by midsummer, settled into a small hotel on the Left Bank, and plunged into *la vie Parisienne* on a scale he could have only dreamed of at the time of his first period of residence in the city almost thirty years before. Connections established during the wine junket of the previous year—from Louis Vaudable, proprietor of Maxim's, to wine magnate Alexis Lichine—served him well, but his constant companion was Alexander Watt, a Scottish journalist whose acquaintance he had made at the same time.

Watt was a gentleman of classic crystalline elegance. He was supremely educated, urbane, polyglot, well-versed in the arts, and, although nominally a journalist, lived a leisured life on the Île St.-Louis in a flat overlooking the Seine and the Left Bank. He knew food and wine, had a Danish wife and an infant son, and was staggeringly handsome. Watt had everything Bill Rhode had (save Rhode's penchant for icy manipulation) and more—in particular a refined Britishness upon whose easy charm the sun never set. In the estimation of one of James's closer friends, he was the love of James's life.

Their relationship took place in, around, and among the Paris bistros and *restaurants du quartier* that were Watt's greatest passion. Although James had made the acquaintance of such places by necessity in the 1920s, like most American epicures he tended at least initially to be drawn to the truffle- and quenelle-encrusted three-star palaces glorified by the Guide Michelin and typified by the pressed duck of La Tour d'Argent and the gratins of shellfish served at Lapérouse. Watt, by contrast, reveled in unprepossessing places like the later-renowned L'Ami Louis or Les Cigognes in the down-at-the-heel fifteenth arrondissement, at which film stars and financiers might slum deliciously on rabbit and country wines. Prices at such bistros could approach those of glossier restaurants, and their menus flirted with distinctly upscale ingredients and treatments: A "simple" presentation of grilled foie gras at L'Ami Louis might seem less ostentatious than one sculpted, studded with truffles, and girded with amber cascades of aspic at La Tour d'Argent, but it nevertheless sported the equally compelling virtue of being "a diamond in the rough"; the sort of snob appeal that could be savored by a knowing few in an atmosphere that shielded the consumer from any awareness that he himself might be a snob.

If Watt was therefore not exactly a genuine populist, neither was he a trendmonger amusing himself with condescending or sentimental forays into the culture of peasants and the petit bourgeois. As a journalist he was hardly unique in his appreciation of this kind of relatively earthy food and the no-nonsense places that served it, for they were already very much part of the manly epicureanism associated with foreign correspondents like Liebling and Hemingway. But Watt also believed that here was food in its most direct and pure form, and he cultivated the cooks and proprietors of such establishments as the keepers and guardians of gastronomy's true essence. They in turn made him part of their families, sharing recipes or creating dishes in his honor such as Les Cigognes' "Sole Farci, Alexander Watt."

In all this James and Sandy, as he was known to intimates, were culinary soul mates, not only in the catholicity of their tastes but in the straightforwardness of the food that resonated most strongly for them, whether that of France's provinces and family tables or of the beaches, valleys, and streams of Oregon. Together they prowled the markets, dining rooms, and kitchens of Paris, sometimes accompanied by Ate, who left New York to join James for a number of weeks later in the year. In any case, a collaborative work based on the meals James and Sandy had shared—a restaurant guide with recipes—seemed a natural outgrowth of their time together. Sandy's knowledge of the restaurants and cooks of Paris was unchallengeable, as was James's ability to construct a recipe and to present foreign food to his countrymen in such a way that it became accessible while losing little or none of its exotic, exclusive cachet.

Moreover, with *Paris Cuisine,* as the book was to be called, James once again displayed his knack—or luck—for predicting and servicing emerging consumer appetites. With his expertise in outdoor cooking and entertaining, James had been perfectly placed to cater to the "station wagon way of life." By the mid-fifties, those same affluent and now food-conscious Americans were traveling abroad in increasingly large numbers thanks to the rise of commercial aviation and to a real curiosity about the larger world in which the United States was now the preeminent force. The European tour—once the exclusive circuit of bohemians and the wealthy—was now a requisite part of the postwar life-style to which middle-class Americans aspired. Gastronomic exploration had always been one of its major components, and as he had been in Westchester and Shaker Heights, James was now in Europe to teach them how and where to eat.

• • •

On his return to New York after seven months abroad, James—still without an agent—struck a deal with Ned Bradford of Little Brown, and ensconced himself in Cheryl Crawford's Connecticut house for the summer of 1951 to undertake a labor that the introduction of *Paris Cuisine* likens to the decoding of the Rosetta Stone:

> The unique creation of these individual chefs is here and only here set down in print. The quest for these recipes was not, as some might think, just a gay and casual gastronomic holiday, You do not, as a stranger, go into any restaurant, order a meal, ask for and get the recipe for a particular dish. It took years of becoming acquainted, of finally making firm friends of chefs, proprietors and their wives and colleagues. It took months of testing, comparing, evaluating and rejecting to acquire and to sift the recipes we wanted.

In truth, it was difficult work, involving the translation not only of words but of ingredients and instructions—themselves designed by and for professional rather than home cooks—for dishes running the gamut from standards like steak au poivre, coquilles St.-Jacques, and chocolate mousse to exotic specialties like soufflé de homard Plaza-Athénée. The resulting book is, if free from gourmet pomposity, rather grave in tone: This is serious business, it seems to say, which—given the load of psychic and cultural baggage Americans continued to bring to France in general and French food and drink in particular—indeed it was.

That solemnity may have in part reflected James's own circumstances through 1951. The success of *Fireside* had not produced any offers to create a similar blockbuster with a correspondingly high advance, and James's economic life, based largely on grinding out articles for *Argosy* and, more recently, *Apartment Life* for two-hundred-dollar fees seemed unrelentingly hand to mouth. James was adept at reducing the actual cash costs of living by amassing trade-offs, favors, and freebies—the tribute paid to Air France in *Paris Cuisine,* for example, would defray travel costs to Europe for the next few years—but James wanted real money in his pocket that he could spend when and as he saw fit. The only solution seemed to be to vastly increase his writing work while further exploiting his reputation as a food expert and celebrity. The connections he had forged in the wine business through Sherry Wine & Spirits, his friendships with Alexis Lichine and Frank Schoonmaker, and his editorship of National Premium Beer's *Journal* gave him some sense of how he might accomplish the latter, but to increase further his journalistic output would have seemed a physical impossibility. To James— driven by urges whose acceleration had grown ever more compelling with each of the last forty years—limits, however much they might affect his bodily and emotional health, were beside the point. In the next few years his ambition would become nearly boundless.

Paris Cuisine, published in June 1952, was well received— "highly recommended" was the verdict of the *New York Times Book Review*—and was reprinted twice over the next twelve months. Sandy Watt came to New York for the launch but felt overshadowed by James in the full flush of his social element. While James was generous and kind to a fault, he had a tendency to be less mindful of the presence and contribution of his collaborator than he might be. Over the coming years Sandy and James would see each other in Paris from time to time, but without the personal and professional intensity of the months that produced *Paris Cuisine,* each encounter more distant than the last. Watt himself would become food and wine correspondent of the London *Daily Telegraph* and write two further books, *The Art of Simple French Food* and *Paris Bistro Cookery,* both models of their kind and prescient in their appreciation of French food in its earthier and less embellished mode.

James, meanwhile, found other collaborators. In particular he reestablished contact with Isabel Callvert, with whom he had worked in radio in Portland. An actress by profession, Callvert had built up a sideline in script writing and editing as well as a keen interest in food and drink, shared by her AT&T executive husband, Ron. James knew he needed something or someone to help him increase the quantity of journalism he produced, and it seemed natural enough to ask Isabel—for whom he had first cooked when she was a teenager in Hawthorne Park—to help with his recipe development and writing.

Although their work arrangement was informal in the extreme, within months Isabel had become the indispensable factotum who allowed James to become James Beard—who researched recipes and lore, reworked his frequently stuffily congealed and precious prose into smooth if often characterless magazinese, fended off or reassured editors as circumstances might require, corresponded with the IRS, made reservations and bought tickets, and ordered suits and jackets from Toronto and shirts from Barcelona. During the first three years of their collaboration they would create six books and a minimum of three magazine features a month, producing articles for *McCall's, Gentry, Vogue, Harper's Bazaar, Woman's Day, Collier's,* and *This Week* as well as regular columns for *Argosy, House & Garden,* and *Apartment Life,* together with sundry Sherry Wine & Spirits newsletters and National Premium Beer *Journals.*

During the spring of 1952, James also became acquainted with Helen Evans Brown, a California food writer who had been making a name for herself first at West Coast publications like *Sunset* and more recently at *House & Garden, McCall's,* and even *The Atlantic.* She had written six cookbooks, four of which had been published by the Southern California craftsman printer Ward Ritchie. Like Ritchie's typography, graphics, and binding, Brown's culinary sensibility was both innovative and yet solidly rooted within the best traditions of the artisan; its novelty was restrained by an appreciation for classical purity and simplicity. As for her food, Brown's menus rang with freshness and fire, even when built on apparently banal "high-concept" women's magazine ideas inflicted on her by her publisher. For example, *The Holiday Cook Book,* devised around the unpromising premise of a set of menus for the year's major holidays, is full of unhackneyed pleasures: a summer dinner of chilled mushroom soup, grilled broiled shrimp, onion turnovers, and green-bean-and-dill salad; or a Valentine's Day lovers' supper of bacon-wrapped chicken livers and ripe olives, a dark braise of lamb shanks, carrots sweetened by a brandy glaze, and mashed potatoes.

A pretty, dark, and tireless woman a year James's junior, Brown was direct yet gentle, a self-deprecating perfectionist with a level of ambition and drive that was akin to his own creativity and energy if not compelled by his inner ghosts and terrors. Given such talent, burgeoning reputation, and the claim she had staked on James's native turf of the Pacific Coast, they were destined to be great enemies or great friends. But when James received the galleys of her *The West Coast Cook Book* from Ned Bradford at Little, Brown, he was stunned by its quality. By the standards of other books—whether bestselling home-ec tomes like *The Better Homes and Gardens Cook Book* (5.5 million sold) or James's own *Fireside*—the food was vibrant with colors, scents, and bracing flavors beside which most dishes presented in New York–based magazines and books seemed pallid, contrived, and a little lacking in heart and sense of place.

There were Hispanic dishes from California like guacamole, quesadillas, and salsas—at once cool and piquant; grills of meat, game, and fish—from salmon to albacore to abalone; salads whose composition suggested not helmets cast in gelatin but acres of meadows and fields; and vegetables and fruit—artichokes, avocados, asparagus, papayas, oranges, lemons, and tomato upon tomato—that bespoke a life of pure possibility under the constant western sun. There was foreign food, too, but foreign food subsumed into the creative milieu of what might be called California classicism: pizzettas and won tons reinterpreted with local ingredients; cassoulet, gnocchi, curries, and quiche; and steelhead trout baked en papillote and a roast haunch of venison with chestnuts and red California wine.

Helen Brown's husband, Philip, was a rare book dealer, and she was well versed in antique recipe books, some of whose titles were compiled in a bibliography at the back of *The West Coast Cook Book*. Among those listed are *The Web-Foot Cook Book,* the Portland Council of Jewish Women's *Neighborhood Cook Book,* and the 1924 *St. Peter's Guild Cook Book* from La Grande, Oregon. That anyone knew or cared about such recipes was more than James normally dared hope, and Helen's recipes for "Dutch Babies," Huckleberry Muffins, Vancouver Cream Scones, an Oregon cake of cherries and filberts, razor clams, and the fried crab legs served at Dan & Louis's Oyster Bar in Portland made him swoon with hunger, longing, and the realization that he was not alone in the world.

He dashed off a letter to Brown, introducing himself as an Oregonian and the author of Little, Brown's forthcoming *Paris Cuisine,* adding a gentle suggestion that the cooking time in one of her recipes might be a little long. He asked if Philip might track down a copy of Montagné and Salles's *La Grande Cuisine Illustrée* and reported on a series of dismal home economists' lunches—the most recent hosted by the Banana Council—he had been attending. Brown typed an enthusiastic reply, recounting her own trials as a judge at a cooking contest held by *Western Family,* a magazine at which she was a contributing editor, and her encounters with the Olive Advisory Board.

Most crucially, she inquired about the publication date of *Paris Cuisine* and swore her aid in promoting it. Brown edited a newsletter for a gourmet grocery store called Balzer's, at which, she noted, *Fireside* had sold "like bananas in England" and enclosed some bookplates for James to sign. As a comrade in what James would more and more frequently call "the wars," she understood that publicity was the staff of life; that the logrolling of mutual promotion was the highest intimacy and gift two food writers could exchange.

By summer James had found reasons to visit the West Coast, arriving at the Browns' in the afternoon and talking far into the night. If James found in Helen his ultimate culinary alter ego, he was equally enchanted with Philip, a patient, wry, and dapper gentleman who shared many of James's cultural and literary enthusiasms. On his return to New York, parcels flew back and forth between the coasts: from the Browns, abalone (then unavailable outside California), antiquarian books, and eventually the kimono-style robes that became James's habitual indoor costume at his Twelfth Street apartment; from James, wines and spirits (which, by virtue of his work with Sherry and its ilk, he was increasingly in a position to dispense as largesse), a torrent of books and clippings, and larder items such as truffles that were, if not commonplace, more readily obtainable in New York.

With *Paris Cuisine* showing respectably, Little, Brown commissioned another book, to be titled *James Beard's Fish Cookery*, from James that summer. The incorporation of the author's name into the title was a curious but persistent tradition in cookbook publishing that asserted not so much the author's manifest celebrity as his or her expertise as a food "personality" whose experience and good sense could be trusted. Helen Brown, less known than James, was given this treatment by Little, Brown for her first book. In any case James was now enough of a force to be reckoned with to be introduced by Cecily Brownstone to Irma Rombauer, author of *The Joy of Cooking*. He confided to Helen: "I have never cared much for *Joy of Cooking*, being a tried and true Fannieite. But the woman herself is wonderful and I adore her."

A good measure of Beard's admiration for Fannie Farmer was based not on her food but on what he saw as her consummate mastery of the business side of food writing, consulting, and teaching. Farmer's dealings with her publisher, the Boston Cooking School, and the corporate food producers and manufacturers to whom she gave endorsements were still, in James's eyes, a model for food professionals fifty years later. By his own reckoning, he had established himself as a writer; teaching was an area he was beginning to give some thought to; and he was even now assiduously looking for consulting opportunities, particularly in the wine and spirits business, where his connections—furthered on another trip to Europe that autumn—had become considerable.

Despite his desire to tap the wealth of the food industry for himself, James had misgivings about what was, in many ways, the joint legacy of American big business and Fannie Farmer and her ilk. For the fall issue of the National Premium Beer *Journal* he wrote an editorial citing a USDA study showing that meals prepared from scratch were both tastier and cheaper, as were natural cheese as opposed to processed and homemade or neighborhood-produced bakery goods as opposed to regional or national brands. "Why is it that each year our bread gets less and less palatable, more and more flabby and tasteless?" asked Beard and waxed ravenous: "Where, oh where, do you find a real apple pie, oozing with juices and covered with a flaky brown crust? Or a fine, well-grained chocolate cake? Or a buttery piece of genuine pound cake? All these old standbys are disappearing from our lives."

A few months later Beard would write Helen from the National Restaurant Show, where he manned the National Premium Beer booth, several furlongs down the interminable length of Chicago's Navy Pier, reporting:

> More ways to imitate food and less good food than you can imagine. There were artificial onion soups, ice cream made from old rayon petty coats [*sic*], barbecued(?!) sandwiches heated with a steam pipe in one second, . . . artificial charcoal and little doots to keep potatoes white. . . . But as far as anything to make food better or truly more flavorful there was nothing. A sad commentary on the future of food in this country. If the restaurateurs are intent on cutting quality . . . there is no chance for any of us to do any missionary work at all.

In the minds of most writers and editors, however, any "missionary work" they might do consisted precisely of promoting the advances of the food industry to the nation's growing regiment of credulous housewives. In October Beard attended the annual Food Editors' Conference in New York, an industry-sponsored event at which he was able to consolidate his position among his peers by providing affable company and amusing commentary while the nation's magazine and women's page editors ruminated on the newest miracles wrought by corporate America's food engineers and home economists. Breakfast saw a National Dairy Products Corporation promoting ice cream with fresh fruit or French toast as a "really exciting and glamorous" breakfast trend, followed by a mid-morning homily on the technical virtues of Minute Maid orange juice. At a lunch sponsored by Procter & Gamble, makers of Crisco, an MIT biochemist proclaimed obesity the country's most crucial nutritional problem.

A later presentation on the psychology of the American housewife explained that the housewife's "reward in living" lies in the feeling of closeness she attains with her family through her domestic duties, and in particular in conferring rewards on the family through the provision of favorite foods (and especially desserts and sweets). The editors were cautioned that although they themselves might be intrigued by exotic dishes, they would best serve their readers by providing new twists on familiar foods. Women might prefer casseroles on the basis of cost and convenience, but men would continue to insist on meat and potatoes, and that was the unalterable fact of the national diet.

After the Food Editors' Conference, Beard put the finishing touches on his December *Argosy* article, a piece whose roast beef and hot Christmas drinks did little to change the ineluctable patterns of American men's lives. But in other issues, "Jim" Beard fostered a more imaginative and diverse style of cooking, one whose brassy and sometimes bizarre flavors might gain acceptance because they formed a culinary counterpart to the appetite for rough-and-tumble adventure and square-jawed heroics that was the supposed stock-in-trade of the American male. Octopus in wine, carnitas, clam hash, and duck on a spit were brawny dishes that might be flung on the table like a challenge to a duel, a far cry from the safe and comforting menus a woman might provide.

Early 1953 found Beard and Isabel Callvert most of the way through a first draft of *Fish Cookery* and, in the grip of the seasonal asynchronism that is the food writer's lot, grinding out magazine articles for publication later in the year, writing about picnics in February and Christmas dinners in July. But with Isabel firmly in control of his journalistic enterprises, James was at last free to explore the possibilities of consulting. He made the acquaintance of Phil Klarnet, a public relations man who represented the French cognac and champagne industries on behalf of Edward Gottlieb Associates. James would eventually go to work on these accounts for Gottlieb but was initially a free-lancer on projects of his own devising. By summer he had put together a Pernod recipe booklet for liquor store distribution and secured the endorsement of the extraordinarily imperious and difficult Waldorf-Astoria chef Claudius Philippé for five hundred dollars cash. At the same time he promoted a line of stainless and copper cookware and established a relationship with the manufacturers of the Skotch Cooler—an insulated tartan-plaid canister that became a fixture of 1950s picnics and cookouts—and helped plan a promotional campaign for the forthcoming Skotch Grill. As the United States was gripped by the impending coronation of Elizabeth II in the spring of 1953, the quasi-British James was rolled out by tourism promoters to assure his countrymen that delicious food could indeed be found in the United Kingdom.

In one of his first paid endorsements, Beard appeared in magazine advertisements for Adolph's Meat Tenderizer as "Jim Beard, *Argosy* food editor, author of many cookbooks, food consultant, radio-TV notable. But James was no mere front man: Like an impresario staging the show to end all shows, he was full of ideas for his employer for parties, receptions, media promotions, booklets, and magazine and newspaper tie-ins in which his own presence was the essential catalytic vortex. But he was equally mindful of finding supporting roles for close friends and associates—such as the illustrator he signed up to work on an Adolph's booklet whom Adolph's subsequently refused to pay—and above all Helen Evans Brown.

Even as he gained the recognition and money he craved, James sensed that he was in many ways moving further away from what genuinely mattered to him: He could now write for virtually any editor in the business, but those same editors were inclined to excise his memories of Gearhart from the final text; his endorsement might be seen as a valuable marketing tool, but for products that meant little to him; and his status among his fellow food professionals was unquestionable, but whether that profession was of any genuine service to either food or its consumers was questionable indeed.

As the manifold complexities of his own labors grew more unmanageable, James often dreamed of a simpler and purer life; of running a small restaurant in the country or of writing the kind of literate food books authored by Helen Brown's friend and fellow Californian M. F. K. Fisher: "If only I were really a good writer I would do something fantastic and fabulous in that direction," he wrote Helen, "but maybe I shall find someone to ghost it for me or to do it with me."

In fact friends from Manhattan had persuaded him to act as manager and head cook that summer at a restaurant they owned on Nantucket, called Lucky Pierre—"a real west coast hamburger and sandwich job" serving honest beach food—which, James wrote Helen, could be parlayed into a chain in New York if he and the owners played their cards right. Even James's fantasies of a quiet and decent life of craftsmanship were, as he would be the first to recognize, tinged by a purplish undercurrent of grandiosity, greed, and cynicism.

In April James headed west to California and Oregon—always a place of renewal, healing, and purification for him—and to Helen Brown in particular. Collaboration with Helen and her inspired food seemed both an imperative and a kind of refuge, and he left Pasadena at the beginning of May with the idea of a published exchange of letters between Helen and himself, an epistolary essay on cooking and gastronomy. He spent May 5, his fiftieth birthday, eating at Jack's in San Francisco, as he had done on several occasions as a child, and continued north to Portland, to old friends like Mary Hamblet and Jerry Lamb and to all the attractions and awkwardnesses of coming home after a long absence.

His return was not what he might have hoped: Not only were there no copies of *Paris Cuisine* to be had in Portland, but few people seemed aware of its existence. The ladies of Trinity Church were wrapping up their most successful rummage sale ever, and local asparagus and rhubarb awaited canning. *The Oregonian* food pages featured pressure-cooker Chili con Carne, Rainbow Cake with Lemon Butter Frosting, and "Pineapple Betty" (a baked impasto of graham cracker crumbs and nuts surmounted by marsh-

mallows and pineapple rings). Portland, in short, was its perennially infuriating self, both an inbred enclave of self-satisfied know-
nothingism and a slave to the most debasing and soulless of
national trends. James left for Chicago and dinner at the celebrated
Pump Room ("Hot and cold running waiters in their hunting pink
jackets and their black satin knickerbockers and nylon hose and all
the usual pomp and glop to make it more chi-chi than ever"). By
the end of May he was back in New York, having a good gossip
with Ann Seranne about Jeanne Owen's latest slanders against him
and about Earle MacAusland's impending Nevada divorce. He
issued instructions for the summer's labors to Isabel and packed his
bags for Nantucket.

Lucky Pierre's proved to be a nightmare, featuring, by James's
account, a clientele of vulgar, braying ingrates who refused all his
attempts at fresh and decent food save for hamburgers. In the swel-
tering kitchen, James threw out his back and was constantly abused
by his onetime friends, the owners. In the midst of it all he continued
to send outlines and notes to Isabel, such as these for an outdoor
cooking paperback original for *Argosy*'s Jerry Mason:

> Here is the idea: 1. Definition of culinary terms and barbecue terms
> and certain dishes . . . some of the mouthwatering terms men like.
> 2. Cold and hot weather menus and recipes featuring masculine
> dishes and fish and meat. 3. Recipes for sizzling platters and rotis-
> serie junk. 4. A glossary of drinking terms—also how to use
> whiskey with recipes and man-sized portions (most men drink less
> than women but I suppose we must say man-sized—and be male).
> No fancy schmancy drinks but drinks which are good and full and
> really wonderful.

He took a weeklong hiatus from Nantucket at Cheryl Crawford's
country place (where a bedroom was now permanently reserved for
him) and started work on the epistolary exchange with Helen. The
concept had been one of a lively, argumentative, and at times icono-
clastic dialogue on food—a counter to the usual pomp and senten-
tiousness of gourmet society prose. Unfortunately it seems that the
very attempt to be self-consciously serious about food infected
James's writing with exactly the faults he set out to avoid:

Your letter brings up so many interesting questions and ideas that I
have a thousand thoughts all clamoring for expression at once. First
off, I share your feeling about too much gastronomic delight in too
little time. Only my most recent experience, last week to be exact,
was really an unpleasant one. I attended a dinner given by a very
famous person in the food world and I was amazed at the lack of
balance in the meal. Helen, would you ever serve two dishes with
Hollandaise at one meal? I'm sure you wouldn't.

It was not that Beard could not write in an opinionated yet plainer
style, as this genuine private letter to Brown, written a few months
later on a similar occasion, made clear:

Confidentially, Brown, if you and I had the kitchen, the raw materials and the time and all the rest of it, we could have produced a
meal which would have been a milestone in American gastronomic
history and which would surely have brought the spirits of Carême
and Montagné buzzing around to make us Chevaliers of the Heav-
enly Host of Cook Book writers with double halos piped with phos-
phorescent Duchesse potatoes. I really think no one—and I haven't
tasted yours yet—can cook a goose as well as I can. Period.

In the formal letters, James touched on important subjects—the
necessity to educate the nation's schoolchildren on the sources and
traditions of their food as well as the need for "a real and complete
book of the whole country which would equal what you have done
for the Pacific coast." He continued:

It has to be done. Mrs. Hibben's regional book is anything but
that—being a book of her prejudices which are too many for the
average person. Imagine giving one regional dish for the state of
Oregon and making that one buttered leeks?

The latter lines, one of the few lively moments in the exchange, were
judiciously expunged in an early revision, but the idea behind them
would preoccupy Beard long after he had ceased to worry about settling scores with Sheila Hibben—or, for that matter, with Jeanne
Owen, whose Francocentric pretensions were an inviting target.

Eventually both James and Helen agreed that the letters were "smug" and "high-hat," and should be shelved for the moment and perhaps abandoned. But if nothing else, Beard gained, at long last, an agent as a result. Helen Brown's agent, John Schaffner, summered on Nantucket, and in short order Beard had signed on to a list that would eventually include not only Brown but Craig Claiborne. Schaffner may or may not have made Beard as rich as another agent might have, but he was an infinitely patient and courteous man who worried about James's health and welfare at times when James himself, hurling himself into yet another project, would not.

With the thankless summer at Lucky Pierre behind him and his collaboration with Helen stalled, James boarded a ship for France at the end of September on an Alexis Lichine–sponsored tour of France, followed by stops in London and Lisbon. In going to Europe, Beard missed the 1953 Food Editors' Conference, whose speakers urged their audience to abandon their "nostalgia" for the traditional loaf in favor of the nutritional virtues of modern enriched bread. Helen Brown was in New York on his return in November, and although they continued to hope something might come of the epistolary exchange, they conceived the idea of working together on a book on outdoor cooking, something Helen had already been approached about by a publisher. Beard was hardly short of work: In addition to the completed but unpublished *Fish Cookery,* he had contracted for a book on economical eating to be cowritten with Sam Aaron as well as three paperback originals for Maco Magazine Corporation, a publishing house started by *Argosy*'s Jerry Mason.

Other collaborations seemed to be on the horizon, but none stranger than the one Beard claimed to Helen had been proposed to him by Dione Lucas. More than Beard, Jeanne Owen, or any of the food editors, Lucas was the most visible figure on the New York food scene of the early 1950s. A severe, thin-lipped Englishwoman with hawklike features, Lucas had parlayed her magisterial demeanor and attendance at Paris's Cordon Bleu into two successful cooking schools, first in London and then in New York, and had since 1948 had her own cooking show on local and, later, national CBS television. But she was best known as the queen of the omelet, the dish that—far more than quiche or fondue—symbolized culinary attainment and refinement from the fifties until almost the mid-seventies, embodying both technical prowess and, in its outward purity of form, modernist sophistication.

By James's lights Lucas was a strange bird. The creator, in fact, of the dinner mocked at the start of his epistolary exchange with Helen Brown, she maintained an entourage of fanatical hangers-on that James described as a religious cult. What she had in mind for herself and James—a union he likened to Helen to the battle between the *Monitor* and the *Merrimac*—was an omelet bar and a cooking school. He considered the idea carefully, if only to relish what he imagined would be Jeanne Owen's reaction.

Helen Brown, usually restrained in her advice, wrote back and suggested that he must be out of his mind to consider joining forces with a woman so roundly disliked—or at least so roundly envied—in the food community and one whose reputation rested on what Brown believed was her fraudulent appropriation of the Cordon Bleu name. Moreover, Brown was concerned not only for the future of her own collaboration with Beard, but for his well-being generally, which (he admitted to her with growing regularity) was under increasing assault from feelings of depression, anxiety, and emptiness. Before Christmas he wrote:

> I cannot face this life here any longer—it bores me and I see no point in it at all. . . . All the Home Ec side seems like such crap and all the other sides of life here seem so futile and so empty. And I can no longer bear the traffic and the tempo of the life. Maybe I am just suffering from the return of the traveller blues, but somehow it feels deeper than that to me.

The first days of 1954 were enlivened by the Goddard Gala on January 20, an epically scaled food and wine-tasting event of mammoth proportions, held in the Grand Ballroom of the Plaza, featuring some thirty-five dishes, a similar number of wines, and, with a certain inevitability, Dione Lucas fabricating omelets. Beard was a keen supporter of the event, if only because the gala by accident or design increasingly stole the limelight from Jeanne Owen's Wine & Food Society as one of the centerpieces of New York's gastronomic year.

But Beard was not ultimately a joiner, and he kept himself above the fray and equidistant from both the Owenite and Lucasite fac-tions. In any case, he was much too busy: In addition to an endless cascade of magazine work, during the late winter and early spring he corrected the proofs of *Fish Cookery* and put the finishing touches on *Jim Beard's Complete Book of Barbecue & Rotisserie Cooking* for Jerry Mason, simultaneously developing the initial texts of the two further paperbacks for which he had contracted. John Schaffner was meanwhile pitching the Brown-Beard collaboration on outdoor cooking—what would be James's third book on the subject—to two publishers, Holt and Doubleday. By March the book was signed by Doubleday, with the manuscript to be in the hands of its editor, Clara Claasen, by the fall.

Both Beard and Brown approached the project less as a book than as a personal and professional manifesto, the launch of a culi-nary revolution that would banish both effete gourmets and bovine home economists to the outer reaches of the gastronomic universe. As James wrote to Helen when she, too, confessed to some despair:

> You are one of the few people in this country to have what it takes to make gastronomic history of what we are living through and never forget it. We all have to take some shit from people sometimes which makes us feel like the traditional dime's worth of ground up dog meat. But the important thing is know your power and your strength and above all that you are one of the instruments through which the knowledge flows. You are not a trained homemaker nor a home economist but a true prophet in a world where prophets are needed.

Although both knew they could easily produce a manuscript with material already in their possession, they were determined that the book be not only highly authoritative and original but a sort of odyssey. Their collaboration would begin, they and Philip Brown decided, with a tour of food and drink producers in California, Ore-gon, Washington, Idaho, Utah, and Nevada—a preproduction immersion in the United States, but more specifically in the foods and foodways of its Pacific and western regions. They would then return to Pasadena, and, on a battery of grills and broilers cadged by James from various manufacturers, show the benighted food world their stuff.

Helen and James were both adept at extracting hospitality from producers and at making private activities yield professional dividends. Helen would therefore work up some free-lance assignments from the trip while James arranged a publicity party for the Skotch Grill to be held at the Browns'. He had also recently signed on with Edward Gottlieb Associates as a representative of the French cognac industry and therefore scheduled lecture-demonstrations of cocktails and flaming foods in several cities on his way to and from the West Coast. Helen also arranged book signings along the route and television appearances in San Francisco and Seattle.

Despite all these commitments, the monthlong tour was both inspiring and restful, the latter an important consideration given the varying degrees of obesity, high blood pressure, and other ailments that afflicted all three. James was reunited with his onetime mentor Bess Whitcomb in San Francisco; reacquainted himself with Astoria and Gearhart; had book jacket photos with Helen taken in Seattle; and ended the circuit in Virginia City, Nevada, with a gin-soaked idyll at the home of the aging Lucius Beebe and his lover.

Back in Pasadena, James and Helen set to work, smoking pork tenderloins, stuffing and grilling chicken necks, barbecuing crab over charcoal, experimenting with a backyard lobster-and-clambake, and testing cooking times for dozens of varieties of meat, poultry, and fish on the Skotch Grill, the Smokadero, the Bartron, and sundry other grills and hibachis. By mid-June, they had finished a chapter and sent it off to Clara Claasen, whose "Prussian soul," in James's phrase, decreed it too chatty and impractical. At that point the book ceased to be a personal statement in the mold of *The West Coast Cook Book* and became something closer to a manual. Much of the unique, groundbreaking character Brown and Beard had strived for was consequently lost, save in the sheer breadth of ideas and juxtapositions the book would contain.

When the recipe development and testing were largely complete at the end of June, Beard left for home with a few stops on the way for cognac promotional appearances. Helen would for all intents and purposes write the book (a task she undertook while mastering, as all serious cooks now had to, omelet making) which Philip in turn would type and index. By September the manuscript, of which the Browns were exceedingly proud, was finished, only to be subjected to unending editorial indecision, inattention, and second-guessing by

Clara Claasen: What she had once decreed needed to be encyclopedic was now deemed too long; what once was praised as fresh and innovative now seemed in danger of being another run-of-the-mill book on grilling.

Helen was hurt and incensed, and tension increased between her and James as he took on the role of mediator between her and Claasen. As sensitive as any free-lancer to a competitor's expropriation of her story ideas, she grew increasingly concerned about areas in which James's recent magazine work seemed to overlap with hers: Wasn't the story he was planning on cheese a little close in content to the one she had researched on their western tour? Didn't the home entertaining guide he was doing for Jerry Mason seem a little similar in style to the next book she was planning to do herself? And mightn't his paperback barbecue book steal sales from their joint effort?

However infuriating Beard himself found Clara Claasen, it was a conflict from which he was inclined to distance himself. He was sanguine about his own career, and with reason: *Jim Beard's Complete Book of Barbecue & Rotisserie Cooking* was doing well; his collaboration with Sam Aaron looked to be a success even before the book's publication, with both hardcover and paperback editions being rushed into print; he had more free-lance work than he could deal with; and his consulting work was increasingly lucrative. In its review of the barbecue book on August 22, the *New York Times* reviewer declared: "Jim Beard is considered by most to be the Dean of American Cookery," a title that stuck to him for the rest of his career. When *James Beard's Fish Cookery* was officially launched—together with Kool-Aid and Good Seasons Salad Dressing mix—at the Food Editors' Conference in New York during the first week of October, it was in effect a coronation.

James had to share the attentions of the editors with others, of course. The keynote speaker was Duncan Hines, who combined a career as the publisher of the nation's first coast-to-coast restaurant guide with that of cake mix manufacturer, and who enthused, "Eating is more fun than anything else in the world." In a now-annual fixture, the editors also heard from a representative of Minute Maid orange juice, who detailed the success of the company's efforts to convince Americans to increase their orange juice consumption and to try pineapple juice as well. But despite the attention *James Beard's Fish Cookery* received at the conference, fish, unlike orange juice, was of decreasing interest to Americans, and fish consumption would drop in tandem with the rise of beef eating. *Fish Cookery*—an exhaustive compilation of recipes that James described to Helen as "one of the few things I have ever done I really like a great deal"—would do moderately well, but unlike much of James's work it did not successfully catch the wave of the public's current taste.

The true blockbuster of the early 1950s, *Betty Crocker's Picture Cook Book,* had only four pages of fish recipes and sold more than three million copies between 1950 and 1955. Produced by a miller in landlocked Minneapolis—and therefore with a vested interest in promoting baked goods, cereals, and noodles—it ranged from such home-ec inspirations as "Bit O'Walnut Chiffon" and "Baked Prune Whip" to several varieties of omelet. Its success reflected not only the perennial appeal of the recipe compendium and the pie-centered cooking of the Midwest combined in *The Joy of Cooking,* but also the need for a basic cookbook pitched at the burgeoning number of women who practiced or aspired to "the station wagon way of life." Designed in a photo-laden style that owed much to *Life* and *Look* magazines, with recipes limited to a paragraph in length, *Betty Crocker's Picture Cook Book* suggested that the housewife could learn to cook by the numbers rather than at mother's flour-dusted elbow, and that she could do so in discrete, TV-commercial-size nuggets of time.

These may not have been laudable or even achievable goals in culinary terms, but they seemed socially desirable. As the food editors were feted with the latest convenience foods at the Waldorf-Astoria, the third annual Family Life Conference, being held upstate, agreed that, in theory, "Women could combine marriage, career, and citizenship successfully" as a result of the changing definition of homemaking, time-saving household appliances, and "the new attitude of men who now accepted the modern role of women." The latter contention might have been gainsaid by the women who constituted the overwhelming majority of the attendees at the Food Editors' Conference, and who as journalists and editors found themselves confined for life in the thankless and low-paid ghetto of the women's page and the service magazine. As was the case with race relations in the American South, in the 1950s the male and female spheres were in theory separate but equal, a system extended to food in James and Helen's by-no-means-remarkable assertion in their grilling book: "We believe [charcoal cookery] is primarily a man's job and that a woman, if she's smart, will keep it that way." As Helen would often say to James, "As usual, the boys win."

Helen's assertion of masculine hegemony, as James knew all too well, did not necessarily extend to gay men. They were unlikely to reap the rewards available to heterosexual males, having been drawn or forced into work that, like women's, was marginal in both status and remuneration, such as window dressing and hairstyling. Survival as a homosexual depended on concealment and the manipulation of outward appearances, and gays quite naturally came to excel in endeavors involving artifice, such as the theatrical and decorative arts, among which cooking was numbered.

Gays shared this oppression with women, who also found themselves at the outer margins of the nation's economic life, largely barred from what society considered important occupations and the channels of power through which careers were advanced in them. In the worlds of cooking and gourmet dining, women and gays found themselves both allies and rivals in an arena that was itself viewed by the rest of society as the most trivial of the decorative arts. Given its position as a nexus for gays, women, and their very real discontents—together with social-climbing gourmets and their more frivolous but-no-less-earnestly-pursued agendas—it was perhaps unsurprising that the New York food scene was a vortex of resentment and fevered competition over what most of the world would regard as paltry spoils. By late 1954, the by-no-means-unique envy borne James by Jeanne Owen—whom Beard now referred to simply as "the madame"—had effloresced into a Manhattan-wide matrix of innuendo and spite. Its every manifestation was instantly relayed back to James by *Gourmet*'s Ann Seranne, whose penchant for gathering salacious and damaging intelligence made her the J. Edgar Hoover of food. But by this time James took a kind of wicked delight in hearing Owen's latest slur on his mental health, his sexual habits, his cooking prowess, or that of friends like Helen Brown, whom Owen had that fall publicly blessed with an admiring letter and privately blasted as an obvious culinary incompetent. Beard's stature was now secure enough that he could afford to ignore her, or even—through back-channel gossip of his own—to taunt her, as he might a rattlesnake in a box whose furious but ineffectual buzzing could be safely provoked with a stick.

James spent Christmas and New Year's of 1955 in Europe on a junket of Odyssean scope, flush with the conclusion of a consulting deal with Old Crow whiskey and the successful launch of *How to Eat Better for Less Money*. Produced as a quick cash maker, the collaboration with Sam Aaron proved to be a steady seller in the unique and compelling mold of *Fireside*, based on an approach to economical eating that owed little to the purse-lipped bean counting of the home economists. Instead of discount versions of conventional American favorites, *How to Eat Better for Less Money* proposed a steadfastly bohemian cuisine of innards, offcuts, curries, peasant braises, and ethnic stews—bold, exotic food suffused with integrity and sweaty cosmopolitanism.

James himself dined in Paris that December on lobster a l'américaine, a Provençal tomato-and-garlic dish gussied up by immolation in cognac. If the promotion of this concoction was for James something of a personal crusade during the 1950s, the promotion of cognac itself was increasingly his main consulting job—it was Edward Gottlieb Associates that had sent him to Paris. His escort there and in the Cognac region was Henry McNulty, Gottlieb's Paris representative, whom James described to Isabel as "a delightful person who is completely a part of France." McNulty and his future wife, Bettina, were to become among James's most intimate lifelong friends.

In addition to Gottlieb's cognac and champagne accounts, Beard had business in Spain with the sherry industry, in Italy with Cora vermouth, and back in Paris with Louis Vaudable of Maxim's, all the while noting on Isabel's behalf "enough good food ideas to sink a ship of some size, I can assure you." Still, there was time to spend Christmas in Florence with the Browns' writer friend Bill Veach, followed by a side trip to Tangier in the first few days of January 1955. In Morocco opportunities abounded for liaisons with men, with yet more thereafter back on the Continent—European men in the mold of the Dutchman Ate, who was now no longer a part of James's life. In Milan, for example, there was Pinot (sighed James in his datebook, "The mystery of Pinot!!") and back in Paris, André, the ultrafop.

In Paris, too, Beard was introduced by Henry McNulty to Alice B. Toklas, Gertrude Stein's lifelong companion. Beyond their affinities as westerners and well-connected members of the international gay, lesbian, and arts communities, Toklas and Beard shared a passionate interest in food. *The Alice B. Toklas Cookbook,* reviewed by *New York Times* food editor Jane Nickerson in tandem with *How to Eat Better for Less Money* in November, was at once whimsical ("One day when Picasso was to lunch with us I decorated a fish in a way that I thought would amuse him") and rigorous. Toklas was a stalwart defender of Gallic tradition; patient, careful selection of ingredients; and painstaking preparation; instinctively eschewing shortcuts and compromises of any kind. Ironically, her editor and collaborator for the U.S. edition of *The Alice B. Toklas Cookbook* was none other than America's first lady of the freezer, Poppy Cannon. Cannon, food editor of *House Beautiful,* regular fixture on CBS's "Home" show, and author of *The Can Opener Cookbook,* was to 1950s labor-saving food—from tuna casserole to puffed rice bars to onion dip to sloppy Joes—what Edward Teller was to nuclear fission: a proponent of a something-for-nothing ethic based on the proposition that food, or energy, could be had cheaply and quickly without compromising quality, safety, or the deep-rooted but fragile patterns that comprise culture and community. On "Home," Cannon demonstrated such mutant fare as a vichysoisse made from frozen mashed potatoes, a solitary sautéed leek, and a can of Campbell's Cream of Chicken soup.

It was an approach that proved irresistible not only to the editors of women's magazines—who were, after all, the inheritors of the science and efficiency-obsessed domestic science movement—but even to some people catering to the upper tiers of the gastronomic heap. One of James's European assignments, for example, was to develop a line of quick "gourmet" sauces to be sold in the United States under the label of Maxim's of Paris. Beard hated Maxim's owner, Louis Vaudable, and was contemptuous of Maxim's itself, which he felt had degenerated into a self-parodying tourist trap and fin-de-siècle theme restaurant.

The term "theme restaurant" had yet to be coined, but back in New York, Beard was already in the employ of the company that would become synonymous with it, Restaurant Associates. The previous summer James had traveled out to the Newarker, Restaurant Associates' property at Newark Airport. More familiar than most with the state of cooking at the nation's air and rail termini, James expected little. But the Newarker was, if not perfect, an arrestingly different place founded on the formal principle that more is indeed more and that different is better still: Where most restaurants served oysters in sixes and lobster claws in twos, the Newarker served them in outsize sevens and threes, with napery and cutlery brought on by the sherpa-load and a veritable arsonist's tea party of flambéed dishes to follow. But there was substance behind the style—a genuine concern and understanding of service, ingredients, and cooking.

The creator and guardian of this seemingly revolutionary approach to public feeding was Restaurant Associates' idea man, Joseph Baum. Born into the hotel business in the resort town of Saratoga Springs, New York, he grew up surrounded by bars, clubs, and restaurants and attended Cornell's School of Hotel Management. He was a small, dapper, distinguished-looking man whose honeyed if never unctuous speech and calm demeanor concealed a restless perfectionism and a head full of hospitality ideas seemingly drawn from just this side of Ludwig of Bavaria. But Baum's imagination was tempered by a sure sense of good taste, and few of his notions were wholly untried. Flambéed food of the kind served at the Newarker, for example, had—according to the Duncan Hines restaurant guide, *Adventures in Good Eating*—reached not only Minneapolis but Duluth by 1952, and Restaurant Associates' next project, The Hawaiian Room in Manhattan, was a relatively late example of a trend that had begun in California at Don the Beachcomber in Los Angeles and, most successfully, at Trader Vic's in Oakland.

Such "Polynesian" restaurants both epitomized dining out in the 1950s and marked the beginning of the dominant place theme restaurants would hold in the nation's gastronomic life for the next twenty-five years. In truth, all restaurant eating in America—save in the most unself-consciously American places—was theme dining and had been since the days of Delmonico's and the Broadway lobster palaces: Then, as in the early 1950s, dining out was not so much an intrinsic part of American culture—of life as it was lived—but an escape from it, and eating foreign food was not designed to be an experience of the flavors of another country's cuisine but a synthetic experience of the country itself. To visit a Chinese, French, or Italian restaurant was to take in a kind of travelogue or amusement park ride that was a simulacrum of China, France, or Italy that really had very little to do with food or—given the narrow and often inauthentic choice of dishes and decor found in most "foreign" restaurants—the reality of the country and culture in question.

Polynesian food was in this sense the ultimate theme cuisine: Claiming inspiration from points in and around the Pacific from Hawaii to China, but with no genuine connection to any one place in particular, it was an entirely artificial genre: a fantasy cuisine based on marinated steak, chicken, and fish with pineapple chunks, accompanied by fruit juice–based cocktails whose much-vaunted potency conjured up images of uninhibited, premissionary sexuality, torches, tiki gods, and—geography being utterly beside the point— Caribbean voodoo. The Polynesian food craze was also fed by memories of World War II—already being sentimentalized through such vehicles as Rodgers and Hammerstein's *South Pacific*, itself based on a bestseller by James Michener—and by a general fascination with Hawaii and the Pacific islands that seemed to represent a new frontier to be conquered and mined not for its economic resources but for its leisure opportunities. It also jibed nicely with many aspects of the emerging 1950s culture: There was smoke, firelight, and the sizzle of outdoor food wrestled into submission—pummeled, drowned in marinade, trussed, skewered, and seared—by men and served by compliant, beautiful women on the beach or by the pool. In the end Polynesian restaurants represented the expropriation of food as a life-style commodity: To own the objects associated with a life was to live the life—however much a marketing man's bogus concoction the life might be—and with a grill, some juice, some rum, and some torches, anyone with the means could shed the button-down existence of suburban life for that of an indolent and sated beach kahuna.

• • •

If Joe Baum was going to do a Polynesian restaurant—and then probably only at the insistence of the corporate officers at Restaurant Associates—he would do it right. In 1955 he put his brilliant, inebriate, and temperamental executive chef Albert Stockli to work on food and drink that would bear some resemblance to that of Hawaii, and signed on James, now returned from Europe, as a consultant to work with him. Beard had already done some work devising menus at the Newarker, and he, Baum, and Stockli worked fabulously together, even as the year wore on and James confessed to Helen that he was sick to death of papayas and rum.

Nineteen fifty-five had not begun entirely auspiciously. After his return from Europe, Beard spent the better part of a week in the hospital in a state of collapse with shingles and hemorrhoids, together with varicose veins and incipient phlebitis in his legs. As ever he was warned about his weight, and as ever he did little about it, returning after his release to a daily round of lunches at Quo Vadis, "21," Chambord, and lesser spots followed by dinners for from two to eight guests at the apartment on Twelfth Street. He had remodeled the still-tiny kitchen the year before, painted the apartment forest green—the color for all apartments in Manhattan with pretensions to style at the time—and started to establish the collection of majolica pottery that became a lifetime obsession.

Dinner guests regularly included Sam and Florence Aaron, Helen McCully, *Gourmet* contributor Alvin Carr, decorator Freddie Shrallow, Isabel and Ron Callvert, arts administrator Mateo Lettunich, Cheryl Crawford and Ruth Norman, book editor John Ferrone, and a *Gourmet* staffer from Mississippi named Craig Claiborne, whom James had met through Ann Seranne. Seranne, a constant guest herself, had been fired that February in one of Earle MacAusland's periodic attempts to regain his fragile sense of control over the magazine. Claiborne would join her at the public relations firm she launched after her departure before himself moving on to bigger things.

Dinner at James's could feature cassoulet, or roast chicken with braised endive; cracked crabs followed by steak and asparagus; lamb curry or, with some inevitability, lobster à l'américaine, for which the Swiss-hotel-school-trained Claiborne might produce a pastry case. A book or magazine article in progress often dictated dinner for a succession of days—a week of shrimp or of vermouth-based dishes, for example—with Ferrone and Shrallow serving as guinea pigs. Recipes might also be developed in correspondence with Helen Brown, who had access to the West Coast ingredients that were his flavor touch-stones.

With *The Complete Book of Outdoor Cookery* now ready for publication, he and Helen also volleyed ideas for their next collabo-ration between Pasadena and Greenwich Village. They had no inter-est in working for Doubleday's Clara Claasen again, but a clause in their contract gave the publisher right of first refusal on their next book (should there be one). At various times they considered a book of classic recipes and their variations, a complete guide to home entertaining, and a revival of the epistolary exchange in the form of *Recipes and Reminiscences,* a book of recipes based on mutually rec-ollected "taste memories" and the recounting of their origins.

House & Garden had meanwhile begun paying Beard $200 a month for a column on wines and spirits called "Corkscrew," as well as $350 for longer "cookbook" features that appeared several times a year. With this relationship and a similar one with *Woman's Day* apparently well cemented, James was able to drop his commitments to *Argosy, Apartment Life,* and the National Premium Beer *Journal,* assignments that in any case paid badly and that he now regarded as somewhat déclassé. Of late he and Helen had conspired to crack national magazines on the order of the *Saturday Evening Post,* and succeeded in placing two articles with the *Post* and *Life's* ill-fated rival *Collier's.* Now James was in pursuit of the nation's biggest-cir-culation magazine, *Reader's Digest,* and its uncommonly rich fees of fifteen hundred dollars per feature. A March meeting with a *Digest* editor yielded an assignment for an article titled "How Good Is American Food?" which would gently suggest that the nation's appetite for big, out-of-season produce and embrace of frozen and convenience foods and supermarkets were all that stood between the United States and its rendevous with gastronomic greatness.

But much as Beard had opinions about these matters, he was no polemicist, and for the *Reader's Digest* assignment he produced prose of unequaled lassitude: "It is wise to appreciate what is in sea-son for what it is. If one has spent winters in France or Italy it is easy to accustom oneself to the winter vegetables, which are truly very good in their own form and which for the most part have wonderful

variations which many of us miss." Despite such writing, the piece
was full of wise and prescient thoughts about the importance of producer, retailer, and consumer getting to know one another and one
another's interests; on the pleasures of truly seasonal cooking; and
on the debilitating effects on the nation's larder of pink tomatoes,
iceberg lettuce, and cosmetically perfect gargantuan produce. But
any genuine ideological fire the piece might possess was dampened
both by the *Digest*'s innate conservatism and James's sense of where
his own future interests might lie. James could hardly condemn processed food and simultaneously plug canned petits pois from Green
Giant—as he did in the article—with whom he hoped to reach a consulting agreement after being introduced to a company executive by
Cecily Brownstone. Despite his lifelong left-wing politics and his
heartfelt desire "to make this a better world for honest cookery,"
James was disinclined to make enemies for economic as well as psychological reasons: Out-and-out disagreement, with its potential for
alienation and even hostility, was antithetical to the affable persona
through which he purchased the world's professional and personal
regard.

In the end the *Reader's Digest* piece was watered down to "How
to Buy Good Food." When the editor who assigned it left the magazine, it was killed, and a much-improved version was eventually ped-
dled to a new food magazine called *Bon Appétit*. But that spring
John Schaffner was working on a deal of much greater consequence
with Dell paperbacks, where John Ferrone was an editor. Ferrone
had mentioned his acquaintance with James to Dell's president,
Frank Taylor, and, in part through the intervention of Taylor's food-
savvy wife, a paperback original tentatively titled *James Beard's
Basic Cook Book* was conceived, with Ferrone as editor. The
advance was to be three thousand dollars, hardly a stunning sum but
one that in part assumed the potential of a mass-market paperback
bestseller to generate much greater royalties and to make Beard's
name a household word. Isabel Callvert would receive half the
advance and credit as an assistant on the title page but would not
participate in the royalties themselves. Still, her share represented a
windfall in comparison with her usual 10 percent share of James's
magazine fees.

Publication of the paperback was not, however, a high priority
for Dell and, despite being completed by the autumn of 1956, the

book would not appear until early 1959. But with two further paperbacks done for Jerry Mason now on sale, *Jim Beard's Casserole Cookbook* and *Jim Beard's Complete Cookbook for Entertaining*, and *The Complete Book of Outdoor Cookery* on the eve of publication, Beard was more than ready for a hiatus from book writing—barring a further collaboration with Helen Brown. He had in any case been disappointed by the modest sales of *Fish Cookery*, a book he numbered among his best efforts, and by what both he and Helen admitted was the dry and impersonal final draft of *Outdoor Cookery*.

When it was published in June, *Outdoor Cookery* received fulsome reviews ("Far and away the best thing yet that has been printed on outdoor cooking," wrote Jane Nickerson in the *New York Times*). James's mind, however, was focused not on writing but on business schemes and television and radio appearances. Despite his low opinion of Poppy Cannon's vulgar, technical approach to food, he was a regular guest on "Home" and was of sufficient note to garner appearances on the Ted Mack and Arthur Godfrey shows, as well as innumerable local homemaker and talk programs. With these, his magazine work, and his consulting work for Edward Gottlieb Associates, Restaurant Associates, Sherry Wine & Spirits, and a half dozen others, he was as busy as he had ever been.

But Beard in the meantime had become convinced that he should open a shop, a restaurant, or a cooking school—or possibly all three—as both a source of a steady income and a hedge against old age. As the summer wore on, he wrote Helen less about book ideas than of what a good plan it would be for her to move east and set up in business with him. Meanwhile, he conferred with French chef André Surmain, Ruth Norman, and others about starting a cooking school, and in July signed a lease on a storefront on lower Fifth Avenue with his old Portland decorator friend, Agnes Crowther, and her real estate developer husband. The business, which was to be named "Boutique Gastronomique," was never launched, and Beard retired to Cheryl Crawford's place in New Canaan, where he cooked for Marilyn Monroe ("so quiet and unassuming and little girl I couldn't believe it," he wrote Helen), followed by a trip to Mexico with a wealthy epicure friend.

On the way down he stopped in Pasadena, and he and Helen inspired each other to the creation of what was for them comparatively fussy food. Ideas from letters they'd exchanged—a Dungeness crab imperial gratinéed with béarnaise sauce, onion, and bread crumbs—were followed up on, and new dishes—mayonnaise gazpacho and snails with mushrooms—were put to the test. When Helen and Philip visited New York at the end of September, Helen in turn brought along three new variations on oysters Rockefeller. In the interim parcels of cheese, morels, truffles, and fruit made their customary transits between the coasts. James was also a sensitive and generous giver of gifts—not only of cookware, pottery, and china, but of items like the extraordinary shawl that Helen wore continually through the latter half of the year.

During the autumn, Beard worked for Restaurant Associates and on three pieces for *Collier's* that in retrospect epitomize middle-class life in the mid-1950s: beans, meatballs, and station wagon picnics. But James's own tastes—perhaps foreshadowing those of the middle class's betters—continued in their now rococo, lobster-obsessed mode. At the end of 1955 he left for Europe and on his arrival wrote Isabel a fevered note about two new discoveries:

> One is an omelette with a sauce cardinal made for the bits of lobster with orange juice added and orange sections and anchovies. This is folded into the omelet and served so. Fabulous combination of flavors. The other is a lobster in large pieces poached in the shell of an orange and served with orange sections, a sauce cardinal and rice—the orange is cut in quarters about two-thirds of the way down, then the meat removed and when the lobster is put in, the four pieces are put together and little bits of lobster peek out through the incisions in the fruit. It is something unbelievable I can assure you.

Regardless of his current feelings about the virtues of such couturier assemblages as opposed to the more direct pleasures of American food, Beard continued to be a formidable absorber and generator of ideas. While in Paris, he corresponded with Isabel about his promotional work for Cora vermouth:

> Here are the various things about vermouth that I thought of—Sole au vermouth, baked salmon stuffed with onion, pepper, tomato slices, dill and basted with vermouth and a sauce similar to the one with the sole, Salmon in jelly as you do it with a vermouth jelly,

Mexican chicken—like the molé with vermouth, chicken with vermouth for basting with butter and green olives, basted turkey, veal with vermouth and tarragon and noodles for accompaniment, lobster vermouth, ham slice in vermouth aspic, shrimps with vermouth—your pickled shrimps but with that—short ribs with vermouth and soy and garlic and fresh ginger, duckling with vermouth and young turnips and peas, baked swordfish with mushroom stuffing and basted with vermouth and a vermouth sauce, spareribs Chinese, squab with pignolias and vermouth, chicken, black olives, peppers in vermouth flavored cream sauce. Kidneys with vermouth and mushrooms and a bit of mustard and cream.

Following several intervening paragraphs of news, gossip, and a rundown of Beard's itinerary, the letter closes, "Oh yes, sausages in vermouth for Sunday breakfast with poached eggs with a sauce espagnole flavored with vermouth. Love and kisses, JB."

At the New Year Beard went to Bordeaux to be inducted into the Commanderie du Bontemps du Médoc, a renowned wine society given to more than a little pomp and pageantry. ("Wait till you see papa in those medieval hats!" he wrote Isabel.) But no sooner had he returned from Bordeaux than he appeared in then Paris-based humorist Art Buchwald's column as the putative head of a "Society for the Suppression of the Word Gourmet in America." Part in jest, part in seriousness, and part in spite against any and all manifestations of the Owenite tendency, Beard proposed the substitution of "epicure" for "gourmet," arguing, "The epicure is a man who likes food, the gourmet is a man who talks about liking food." Damning the status-conscious members of eating societies—the difference between a gourmet and an epicure is "the difference between a social climber and someone who has arrived"—and the snobbish attractions of culinary "chi-chi," James opined that American home cooking was in fine shape and that as a result of foreign travel and the fashionableness of food as a topic, Americans were more food conscious. He was less sanguine about American restaurants, which suffered as a result of being run by graduates of courses in restaurant management. In closing he offered a list of the ten best restaurants in the country: Le Pavillon, "21," and Quo Vadis in New York; Jack's in San Francisco; Brennan's in New Orleans; Locke-Ober in Boston; Perino's and Musso and Frank in Los Angeles; the London Chop

House in Detroit; and, in a burst of impish nostalgia, the Pancake House in Portland.

Much of Beard's interview with Buchwald was tongue-in-cheek, but he was not incorrect in his observations. Although James himself might view the gastronomic universe in terms of quality versus convenience—himself and Helen versus Poppy Cannon and the home economists—for most of the country it did not consist of two mutually exclusive options, but of a range of choices whose incompatibility was in the eye of the beholder. True, at the beginning of 1956, the nation's diet was growing relentlessly more homogeneous, but Americans were also purchasing and dining on ethnic foods—even if only chow mein and pizza—with increasing regularity; the growth of frozen and canned food business was unstoppable, but so too was a palpable turn toward natural as opposed to processed cheeses; supermarkets and shopping centers may have continued to steamroll the neighborhood grocery store, the urban market, and the farm stall out of existence, but the gourmet shop, whether free standing or as a department within another store, was ascendant; and the counterpoint to the TV dinner—itself foreshadowing the potential of a twelve-hundred-dollar appliance called the microwave oven Tappan announced that year—was a fresh green salad and a steak grilled outside over coals on some of the thirty million dollars' worth of grilling equipment sold in 1955. With their incomes at an all-time high, Americans saw nothing but an infinitely bountiful supermarket of options: In the course of a day you could emulate, as whim or need demanded, the domestic dynamo Poppy Cannon at lunch and the tweedy cosmopolite Beard at dinner.

On Beard's return home in February 1956, the idea of a cooking school continued to preoccupy him, as well it might. While convenience foods and new appliances might mean that, for practical reasons, few were compelled to acquire an advanced culinary education, the nation's new leisure and life-style imperatives decreed that one might want to know about food and cooking anyway, perhaps not so much as a domestic as a social skill. But with the extinction of the great domestic science academies of the turn of the century (save in the remnant preserved in high school home-ec classes, in which generation on generation of girls learned to make Jell-O), there were, in fact, surprisingly few places to learn cooking. An article in the *New York Times* published the previous autumn listed five in New York, excluding the YMCA, and of these perhaps only one—the Helen Worth Cooking School on East Forty-fifth Street, which James lost no opportunity to excoriate—could be said to teach the kind of high-style cooking sought by the emergent consumer-leisure class.

If classes were few, cooking demonstrations had become commonplace. In addition to the television performances of Dione Lucas, Poppy Cannon, and James himself, department stores and other retail venues frequently offered nuggets of culinary instruction in the course of promoting products and ingredients. At a more ambitious level, Bloomingdale's presented six weeks of demonstrations in the fall of 1955 in its Au Gourmet department, featuring what the *Times* called a "rather round-faced young man," Craig Claiborne, who was now an employee of Ann Seranne's food-consulting and public relations business. Already speaking with some of the authority and belief in a systematic approach that would characterize his later career, Claiborne counseled: "Adequate equipment costs little and correct procedure costs nothing" and cited the value of "sound gastronomical influences," chief among these being good restaurants and cookbooks by such authors as "Irma Rombauer, James A. Beard and Helen Evans Brown."

By summer 1956 a partnership between James and André Surmain was taking shape, with Ann Seranne's new business serving as a model, combined with features drawn from Dione Lucas's idea for a collaborative cooking school and shop. James spent June in a house obtained through Frank Schoonmaker (with whom he was to write a wine book that would gestate for the next six years but never appear) at Palamos on the Spanish coast, breezing through the marketplace in oversize shirts and espadrilles, working in the kitchen with the gifted resident cook Mercedes, and conferring with Surmain, Henry McNulty, and other visitors who passed through. He wrote Helen and served notice that for the moment art—and perhaps their dreams of serving the greater gastronomic good—would have to yield to commerce: "I am sick of being poor. I want to earn some really big money for a few years and see what happens then."

The business would be called "André Surmain Associates," with James's name on the letterhead as a consultant rather than partner, an arrangement necessitated by his continuing employment with Edward Gottlieb. But in the end, whether as a result of pressure from Gottlieb or simple practicality, only the cooking school aspect of the business survived. By August James had set up an office in Surmain's town house at 249 East Fiftieth and enrolled some twenty-five initial students, among them Helen McCully of McCall's; Paula Peck, who was to become America's doyenne of baking; and Rita Wynn, whose photographer husband, Dan, would become the more-or-less official recorder of Beard's life and milieu. More crucially, Beard persuaded Jane Nickerson of the *Times* to make the school the subject of a *New York Times Magazine* story, featuring a menu of Ham Cornucopias, Leg of Lamb Lucullus, and Boules sur Chocolat.

A triumph of equal, if more personal, importance for Beard was the glowing account of the school produced in *The New Yorker* that November by Sheila Hibben, who praised "the singularly relaxed but at the same time authoritative attitude of the two instructors and ... the lucidity with which they directed the proceedings." Hibben also extolled the food cooked at the school; on her visit, a terrine of veal and Canadian bacon; spinach pasta with cabbage, bacon, and poppy seeds; sautéed green peppers; potatoes fondantes; dinner rolls; and a dessert called Diplomate au Grand Marnier. Classes at both the basic and the advanced levels were limited to ten students and consisted of six lessons for $100 (raised to $125 in the new year), during each of which students prepared and served a complete dinner.

From the start the lessons were participatory rather than demonstrations, and students were encouraged to get their hands dirty while the instructor looked on as a discreetly omniscient but never overbearing presence. It was an approach to teaching that James would enlarge on and refine over the years, in the process both making it his own and creating what became the standard method of culinary education. The school was an immediate success, so much so that James set up consultations with two investment advisers and made plans for yet another remodeling of his home kitchen. By November he and Surmain had persuaded Frigidaire to furnish the school kitchen with new electric appliances, prompting James to covet an electric range for himself. The smell of gas—"that horrible natural gas—what a stinking thing it is!" he wrote Helen Brown more than once—produced a furious and almost primal revulsion in James as few other things could. At 36 West Twelfth, where he had lived for sixteen years, James was now the proprietor in part of two apartments; his own at the rear and another at the front, now occupied by an Italian architect named Gino Cofacci. They had met that spring at Felix's on Thirteenth Street, a restaurant favored by the gay arts community, where Beard had joined a mutual friend, at the time Cofacci's lover, for dinner. At forty, some twelve years younger than James, Gino had a strong, cleft chin; hooded, piercing eyes; and the distracted look of a man buttonholed by a distant acquaintance while late for a train. Although his conversation careened uneasily between sullen silence and reckless volubility, Gino had a lean and edgy beauty about him and, at times, a kind of European refinement and elegance.

James was recovering from a disastrous affair with a black lover whose rejection had left him nearly suicidal, and Gino's attentions—whether they were stolen from or willingly surrendered by his previous lover is unclear—were a badly needed solace. And while Gino had his shortcomings—chiefly an inability to keep a job or provide for himself for long—he was someone who accorded with James's own sense of what he desired and deserved in a lover. Gino was someone he could enjoy, admire, and feel affection for, even if never entirely love without reference to how Gino reflected on him. Within months Gino moved in, and though at times he flayed James's soul with embarrassments and failures that would have driven Mary to the next outbound steamer in an instant, Gino never left, nor did James ever truly ask him to.

Despite his other failings, Gino was largely uncritical of James's body, and that alone was for James a singular consolation. Through 1955 and 1956 James, like Helen Brown, could not lose weight—or perhaps it was that he could not stop eating—despite being under doctor's orders to do so. Helen was stuck at 135 pounds and could loose at best ten pounds, and that mostly water. James, who brushed 300 at times, was comparatively wizened at 250. His legs, ankles, and, more seriously, his heart could hardly bear the strain, but to him forgoing food was not so much deprivation as drowning—like suffocation in thick, blue, stinking gas. Throughout his life Beard could effectively lose weight only as a captive in hospitals and clinics, a Ulysses of appetite lashed to the mast.

Helen, like most Americans, could persuade herself to set aside certain foods and to lower her caloric intake. In a May 1956 article in *McCall's*, she described her years of yo-yo dieting under the heading "I lost 5 pounds in twenty years"—the same 5 pounds over and over again. The McCall's piece, however, was meant to represent a success story: "We Diet Together" described the reducing plan imposed on both Helen and Philip by their doctor, through which Philip lost twenty pounds. Although the high-protein, low-carbohydrate regimen was the standard program of the 1950s and 1960s, in McCall's it seemed both effective and compatible with good food and entertaining. As ever, the underlying message was "You can have it all"; in this case, you could eat deliciously, live the lush and sunny Californian life of this happily married couple, and lose weight simultaneously.

But for most people such a program would prove too good to be true, and Helen herself could not maintain her weight on it, although her declining health—manifested in a steady onslaught of inexplicable and untreatable minor ailments—was as much a factor as her lack of effort or will, as were the obvious exigencies of being in the food business. The problem of weight gain in fact belied the consumerist ethic as few realities could: You might range as you saw fit from TV dinners to veal terrine, but barring an extraordinary accident of metabolism you could not eat indefinitely without gaining weight. Consumer society was predicated on the belief that no choice precluded any other, and yet eating—the essence of what it meant to consume—proved that consumption had consequences; that the consumer value of infinite appetite infinitely satisfied was at odds with the consumer value of slimness as well as the more fundamental values of individual well-being and—as Americans discovered the economic and environmental costs of unrestrained consumption over the next thirty years—the common good.

Unsurprisingly, interest in reducing rose in tandem with interest in food, as it had been doing in fits and starts for the last fifty years. For each new food product, restaurant concept, or taste and entertaining trend, there seemed to be a countervailing diet or slimming aid. In 1955 a diet book (published by Better Homes and Gardens, the font of cookbook blockbusters) became for the first time one of the ten national bestselling titles of the year, joined by self-help titles from Norman Vincent Peale and Billy Graham (as well as a catalog of the popular photo exhibition, The Family of Man, from Jerry Mason's Maco Magazine Corporation). Over the next twenty years, the sales of diet books would in fact come to surpass those of food books; a cookbook in the top ten became an increasingly rare event, while every year featured at least one new slimming bestseller. The diet—a program of abstinence designed as an antidote to the excesses of the consumer society—itself rapidly became yet another object of consumption.

In a more rational world, eating and slimming might be seen as two sides of the same nutritional coin, to be viewed in an integrated, holistic manner in which the needs of appetite and health were balanced rather than opposed. But even with its inherent promise of a compromise rather than a conflict between desire and restraint, that concept would in a society predicated on unlimited, heedless consumption be not only subversive but somehow unspeakable. As it was, one led a normal life and ate as one pleased, intermittently submitting oneself to the flensing and purdah of weight reduction, only to return to real life to begin again like a lost soul condemned to a hellish cycle of eternal recurrence.

In their letters James and Helen continued to commiserate with each other not only about their chronic weight and health problems, but about the incessantly cannibalistic mores of the food business. As the food editors held their annual conference in New York and discoursed on new uses for one of the boom foods of the fifties, frozen fish sticks, their ad-starved employers plotted the forced removal of many of the most eminent in their company—among them Poppy Cannon of *House Beautiful* and Charlotte Adams of *PM*. Even in the comparative calm of the West Coast, Helen found friends and colleagues being betrayed and sent packing at *Western Family* (where Merle Armitage of *Fit for a King* had displaced her editor, only to be deposed himself a few months later). Her own new position as a contributing editor at *Sunset* was proving to be a minefield of pettiness and provincialism, in which a one-hundred-dollar fee was expected to purchase eternal fealty. Helen herself became jealous and resentful of James's failure to promote their book with sufficient fervor, while James in turn considered abandoning John Schaffner for a new, more dynamic agent.

Beard spent the Thanksgiving and Christmas holidays at home with Gino, whose fondness for cranberries grew with an intensity equal to James's loathing of them. By the new year of 1957, the pace and fury of his professional life—what he now routinely referred to as "the wars"—had accelerated further. He felt increasingly frustrated at having to share the success of the cooking school with André Surmain and began to think of ways he might break away. At the same time he felt (or imagined he felt) that Helen McCully was disaffected with him. McCully had served as a benevolent older-sister figure to James, an angelic version of Jeanne Owen, who selflessly advanced his career and expected nothing in return. He also felt encroached upon by competitors who, he believed, either stole or unfairly acquired work that should have been his. In particular he became obsessed with Myra Waldo, a handsome, dark-haired, food-and-travel writer who had just published a book called *The Slenderella Diet Book* and was putting the finishing touches on *1001 Ways to Please a Husband*. Regardless of her taste, Waldo's capacity for work and the pursuit of commercial opportunities seemed to be every bit the equal of James's, and he imagined her lurking around the corners of every editorial and consulting opportunity he cultivated, waiting to pluck the spoils from his hands.

Beard himself confessed to Helen Brown: "I have a poisonous personality that undermines everyone. I'm getting bitter and disagreeable and horrid and perhaps should just fade out of the picture completely." Nevertheless James was less inclined to find solace in self-pity than in action and in fantasies of a quieter and purer life. He became determined to move himself and Gino to a better apartment with an electric kitchen—"This awful gas is beyond belief"— and to open a restaurant, perhaps in the country, serving the simple cooking that he once again felt was the epitome of food at its elemental best:

> Gino's and my menus here are the simplest quickest things in the world—but good. We eat, for example: last night a halibut steak with batter onion slices and lemon slices baked at 425 for 18 minutes. With this merely a grand salad and cheese—nothing else. The night before we ate a flank [steak] with rice and salad and cheese and fruit. This time it was an avocado tomato salad and simply heavenly. . . . Well, this is not peasant food but it is good simple food which tastes of the natural foods. That is what I want people to realize. That natural foods without embellishment taste wonderfully if they are well cooked. Maybe I will write a book some day soon and say all these things.

James's interest in this idea was sufficient to ask Helen what she knew of organic gardening, which she replied was little indeed. But through the spring and summer—part of which he spent with the Browns on their first trip to Europe—a life in the country was on his mind. On her return Helen found a long letter from James about a place he envisioned himself, Gino, and the Browns establishing—on the surface a restaurant but in its bones something more:

> I want it to be on the ocean and have been thinking of somewhere between Monterey and the California line. I have come to the point where I think I want the ocean and by that I mean the Pacific which to me is the true ocean.... [I want] a limited menu with specialties and almost the same thing every day with some seasonal changes which are at the height of the season.... Wish of all wishes that you had the same idea—but keep telling myself that someday you may. It is really the thing and I want to look for the place when I am there. Think and think and see what you can come up with. But the ocean must be in the picture I think for some reason.

By summer James was considerably more sanguine about his life. He had gone to the Leo Burnett Agency in Chicago, representatives of Green Giant, and returned with a lucrative deal to promote and write recipes using Green Giant products. The first set of recipes for Niblets corn earned him fifteen hundred dollars—as much as five or six magazine stories might—and that was just the beginning, with promotional articles with titles like "Good Vegetables Mean Good Eating" to follow. He also arranged to separate himself and the cooking school—thereafter known as the "James Beard Cooking School," with Ruth Norman serving as director and chief dishwasher—from André Surmain with little rancor and to hold that autumn's classes at the Lexington Avenue kitchens of Restaurant Associates, for whom he continued to consult. The school held classes on wine for RA staff, and in turn RA's executive chef Albert Stockli became the first member of James's guest faculty, a dervish with a whisk who at one class "got started demonstrating sauces and couldn't stop."

Meanwhile the game of editorial musical chairs that had preoccupied the New York food set that year reached its culmination with the announcement that Jane Nickerson, food editor of the *New York Times,* had resigned her post. It attracted applications and suggestions from every corner of the food business, with James promoting Helen Brown. But the decision reached by the *Times* that July caught almost everyone by surprise, as Beard informed Helen:

> I am shocked to tell you that Jane's successor is to be Craig Claiborne who worked with Ann for so long. Jane and I had a long talk about it last night and between ourselves both agreed that we felt you were the only person who could have done the job as well as we both feel it should be done. But this is in the family and never breathe it. It seems to be a shock all over town.

As would often be the case, once he ascertained which way the wind was blowing, James was capable of quickly revising his opinion, and in any event Helen's candidacy for the job had been more his idea than hers. Within a few weeks he was affably commenting on the first-rate job the ingenue food editor was doing and on the well-deserved raise he had received. Beard could only benefit from having a friend, and something of a protégé at that, in so powerful a position. Under Nickerson the *Times*'s food coverage was similar to that of most papers, if rather less dowdy and possessed of something of the paper's characteristic sobriety and journalistic rigor. With Claiborne the *Times* would become perhaps the country's premier vehicle for fostering the idea that food and cooking were culturally significant. The appointment of a male—and one with professional European culinary credentials—as food editor was notable in itself and by so doing, the nation's most respected newspaper could not but suggest that food might be worthy of serious attention.

At Restaurant Associates' latest project, which James had worked on and which opened that autumn, food had indeed attained nearly epic seriousness. The Forum of the Twelve Caesars was theme restaurateuring of the highest order, a Baumian spectacle that played to New York's fantasy of itself as the new Rome of the postwar era toward which all the world's money, power, and media irresistibly flowed. With toga-clad waiters, wine coolers shaped liked centurions' helmets, and a menu featuring "Pheasant of the Golden House on a Silver Shield in Gilded Plumage Roasted with an Exquisite Sauce—for two," only Baum's dead eye for the boundaries between taste, irony, and kitsch could save the Forum from being crucified on the beams of its own audacity. In fact both the restaurant and its food were well received, and the Forum became a bolthole for tycoons from banking and television well into the 1970s.

James and Gino ate a Christmas Eve dinner of oysters, lamb, and venison there with Cheryl Crawford and Ruth Norman, and then the four walked together the short distance to the massive Christmas tree at Rockefeller Center, where skaters circled in the cold. There the couples went their separate ways, James and Gino returning to their new apartment in the Village at the corner of Twelfth Street and Sixth Avenue, where they opened presents, toasted each other with champagne, and watched the dawn of Christmas day form from the blue-black night.

Pained by further ankle and leg problems, James spent the early weeks of 1958 working up recipes for Green Giant peas as well as their Niblets, Cream-Style Corn, and Mexicorn. Meanwhile, the cooking school moved yet again, this time to the test kitchens at *McCall's,* courtesy of Helen McCully in what were to be her final days at the magazine. In addition to classes at the school, James had begun giving private lessons at twenty-five dollars each and numbered Mrs. Ernest Hemingway and both Henry and Clare Luce among his students. By summer he heard rumors that the *Time-Life* magnate and his author wife were on the verge of offering him a job as a sort of gastronomic private tutor and court jester, but nothing came of it.

By now his magazine work consisted of the comfortable routine of the "Corkscrew" column at *House & Garden* plus regular features there and at *Woman's Day* (which paid him a handsome five hundred dollars per piece), although he often felt his tenure with both of them was shaky. He believed a recent editorial putsch at *House & Garden* could only bode ill for him, and he continued to worry about competitors, writing Helen: "I hear Myra Waldo goes around to half my jobs and asks why she can't have the job instead of me. Craig told me this, but don't breathe a word of it."

But it was not only James whose territorial instincts were aroused. Alarmed by an announcement in *Publishers Weekly* of a forthcoming title called *The Complete Book of Outdoor Cooking,* with James listed as sole author, Helen sent Beard a swift and sharp letter demanding an explanation. In fact the book was nothing more than a reprint of the outdoor book James had done for Jerry Mason four years earlier, and the title was quickly changed and the matter largely forgotten. But in her letter Helen rehearsed several incidents in which she felt James had been too free in his use of material belonging to her or to both of them, in which he had been less than forthcoming about his other pending projects, or in which he had failed to accord her equal billing.

The bonds between Helen and James were far too strong to be broken by such a misunderstanding, and that summer found them sharing jokes about "Miss Waldo," by now their mutual nemesis and in their imaginations the Professor Moriarty of food journalism. More seriously they also found themselves puzzling together over how recipes remarkably similar to some they had jointly produced for the recently defunct *Collier's* had turned up, unattributed, in *House & Garden*. Such events gave some rational foundation to the mistrust and suspicion that the buyer's market that was food writing could inspire among those competing for its relatively scarce and meager rewards, an atmosphere that no doubt exacerbated Beard's real if not entirely conscious tendency to keep the limelight to himself and his projects secret.

Magazine and book work in any case no longer provided the largest share of James's income. Although Edward Gottlieb had been compelled to cut his salary when two accounts left at the New Year, Beard continued to plug cognac and champagne through such outlets as the Arthur Godfrey television show. Moreover, by summer Beard was on the verge of completing an arrangement with Nestlé that could pay him up to twenty thousand dollars per year for a combination of promotional work, product development, and consulting. On a humbler scale, he contracted with a blowtorch manufacturer to do a recipe book of flamed dishes, an imaginative stroke that brought together James's cognac and outdoor cooking work with current national fixations on time-saving culinary gadgetry, torches in general, and the subjection of food to incineration, whether in restaurants or on the patio. He persuaded Helen Brown to contribute some recipes to the project, although she pronounced herself somewhat stumped for ideas.

Beard continued to be enraptured by the idea of a country restaurant, whether his own, or at a remove, as a consultant to Chillingsworth on Cape Cod and to its chef, John Clancy. He spent several weekends that July in and around the Choptank River on Chesapeake Bay with Henry and Bettina McNulty and came close to buying a restaurant with them there. By September the idea had been revived but transferred to a location somewhere in Arizona, an up-and-coming resort destination whose landscape, however, had little resonance for James. In the end retirement to the country was an idea with which Beard would endlessly flirt but to which he would never ultimately commit. Despite his complaints of being "Home Ecced all over the place" at Green Giant functions for hundreds of dietitians, caterers, and food reporters, the irritations of too many engagements with too many people were outweighed by being the center of attention at the center of things in New York.

He did find time for privacy and leisure, chiefly at Cheryl Crawford's Connecticut hideaway, where he could lounge in his Los Angeles–made kimonos and indulge his still-voracious appetite for books, currently running from Dumas's *Grand Dictionnaire de Cuisine* to Vladimir Nabokov's *Lolita*. But by autumn, days that began on board a night sleeper to Washington, D.C., and continued through a champagne breakfast, two TV shows, a radio interview, and an afternoon tasting were not uncommon. James's chief respite was travel, whether to Europe (where he had gone for a few weeks in May) or to the West Coast and the Browns, where he spent Thanksgiving. He returned to New York to a chaotic round of engagements and a book contract with Jerry Mason for a "colossal" advance that would free him, he assured friends, to do less rather than more. Beard's friends and close followers of his work were unsurprised to find it was to be titled *James Beard's Treasury of Outdoor Cooking*, yet another mining of the vein that had served him so well.

With perhaps equal inevitability James began 1959 with health problems. An electrocardiogram revealed an irregular heartbeat, and his doctor ordered him to work, eat, and drink less, a regime he managed to stick with through much of January and February, aided by his hiring of an assistant and typist named Dick who took over his now-considerable business correspondence. Perhaps motivated by a heightened sense of his own mortality, he also drew on a new well of generosity, which had never been entirely absent in the past but had lain dormant in recent years. In January he had received a letter from a mission in India asking for cooking utensils and books and promptly organized a drive among his food-writer friends which resulted in crates of pots, pans, utensils, and recipes from America's most eminent cooks being dispatched to the subcontinent.

He had also begun to promote the careers of, and act as a mentor to, people getting started in the food business. One such was a young woman who had been working for Dione Lucas and to whom "Dione was being down right cruel . . . as she often is with people." With perhaps a certain measure of self-satisfaction, he invited the woman, Paula Wolfert, to cook for him, instructing her—despite having received his doctor's warning only six weeks before—to prepare a menu that was a symphony of fat, including both a lobster bisque of sclerotic richness and a congestive chicken dish incorporating six egg yolks and a cup of heavy cream. Pleased with her performance, Beard arranged a job for her at Chillingsworth at Brewster on Cape Cod. Wolfert was to become one of leading food writers of the next generation, noted for both the rigor of her research and the bright flavors of the recipes she culled from around the Mediteranean littoral.

James might well feel expansive, whether in his appetites or his altruism. Spring 1959 saw at long last the publication of the Dell paperback, now titled simply *The James Beard Cookbook,* with an aproned, bow-tied, and now largely bald James hovering over a plate of choucroute garni and wearing the happy, solicitous look of a dog eager to play fetch. Americans accepted the invitation, buying up the first printing of 150,000 copies over the next nine months and close to 500,000 during the first five years of the book's life. Beyond the customary television and radio appearances associated with publication of a blockbuster, Beard was interviewed by *Publishers Weekly* as an exemplar of the successful, market-wise author whose current offering was outselling even Dell's own *Anatomy of a Murder,* a hardcover and movie hit. Although James earned only three cents per copy, the book made him, if not rich, a mass market star. Craig Claiborne, admittedly a friend and regular dinner guest, told *Times* readers that "there is not a gastronomic cliché in the book" and that it was "a work that is fired with recipes culled from the finest kitchens of Europe and America." James himself was both "deadly serious and genuinely inspired," a "kitchen wizard."

Although James could not help but be pleased with and indeed craved such status, *The James Beard Cookbook* was not an effort he himself was inordinately proud of. The work was at least half Isabel Callvert's—a fact both its title page and the division of the advance made clear—and Beard himself pronounced it rather dry, an opinion confirmed by Helen Brown, who lamented the absence of James's own character and taste in his more recent books. But if it was not the intimate, creative work in the vein of M. F. K. Fisher or Helen's own *The West Coast Cook Book* that Beard still hoped to write, *The James Beard Cookbook* was a triumph of niche marketing, perfectly positioned between the frumpy domestic ethos of the *Better Homes and Gardens* and *Betty Crocker* encyclopedias and the condescending, forbidding reaches of *Gourmet*. The recipes were written in what Beard liked to call a "narrative" style, addressing the reader as "you" and guiding her or him—there being remarkably little presumption for the period about the sex of the cook in question—on the journey that was the recipe. The tone was unpatronizing and presumed that the reader was interested in learning to cook not out of duty or inadequacy but because food was inherently interesting and was therefore the natural purview of intelligent, interesting people. Moreover, there was no shame in ignorance:

Anybody who is conscientious enough to follow simple directions can learn to cook. For example, if you are among those who have never boiled water, this is what you do: Fill a saucepan with cold water and put it on the stove. Adjust the burner to high. Let the water heat until it bubbles and surges—and that is boiling water. I assure you in all seriousness that many of the recipes in this book are not much more complicated than these instructions.

From hamburgers to consommé to, yes, lobster a l'américaine, this was largely the case, and perhaps the book's greatest achievement was to suggest that all these dishes were equally legitimate and worthwhile. Similarly, while the technical difficulties of omelet, soufflé, and sauce making were acknowledged, they were not presented as rites of passage that separated real food and real cooks from amateurs or poseurs. The book offered itself as a resource rather than an icon: Try this if you like; if not, fine. And while Beard and Callvert condemned cooking shortcuts, convenience foods, and ingredients like iceberg lettuce, they did so gently and thereby fostered the notion that flavorful food prepared from fresh, local, and seasonal materials was not a privilege or elite preference but a natural birthright and rational choice to which everyone was entitled and ought to be educated.

James himself may have regretted that he had yet to produce either a work of gastronomic belles-lettres or a classic reinterpretation of the culinary canon, but in both form and content *The James Beard Cookbook* was a genuine if perhaps unintended gesture toward the much greater good of furthering gastronomic democracy—if not to all Americans, at least to the middle of the middle class rather than its upper margin. The book asserts the primacy of flavor and freshness; the importance of the necessarily local economic and social community that must exist among cook, retailer, and producer; and the validity of simple, regional, vernacular foods and ingredients. In so doing and by using the tools of consumer capitalism—the mass market book written by the expert "personality" pitched to a status-anxious middle class—*The James Beard Cookbook* was an effective counter to some of consumerism's most pernicious effects.

Some of the same ideals promulgated in *The James Beard Cookbook* were also apparent to Joe Baum. What James understood viscerally about food—the importance of its provenance and season and the way in which, within one's life, they might swing like the pendulum in a grandfather clock, measuring the movements of the year, marking the gravities of the place—Joe understood conceptually, if with no less conviction. But Baum's current assignment at Restaurant Associates—with James again serving as consultant—was hardly to bring food to the masses but to create a restaurant consistent and commensurate with the ground-floor space of the Seagram Building on Park Avenue, by definition and by its Mies van der Rohe design a cool and elite temple built to celebrate power. Baum understood power—how to intrigue and win over the powerful through the mastery of surfaces and surprise—and he understood the modernist aesthetic of the Seagram Building. Where some might see in it an austerity based on a pursuit of pure form, he saw simplicity in search of essences, and in that he found his theme. He had been reading haiku, whose own formal spareness reduces the world to the flow of seasons and the elements within them. The restaurant to be called the Four Seasons would become the most significant restaurant founded in New York since Delmonico's.

The menu would of course be seasonal, too, and, Joe Baum being Joe Baum, so would the uniforms, the napery, and a dozen other details. But if seasonality was the raison d'être of the food, then its identity came not from belonging to a particular national cuisine but from its ingredients: The food couldn't be categorized as French or Italian or Polynesian, as restaurant cooking almost always was. It was simply the food that resulted from the fact that in autumn one had game, in winter oysters, in spring salmon, and in summer tomatoes: It was necessarily nothing more or less than the food that was at the moment *there,* and since this was the United States, it was by a sort of default American food. True, as in *The James Beard Cookbook,* there was ample room for foreign dishes (as well as flamed food, then entering middle age), but national origin was beside the point and, no matter how glorious, never privileged. Thus might a menu record without apology wild mushrooms; a salmon soufflé with an onion sauce; quail stuffed with mandarin oranges and nuts; casserole of pigeon, green almonds, and tomatoes; bluefish with flaming fennel; and perhaps most significantly a rich house "velvet" chocolate cake that may have launched the fashion in restaurants for shamelessly intense proprietary desserts.

The Four Seasons was also a groundbreaking restaurant in a number of other respects: It grew its own herbs; established direct connections with local farmers from whom it might contract for an entire crop of, for example, baby vegetables (in itself a pioneering stroke); and made a point of showcasing the origins of its ingredients, many from Europe but principally American. But however much simplicity, seasonality, and a Beard-like cosmopolite eclecticism with deep American roots shaped its food, the Four Seasons was both expensive and exclusive: The restaurant itself cost an unheard-of $4.5 million, while dinner for two ran about $40, an exceedingly stiff tab by the standards of 1959.

Craig Claiborne would note some of this excess in a largely glowing review in the *Times,* commenting in particular on the restaurant's penchant for indulging in the "vulgar" custom of overloading plates with food—a tendency Claiborne saw as American in origin. But if Claiborne caviled, he did so based on a perhaps uneasy recognition that "the cuisine is not exquisite in the sense that la grande cuisine française at its superlative best is exquisite." Exquisiteness was not what Baum, Beard, and Stockli were aiming for, but they did strive to create something that promoted values of equal or, in the eyes of many, of greater importance and seriousness. But in New York a restaurant's seriousness was still a function of its Frenchness, an attitude Claiborne himself embodied and promulgated to the nation through the pages of the *Times*.

Indeed, despite the publication of books like *The James Beard Cookbook* and the opening of restaurants like the Four Seasons, which might add new life to the nation's culinary scene, Claiborne and a host of others were pessimistic in their outlook on the future of good food in America. As much as gastronomy applauds novelty, it is based in equal part on nostalgia. In the mind, food, being an ephemeral creation prepared from ephemeral materials, is necessarily located in the past, and there is a tendency to believe that the best must be behind us; that, in a sort of theory of epicurean entrophy, flavor and goodness are ebbing as time moves forward. But Claiborne's *Times* article of April 13, 1959, headed "Elegance of Cuisine Is on Wane in U.S." and placed on page 1, was no mere case of routine gourmet whining, but a news report of a national crisis of some import, at least for the well-heeled readers of the *Times*.

The piece opened with a quote from Beard: "This nation is more interested in preserving the whooping crane and the buffalo than in perpetuating classic cooking and table service. We live in an age that may some day . . . be referred to as the time of the decline and pall of the American palate." According to Claiborne and the experts he interviewed, the source of the problem lay in the aging and retirement of European-trained chefs; the lack of a new generation of trained replacements for them from either Europe or the United States; and the rise of corporate, cost-conscious restaurant ownership. The liberal immigration laws that permitted Henri Soulé and his ilk to come to the United States in the 1930s had been tightened, while the only place in America training chefs in restaurant cooking at a truly rigorous level was a small, nonprofit academy then in New Haven, Connecticut, called the Culinary Institute of America. Meanwhile, both corporate and individual restaurateurs sought to lower labor and material costs through portion control, frozen ingredients, and prepackaged dishes. By way of illustration, Claiborne compared a bass stuffed with sole mousse and covered with champagne sauce as prepared by Le Pavillon's Pierre Franey (who had come to the United States as Soulé's teenage sous-chef in 1939) with a typical restaurant steam table laden with Swiss steak, candied yams, and lima beans.

But the heart of the malaise lay not so much in the decline in the quality of food generally as in the decline of its Frenchness. For Claiborne and perhaps most of the nation's old guard of restaurateurs, hoteliers, and gourmets, French cuisine was not simply a taste preference but the gold standard of food against which everything might be judged. In November at the 1959 Salon of Culinary Art, a cooking exhibition then in its ninety-first year, old-school restaurateurs stood among the molded aspics, galantines, and pastry cases like senescent curators at a museum. Remarked one to a reporter, "Concoctions like these take imagination, skill, and time. But the haute cuisine here is a dying art." There were at most fifty great chefs still active in the United States, and every week more of them were taken by old age or the public's indifference.

Gastronomes saw little to like and much to fear in the dawning decade of the 1960s. Like colonists in the darkest days of the American Revolution awaiting aid from Lafayette, they sought salvation from France and, after a fashion, would receive it within a few years. James himself spent the final days of the fifties swinging from exaltation to depression amid the remodeling detritus of a new house, obtained through Agnes Crowther with a five-thousand-dollar advance from Dell for a book to be titled *James Beard's International Cookbook*. The small, three-story brown stucco row house at 119 West Tenth Street was across the street from the New York City women's prison, whose inmates greeted those entering or leaving the house with a harpies' chorus of obscenities. Female visitors in particular were often subjected to salacious tirades of extraordinary vividness, and, once they were safely inside the door, James debriefed them with painstaking, voyeuristic delight.

By Thanksgiving, spent with Craig Claiborne ("really a sweetheart," James confessed to Helen) and Gino, the house was in relatively good order, but the refurbishment of the kitchen—which would also serve as the new James Beard Cooking School—was beginning to cause James considerable concern. Despite obtaining appliances and furnishings via numerous trade-offs and freebies, Beard found his cash reserves dwindling, and by December he was close to exhaustion once more working full-time for Edward Gottlieb as well as for Restaurant Associates. As the New Year approached, he felt himself overtaken by ravenous dread, pursued through the shortening days by an anxiety he had thought he had at last laid to rest but that could be truly assuaged only by more time and more money, and then, only momentarily.

he kitchen at 119 West Tenth, perhaps twenty by twenty feet square, had lofty ceilings, two windows at its northern end, three walls covered in a green-and-red-checked wallpaper, and a fourth postered with enormous pineapples from a book of antiquarian botanical prints. The pineapples became the customary background for photographs of Beard, much as the bow ties, aprons, and enormous hands and braceleted wrists formed the foreground, the whole dominated by Beard's head, now as bald and ovoid as that of a eunuch or a Tartar warrior.

The walls were studded with hanging copper and majolica pieces and the counters jammed with mixers and blenders, baskets of ingredients, jars of wooden utensils, mortars and pestles, crocks, and scales. The center of the room was filled by a horseshoe-shaped counter with five electric cooktops, inside which James might sit in a director's chair, overseeing a flock of affluent Junior League housewives one day or a group of would-be food professionals the next. The classes were increasingly oversubscribed, aided by publicity like Craig Claiborne's fulsome spread in the *Times* at the beginning of 1960. The first sessions of the year would consist of six lessons apiece for a basic and an advanced group. The basic course would cover bread making, sauces, crepes, soufflés, and omelets; the advanced, menus from France, Italy, Mexico, and an additional cuisine to be chosen by the students.

Ruth Norman, who was an accomplished cook in her own right with a book in the works to prove it, continued to manage the business side of the school. But her role as an assistant teacher to Beard was taken over in the New Year by Paula Peck, whom James believed was extraordinarily talented and regarded as a protégée if not in fact an equal. A gifted teacher and author, Peck became something of a legend in the food world after her premature death in 1972. But the obvious favor she enjoyed with Beard left the now-displaced Norman jealous and angry, and the two women feuded with greater and greater vociferousness as the year wore on. James himself was distressed by the rancor between them but, as a connoisseur of gossip and social intrigue, also seemed to take a certain pleasure in stepping back and viewing the pageant he had set in motion.

Nonetheless 1960 was promising to be a sour, luckless year. In February James cut himself badly with a knife in the kitchen at Tenth Street—a disconcerting thing for a professional cook to have done. Then he was galled to discover that Myra Waldo had found her way onto the payroll of Restaurant Associates as a consultant to La Fonda del Sol, a place that would feature the food of Central and Latin America and that promised to be one of RA's most exciting projects, a thoroughly contemporary bazaar of zesty food and arresting design concepts done up in purple, orange, and black. James himself was working on menu changes at the Four Seasons with Joe Baum—by now a little full of himself, by James's lights—and fighting with the mercurial Albert Stockli, still a regular guest instructor at the James Beard Cooking School. Like James, Helen Brown was growing disenchanted with John Schaffner, who worried about James's willingness to finish the collaborative work on wine with Frank Schoonmaker that had been under contract with Random House for the last several years. And Schaffner could do nothing to dispel Beard's nervousness about the financial effect on him of the editorial housecleaning under way at *House & Garden*. Meanwhile Helen McCully, whose personal and professional life seemed to have been undergoing an inexorable collapse over the previous eighteen months, waited out her final few weeks at *McCall's*, her termination there imminent if not yet precisely scheduled.

Happily James was scheduled to travel to Europe in April and took his leave of Manhattan and its bloodlettings. In the dining room of the SS *United States* he found himself at table with a quintessential group of late-fifties American celebrities, among them Margaret Truman; her husband, *New York Times* reporter Clifton Daniel; and bestselling writer John Gunther. The ostensible purpose of the trip was to visit the Nestlé factories in Switzerland, but Beard was able to work in side trips to Paris and Venice, where he exulted boyishly to Isabel about his plans:

Tomorrow I go to the great Fenice restaurant at ten in the morning for a pasta lesson—this should be fun!! We can use it!! Such fish and seafood as they have here! The scampi, the tiny little squid, the crab, the sole and the St. Peter—all of them are fresh as the day they were born and delicious beyond belief.

With this letter he enclosed the picnic section of the forthcoming *Treasury of Outdoor Cooking,* also written in Venice in the same ebullient mode:

I think my first picnic memory was a thriller! We were invited by the Hamblets to go out in a great touring car which opened at the rear. Everyone had their dusters and the ladies had their veils and we were a gay group that chugged off to the countryside around Vancouver, Washington!! We had a great hamper of club sandwiches specially made for Harry Hamblet by the Royal Bakery and elegant and wonderful they were!! . . . What a whirl this first automobile ride seemed to me!! It was as if I had been thrust into another age.

He continued for four pages in this vein, rehearsing the train ride to Gearhart ("with a little box of marmalade sandwiches and a hard-boiled egg"), the beach cookouts at Tillamook Head, the crayfish hunting on the Necanicum, and the birthday parties at the Oaks in Portland, each rendered with an awestruck and unself-conscious delight at his good fortune to have lived such moments in such places with such people. For some time he and Helen Brown had discussed the idea of his writing a book of memoirs, not so much a biography as a set of gastronomic recollections. Now in Venice, he had begun to do something along those lines, and as he recounted his life to himself, he recovered some of his appetite for living.

On his arrival home he found that most of this material was to be excised from the finished book to make room for artwork and photography. All his books had been compromises—a reality of publishing he had in the past accepted with grace and good humor—but this time he was genuinely hurt and angry: "I have read the book through and I feel they have just murdered it to make way for the pictures," he wrote Helen Brown. "I hate it more than ever now and have no interest whatsoever in doing it any publicity." Despite enthusiastic reviews from Claiborne and others, *Jim Beard's Treasury of Outdoor Cooking* was indeed a hostage to its lavish and often bizarre photography: A glass of wine hangs inside a birdcage while meat is suspended in the air or on vertical racks, variously impaled, gibbeted, strung up, and run through with knives, spits, and skewers. Isolated from any real context, the arty ghoulishness of the photography suggests a sort of culinary charnel house in which the art director sadistically set out to humiliate the ingredients.

That May Beard undertook an exhausting work schedule and entered a further cycle of depression, losing interest in both the Schoonmaker wine book and the Dell International paperback, for which John Ferrone had sent him an outline in April. John Schaffner openly voiced his concern to Isabel Callvert about Beard's capacity to meet his book and magazine obligations. Life was affording Beard few pleasures: Normally an enthusiastic liberal and a follower of politics, he viewed the presidential election simply in terms of keeping "that shit Nixon out of the job." Dinner with Claiborne at Quo Vadis, normally one of his favorite places, prompted a tirade on how few restaurants gave him any satisfaction and how "sick to death" he was "of gourmets and gourmet food." And the people around him offered him little solace:

> I am so rushed I have nothing of myself anymore. Gino gets increasingly busy and although we have a delightful understanding, it is not a companionship where things are shared. Ruth and I are on a business basis now. Paula and I are close but outside of food there is no common ground. . . . I know dozens of people but I am not close to them. . . . There is really no one in New York with whom I can have a fine close talk. I'm really terribly alone and terribly distrait about the coming years.

Still, he found consolation in some of his long-standing dreams—the country restaurant and a genuinely important book—as well as the newly discovered notion of a kind of experimentation coupled with teaching that would enable him to "train people for something beyond just the ability to make certain dishes"; to act as a mentor and to foster a kind of culinary culture that would be genuinely creative and a part of the best gastronomic tradition. But creativity in the food business continued to be accepted for the most part only within the traditions of what Helen Brown liked to call "the mix gals and Jello people": The food editor of *Sunset,* determined to further the boundaries of West Coast cuisine, had recently come up with "Tortillas Suzette," tortillas spread with butter, sprinkled with sugar and grated orange peel, and rolled with frozen peaches.

High seriousness was unlikely to fare better elsewhere. In publishing, for example, the early sixties saw a turning away from such earnest, uplifting titles as Catherine Marshall's *A Man Called Peter* in favor of humor and whimsy, variously sentimental, satiric, or arch, with Charles Schulz's *Happiness Is a Warm Puppy* and Virginia Cary Hudson's *O Ye Jigs & Juleps!* among the top five bestsellers by 1962. The biggest-selling cookbook of the early sixties embodied exactly these traits: *The I Hate to Cook Book* by Portland advertising copywriter Peg Bracken (drawings by Hilary Knight, illustrator of Kay Thompson's mordant children's and adult bestseller *Eloise*) was a smart-aleck, plague-on-both-your-houses rejoinder to both home economists and gourmets that sold nearly three million copies. Adopting the persona of the harried but drolly resigned housewife, Bracken proclaimed that for most women, cooking was nothing more than a necessary drudgery that, once acknowledged as such, could be made bearable. Her recipes had only one goal: the unrepentant pursuit of quick and effortless preparation, as epitomized in "Sweep Steak"—beef dumped onto a sheet of aluminum foil, topped with a packet of onion soup mix, sealed, and thrust into an oven for a few hours—or "Portland Pilaff," rice cooked with bouillon cubes and canned shrimp. For Bracken, cooking was neither interesting nor fun, as Beard suggested, nor did she pretend, like Poppy Cannon, that truly delicious food could be prepared using shortcuts and convenience foods. Bracken's food was good enough to keep a woman's husband and kids out of her hair—and no more than that.

Bracken's pie-in-your-face gastronomy no doubt offended almost every segment of the food community, whether home economists bent on ennobling the science of homemaking; flavor primalists like Helen Brown; or even promoters of canned, frozen, and "instant" foods who felt their labors on behalf of the consumer were entitled to a modicum of respect. But none of these could claim to be purists in a universe dominated by plugs, promotion, freebies, and appeals to consumer feelings about family, community, and tradition from an industry that cared little about such values. Even as James lamented the "decline and pall" of the American palate, he collected his checks from Nestlé and Green Giant and embroidered his biography in press releases and interviews, relocating his childhood food experiences from Salmon Street to the kitchens of the Gladstone Hotel and his professional launch to an Hors d'Oeuvre, Inc., housed on Fifth Avenue with himself as sole founder and proprietor. In a speech on "The American Food Writer"—an expunged portion of which suggested that even Claiborne and the *Times* availed themselves of free photographic and recipe development services from the food industry—James described the symbiotic relation among food producers and processors, their flacks, and journalists in glowing terms, permitting himself to remark: "I think it is safe to say that in the majority of our homes food is appetizing, healthful and tasty. Without our food writers, backed by our great food industry, this would not be true."

Purity was not only an ethical but a practical concern. Questions arising throughout 1960 about the safety of food colorants, hormones, and pesticides caused concern in government and among consumers; the head of the FDA was vilified by farmers and food processors; and a book called *The Poisons in Your Food* attracted considerable comment. For a public now sensing the whiff of sham in the cozy fantasy of farm, hearth, health, and home sold it by the food industry and its friends in the press and government, Bracken's lightly put contention that food and cooking were in fact a grind was refreshing in its candor.

In January 1961 the nation got a new president with new tastes in food. Within days of John Kennedy's inauguration, press reports made clear that he was no Dwight Eisenhower, whose tastes ran to stew, steak, and baked potatoes. Kennedy, by contrast, was a habitué of La Caravelle in New York, which had supplied his campaign airplane with stocks of vichyssoise and chicken in champagne sauce. In February a diplomatic furor erupted when it was revealed that the White House had made an unsuccessful attempt to hire away the legendary Vietnamese chef Bui Van Han from the French Embassy in London. Kennedy's press secretary, Pierre Salinger, attempted to dampen public reaction and furnished recipes to UPI for the haddock-based fish chowder that, as supposedly cooked by First Lady Jackie, was said to be the president's favorite dish.

But by the beginning of April, the White House formally announced the hiring of René Verdon, an impeccably credentialed French chef who had been indoctrinated into the Kennedys' preferences while working at La Caravelle and whose appointment was greeted with a page one tribute by Claiborne in the *Times*. For the next two and a half years, French cuisine was a fundamental part of a glittering White House culture populated by Frank Sinatra, Leonard Bernstein, and a panoply of stars both popular and highbrow. The Kennedys' insouciant yet athletic embrace of a life that incorporated fifty-mile hikes, vichyssoise, and black-tie socializing suggested that you could in fact play with the appurtenances of high society and culture while mocking their stuffiness and soi-disant seriousness. Every cultural artifact and sensibility was grist for the mill, the object of style obsession one week and satire the next: Even the Kennedys themselves were not sacred, their own quirks and pretensions spawning record albums and collections of photos embellished with comic dialogue in cartoon balloons.

As for food, the Kennedys were no more awestruck by gastronomy than was Peg Bracken, and their example did more than James Beard or Helen Brown ever could to convince Americans that food, like every other style icon with which they toyed, might be fun. French food, like Jackie's couturier clothes, embodied the ethic of lightly worn, tasteful trendiness: not the homely joy of cooking but the sexy, moneyed, youthful joy of chic. With the Kennedys in the White House, 1961 was the *annus mirabilis* for French food in particular and for food in general that might be deemed foreign, exotic, or daring; for food that could claim to be not just cooking but cuisine. This is not to say that there were no rules or that a spirit of anything goes prevailed: For every taste there was an arbiter, a tastemaker—usually a journalist or editor—and within the Manhattan-oriented precincts of the affluent and the aspiring, what Diana Vreeland was to clothes or Clement Greenberg to art, Craig Claiborne—even more than Beard, who lacked the unique cachet of the *Times,* the top people's paper—increasingly was to food.

When André Surmain, for example, opened a restaurant he named Lutèce in March 1961, in the town house once occupied by the original James Beard Cooking School, he expected a New York feverish for the latest word in elegant feeding to crowd his tonily understated foyer. But Claiborne weighed in with a review Beard felt would surely put Lutèce out of business completely, cautioning *Times* readers against Surmain's mind-boggling prices and summing up with the judgment: "It is this reviewer's opinion that the food at Lutèce could not be called great cuisine." Despite that initial reception, however, Lutèce eventually earned Claiborne's approval and became the most celebrated French restaurant in the country.

Claiborne was also strongly associated with two other significant events of 1961 that furthered the internationalization of the American palate: the publication of *Mastering the Art of French Cooking* and Claiborne's own *The New York Times Cookbook,* both in October. Simone Beck, Julia Child, and their collaborator Louisette Bertholle had been awaiting the Francophile atmosphere that took over America in 1961 for nearly ten years. Child, the California-born wife of a foreign service officer, and Beck, a Frenchwoman from Normandy, met in Paris in 1951, launched a cooking school, and above all dreamed of creating a book on French cuisine for American homes. Using Paul Child's PX privileges, they reconstructed the French repertoire with American ingredients and an approach to recipe writing that in its structure and detail appealed to the American sensibility. But their early efforts to find a publisher met without success, despite the steady appearance of titles on French cooking from *Gourmet* and other sources throughout the fifties.

In late 1959, however, a friend of Child's named Avis DeVoto passed on the now well-thumbed manuscript to an editor at Knopf. Judith Jones, a patrician New Englander whose sunny, hair-ribboned demeanor overlaid shrewd editorial and marketing instincts, loved food herself and saw the genius of the book's concept as outlined in its foreword:

> This is a book for the servantless American cook who can be unconcerned on occasion with budgets, waistlines, time schedules, children's meals, the parent-chauffeur-den-mother syndrome, or anything else that might interfere with the enjoyment of producing something wonderful to eat. Written for those who love to cook, the recipes are as detailed as we have felt they should be so the reader will know exactly what is involved and how to go about it. . . . No out-of-the-ordinary ingredients are called for. In fact the book could well be titled "French Cooking from the American Supermarket."

The foreword ends some three pages later with the advice, "Above all, have a good time."

Jones was a gifted editor who understood the possibilities of cooking as a form of high-style recreation that was simultaneously demanding enough to be intellectually stimulating, creatively satisfying, and consistent with the status needs of affluent, educated Americans. The title, a Jones masterstroke, suggested not the Pyrex-measuring-cup-and-porcelain-steel frumpiness of most cookbooks but the refined fun and rigor of a painting course or a junior year taken abroad from Wellesley or Smith. Superbly organized, designed, and produced, the book bestrode the middle ground of French cooking with a catholicity that expanded the repertoire of many American cooks beyond the tried and tired triumvirate of omelets, soufflés, and crepes to include both star turns like pâté de canard en croûte and humble, upright stews and braises. *Mastering,* which struck with perfect pitch virtually every chord in the early sixties sensibility, would undergo twenty-one printings over the next ten years.

Claiborne was instrumental in promoting the book and its creators, declaring with an authority that few institutions save the *Times* can muster that here was the true gospel of French cuisine. But in the same month that saw publication of *Mastering,* that authority was itself made manifest in the release of *The New York Times Cook Book* with Claiborne as editor-author. Although it could not claim ancestry from the venerable canon of French cookery, its pedigree as a product of the *Times* was, in the eyes of many Americans, nearly as distinguished.

The book was for the most part a compilation of recipes that appeared in the *Times* during the previous ten years, the bulk of them under Jane Nickerson's editorship. Despite its origins as a grab bag compiled from *Times* correspondents, New York society hostesses, and sundry food writers from Brownstone to McCully to Beard, the book had a definite shape, if only in its global "All the News That's Fit to Print" scope: There were two versions of borscht, three avocado soups, two boeuf bourguignons, three goulashes, *hallacas* from Venezuela, *pastel de choclo* from Chile, steak-and-kidney pie, and Chinese spareribs. This being Claiborne's book, there were also caviar, foie gras, and truffles, either on their own or incorporated in dishes like Lobster en Bellevue Parisienne, in which an entire eviscerated lobster was made to sit regally astride a bed of salad greens surrounded and surmounted by an entourage constructed from its aspicked and mayonnaised flesh accompanied by stuffed eggs and artichoke hearts.

Despite such excesses *The New York Times Cook Book* had a deservedly wide influence, perhaps wider than any other cookbook of the sixties. Neither a primer nor a course of instruction like *The James Beard Cookbook* or *Mastering the Art of French Cooking,* the sheer volume and variety of recipes presented in it fostered the notion that food was an infinite universe, inexhaustible and forever explorable. Given Claiborne's role during the next two and a half decades as the nation's mediator between the best people and the best food, it is tempting to credit him with these qualities as they appear in the book. But although the perhaps-unintended generosity of the *Times* management (who may have underestimated its potential sales) granted Claiborne sole rights to the book and its recipes, *The New York Times Cook Book* represented as much the intelligence and curiosity of Claiborne's predecessors during the supposed dark age of gastronomy of the fifties as that of Claiborne, however formidable his own talents proved to be in later years.

James, too, published a book that October, although it was nothing more than a hardcover edition of *The James Beard Cookbook.* His own reactions to *Mastering the Art of French Cooking* and *The New York Times Cook Book* were positive, even if he failed to grasp how influential they would become: "I think the new Knopf French book is wonderful until they get into the chicken and meat department," he wrote Helen Brown. "Otherwise it's a great book. Nothing new or startling, but a good basic French cookery book." Similarly, what most impressed him about *The New York Times Cook Book* was Claiborne's good fortune in having sole rights to the royalties, noting to friends that by the end of the year the book had sold thirty thousand copies at $8.95 each, a fairly princely sum for a cookbook.

On their arrival in New York in October, Julia Child and Simone Beck had made their wish to meet Beard known to Judith Jones, who arranged for them to visit him on Tenth Street. They sat in on a class and found themselves both amused and taken aback by some of Beard's classroom tours de force, such as compelling his students to fold egg whites into soufflés with their bare hands in order to get "the right feel." But Child herself would join Beard's visiting faculty the following year, and in the interim Beard was generous with his contacts and connections, sending Child to visit Helen Brown on her next trip to California. By December Julia Child was a member in good standing of the Manhattan food milieu and was feted at a reception put on by Dione Lucas, which she attended with Beard, Clementine Paddleford, Jeanne Owen, and other luminaries. It was a club that welcomed her but whose habitual viciousnesses and intrigues she neither wanted nor needed to be a part of, thanks to her residence in Cambridge, Massachusetts, and Provence, and to the unparalleled momentum of her own fame.

Like virtually everyone working in food in late 1961, Beard was in high spirits, sharing a sense that the food scene's collective ship had finally come in and that there just might be, contrary to long-standing belief and tradition, enough provisions to go around. In particular Beard was enthused about his latest writing project, a "narrative" work to be done for Pat Knopf at Atheneum, which by spring had the working title *James Beard's Delights and Prejudices*. Beard spent the better part of May, June, and July writing in Europe—mostly in a hotel room in Lausanne, with side trips to England, France, and Spain—and the pages flew off the typewriter, some thirty thousand words in excess of what had been contracted for. The book was intended to be a collection of gastronomic highlights from Beard's career, joined to a summation of his opinions on food, wine, and restaurants.

What emerged, however, was a repetition of the damburst of recollection that had occurred in Venice the previous year: a laying open of James's gastronomic ledgers and diaries to be sure, but more crucially a sweet and bitter rhapsody on childhood, memory, and Mary Elizabeth Beard. At summer's end the results were unwieldy and amorphous, but Beard was pleased by both his sheer productivity and the fact that he was at last writing in a more personal and literary mode, in which food, ideas, memory, and the contents of his heart might merge. He had finally discovered the novel gastronomic medium that he and Helen had been discussing for years but never succeeded in exploring.

What small interest he had in the Schoonmaker and Dell projects paled, and the latter half of 1961 was occupied with a September travel writers' junket to London with Helen Brown, work for Green

Giant, and another round of cooking classes. Beard also offered what assistance he could to Helen McCully, now deposed from *McCall's* and floating a proposal for a new food magazine to be called *Food and Drink,* with herself as editor and James and Helen Brown as chief contributors. With the $2 million the launch of such an enterprise would require nowhere in sight, McCully seemed an increasingly pathetic figure, a once-important person cut loose from the money and power of publishing whose now often-fragmented phrases still rang with the force of an influence she no longer possessed. Writing James in Europe, she strategized on dieting, product development, and demographics:

> I just got these figures: gross food sales (consumer) in U.S. are better than 79 billion dollars. Gross sales on dietetic foods (estimate) are $250,000,000. . . . Percentage wise, dietetic foods are very low. If my figuring is correct and since I'm not used to dealing in billions or even millions, it's a little better than 3% which seems to me like peanuts.
>
> So on this basis if I were a food manufacturer I'd just go ahead and bring out the finest foods I could and to hell with the fad trends. . . . One thing I think is of concern is the very fact that allegedly good companies will get on any bandwagon just to make a fast buck and they say, or so it seems to me, to hell with the national health. If everybody who was too fat started drinking these liquid diets or eating dietetic foods or chewing up cellulose, the food market would be in something of a fix. Integrity is something we could have a little more of in the food business, believe me. . . . So more and better food is my motto.

Helen Brown, her weight unchanged even after a six hundred-calorie-a-day stay in the hospital for yet another round of inconclusive tests, went on Metrecal, the low-calorie repast in a can. But others, from often surprising quarters of the food business, were responding to the mounting swell of sixties taste for the honest, the ethnic, and the authentic that McCully had sensed: Poppy Cannon, for example, produced a well-written and -researched book on regional European food, which Helen Brown could enthusiastically recommend to James, barring some unerringly Cannonesque notes such as employing popover mix for crepes.

Americans' curiosity about new or foreign foods varied, of

course, by income, education, and class. An article by June Owen in the *New York Times* the previous March surveyed New Yorkers and found most citizens, whether rich or poor, consuming a relatively bland and narrow diet based on meat and starch. Two exceptions were in Harlem, where grits and hog jowls might still surface, and among the city's burgeoning Puerto Rican population, in whose diet chicken, rice, and beans were heavily featured. In only two neighborhoods was the kind of cooking the "gourmet revolution" was to be built upon in much evidence: In the East Sixties, a housewife—or her cook—might impress guests with a Claibornesque spread of fish mousse, crown roast of lamb, eggplant and asparagus sautéed in the Chinese style, and a poached peach with raspberry sauce. It was in Greenwich Village, however, that June Owen found a couple whose habits approximated those of James's ideal reader: They shopped in street markets and ethnic shops and experimented with recipes from Italy, France, Germany, and the Middle East. "Although this couple may be a minority," Owen summed up, "there are many New Yorkers like them who look on eating as an adventure. They are the people who take advantage of one of New York's best attractions—foreign restaurants and food shops that offer delicacies from every corner of the globe."

That willingness to explore not just French but genuinely "ethnic" food was not lost on Joe Baum and Restaurant Associates, which had tapped the upper reaches of that market with the Latin American La Fonda del Sol and its middle with the purchase of Mamma Leone's, a gargantuan, epically vulgar Italo-American hash house that became a major New York tourist attraction. Still, this transformation of what once was considered greasy and noxious immigrant slop into a colorful and compelling cuisine was indicative of a wider willingness to examine and even enjoy the food and culture of America's minorities and immigrant groups.

Thanksgiving at 110 West Tenth Street that November found Gino delving further into American food by persuading and helping James to make crystallized cranberries for dinner. Much to James's pleasure, Gino was beginning to make a social and professional life for himself independent of James, despite his difficulties with passing the American architectural examinations. There seemed much to give thanks for, excepting perhaps Helen McCully's situation, and even

that looked brighter with some test mailings of *Food and Drink* set
to go out in the new year and dummies of several issues put to bed.
It may also have been some comfort and vindication for both Beard
and McCully to hear that *McCall's* publisher had admitted at a party
that he might have made a mistake in firing McCully, but that she
wanted to keep the magazine's food coverage "too gourmet."

Beard himself was in no danger of appearing too gourmet in a
series of ads for Nestlé's Crosse & Blackwell division, launched at
the New Year of 1962 and headed "Jim Beard says":

> Meals can be exotic. I found this glazed frankfurter recipe in a vil-
> lage in Europe. Cut 1 lb. frankfurters in strips. Put in a heavy pan
> with one-half cup Crosse & Blackwell raspberry preserves, 1 tea-
> spoon vinegar, and 2 teaspoons black pepper. Toss over low heat
> until glazed. Serve on crackers or toast as appetizers. It's sensa-
> tional!

In another ad Beard implored "Do try my Sloppy Joes—slightly dev-
ilish and definitely delightful with Crosse & Blackwell Seafood
Cocktail Sauce." The words were not, of course, James's but those of
an ad agency copywriter, and although he had to take some credit
for the recipes, the income—together with that from Gottlieb and
Restaurant Associates—allowed him to pursue more serious work
and kept him in lunches at La Caravelle on those occasions when he
was obliged to pick up the check.

In February he did "a Julia Child job" on all his teaching recipes
for the school, bringing them closer to a *Mastering* level of precision.
Peace had returned to the school, with Ruth Norman (now author of
a book called *Cook Until Done*) acting as Beard's second-in-com-
mand, assisted by Clay Triplette, the cherubic ex-dancer Beard had
hired as houseman at the time he purchased 119 West Tenth. The
routines of the school, now in its fourth year, were well established:
Classes began for the most part at six in the evening and ran until
nine or a little later; the first basic lesson was for crepes; and Albert
Stockli was the regular guest chef with Julia Child and Helen Brown
signed up as "associates."

As at other New Years, James injured himself in January 1962—
a strained ligament resulting from a fall—and went on yet another
diet, pledging to Helen Brown not to drink hard liquor, butter his

bread, or eat his customary double portions. He went to fewer restaurants during February and more plays, seeing "A Man for All Seasons," "A Passage to India," and "The Aspern Papers," plus *Turandot* and several other operas in the space of a few weeks. Helen Brown, James's partner in dieting as in cooking, was subsisting on two ounces of steak in place of breakfast and lunch. Neither had much to show for these efforts.

Other Americans were being offered and taking up more extreme measures. Copies of *Calories Don't Count*, the number-eight bestseller of 1961 and number one through 1962, were seized in January by FDA agents because of dietary supplements being sold in conjunction with the book. In February the agency also condemned broadcasts by dieting expert Carlton Fredericks and stopped distribution of diet aids marketed by him, provoking outraged cries of censorship and restraint of trade from both Fredericks and a public whose hunger for weight loss was reminiscent of the Americans' thirst for booze during Prohibition, yet again thwarted by zealous G-men.

Concomitant with their obsession with reducing, Americans' fascination with food escalated in 1962, which produced, in the wake of Peg Bracken, the perhaps-inevitable *I Love to Cook Book* as well as *Magic with Leftovers; The Gourmet in the Low-Calorie Kitchen; The Playboy Gourmet*, a spin-off from Hugh Hefner's men's magazine; a revised edition of *The Joy of Cooking;* and Helen and Phillip Brown's *Breakfasts and Brunches for Every Occasion*, which would help launch the eggs-benedict-and-quiche brunch craze of the late sixties and seventies. Myra Waldo, with whom Helen McCully and James lunched that spring, produced a mere two books in 1962 but was featured along with James in a special issue of *Life* published in November, devoted entirely to food and containing photo essays on farming, food processing, a day in the culinary life of a typical suburban housewife, and recipes of the stars, including one from a twenty-five-year-old Jane Fonda. *Life* also brought over an inspector from France's *Guide Michelin*, who ranked American restaurants just behind those of France and Britain and pronounced Le Pavillon worthy of two and possibly three stars. Meanwhile *Time* reported the death of Irma Rombauer in October with a full feature on her career, and the next month *Newsweek* followed up on the impending chef shortage facing the nation and what was being done about it. The *Saturday Evening Post* regularly ran not only recipes but gastronomic opinion and humor pieces: One decried the scant attention paid to American regional traditions in the rush toward the gourmet revolution; another by a then-unknown magazine writer named John McPhee recounted his decision to burn copies of *The Can-Opener Cookbook, Instant Haute Cuisine, The Electric Epicure's Cookbook, Economy Gastronomy, Mary Meade's Magic Recipes for the Electric Blender,* and *The Instant Epicure* that had found their way into his home.

Food books in particular were news, with cookbook reviews becoming a standard feature not only on newspaper food pages and in women's service magazines but in publications like *Esquire, Newsweek, Time, Look, Life,* and the *Saturday Evening Post,* where Craig Claiborne commended *The James Beard Cookbook* together with *Mastering* that December. There also seemed to be a genuine revival of interest in gastronomic literature as distinct from recipe books: Scribner's published a modern edition of an English fifteenth-century treatise on cookery; a new volume reminiscent of *Fit for a King,* called *The Artists' and Writers' Cookbook,* prompted an essay in *The New Yorker;* and works like Angelo Pellegrini's *The Unprejudiced Palate*—essays on food, wine, gardening, and the good life by a Seattle college professor of Italian immigrant stock—were brought back into print.

It was against this background that James, now working closely with John Ferrone, was able to place a section of the still-unmanageable manuscript of *Delights and Prejudices* with *Harper's* magazine for publication in November. Ferrone, who would become a distinguished editor of novelists and of the diaries and letters of the Bloomsbury group, was able to help James find a middle ground in his prose that was neither effusive nor stuffy. The piece, called "Life at Its Best: Summer Eating on the Oregon Coast," was largely an account of Beard's childhood days at Gearhart and its rounds of picnics, food gathering, and innumerable meals with the Hamblets. Still driven by the intense process of recollection he had begun in Venice and an opinionatedness that now seemed born of wisdom rather than pomposity, it was a worthy companion to the essays by Arthur Miller and Paul Goodman with which it appeared.

Despite the piece's reception at one of the nation's leading magazines, Pat Knopf at Atheneum had grown unsure of whether he now wanted the book from which it had been taken, and Beard and

Schaffner in turn threatened to take it to another publisher. Beard was able to stanch his fury to some extent with a trip that summer to Europe and to the West Coast, where he rendezvoused with Helen Brown, Claiborne, Paula Peck, and other food people leaving on a junket to Asia. In Oregon he sat meditatively on Gearhart Beach in a Jeep with Mary Hamblet—a moment that was to constitute the final lines of *Delights and Prejudices.*

On his return, he held meetings with Green Giant, the Bourbon Institute (for whom he was to develop a set of recipes), and Ned Bradford of Little, Brown, who showed no interest either in providing a home for *Delights and Prejudices* or in doing a revised edition of *Paris Cuisine.* Feeling stuck on *Delights and Prejudices,* Beard was in little mood to toil on other writing projects, whether the Dell international paperback, the Schoonmaker wine book—which was shortly to be abandoned altogether—or the work on wines he had agreed to do for a book on California cheeses and wines Helen Brown was doing for California publisher Ward Ritchie.

Helen herself arrived in New York in November to teach at James's school, following sessions with Julia Child in what was the school's busiest and most oversubscribed term ever. Increasingly the school also went on road tours, with James—sometimes accompanied by Ruth Norman—giving demonstrations and classes that autumn in Columbus, Chicago, and Seattle. As usual Thanksgiving was by habit or necessity an all-male affair for six, with Claiborne; Claiborne's companion, Henry; Gino; and Beard being joined by a third couple for a dinner of turkey with tarragon stuffing, parsnips, potatoes, and onions, a pumpkin dessert, and cranberries for Gino.

Through December James became increasingly despondent, writing Helen Brown, "My mood is becoming more and more depressed all the time and I don't even want to live much any more." Still, he cooked and entertained impressively during the holidays: a lunch for Claiborne and John Schaffner of clam bisque, veal with truffles, barley in mushrooms, and a pistachio ice; a Christmas spread—composed of vodka and champagne, with rillettes, foie gras, zampone, codfish, ham, croissants, and stollen for nibbling—for the better part of his New York friends. Three days later he served a dinner of deviled crab, sirloin of beef bordelaise, pommes Anna, and dacquoise, all dishes (excepting the beef) that he played a large role in introduc-

ing to Americans or in repopularizing in the United States. He spent
New Year's Eve quietly with Gino and Craig Claiborne.

By January 1963 Pat Knopf had agreed to accept *Delights and
Prejudices* more or less as written, with John Ferrone as editor, a
condition that delighted James: "John senses the idea of the thing at
once," he wrote Helen Brown, "and I feel confident that it is going
to take shape from now on." His financial burdens, heavy ever since
the purchase of 119 West Tenth, lightened considerably with the
signing of a contract to oversee "The Theatre of Food" at the 1964
New York World's Fair for a fee of twenty-five thousand dollars.
With another successful cooking school session completed, he left
New York for Europe in April for an extended tour that began in
London with a visit to Henry and Bettina McNulty and a series of
meals with Elizabeth David.

David had come to James's attention through a book column in
the *New York Times* that reviewed both her *French Country Cooking* and Helen Brown's *The West Coast Cook Book,* and in many
senses David and Brown were linked in his mind. Like Brown, David
had established herself with a collection of recipes drawn from a relatively unexplored territory—in David's case the rustic cooking of
France, Italy, and the Mediterranean—and was both a better writer
than James and seemingly more of a purist, with a taste for honest
and direct flavors. A rigorous researcher and gatherer of food lore,
David was as much a historian and anthropologist as a cook, and by
American standards her terse recipes were impossibly vague. But the
point of David's books—*A Book of Mediterranean Food* (1950),
French Country Cooking (1951), *Italian Food* (1954), *Summer
Cooking* (1955), and *French Provincial Cooking* (1960)—was not in
the recipes but in the writing. They seemed to be less about eating
than the evocation of salt-glazed pots of rustic food that represented
the gastronomic equivalent of William Morris and the Arts and
Crafts movement; a peasant cuisine that was extraordinarily compelling for those of an artistic and intellectual socialist sensibility.

David's cooking, born amid the experience of Britain's postwar
food shortages, was austere in its aesthetics but rich in flavor, drawing its goodness not from rare ingredients or technical wizardry but
from the venerable traditions of patient attention paid to well-made

and well-chosen materials—dishes that gained their earthy savor by
long, patient cooking on the stove. Although David showed little
appetite for stardom or wealth and, like James, was given to bouts of
ill health, depression, and reclusiveness, she unleashed an approach
to cooking and eating that was profoundly influential in Britain
through the sixties and among food professionals in the United
States during the seventies and eighties.

James reached London that spring of 1963 on his way to a house
in Provence rented through Naomi Barry of the *International Herald
Tribune,* and his time with David was an introduction to a life that
was to seem reminiscent of his boyhood summers on Gearhart
Beach. At the house, called Lou Barcarès and situated near Saint-
Rémy-de-Provence, he was visited first by Mary Hamblet, with
whom he marketed, cooked, and walked the lavender- and thyme-
bordered roads and paths surrounding the farmhouse. James had
never learned to drive, but he and Mary were chauffeured by the
owner's son in a Citroën 2CV to nearby olive mills, farm stands, and
the shops of nearby towns, whose produce was turned in the
ramshackle kitchen to David-inspired food redolent of herbs, garlic,
olive oil, and tomatoes. They also visited Provence's most vaunted
restaurants, such as Oustaù de Baumanière, which James found
"tremendously overrated" and "dull" after a lunch there on May 10,
a few days after his sixtieth birthday.

But this was to be a working vacation, and, primed by Mary's
visit, James was joined by John Ferrone, with whom he was to finish
the final draft of *Delights and Prejudices.* The day began at seven—
late for James—with breakfast and a few hours of writing, followed
by lunch, marketing, and perhaps a bullfight, an afternoon nap back
at Lou Barcarès designed to defy the farm's afternoon heat and its
squadrons of flies, and then cooking, drinks, dinner, and sleep. It
was an atmosphere in which James came as close to peace and con-
tentment as he was capable, although the flies and other inconve-
niences of rural life could drive him to tantrums as consuming as
those he would recount from his childhood in *Delights and Prejudices.* However, what was to impress the many visitors who saw him
that summer was the general evenness of his temperament in the
weeks following his sixtieth birthday. At home in New York James
could in private, unguarded moments with Ruth Norman, Gino, or
Clay pass in a flash from his customary humor and congeniality to

terrifying eruptions of sarcasm and anger, released from a normally concealed well of fury.

Beard returned to New York in June with a head full of Provence from which story and menu ideas burst full blown. Within days he had persuaded José Wilson, the recently appointed food editor of *House & Garden,* with whom Helen Brown had been battling during the last few months, to accept a Provençal food story. Provence also brought out a revival in his interest in a country restaurant, which he imagined might bolster his own zest for life and the waning excitement of his relationship with Gino, who had during the last year won and then lost an architectural job and now seemed aimless and increasingly dependent.

The summer in any case continued at a comparatively leisurely pace, with regular escapes to Cheryl Crawford's place for relaxing and writing between bouts of Nestlé and World's Fair work in town. In September James served as a judge at the Pillsbury Bake-Off in California, where he visited the Browns and Chuck Williams, proprietor of a newly founded culinary equipment shop called Williams-Sonoma.

October brought another round of classes, with demand for the basic course exceeding the available space. Beard's school continued to prosper even as that of Dione Lucas faltered under the weight of financial distress and lawsuits, and Lucas herself looked more and more haggard and irrelevant. But James nonetheless had new competition, in New York chiefly from Michael Field, an intense, hyperkinetic, chain-smoking ex–concert pianist and restaurateur who was operating a cooking school out of his apartment. The most significant event in cooking teaching in 1963, though, was a series of programs produced on a shoestring at Boston's educational television station, WGBH, called "The French Chef," with Julia Child.

Like most products of what was then known as "educational" television, the audience for "The French Chef" should by all accounts have been a tiny local group of Cambridge, Massachusetts, students, academic families, and crackpots. But no one reckoned on the chemistry between television and Child, a droll six-footer with a Seven Sisters tone whose hearty and unself-conscious aplomb was the perfect foil to the pretensions of both fancy food and television. Child's predecessors in the medium were less Dione Lucas or Poppy Cannon than Steve Allen and Ernie Kovacs, whose brilliance lay in determining exactly what the public believed one could not do on television and then doing it. Television had predictably sought dignity in its upstart years and borrowed its style from the stuffier regions of radio and newspapers, which specialized in basso-voiced pundits and well-bred glamour girls of the Betty Furness and Bess Myerson school.

What was therefore captivating about "The French Chef" was the novelty of highbrow culture being promulgated in a casual and even offhand manner by a host who was not embarrassed by but embraced the flubs and messes of real life. Julia Child became a star by taking material of the most intimidating sort and treating it like creamed chipped beef—scorches, curdles, and all. It was, in this respect, perfectly matched with the Kennedyesque sixties ethic of sophisticated amateurism and with the era's appetite for satire and ironic comedy: Child's affection for food and France was unmistakable but so, too, was her native inclination not to take it or herself overly seriously. As a result sixties people might watch "The French Chef" for instruction and entertainment, to see just what rule of gastronomic or television decorum Julia might break tonight. Her performances became the stuff of legend, accompanied by apocryphal stories about her guzzling wine on the set or retrieving food off the floor.

Just as *Playboy*, the birth control pill, and a legion of books and magazine articles were teaching Americans to relax about sex, Child's easygoing persona taught the nation to relax about food. She also changed the way the upper-middle-class stratum of society entertained, bringing food back into the dining room from the patio and shifting attention from the atmosphere the food partook of— fire, smoke, and the outdoors—to the aesthetics of the food itself. And even if Child herself was in many respects a force for a more relaxed and casual way of life, she promoted the idea of the ambitious dinner party as entertainment and of formality as fun. Finally, she confirmed the role of French cuisine as the paramount expression of good cooking.

Despite the interest in food Child and others created among the affluent, as well as the increasingly impressive skills of amateur cooks, the nation's restaurants did not seem to be sharing in the great gastronomic progress of the early sixties. In the *Times* that September, while "The French Chef" began to play to a national audience and

James rounded up his fellow culinary stars to appear at the 1964 World's Fair "Theatre of Food," Craig Claiborne lambasted the quality of restaurant cooking in New York, which on another occasion he characterized as a gastronomic "hick town." In a prominently featured piece in the *New York Times Magazine,* he suggested that New York's leading restaurateurs—at that moment protesting impending restrictions on expense account dining—were foisting unimaginative menus, surly service, factory-produced desserts, and unconscionably marked-up wine lists on an increasingly savvy and fed-up public. The piece prompted a flood of letters, a reply from Claiborne, and further letters. It was, as Beard wrote Julia Child that September, an article "that stood New York on its ear."

The quality of restaurants in the rest of the country was even more dire, the vast majority of them peddling variations on steak, baked potato, and salad, their culinary affinities less with Beard, Child, or David than with Poppy Cannon. Although the country at large might be beginning to grasp the idea that food could be appreciated entirely on its own terms, in restaurants it was no more than one element in the dining experience, no more—and perhaps sometimes less—important than decor, service, and cocktails. Other factors also augured poorly for the development of good food in restaurants: the rise and influence of corporate and theme restaurants run by people less able than Joe Baum; the decline of regional and seasonal foods in favor of a homogeneous and ever-more-processed national larder; and an understandable tendency among both the public and restaurant professionals to confuse the outward accoutrements of "gourmet dining" with genuinely interesting and satisfying cooking. All this arguably marked the better part of the fifties and sixties as the nadir of American restaurant dining.

In a sense, there was little reason it should be otherwise, given the fact that there were no organized public voices to plead for change. Restaurant writing, where it existed, usually consisted of a column of news bits and plugs supplied by restaurateurs themselves placed in the entertainment section of the local paper adjacent to restaurant advertisements or a "dining guide." The latter might appear to be a list of establishments recommended by the paper or magazine in question on the basis of their quality but in fact was fabricated from paid entries solicited by the advertising department, a practice that still flourishes today. It was therefore a nearly revolutionary event when Craig Claiborne began reviewing restaurants in a truly critical manner at the *Times* in the late 1950s. When Claiborne's review was made a weekly feature in May 1963, his consumer-oriented approach to restaurant writing became the norm, forever altering not just newspaper dining columns but food journalism in general. If restaurants were to be reported on and evaluated according to the same journalistic standards that applied to the gathering of "hard" news, so too must coverage of food products, books, and services. The marriage between the food industry and the food writer—solemnized at the end of the last century and consummated through an ongoing exchange of freebies, junkets, and plugs—was slowly headed for an inevitable dissolution.

James's second World's Fair, which began in early 1964, seemed to resemble his first. Like the fair of 1939, the 1964 edition was based on the notion of international understanding, prosperity, and, not least, progress: There was an underground house; a home dispenser of custom-made disposable plastic dishes; a cooking-serving cart that both refrigerated and cooked; and an oven that broiled, baked, roasted, browned, and defrosted in any sequence the user might direct. But the earnest, almost hayseed belief in the possibilities of the "World of Tomorrow," so apparent in 1939 among a citizenry still reeling from the depression, was gone. In 1964 the vision of the future seemed to consist not of the realization of ideals but of better and more marvelous consumables of the kind showcased by the fair's corporate sponsors, irrespective of how small a portion of humanity their use might be confined to, or of the effects of their production and use on the larger world.

The fair, dominated by a "Unisphere" globe of metal, was also the jewel in the crown of Robert Moses' lifetime project of rehabilitating New York City by razing vast pieces of it. As for food, cooking at the level of the 1939 French, Belgian, and Swiss pavilions was not the aim of the restaurants created by Restaurant Associates under contract to various foreign tourist authorities. But relative to what might be offered at the 7-Up Pavilion or the General Motors Futurama, their efforts—often working, for example, in the culinary vernacular of countries like India and Indonesia—were worthy. Beard found himself conducting his demonstrations at the epicenter of a pavilion consecrated as "the Festival of Gas."

That indignity was eased by the opportunity to leave New York in April 1964 to publicize *Delights and Prejudices*, and in particular to do so in Portland: "The return of James A. Beard will be," the society editor of *The Oregonian* predicted, "in the nature of a triumph." But Portland was both less than it was and exactly as it always had been. The markets of James's childhood had been displaced by the supermarkets of former Yamhill stall holder Fred Meyer; the great hotel dining rooms had long ago resigned themselves to the provision of blue-plate specials and convention dinners; and Tillamook Head above Gearhart Beach, pictured on the cover of *Delights and Prejudices*, had been logged. Portlanders attended James's demonstrations and book signings at Meier and Frank in droves, but dishes like deviled crab, potatoes hashed in cream, huckleberries with sweet Hood Valley cream, and salmon cheeks did not figure much on their tables. The great salmon runs of the Columbia and other Pacific Northwest rivers had in any case been decimated by damming and logging, and a picture of the diet of Portlanders could undoubtedly be most accurately gleaned not from the books of Helen Brown or James (to say nothing of Child and Claiborne), but from spiral-bound fund-raising tomes like *Favorite Recipes of the Great Northwest*, published that year and boasting nine hundred recipes culled from the region's "women's club leaders" and "modern homemakers."

At least among this presumably representative group of Oregonians—women running the gamut from the wife of Governor Mark Hatfield to members of the Home Demonstration Club and Christian Women's Fellowship of Hillsboro—salmon, crab, clams, oysters, and pies of berries and orchard fruit had been inundated beneath a deluge of mushroom soup, ground beef, and chicken chunks. The casserole swept all before it, either pushing other kinds of cooking aside or appropriating them into its swelling, glutinous, four-hundred-degree-fired corpus of recipes: Thus hamburgers were transmuted into "barbecued burger beans"; pasta into "sour cream-noodle bake"; the cuisine of Asia into a dozen variations from "African chow mein" to "Chinese hamburger dish"; and the pinnacle of Dione Lucas's art into "baked Spam omelet." The aesthetic that informed such recipes was not displayed in their flavor but through creative juxtapositions of ingredients or transpositions from one tradition to another (as in "vegetable soup sloppy joes"); adaptations and modernizations ("electric skillet dinner" and "refrigerator rolls"); and the addition of ingredients like curry powder, pineapple, maraschino cherries, or miniature marshmallows. A tribute to the enduring force of domestic science, it was food that had more in common with a handicrafts project than with cooking as James understood it—it was assembled in steps and repetitions, like a potholder formed from loops of multicolored cotton stretched across a brightly colored metal frame.

In these respects Beard's return that spring was not so much a triumph as the unveiling of a memorial to an Oregon that was gone. *Delights and Prejudices* was an essay in memory, ostensibly the tale of the education of Beard's palate, but in fact a meditation on places and persons whose absence now dominated James even as their presence in his childhood had formed him. Towering above all of them was Mary, whose floods and ebbs could be as cruel and inconstant or as gentle and bountiful as the sea at Gearhart: "I grew up in the helter-skelter of her life. For periods I saw her constantly, and at other times she disappeared for a long stretch into one of her projects."

James's Portland friends were shocked at the picture he created of Mary, who often seemed less an angel of the cast-iron stove than a coolly efficient, controlling steamroller of a woman:

> I have always said that Mother brought me up in the same way she ran her hotel—more manager than mother. She gave instructions on how I was to be fed, what I was to wear, what I was to see and do, and somebody else—at first a nurse, then a Chinese amah, whom I adored—carried out her plans. . . . I was alone frequently, but I was enterprising, and I read a great deal, far beyond my years. And perhaps I spent too much time in the company of [mother's] guests, for I listened to a lot of adult talk, adopted snobbish ideas and expressed myself freely on almost any subject. I could toss a remark into mixed company that unnerved the entire gathering, which, I have always imagined, secretly delighted my mother. I soon became as precocious and nasty a child as ever inhabited Portland.

James's portrait of himself as a petulant, manipulative, and ravenously demanding child was no more sparing than the one he drew of Mary. But while he may rightly have blamed and hated her for his unhappiness, he also understood that they were bound together as coconspirators and partners in crime not only against the stuffy provincialism of Portland but as the joint authors of James's own grandiose character. By contrast he had nothing but good to say about Jue-Let, the Summerses, and the Hamblets. Of his father Beard spoke only to underline his absence.

Although it is debatable whether *Delights and Prejudices* was the masterpiece of gastronomic literature James hoped he might someday write, its virtues are clear enough. Although its chapters wander among the events of Beard's life without much regard for their temporal sequence or logical connection, they return again and again to Mary, to Gearhart, and to the succor and wonder of meals peopled by kind and magical companions. Beard's long preoccupation with the idea of "taste memory" came to fruition in *Delights and Prejudices*, enabling him to evoke not just what he ate and the circumstances under which he ate it but the entire constellation of his life, in all its hungers and satisfactions.

That thread of appetites, both satisfied and unsatisfied, led the sixty-year-old Beard at the book's end inevitably back to Gearhart, to his mother, and to a kind of reconciliation that would at least in part lay the ghosts of long ago to rest:

> More and more I think of Mother's small wood stove at Gearhart and the dishes that issued from that tiny kitchen. . . . I remember how quickly she would start a fire on the beach with fine kindling, adding split wood and then bits of bark. In no time she would have breakfast going. . . .
>
> In the spring at Gearhart, when the meadows were purple with violets and bluebells and the woods filled with new skunk cabbages and the first shoots of ferns, life was at its most tranquil. One could wander alone for hours on the beach, gaze at Tillamook Head and watch the surf. Only last spring I spent a weekend there with two old friends, and we did these same things—only instead of walking, we drove in a jeep!—going far up the beach to the jetty, searching for the Japanese floats we remembered from our youth. At night, when it was raining and blowing slightly, we went out once more in the jeep and drove along the beach, reminiscing about berrying, clamming, picnicking. Then we parked and sat for a long while in silence, looking at the surf, longing for the floats to come in.

• • •

Beard returned later that spring to New York, that summer to Europe, and then back to New York for fall classes and final work on a book that would fulfill his broken contract with Dell. But, overshadowing all these things, he returned to face the worsening illness of Helen Brown and, at last, her death on December 1. Although her native vivacity disguised her condition, she had been sick for years, with sores and swellings and inexplicable pain and fatigues finally crystallizing into the awful fact of her cancer. At sixty, she was not young, but her life, like James's, seemed in so many ways to be just beginning.

Beard was unsurprised but devastated. He had finally written the book she had wanted him to write, and he could recall how large a role her goading, sympathy, and impatience had played in leading him to the point in his life where he could at last bring it forth. She and her effect on him were not easy to categorize—she was by turns girlish and severe, earnest and world-weary, genteel and brassy—but their friendship felt fated, and they were drawn into each other's gravities irresistibly. They could tell each other who they really were and who it was that they wanted to be. James could look into her quizzical hazel eyes, her head slightly tilted, and see the unseen good in himself.

NINE

1965–1969

By the middle of the sixties, James found himself astride two of the decade's emergent trends: home entertaining with food and the television cooking program. The two were not unrelated: On television food had become entertainment and the cook a star whose good-humored mastery was in turn a model for home cooks who might impress and amuse their own guests in their dining room or kitchen. Magazines and books increasingly featured dishes with which ambitious hosts might display their culinary skills and sophistication: Flaming food moved out of restaurants and onto the pages of the *Ladies Home Journal* and *House & Garden* by 1965, and at about the same time a dish called quiche lorraine had popped up in *Look* and quickly migrated to *Sunset* and other middlebrow service outlets.

Beard's contribution to the buffet-and-dinner-party Klondike was *James Beard's Menus for Entertaining,* the book he had begun in the summer of 1963 with John Ferrone in Provence. Produced without much enthusiasm as a means of fulfilling his contract with Dell for a paperback about the world's cuisines, it was nevertheless a vastly more intelligent and interesting work than such hostess fodder as *A Million Menus for Dining and Entertaining at Home* or *Zodiac Parties. Menus for Entertaining* included flambéed steak, kidneys, and peaches as well as a quiche (lurking under the name Swiss Tart l'Oignon), but the distinctive preferences and tastes of Beard in the latter half of his career were also apparent. Lobster l'américaine had given way even in the most formal situations to simpler preparations of roast chicken and filet of beef with side dishes like a garlicky gratin of potatoes, gnocchi, or corn bread serving as foils to the pièce-de-résistance main course. The rustic and relaxed influences of Elizabeth David and Helen Brown were present in dishes from

France, Italy, and Mexico as well as in cold buffet and picnic items and salads.

Although in *Menus for Entertaining* he could appear fogeyish—particularly in anachronistic discussions of the "servant problem" and of such nearly extinct social occasions as ladies' luncheons and teas—for the most part a clearly less formal and more adventurous Beard was visible: a sixty-two-year-old who was capable of learning new tricks, was more willing to mix and match as he pleased, and who may have been rediscovering some of his own forgotten cooking instincts. If there was admittedly no evidence of the chianti-bottle ethnic food that the Greenwich Village outside his door was helping to spread among students and bohemians and thence to the nation at large, neither was there much French food on offer, nor were menus constructed to suit French or Franco- and Anglophile notions of decorum, beyond the suggestion of an appropriate wine for each menu. In a color spread inside the book, Beard was shown in his kitchen and at table wearing evening dress and sporting what were rapidly becoming his stock assortment of expressions, from contemplative bliss at a flavor or smell to twinkle-eyed bemusement to uproarious geniality. Another photo revealed the Beard-Cofacci dining salon in all its Wildean bordello classicism: Terra cotta statuary and purple-shaded lamps tower over a table set with a *putti*-encrusted candelabrum, vermeil, Wedgwood majolica, and green wineglass rinsers from a collection that would eventually number four hundred.

"The James Beard Show" was in an altogether less flamboyant mode, a sort of newspaper women's page of the air. Produced by a Canadian syndicator in Toronto and Vancouver, the five-day-a-week series occupied the better part of James's time during 1965 and 1966 and involved him not only in demonstrating cooking but—assisted by an attractive young female sidekick—in discussing and advising on travel, decoration, homemaking, and fashion with an audience of housewives. The taping schedule was grueling, and in the course of it Beard's weight reached such a formidable summit that virtually every press account of the program commented on it. Through the early part of 1965, he was rarely at home, and class schedules were constantly shuffled by Ruth Norman in order to accommodate James's stints in Canada, promotional tours, and consulting forays to Green Giant in Minnesota. His writing assignments consisted mostly of work for *House & Garden,* whose food editor José Wilson now listed Beard on the magazine's masthead as its food and drink consultant. He had also reached an agreement with Ned Bradford of Little Brown to produce a book on American food, although there was little time to begin work on it.

In May he was at last able to get away for his now-traditional late-spring trip to Europe, leaving for London—where his friends Henry and Bettina McNulty were permanently settled—and Paris, followed by a sojourn at the home of Simone Beck, Julia Child's collaborator and neighbor at Plascassier near the Côte d'Azur. For the first time, however, Gino joined him in his travels, and by the time the two had left France for a week in Spain, Gino's company had begun to wear on him. Gino was discontented in France—"[He] likes Nice, but resents the rusticity of Provence," Beard wrote John Ferrone—and by the time they arrived in Barcelona, where James attempted to rouse Gino from his habitual sulks by taking him to see "his first Gaudi," Beard was thoroughly exasperated. They returned to New York via London and a series of meals with Elizabeth David, who was in the midst of opening a shop filled with rustic and earthy cooking gear. In London Beard also consolidated his friendship with Robert Carrier, an American expatriate of sharp culinary and business instincts, who—free by both nationality and choice from David's hairshirt pastoralism—was establishing himself as one of Britain's most popular and commercially successful tastemakers.

Beard came home to discover that his contract for "The James Beard Show" had not only been renewed but that John Schaffner had negotiated an even higher fee on his behalf. After ten days at home and a weekend at Cheryl Crawford's, he was off to Toronto and Vancouver for another round of taping, working in a few days in Portland on the way to Green Giant. Portland was also on the itinerary of Craig Claiborne, who was traveling the country that summer reporting on the nation's regional foodways. He was introduced by Mary Hamblet to two local cooks whose Oregon bonhomie and recipes for cauliflower with mustard sauce and quick crème brulée he wrote up in the *Times.*

Interest in American cooks and cooking remained, however, a largely marginal affair, and most gastronomically sophisticated Americans continued to look abroad for inspiration. Claiborne reported that *Times* readers' favorite recipes for 1965 were for a

Russian chicken-liver-filled pastry; navarin d'agneau; and paella, perhaps the quintessential mid-sixties dish. Culinary internationalism was, together with folk music and the well-scrubbed Pepsi-Cola panethnicism of the World's Fair, a seemingly inexhaustible trend that could draw on and freely mix cuisines or, as had been the case with Polynesia, simply invent them. Beard, Child, and Claiborne were all forces for this eclecticism, but perhaps its purest practitioner would be Michael Field, who began to attract national notice in the summer of 1965 with the release of *Michael Field's Cooking School* by Beard's old publisher, M. Barrows.

Field's book was serialized in *Ladies Home Journal* and reviewed glowingly in *Life,* and Field was given a monthly column at *McCall's* titled "The World of Fine Cooking." Field's success was understandable: His recipes were excruciatingly precise; he had a knack for spotting appealing surefire dishes; his range was wider than Child's and less scattershot and personal than Beard's, and he had an aura of authority and impeccability reminiscent of Claiborne's. Within months Field's name was being lumped with theirs as a food force to be reckoned with. His approach to cooking was influenced by his background in music: He did not sentimentalize or romanticize food, and he believed good cooking was not an art but the result of technical mastery and practice. In the same vein he assembled what he believed to be a classical repertoire of dishes—boeuf Bourguignon, Caesar salad, osso buco, grilled shrimp with garlic, gazpacho, risotto, pasta with pesto or cream and butter, spinach salad, and the like—most of which look thoroughly appealing and undated twenty-five years later, a rare feat among cookery writers.

Despite his very different way with food, Beard genuinely liked Field, whose hopped-up delirium was in near-perfect contrast to Beard's own lumbering, ursine ease. Field shared Beard's love of the arts and gossip, and they took meals together and accompanied each other to the World's Fair, where James continued to make appearances. But Beard's life during the remainder of 1965 was lived mostly in television studios in Toronto and Vancouver and in offices and test kitchens at Green Giant and, later, Pillsbury and French's Mustard. Although the eternal pilgrimage of North America he made in the service of his career, and his dizzying social calendar, seemed to offer a respite from the escalating friction and alienation between him and Gino, in fact it only deepened it. James resented Gino's dependence on him, but every foot of distance Beard put between them seemed only to inflate Gino's helpless, clutching petulance.

When the year's tapings finished in Vancouver, James returned not to New York but to Oregon and Christmas at Gearhart, in a beach house owned by his old Portland friend Harvey Welch. At the New Year of 1966 he wrote Julia Child in France:

> Went to the beach on the 25th—had a delicious ham and egg Christmas dinner when we got there—just what we had in the car. Then spent five days doing absolutely nothing we didn't want to do. The house was lovely, the weather wild. Mary Hamblet and I both love that type of adventure at the beach from the time of our childhood. We walked on the beach in a 50 mile gale, carried driftwood for the fire, drove to Astoria for caviar and salmon cheeks and picnicked in the car on the road. It was a heavenly time away from everyone. And of course home all too soon.

Mary Hamblet would later say that it was as cold a winter as she could recollect and the first in her memory in which snow covered the beach from the dunes downward, like powdered-sugar frosting on a gingerbread cake, right to the waterline and the sea.

James spent January 1966 teaching classes and working with Joe Baum and his lieutenant, Alan Lewis, on RA's latest venture, Charley O's, an Irish-style grill and "pub" located in Rockefeller Center. The combination of Celtic conviviality set against an Anglo-Irish background of burnished wood and brass proved to be one of the most durable bar and restaurant themes of the next two decades—especially among places catering to the burgeoning population of prowling singles—and was matched in popularity only by the Tiffany-glass-and-hanging-fern Gay Nineties motif pioneered by Warner Leroy's Maxwell's Plum, which opened in New York that April.

Baum was now president of RA and accustomed to unlimited expenditure on consultants such as Beard, Julia Child, and a food writer named Mimi Sheraton, who would succeed Claiborne as the *Times* restaurant critic and—through the exacting and sometimes harsh standards she imposed in her reviews—establish herself for a decade as the avenging angel of gastronomy. Traveling abroad in search of ideas and novelties, Baum brought an often-overbearing sense of urgency to every discovery: In a memo from Denmark he enthused over "an igloo of ice cream with awful chocolate sauce over it and sparklers that burn to a certain point, setting off an American flag which pops, runs up a tiny flagpole . . . horrible . . . we must learn to do this." Baum had finally become too much for Albert Stockli—himself a paragon of ill temper—who quit RA to establish a country inn in Connecticut. Beard was saddened by the rupture, the first of many during the later sixties in which he would find himself uncomfortably positioned between warring friends in the food community.

RA, whose stock was now publicly traded and being touted on a Wall Street well into the frenzy of its "go-go" era, was no longer a hospitable place for artistic and sensitive souls like Stockli or, in the long run, showmen like Baum with Wagnerian notions about food. More generally, the stakes in food writing and consulting were rising exponentially, and habits born during seventy-five years of scarcity were not easily changed. Both money and fame were now increasingly attainable in what once had been the gay and women's ghetto of cooking and "service" journalism. Beard, for example, was the subject of a major *Saturday Evening Post* profile that summer, and in the autumn was described as "the king of gourmets" in a *Time* cover story on Julia Child that also located Claiborne, Field, and the fading Dione Lucas near the top of the epicurean hierarchy. But even with sales of *Mastering* reaching three hundred thousand copies and *The New York Times Cook Book* one hundred thousand since their publication, it still seemed for most people in the food business as though there were too few opportunities and too many rivals. For the major food celebrities themselves, the rewards could be more imagined than real: While *The James Beard Cookbook* might sell 62,000 paperbacks in the first six months of 1966 alone, that impressive tally yielded Beard a mere $3,357.22.

Even then, those at the top—however paltry their fortune might seem by Hollywood or Wall Street standards—continued to enjoy one another's company and to be generous with promising newcomers. Their Olympus was the Beck-Child compound in the south of France, to which Beard retired after a spring of classes, consulting, and tapings. After working in London for three weeks on a projected British edition of *The James Beard Cookbook,* he spent nearly two months in Provence, sketching ideas and outlines for what would become *James Beard's American Cookery* in the Beck residence, even as Julia Child began work on the second volume of *Mastering* across the property in the house she and her husband Paul had built a few years before. In that respect it was a more than appropriate venue: What Beard envisioned was an encyclopedic work along the lines of *Mastering* that would codify American cooking in much the same way as Child and Beck were doing for that of France. But in large part he spent the summer relaxing and receiving visitors from the States; solitude seemed more and more unbearable and so, too, did the solitary business of writing.

In mid-August he returned to Manhattan. "The James Beard Show" had in the meanwhile been canceled, but whatever distress this caused him was moderated by the freedom he now enjoyed to continue to keep the strains of New York at arm's length for a further two months. He embarked on a comparatively leisurely tour of the West Coast, first landing in Los Angeles, where he stayed with Philip Brown. Julia Child's success on television had not only spawned programs like James's over the previous two years but had given a new lease on life to the country's once-ubiquitous local homemaking and cooking shows. In Los Angeles, for example, Beard was a regular guest of "Chef" Mike Roy, an eternal fixture of Southern California radio and TV whose voice, like congealing lard, embodied corpulence. From Los Angeles Beard headed north and south for further media appearances, demonstrations, and classes. Accompanied and assisted by Philip at some points on the route, he visited San Diego, San Francisco, Portland, and concluded with a week in Seattle at the beginning of November.

He returned to New York in time for the release of the *Time* Julia Child cover story, an event that felt like a watershed for the food community, a conferring of genuine legitimacy on gastronomy and cooking after years of mockery and condescension. The *Time* story was of course never absolutely free of either, but even when reported in the magazine's habitually arch prose, it was clear that cooking was a cultural phenomenon that Americans now took seriously. Still, the cult of Julia drew its initiates almost entirely from the most affluent strata of society and the inhabitants of Georgetown, Cambridge, Beverly Hills, the north shore of Chicago, and the Upper East Side of New York. Trends in chic dinner party menus would be followed much like hemlines, and *Time* declared Beef Wellington—

tenderloin of beef slathered with foie gras and mushrooms and cas-
keted within a Fabergé egg of pastry—the current rising star on the
dinner party circuit.

But among the somewhat less affluent and the middle of the middle classes, cost and convenience continued to outweigh style, particularly in 1966 and 1967, during which prices of many foods rose by
almost 10 percent, a stunning surge. Americans were by now long
accustomed to cheap food based on government subsidies, standardization of every aspect of growing and processing, and mass production and distribution of foodstuffs. Accordingly, any demand the
nation might make for better ingredients as a result of a more
enlightened culinary sensibility was countered by a desire to keep
food prices—already absurdly low by the standards of the rest of the
world—at bargain levels. That same impulse further fostered the
nation's casserole complex, served by the ever-present Cannonite tendency at the women's magazines and by book series like *Make It
Now, Bake It Later.*

In fact, the popularity of the casserole represented not only a
search for convenience and cheapness but a perennial urge toward a
sort of culinary monotheism, an ultimate domestic formula of transcendent simplicity born of using one and only one ingredient, vessel,
implement, or method. The continued appearance of such books—
which can be accounted for in part by the willingness of those with a
vested interest in one product or another to directly or indirectly
underwrite them—suggests that they did indeed respond to some
deeper longing. Thus books appeared promoting not only the casserole as the one true domestic savior, but also aluminum foil, the
toaster oven, or the blender; pressure-cooking, low-heat stovetop
cooking, or baking; or ground beef, canned soup, or chicken. As a
result of climbing food costs, the latter ingredient, which Americans
had jilted to pursue their postwar fling with beef, was reborn as the
frugal, unglamorous, but steady girl-next-door ingredient with which
the country now showed every sign of at long last settling down. The
bestselling cookbook of the next two years was neither Claiborne's
The New York Times Menu Cookbook nor the newly revised
eleventh edition of Fannie Farmer, but *Better Homes and Gardens
Favorite Ways with Chicken.*

The lure of simplicity could also lead in directions that had little
to do with cost-cutting or traditional consumerism: Among college

students and the nascent youth culture of San Francisco and New York's East Village, concerns about the healthfulness, purity, and character of the highly processed, "plastic" foods of the sixties led to an interest in a more "natural" diet whose qualities might reflect and even promote personal, social, and political change. The brown rice, bean sprouts, and tofu natural-foods cooking of the late sixties and early seventies was a curious amalgam of influences: recipes from Asia, the Middle East, and India; the domestic health cuisine of Adelle Davis and innumerable cranks; the wild-food gathering of Euell Gibbons; the organic gardening of Rudolf Steiner and J. I. and Robert Rodale; and the ecological eschatology of Rachel Carson and Paul Ehrlich.

In its brown, murky flavors and stodgy, glutinous textures, "natural" food had more in common with prison and hospital cooking than anything that might be connected either with Beard, Child, Field, and Claiborne or *Sunset, Women's Day,* and "the mix gals." But virtually no one in either camp of the mainstream culinary community seemed conscious of the fact that food might be about something more than recipes: that, for example, in the coming year Americans would be shocked to learn that real hunger existed in the United States; that the Federal Trade Commission would threaten action against further concentration of monopoly power among the nation's supermarkets; and that half the country's food supply contained measurable quantities of agricultural chemicals and pesticides. However lacking natural foods might be in the aesthetics of flavor, their proponents were capable of incorporating such issues within their other concerns—a grab bag of impulses that might surprisingly become the stuff of culinary revolution when married to the similarly socially and culturally conscious food of Elizabeth David and her ilk.

If the culinary counterculture often seemed almost tone deaf to the niceties of flavor, presentation, and the great traditions of European cooking, to most food-conscious Americans those features remained paramount, and France in particular continued to be nothing less than the mecca of gastronomy. But voices in both the United States and France urged a relationship less founded on fawning from Americans and condescension from France. In the *Saturday Review,* Joseph Wechsberg, no mean gastronome and *The New Yorker*'s resident food reporter for many years, proposed that Americans impress visiting Europeans with domestic ingredients and dishes rather than the pretentious flambéed kitsch cuisine of "Continental" restaurants. Across the Atlantic the young iconoclasts of French food journalism, Henri Gault and Christian Millau (who would within a few years discover and map out a style of cooking they dubbed "la nouvelle cuisine"), produced a guide to dining in America for their compatriots that conceded the presence of a fair number of estimable kitchens around the United States.

Still, the power and lure of Europe were profound, and as was now his wont, James spent almost half of 1967 there, with four months at the Beck-Child compound at Plascassier. He had encamped there in particular to begin work in earnest on *American Cookery,* a project whose scope and ambition threatened to overwhelm him. In an effort to break through the impasse, he persuaded Catherine Laughton Hindley, an old Portland friend who was now food editor of the *Oregon Journal,* to join him in Provence. The pay would be abysmal, but the south of France and the chance to rub elbows with Child and Beck would surely be some compensation.

It proved to be a long, hot summer devoted solely to baked goods, beginning each day at seven-thirty and working up a regiment of close to 250 cakes, legions of pies and tarts, and an armada of breads and rolls. Hindley, a no-nonsense women's page journalist whose culinary sensibility was entirely Oregonian, found herself clashing with Beard with increasing regularity. Hindley felt that Beard's having spent the last few years macerating in the heady liquor of France while simultaneously obsessed with the idea of producing the last word on American food had put some strange notions into his head—notions of which she as a fellow Oregonian had a duty to disabuse him. For example, James had convinced himself that virtually every dish and technique in American cookery could be traced to France.

Hindley, however, was a considerable food historian in her own right and collected American community cookbooks as James did majolica and wine rinsers. For her it was clear that American cookery was the product of the traditions of various colonial and immigrant groups—none of whom were French other than those in Louisiana and northern New England—interacting with the environments and materials of America's regions. She might point out to him, for example, what the presence of a superfluity of recipes for salt-rising bread in North Dakota community cookbooks said about conditions on the plains and their Scandinavian and German settlers. On the other hand, to contend as James did that Jefferson's French dinners and grape growing at Monticello represented the origins of American cooking was rather like claiming that René Verdon's tenure in the White House was connected to the emergence of McDonald's hamburgers during the same period. But when Hindley argued these points with James, he bellowed, stamped his feet, and retreated to his bedroom, slamming the door behind him. After some time he would reappear, sheepishly admitting that perhaps she might be right, and work would recommence.

For James, however, more than an academic point was at stake: Tracing American cooking to France legitimated American cooking and gave it a destiny, yet another means through which the New World was the fulfillment of the promise of the old. In the wake of one of his tantrums and sullen withdrawals to his chamber, Hindley often felt that James perceived her disagreement as a direct attack not on his thinking but on him. Indeed, for James there was little distinction between his ideas and his identity or between the judgment accorded his performance and the one he believed others rendered on his person.

If James could not tolerate differences and disagreement with other people, neither could he stomach being alone for more than a few moments. Cut off from ready telephone access to his New York cronies, and never having learned to drive, Beard insisted that Hindley work with him seven days a week and that she and her husband keep him company into the night. They were relieved only by the arrival of visitors such as Joe and Ruth Baum, Michael Field, Detroit restaurateurs Lester and Cleo Gruber, and José Wilson of *House & Garden*. Throughout the summer Beard had to be ferried to restaurants, shops, and markets, his phlebitis-ravaged legs at times unable to support him for more than a few steps. Left to fend for himself in Cannes while the Hindleys ran errands, he remained rooted to the same spot for hours.

Gino's arrival in August was a further problem masquerading as a solution. There was little intimacy between him and James, and Gino's lack of social skills and open resentment of others' pleasure flung a pall over the conviviality of even the most animated guests. While James genuinely loved the south of France, much of the time he felt no freer there than in New York, entrapped as he was by his legs, by the dead weight of Gino, by the burden of *American Cookery*, and by a hunger for the company and esteem of other people it often seemed no number of persons could satisfy.

James returned to New York to find the food community there flush with excitement about Time-Life's proposed Foods of the World, a lavishly photographed and researched multivolume series that would cover the world's cuisines using the best food writers and experts available. Their generously recompensed efforts would then be sold by subscription to an audience Time-Life executives calculated to be between 250,000 to 500,000, each of whom would receive three or four volumes a year on approval. Market research and test mailings suggested that these estimates would be more than borne out by a nation ready to lap up global cooking served in *Life* magazine's surefire photojournalistic style.

If *Time*'s cover story on Julia Child had been a kind of media coming-out party for the food community and a public coronation of its leading figures, Foods of the World was nothing less than a potlatch at which Time-Life freely distributed its considerable bounty to New York's food writers, editors, cooking teachers, and recipe testers. In a milieu in which a two-hundred-dollar fee from *Woman's Day* was still met with some breathlessness, Time-Life reportedly paid a thousand dollars a month for the use of a name and the promise to glance at some copy or recipes. From Tenth Street in the Village to the midtown dens of previously unsung and underpaid service magazine drones, it rained gravy.

At the center of this deluge of corporate benison was Michael Field, who at James's urging had been appointed consulting editor for the project. Time-Life's fundamental approach—and an exceedingly congenial one to everybody else concerned—was to go first class, and in that respect Field was a perfect match: He knew food and the best people in it and had the good taste to use them well— launching the series, for example, with a volume on provincial France by M. F. K. Fisher, who could do for a rough-hewn Marseillaise fish stew what her *New Yorker* colleague Roger Angell could do for a rainy seventh inning at Yankee Stadium. Moreover, Field was cultured and literate: He was a serious person, and if he chose to treat food as a serious matter, it was not the subject itself but the fact of his attentions to it that rendered it so. It was therefore natural that Field be hired in 1967 by the *New York Review of Books* to write about cookbooks, and to recommend to its readers the work (if not, to his mind, the maddeningly imprecise recipes) of Elizabeth David.

Ironically, it was Craig Claiborne—blessed with much the same gifts and pretensions as Field—who with a review of the series' first volume punctured Field's reputation much as he might effect the collapse of the soufflé pictured on the book's cover. *The Cooking of Provincial France*—with M. F. K. Fisher as author, Julia Child as consultant, Beard protégé John Clancy piloting the test kitchen, and research culled from Elizabeth David and others—was, in Claiborne's words, "the most dubious sample of the regional cooking of France," which ought to prompt readers "to mourn in the name of Georges Auguste Escoffier, Carême, Vatel, and Ali Bab." Claiborne was careful to excuse Fisher's text but excoriated the recipes, many of which he claimed were incorrect and had no place in a book on regional cooking. As for the person responsible for them: "The consulting editor for this work is Michael Field, a former concert pianist who might be excused perhaps on the grounds that he never played in the provinces."

Claiborne was indeed correct that a number of the recipes in *The Cooking of Provincial France* belonged to the classic rather than the regional table, but the real charge he laid against it and Field—that Field was an inexperienced poseur ("a former concert pianist") who didn't really know anything about food—was a canard as old as the schoolmarms of nineteenth-century domestic science. In a profession—if it could be called that—without credentials or official standards, such an accusation was unanswerable and was in any case as much an assertion of its maker's own expertise as an assessment of its target's deficiencies. Claiborne did indeed know his French cooking and had the unscalable battlements of the *Times* from which to proclaim it, and the review was as accurate as it was petty. Among those whose business was food—or rather the possession of recipes and technical information about cooking, for that is what most of its denizens understood by the word *food*—it caused a sensation.

Normally that sensation, which enveloped the February 19, 1968, launch party for Foods of the World at the Four Seasons in a fog of both dreadful and gleeful anticipation, would not have been shared outside the food community. But the party, the Claiborne-Field melee, and the importance ascribed to it by "the food establishment" were reported in all their self-inflated, histrionic detail by Nora Ephron in *New York* magazine. Like the *New York Review of Books*, *New York* was born out of the ashes of the 1963–64 newspaper strike and was perhaps therefore—with some reason—fixated on the media and the personalities who created them. At its heart *New York* was nothing so much as the weekly disgorgement—often by extremely talented writers—of the self-referential life-style and professional fantasies of its editors, who as with-it, affluent Manhattanites represented the consumer avant-garde at its most style and trend obsessed. *New York* dealt not in presidents and popes but in the fortunes of local television anchorpeople, ad executives, fashion models, chic retailers, and, of course, magazine, book, and newspaper editors and writers. It was, in its effect on the magazine industry, perhaps the most influential magazine of the sixties and seventies, the practical fulfillment both of Marshall McLuhan's assertion that the medium is the message and of the ultimate promise of American consumerism: that style is substance. Traditional notions of journalism went by the wayside: In a world where style was substance, gossip was news.

That obviously included food, whose status in the media *New York* both followed and promoted in pieces like Ephron's. But as a life-style guide, *New York* was also careful to keep the consumer apprised of what he or she needed to know either as streetwise consumer or cultured aesthete. Thus the magazine ran two dining columns. One, "The Underground Gourmet," purported to offer access to places that offered the irresistible virtues of being cheap, unknown, and hip. The other, "The Insatiable Critic," approached restaurant dining as a variety of sensual experience in which the critic was not so much served as serviced by the staff and chef, whose imagination, fervor, and staying power were gauged and rated in a manner familiar to denizens of East Side singles bars. To a public devouring copies of *Sex and the Single Girl*, *Everything You Always Wanted to Know About Sex (But Were Afraid to Ask)*, *The Joy of Sex*, and *The Sensuous Woman*, the confluence of appetites was clear. The column's author, Gael Greene, was perhaps the most distinctive voice to arise in food writing during the sixties and seventies: at once effusive and dissolute, a Henry Miller of dining who'd seen it all and had it twice already on any given day but couldn't resist one more fling.

In every respect, then, the self-regarding sensibility manifested so brilliantly in *New York* was a perfect match for the furious narcissism of the Manhattan food scene, whose internecine feuds and pseudocrises seemed increasingly to be played out from the stock repertoire of gay camp culture: set pieces of bitchery, betrayal, and revenge dramatized by drag clichés ranging from Callas-like opera divas to Bette Davis's Margo Channing. The Foods of the World furor escalated with an attack by Field in *McCall's* on Claiborne's favorite New York restaurants; Claiborne grew ever-more huffy about the matter; and Beard—apparently feeling left out and convinced that Claiborne had not in any case paid him the attention that was his due during the last few years—unilaterally decided that his friendship with Claiborne had cooled and threw in his lot with the Fieldite camp. But Claiborne trumped the lot of them by announcing that he, in fact, would like to join Pierre Franey—former chef at Le Pavillon and Claiborne's frequent if unacknowledged collaborator—to do a volume for Foods of the World on classic French cuisine. Time-Life had no choice but to agree, although Claiborne was saddled not only with Field but Beard as consulting editors. After its completion Claiborne effectively disowned the book, even deleting it from the bibliography of his work contained in his memoirs. As a veteran and slightly befuddled Time-Life staffer involved in the project later confessed, "It was as high strung a group of people as I'd ever met—and that includes the fashion industry too."

It was an atmosphere not confined to Manhattan: In the autumn Elizabeth David wrote James and in the course of her letter asked him to ascertain whether a New York visit she planned to make later that year would coincide with the appearance there of her nemesis Robert Carrier. If so, she wasn't coming. Nor would *The Cooking of Provincial France* affair go away: For the French edition of the book, Time-Life retained Robert Courtine, a French food writer with a reputation for irascibility, to provide notes and commentary. No one in New York bothered to review Courtine's copy, and when the volume appeared in April 1969, his emendations to the original recipes were found to be rather more outspoken than anyone at Time-Life's Sixth Avenue headquarters might have bargained for. To the book's suggestion that quiche be followed by a cold dish, Courtine queried, "Why the hell should it?" commenting on another recipe, "That's a lot of work for a skimpy result. It's a typical dish of the sort that's supposed to surprise and charm a foreign woman, but it is fake grand cuisine and as antigastronomic as can be."

Claiborne and the *Times* gave the incident gleeful play ("Time-Life Cookbook: It's Self Roasting" was the headline), with a story filed from Paris by correspondent John L. Hess. True to the unalterable laws of food journalism, Hess, who briefly succeeded Claiborne as *Times* restaurant critic, would a few years later flay Claiborne in print as one of the architects of what he and his wife Karen termed "the gourmet plague," themselves manifesting one of its least attractive tendencies in the biliousness of their attack. As Beard's friend (and daily telephone interlocutor) food writer Nika Hazelton had told Nora Ephron, "It's a world of self-generating hysteria."

At the end of 1968, James left—or perhaps fled—for France and Christmas and New Year with Paul and Julia Child in Plascassier. Although it was cold and snowy, Beard managed walks around the back of the house and down the hill until he was temporarily immobilized by a fall. He lunched on New Year's Eve with the Childs at the three-star L'Oasis at La Napoule ("a pretty poor example of $50 worth of restaurant," James wrote in his notebook), returned to the Childs, talked to Michael Field, and brought in the New Year of 1969 with foie gras with truffle sauce, fillet of beef, salad, and an apple tart prepared by him and Child. "All superb!!!" James wrote. He was cooking magnificently, enjoying Julia's company, and was as happy as he had been in some time. He rounded out January with a tour of that winter's opera productions in London and on the Continent.

Back in New York, Foods of the World had been expanded from its original eight volumes to nearly thirty. Through Field, James had always been involved in the series, having staged cooking classes for the Time-Life production team and acted as a general adviser. He was also signed as a consulting editor, not only for Claiborne's classic French volume, but also for one on wines and spirits in collaboration with Sam Aaron, and for *American Cooking*. The latter was a general treatment of American food that was, with Beard's enthusiastic endorsement and participation, followed by seven further volumes on specific regions, for which James was consulting editor. The money was good—in the neighborhood of one thousand dollars a month for suggesting recipes and talking about the things he loved to talk about—and he was able to ensure that there would be a Northwest volume. By the book's definition the Northwest included much of the upper Midwest and Canada and culminated in Alaska—a view that made considerable gastronomical and sociohistorical sense—but James was able to counsel an approach heavily oriented toward Oregon, the sea, and the small farmers and suppliers he loved.

He was also influential in securing José Wilson, his former editor at *House & Garden,* a job as author of the Midatlantic volume of the series. Over the past two years, Wilson had gradually taken over the post of Beard's amanuensis/ghostwriter from Isabel Callvert, whose health was rapidly failing. Beard had returned that January to the pages of *Gourmet,* whose editor, Jane Montant, had at long last secured consent for Beard's readmission to the fold from Earle MacAusland, the magazine's aging and increasingly dotty founder. It was not clear whether MacAusland had accepted Beard's rehabilitation, forgotten (like everyone else) what he and James were supposed to be feuding about, or simply acceded to the wishes of Montant, whose stellar good breeding even he found largely irresistible.

In any case James had put José (whose name, despite its perverse orthography, was pronounced "Josie") to work on the *Gourmet* columns, a commission he relished both as an opportunity to serve crow to MacAusland and to try an approach to food writing that incorporated some of what he did in his cooking classes. Titled "Cooking with James Beard," the new series was an attempt to bypass the traditional ad hoc and piecemeal recipe writing of the service magazines and food pages in favor of teaching the fundamental principles of cooking through a series of written lessons that began with "Boiling and Poaching" and continued for the next three years. Although in some sense every cookbook since that of the Boston Cooking School had paid lip service to this approach, it was *Mastering the Art of French Cooking* that had given it genuine expression. Julia Child had come to cookery writing not as a journalist or home economist but as a cooking teacher, and the highly structured, pedagogical style of book she and her editor, Judith Jones, created had quickly become both widely influential and widely imitated. By the end of the sixties, the cooking course had joined the blockbuster compendium, the single-subject guide, the foreign cuisine Baedeker, and the celebrity selection of personal favorites as one of the staples of food writing and publishing.

In contrast to Isabel Callvert, José completed the *Gourmet* columns in fits and starts, and for the first time in his career since the early fifties, Beard had to worry about whether his deadlines would be met. But despite José's unsteady performance, which pitched and yawed on the turbulent seas of her drinking and bouts of depression, in 1969 James gave her further work in the form of a revision of *How to Eat Better for Less Money,* due for publication the following year. Although Wilson could be difficult and unreliable, when she was good, she was very good indeed. Moreover James liked her, and their personalities were a compelling if sometimes awkward fit.

With Helen Brown's death, Helen McCully had become perhaps James's closest confidante. Always James's adoring guardian angel, she was now ensconced as food editor at *House Beautiful* and producing cookbooks with reassuring titles like *No One Ever Tells You These Things* and *Cooking with Helen McCully Beside You* that seemed to embody her comforting, maternal character. It was a role she also played, often thanklessly but also perhaps often unasked, in James's life: the Mary Beard of Gearhart cookouts and birthday picnics at the Oaks in Portland, whose culinary bounties reflected a kind and nurturing soul. In contrast José Wilson—who, like Mary, never lost her native English accent—seemed for James to manifest Mary Beard's other, outlaw side: The sharp-tongued, profane social and artistic sophisticate whose affections were volatile, random, and inconstant. She was most at home in the company of gay men and gossip, in a discourse of mockery, sentiment, and schadenfreude that might accommodate both bitterness and hilarity.

Wilson and Beard were therefore not only collaborators in work but in each other's miseries, sharing the quotidian indignities of the food scene, the interminable and draining chores of writing and editing, and the hell of other people and of their own pasts. As with Gino, while James might complain about Wilson's dependency and weaknesses, he also cultivated them, and by decade's end Wilson was part of the household entourage on Tenth Street: Clay Triplette, the beaming, soothing houseman; Ruth Norman, the faithful keeper and doormat of the James Beard Cooking School; Betty Ward, the secretary and bookkeeper who increasingly functioned as Beard's financial manager and promoter; and Gino P. Cofacci, the cleft-jawed companion and loose end.

Although James found each of them indispensable to his life and appreciated their labors in his behalf, he also felt increasingly drained by his responsibilities to them, which ran the gamut from paymaster to personal counselor and seemed to be without end. As for Gino, his too-often moping, idle presence was a kind of absence to which real absence often seemed preferable. James therefore removed himself once again to the West Coast and Oregon for the month of April, returning at the end of the month to put Gino on a plane to Europe and to undergo a tax audit, a dread-making ordeal that together with jury duty was visited on him every three or four years as though by some capricious design of the fates. He arranged a lunch with Judith Jones, whose editorial gifts looked increasingly attractive as he found himself more and more hopelessly mired in the seemingly unfinishable *James Beard's American Cookery*.

In all likelihood he would suggest meeting at the Four Seasons, an almost daily lunch venue for whose new managers, Paul Kovi and Tom Margittai, James felt a fatherly affection. Under their stewardship the Four Seasons had furthered the excellence of its kitchen while its Grill Room became New York's preeminent site for midday meals at which editors and publishers romanced, cajoled, or made amends to their writers—a custom that would be taken up by the city's business and political elite and enshrine the restaurant as the home of what became known as the "power lunch." James's favorite restaurant for dinner, the Coach House, seemed on the surface to be an upper-middle-class Westchester dinner house that had made a wrong turn on the Thruway and landed in Greenwich Village, serving high-class WASP nostalgia food like crab cakes, black bean soup, lamb chops, and pecan pie in a room of brass chandeliers and wood paneling under the management of a Greek perfectionist named Leon Lianides. But the Coach House's affinities were in fact less with Scarsdale than Paris's L'Ami Louis, which sold extraordinary renditions of relatively banal dishes to a sophisticated crowd willing to pay good money to experience something simple done superbly. Perhaps even more than the Four Seasons, the Coach House embodied Beard's personal food ethic: a mix of forthright—if rather worldly and upper crust—Americanism and good, honest grub with an upstairs "Siberia" to which the ugly, the unknown, and the dull might be relegated.

James's dining experiences were, however, by no means typical of the nation's as a whole during the 1960. Places such as the Four Seasons and the Coach House were striking exceptions to a rule epitomized by the flocked wallpaper, hyperpriapic pepper mills, and wall sconces of the Continental restaurant then in its heyday. There, as in much of the gourmet cooking undertaken in the nation's homes, things seemed to taste better and more interesting not necessarily because cooking methods or materials had improved, but because of the more lavish use of butter, cream, eggs, cheese, and chocolate—in short, of fat. Child, Claiborne, Beard, and the rest had indeed opened the door to a world of aesthetically compelling and soul-satisfying cooking, but they had also and perhaps unwittingly unlocked a candy store of emulsified sauces, mousses, and puff pastry in which richness could be equated with goodness. It was a tendency favored both by the low-carbohydrate regimen promoted by the sixties dieting experts—whose emphasis on protein consumption often obscured the role of dietary fat in weight gain—and by agriculture and the food industry, whose ever-more-bland and uniform products were continuously stripped of whatever distinct and inherent flavor they might possess. Even McDonald's, the most genuinely significant food business of the decade—and one that had thrived by making virtues out of these very demerits—was on the verge of substituting frozen produce for the freshly peeled and sliced potatoes that had produced french fries publicly lauded by Julia Child.

But if food itself at the end of the sixties was in many respects no better, and in some instances worse, than it had been ten years before, the rise in food consciousness was both obvious and newsworthy, the culmination of a movement with enough historical definition to bear chronicling. Sometime during 1969 James himself was moved to take up a pad of paper he had bought in France and draft a list of the leading figures in American food and his assessment of them. The effort seems to have been prompted by *American Cookery*, although the result was surely not intended for general circulation. James's hand volleyed across page after page, marshaling "mix gals," "The PR Girls," the sainted mothers of domestic science, and

his own contemporaries into platoons and battalions in the bloody
crusades of gastronomy:

Helen McCully—[brought] elegance to the women's magazines . . . ;
Myra Waldo—the whirlwind, independence, push, bitchery and
guts; Craig Claiborne—born to be . . . ; Cecily Brownstone—the
researcher and wit; Poppy Cannon—the commercialist (Poppy's
putting everything into a can!!); Julia Child—the lift to great influences; Michael Field—the battlefield; Peg Bracken—the enemy
camp; Paula Peck—the revolutionary; M. F. K. Fisher—gastronomic
writer, humor, sensuality; Sheila Hibben—the intellectual's darling
and a real battleground; Jane Nickerson—another intellectual with
an open mind—*New York Times Cookbook;* Dione Lucas & Le
Cordon Bleu—the battle rages . . . the real establishment is born/TV;
Jeanne Owen—Bitchery incarnate—the beginning of the avalanche:
[Woman's magazine writer] Mary Frost Mabon—Bitcherie; Clementine Paddleford—Purple prose over food; [*Ladies Home Journal* edi-
tor] Ann Bachelder—the beginning of the precious school. The
tyrant!! Bitch—Drunk! But don't let down the Journal!!

According to James's notes, this combative atmosphere had its origins in the previous century with Mrs. Rorer ("Probably the first
commercial gal") and Mrs. Lincoln, the founder of the Boston Cooking School, who in an escalating tide of "bitchery" found herself
overshadowed and finally eclipsed by Fannie Farmer, herself in
James's estimation the target and origin of "Much Bitchery." In a
case of the sins of the fathers—or rather mothers—being visited on
the children, "the Farmer-Rorer-Lincoln Battle" gestated "the general battlefield of Jeanne Owen including JAB, Dione, Sheila . . .
everyone," followed by "the general melee": "*Gourmet,* and its
rather definite avoidance of really good food—the sentimental side
of Earle MacAusland—never have editors who know food! Rhetoric
after a fashion [but] food, no!!"

James's history of his own profession was a curious blend of
bemusement and rage, of genuine appreciation and concern for the
individuals involved offset by an ironic and sometimes camp detachment. But if the conflicts among the individuals mentioned were real
enough, the larger pattern of nearly one hundred years of war that
James saw overlying them may have been more a self-aggrandizing
dramatization than a fact recognizable to the participants. Beard

craved both legitimacy for his field of work and the theatricalization of daily life, inherent in gossip and intrigue: To paint the history of American gastronomy in such grand and tragic terms was to invest it with significance and pathos, worthy of attention and perhaps even tears.

That July, on a night that bristled with crickets and humidity from Provincetown and Chillingsworth on the Cape southward to Greenwich Village, men walked on the midsummer moon. Four weeks before, on June 28, a few blocks from James's house at a gay bar called the Stonewall Inn, other men fought off a police raid, beginning a movement that in social terms was every bit as crucial as that first step of Neil Armstrong. Gay men, together with women, now publicly repudiated their traditional status in American life, and whether or not it wished to do so, the food community—constituted mostly from those two groups—would necessarily and irrevocably change.

It was not that it, or its members, would now be taken more seriously. Indeed, the media then focusing attention on food were as disposed to satire as to high seriousness, as they always had been. The apparent triviality of high-style cookery and fastidious gourmetism in a world beset by hunger was too easy a target, and—when the spats and feuds of James's cohorts were set against the insoluble tragedy of Vietnam—a deserving one. If cooking with Julia, Michael, Craig, and Jim was all the rage in 1966, three years later it was not only old news but a bit overdone. It was hardly any wonder that in November a piece in the *New York Times Book Review* would expose the close ties among food writers, publishers, and food and cooking-equipment manufacturers as well as the cynicism and low estimate of the public's intelligence that underlay the publication of most cookbooks. Given their generally shabby quality, the current proliferation of cookbooks—with twice as many published in 1968 than the year before—was pointless and undesirable.

For the most part, however, the criticism the food community attracted consisted not of open condemnation but simple mockery, treatment with which it was not unacquainted. Much of the positive attention food and cooking had attracted during the sixties was in fact the product of their leading proponents' ability to show that one could take food seriously without necessarily taking oneself seriously, an achievement that belonged in particular to Julia Child, who might be droll and self-effacing but never foolish and silly.

At the decade's end, however, Child found herself sharing the realm of television cooking with someone who was more than willing to be both. Graham Kerr, "the Galloping Gourmet," was a thirty-five-year-old English charmer who had learned to cook in Europe under the mentorship of International Wine & Food Society founder André Simon and emigrated to New Zealand and Australia. There he created a studio-audience show featuring sometimes dubious cooking instructions underscored by an incessant barrage of suggestive, nudge-and-wink witticisms, a downmarket oleomargarine comprising unequal parts of "the French Chef" and the culinary libertinism of Gael Greene. Kerr's manic energy seemed forever to be verging on madness and chaos—indeed, it was rumored whole segments had to be cut when his boundless vulgarity attained warp speed. As with Child's audience, his fans, drawn largely from what President Nixon had dubbed "the silent majority," tuned in just to see what he might do or get away with today.

Kerr's tastelessness and anarchism were anathema to the food community, not just because he was an interloper from Australia who went a little too far (and who, of course, "didn't really know anything about food") but in part because he was subversive, even if only by accident; a prankster who explicitly linked food and sexuality and tweaked the nose of what had recently come to be termed "the food establishment" in front of their inferiors among the masses. In show after show Kerr seemed to treat food and cooking as irredeemably frivolous. But even if he unintentionally threatened a status quo that could have benefited from some frank self-examination, Kerr was more an iconoclast than a reformer. He was interested in exposing and mocking the pretensions of the food establishment but offered little in their place except laughs.

Moreover, with sponsorship by food giants like Hunt-Wesson, he was hardly in a position to deplore what was really wrong with food in the United States: the steady erosion of flavor, diversity, distinctiveness, and quality at the hands of large-scale agriculture, food packers, distributors, and retailers. James and the food establishment might find Kerr silly beyond belief, but they could hardly claim to be grappling with more pressing concerns. Pointing out the public discussion of pesticides and food packaging and labeling fostered by consumer and pressure groups, Mimi Sheraton had wondered aloud to Ephron: "To me it's interesting that not one of these stories began with a food writer. Where are they, these food writers? They're off wondering about the boeuf en daube and whether the quiche was authentic." Ironically it was Kerr, alone among the major food celebrities of the sixties, who fifteen years later would fully take up the issues of health and diet, world hunger, and the environmental costs of industrial farming.

By 1969 the average American had a vastly enlarged awareness of food compared to what he or she was likely to have possessed at the beginning of the decade. Within that mental larder were contained the direct or indirect influences of James and the food establishment, of black sheep like Peg Bracken and Graham Kerr, and of an even larger store of McDonald's hamburgers, Tang, Cool Whip, sangria, salad bars, and bacon bits. The brave new world of popular gastronomy dreamed of by Finck, Mencken, and their successors, in which a large segment of the population had some appreciation of and interest in what it ate, seemed aborning. It was a world James had had more than a hand in fashioning, and it might have suited many people of his age and position to recline on the litter of elder statesmanship and genially wave his pinkie to appreciative crowds.

In fact, it was a role many were already placing him in even as his magnum opus, *American Cookery*, sputtered and simmered on a back burner. James had not published a book of any significance for almost six years, and he feared both the paralysis that seemed to afflict his work on the book and the sense of his growing irrelevance to the materials and forces that seemed to be spinning closer and closer together, on the verge of forming a new culinary universe. He worried not only that he would be left out but that he might fail to grasp what was taking place—that his aching, thrombotic legs could not carry him into the new age. He wrote glumly in his datebook of two-hundred-dollar257

magazine fees and in November recorded the elemental observation: "I'm depressed." He left New York like a refugee for Christmas in Europe, spending the last days of the decade in London with Elizabeth David and Henry and Bettina McNulty.

TEN

1970 – 1974

James passed the first blustery days of 1970 threading his way through the intricacies of London's food community: lunching with David, dining with Carrier, and discerning with his instinctual grasp of such matters where food writer and restaurateur Margaret Costa and wine experts Hugh Johnson and Gerald Asher fit into the scheme of things. Compared to New York, London was a cozily small if competitive place pervaded by a sense that there was far too little in the way of good ideas or money to go around: David would later caution James, "I think I would like to have an ice cream shop, but please don't tell anybody or Robert Carrier will be following me round so that he can settle next door."

By contrast New York had a scope and self-importance that nurtured a heady sense of possibility, allowing Claiborne to close out the sixties with a ringing proclamation: "In almost every respect where food is concerned, the past decade was by far the most impressive since the one that produced the Boston tea party." He backed this assessment by reference to René Verdon's tenure in the White House kitchen; the publication of *Mastering the Art of French Cooking* and the broadcasting of "The French Chef"; and the proliferation of both ethnic and grandluxe French restaurants in New York, starting with La Caravelle in 1960 and continuing with Lutèce a year later, La Grenouille in 1963, and Le Cygne in 1969. Heaping praise on Child and mourning the death of Le Pavillon's Henri Soulé in 1966, Claiborne nowhere mentioned Beard, an omission that James might chalk up to spite but that was probably more motivated by Claiborne's unflagging Francophilia: In a culinary world in which French cooking continued to be the gold standard, being universally acclaimed as "the dean of American cooking" was akin to a consolation prize.

But if James was perceived as being neither at the cutting edge nor the most influential person in the food community, his commercial stature was unarguable. Profiled in *Business Week* as "the man who wears the no. 1 apron," Beard had now launched a weekly newspaper column featured in sixty cities, was a regular guest on "The Mike Douglas Show," and had three books under contract. The column netted him about two thousand dollars a month, as did his work for Time-Life and Restaurant Associates, and he could command five thousand dollars for a short book of recipes for Booth Fisheries and twenty thousand dollars for an endorsement of non-stick cookware. With steady earnings from book royalties and the cooking school, Beard's annual income approached six figures; factoring in the cash value of free airline tickets, hotel rooms, meals, and products, it might be half as much again.

James returned home in the third week of January for winter classes, sessions with John Clancy at the Time-Life test kitchen, and work on his newspaper columns, which he dictated on tape and turned over to José Wilson for transcription and editing. The columns were by no means either literary or gastronomic art, most weeks relying on a stock formula in which a subject was introduced by a question ("Has it ever occurred to you how many different members of the cabbage family we eat?"); expounded on over a few paragraphs of history, lore, or personal reminiscence; and closed with a recipe. Despite such apparent limitations, the column was effective not only commercially—eventually reaching more than one hundred papers—but as a force for creativity and novelty amid the apron, hairnet, and tuna casserole ambience that still prevailed on most newspaper food pages: Beard's millions of newspaper readers—unlikely to be avid followers of Child, Claiborne, or David—were warned off winter supermarket tomatoes, encouraged to rediscover traditional ingredients like hominy, and introduced to bold flavors like that of aioli, the garlicky mayonnaise of Provence.

Aioli also figured in the revision of *How to Eat Better for Less Money*, which José had prepared for publication that summer by Simon & Schuster. The new edition was a considerable expansion of the original, deleting some of the more outré dishes like lamb's head in favor of Caesar Salad, a covey of meat loaf recipes, and new sections devoted to fish, salads, and pasta. Although the book lacked the daring, rough-and-ready qualities of the 1954 model, the revision was more comprehensive and better organized. Despite that Beard was disappointed in it and in José. The final work on *James Beard's American Cookery*, which seemed at last to be reaching an end that year, was entrusted not to her but to John Ferrone, who had so impressed James with his work on *Delights and Prejudices*.

In the six years since the book's publication, James had eaten lunch after lunch with its publisher, Pat Knopf of Atheneum, hoping to reach an agreement for another book. In 1970 Knopf at last contracted, not for another quasiliterary work, but for a menu handbook for overseas tourists. *How to Eat (and Drink) Your Way Through a French (and Italian) Menu*—whose utilitarian title and coy parentheses were doubtless inspired by the bestselling *Everything You Always Wanted to Know about Sex (But Were Afraid to Ask)*—would also serve to bring Gino into the growing family of Beard's collaborators: As coauthor Gino could become James's professional partner and make a genuine contribution to the book through his knowledge of Italian culture and language, attain some measure of purpose in life, and be conveniently dispatched overseas on lengthy research trips.

How to Eat (and Drink) Your Way Through a French (and Italian) Menu was little more than a gazetteer of French and Italian food terms with advice on tipping and the like. The timing of its publication was, however, remarkably prescient. Multitudes of Americans crossed the Atlantic during the 1970s on discount fares and charter flights that made the experience of European food available not just to *Gourmet's* audience of surgeons and executive wives, but to middle-income families and college students. Beard still had a knack for catching the tides of public taste and for producing work that either remained fresh or could be successfully revised or reused: The twenty-year-old *Fireside*, for example, was still in print, and a new paperback edition of *Hors d'Oeuvres and Canapés,* first published thirty years before, sold more than forty thousand copies in six months. But other titles sold under his name did less good to Beard's reputation: Throughout the 1970s, 1980s, and even after his death, legally and illegally recycled paperback originals and promotional recipe booklets produced by him in the 1950s and 1960s created a zombie counterworld of second-tier Beard titles and bootleg editions.

In truth, however, just as there was a separate and different James Beard for each of his friends, so there was a James Beard for each level and sphere of the food business: for corporate clients like Green Giant, Du Pont, General Electric, and Corning; for middle-class consumers who read his newspaper column and might pick up a Dell Purse Book collection of recipes at the supermarket checkout; and for the more affluent suburbanites who purchased the bulk of his books and followed his articles in *Gourmet* and *House & Garden*. The most select group—his admirers and fellow culinary professionals—took his classes, awaited the ever-forthcoming *James Beard's American Cookery,* and received his most thoughtful and considered counsel.

Of all the people with whom Beard worked as a consultant, perhaps none brought out the best in him as easily or thoroughly as Joe Baum. With Baum and RA, James was paid for sheer creativity—for simply tasting and talking without the drudgery of writing—and for refining the ideas he and Baum synthesized together down to the pure culinary gold of a result like the Four Seasons. It was, of course, too good to continue indefinitely: In the spring of 1970 Restaurant Associates, its properties losing money and its once ridiculously overvalued stock decimated, began to collapse. In particular Joe Baum's $75,000 salary, titanic expense accounts, and Park Avenue apartment suddenly looked not like the necessary appurtenances of genius but like overindulgence. Baum was excised, costs were cut, and numerous operations—eventually including the Four Seasons—were sold off or allowed to decline. James stayed on as consultant with Baum's apparent blessing, and Baum himself evened the score against the RA executives who had deposed him, winning a $125,000-a-year consulting contract that autumn to create $10 million worth of food facilities at the twin-towered World Trade Center under construction in Lower Manhattan. Like James, Baum had an irresistible itch to marry art and commerce on the grandest, most operatic scale possible, and as *American Cookery* was for James, so the World Trade Center would be for him.

As Baum began to plan the masterwork that would perch atop the tallest building on earth, he was hindered by neither age nor frailty. But at sixty-seven James found himself the possessor of a lively, imaginative, and ambitious mind fighting a rear-guard action against his failing health, a ceaseless shoring-up of his inexorably and irreversibly disintegrating body. He now made monthly visits to a cardiologist who could dispense prescriptions but no positive long-term prognosis unless James undertook to lose at least fifty pounds. In late November 1970 he made his third visit to Europe in six months and checked into the Clinique Médicale et Diététique in Grasse near the Child-Beck compound in the south of France. Although he might have hoped for a more epicurean and sophisticated view of his condition in France, his doctors there were no more comforting: He had high blood pressure; his breathing was abnormally shallow because of his girth; and his abdominal organs were scarcely palpable through the batting of his gut's adipose tissue. He weighed a fraction under 304 pounds, his prostate was restive, and his legs were a shambles of varicose veins and impending ulcers.

Nor could the doctors at Grasse in all honesty suggest that he go on a cure at their clinic for a few weeks, lose some weight, and thereby recover his health. He could indeed lose some portion of the minimum of fifty pounds they advised, but the effort was pointless without a continuing and permanent change in James's dietary habits—in this case, a slow and steady reduction based on a two-thousand-calorie-per-day regime, a quantity of food about one-half of what he was accustomed to. The doctors were aware of the magnitude of what they proposed and advised their counterparts in New York that only through a sense of winning a "moral victory" over his obesity and the maladies it visited on him could James hope to save himself from the consequences of his appetites. To his medical advisers, it might seem a clear if difficult choice between death and life—between eating and dieting—but to James it may have seemed more a choice between two variations on death; between death by satiation or death by craving and hunger. He could not convince himself that either had much to recommend it.

Back in New York, James entered the hospital in early January 1971 for six days of rest and observation, which confirmed the severity of his condition but replenished his still-considerable energies. By spring the manuscript of *American Cookery* was complete enough to send to Little Brown and with that obligation removed, he plunged into classes, column writing, commercials for Spice Islands and Hecker's Flour, and a syndicated weekly radio show called "James Beard's Dollars and Sense Cookery." He wrote book blurbs and references and made personal appearances on behalf of a coupon magazine called *Homemaking with a Flair* and at the convention of the American Bar Association; at food and restaurant shows in Miami and San Francisco; at women's clubs in Ohio and upstate New York; and at fund-raising dinners in Iowa. He judged newspaper cooking contests, was courted for a possible contribution by *Playboy* magazine, and evaluated the food served aloft by American Airlines, with which he was forming a relationship as a consultant and columnist for their inflight magazine.

Other work—for example, revising the menus for RA's Restaurant America at Kennedy Airport and his continuing relationship with Time-Life's nearly completed Foods of the World series—called on Beard's expertise, but increasingly it was his celebrity that was in demand. The use others now had for James transcended anything he might know, do, or say; he was not so much a force as a monument, a venerable and familiar object next to which people might pose for photographs. If some in the food community considered Beard a little passé—a little too enmeshed with commercial interests and rather unfashionably and parochially American—Beard feigned unconcern and basked in his fame, of which he never tired. He kept his phone number listed, and during his still-frequent-if-now-often-painful walks, he lapped up the glances and stares, the whispers of recognition, the autograph hunters, advice seekers, and stammering adulators. He knew, of course, that the admiration and attention of strangers was simply the product of his work and notoriety, but on the street, with his students, and at personal appearances, it felt like a gift freely and unconditionally given. Provided one was willing to work at it, it was something one could count on, and by simply opening the front door, one need never be alone.

But even as he harvested his fame and the benefits that came with it, he tended long-standing friendships, returning to Portland for Mary Hamblet's birthday and holding dinner parties for Helen McCully, the Grubers from Detroit, and other old friends. But some friendships withered: Ruth Norman and Cheryl Crawford, constants in his life since the 1940s, avoided him after reports reached them of gossip in which James had disparaged Cheryl's producing talent. Norman was embittered by her displacement from the cooking school, but Crawford eventually sought a reconciliation although James remained too embarrassed to pursue her several overtures.

There were also new relationships fostered by mutual need and affinity but equally by Beard's celebrity, his awareness of his age, and a post-Stonewall willingness to be more open about his sexual desires and identity. By 1971 a gifted and strikingly handsome twenty-six-year-old Peruvian named Felipe Rojas-Lombardi was a full member of the Beard entourage and James's steady companion and assistant at demonstrations and in classes. Bearded, wavy-haired, and endowed with the sunny, angelic looks of a Latin shepherd boy, Rojas-Lombardi was as ambitious and willing as he was beautiful, and he absorbed every instruction that passed from James's lips and shadowed every movement of his hands. For James's part sex was beside the point—and probably out of the question given his various conditions—in so seductive a relationship: They blossomed for each other, Felipe absorbing the accumulated wisdom of his mentor and James losing twenty pounds, smartening up his wardrobe, and giving up liquor at his protégé's behest. By spring Felipe had taken over from José at the James Beard Cooking School, and that summer he and James traveled to Europe accompanied by Felipe's mother, with whom James held animated conversations in French and his creaky-but-operational high school Spanish.

James had planned to return to France in December, where he had booked himself into the clinic at Grasse for a bout of weight reduction. But on October 18, shortly after he returned to New York from a junket to Germany to a new round of cooking classes, a sensation like a weight toppling on his chest overtook him, and he was taken to Doctors Hospital, where he was diagnosed with a serious if not massive heart attack. He remained there for nearly a month, while his secretary, Betty Ward, fended off queries with the explanation that he was suffering from exhaustion and overwork. During the first week of November, the galley proofs of *American Cookery* arrived from Little Brown and James reviewed them in his hospital bed. Its gestation had taken nearly six years, but he confessed to Elizabeth David that he felt as though the book was still not quite done and that he was not quite ready to let it leave his hands.

His hesitation was understandable: Not only had he self-consciously set out to write a masterwork that would cap his career, but to cover a subject that was both huge in scale and undefined. On publication, *James Beard's American Cookery* weighed in at 877 pages and contained fifteen hundred recipes, although it might have contained five hundred more or five hundred less and have been much the same book. In establishing the scope of his project, James did not ally himself with the melting-pot theory of American cooking that held that the manifold culinary traditions brought together in this country had produced a recognizably American cuisine. But neither did he take up with the multiculturists who maintained that there was no such thing as an American cuisine, but only a coexistence of ethnic and regional traditions in which the Anglo-Germanic style of the Midwest had some national dominance.

For the most part James sidestepped the question: American food was whatever Americans cooked, and that made the inclusion of recipes for omelets and a variation on lobster l'américaine as likely as hominy grits, if somehow less credible. In his introduction Beard argued that American cooking was not a conscious development but an evolutionary one that took place in the nation's small towns and countryside through the sharing and gradual alteration of recipes among housewives. That evolution could best be traced in community cookbooks, and in the codification of the kind of food contained in them, by Eliza Leslie, Mrs. Crowen, Mrs. Rorer, Fannie Farmer, and the other mothers superior of American domestic cookery—a tradition that had been continued in the work of Irma Rombauer, June Platt, and Helen Brown, to whom he had dedicated the book together with these nineteenth-century antecedents.

Under the influence of Helen Brown and Catherine Hindley, James had indeed immersed himself in community cookbooks during the composition of *American Cookery,* running up at least one hundred dollars a month in charges at Eleanor Lowenstein's Corner Bookshop, which specialized in rare and antiquarian culinaria. Beard's dependence on these books—together with extensive borrowings from Bob and Cora Brown's *America Cooks* and Louis de Gouy's *Gold Cook Book,* which Beard inexplicably failed to credit— was in large part the foundation for the nature and breadth of *American Cookery.* Slight in its offerings from the South, the Southwest, and urban ethnic groups, the book focused on the northern two-thirds of the country, from New England to the Midwest to the Northwest, precisely the white Protestant Anglo-Germanic territory of the church and charity-based community cookbooks on which James had relied.

This orientation reflects not so much Beard's provincialism or racism—he was perhaps the most curious, cosmopolitan, and unbig-

254   J A M E S   B E A R D

oted person in his profession—as the limitations of his sources. In any case *American Cookery* proved to be not even an exhaustive or balanced account of middle-class WASP cuisine. While it contained in excess of one hundred pie recipes and a near encyclopedic treatment of pork, the nation's archetypal protein, the concentration of berry, crab, clam, and oyster recipes joined to elegies for the salmon docks of Astoria and the golden age of Willamette and the Hood River Valley produce revealed that this was ultimately a book about Anglo-Oregonian food, a sort of *Web-Foot Cook Book* redux or a recipe supplement to *Delights and Prejudices.* As an American counterpart to *Mastering the Art of French Cooking,* the book was a qualified success, but as *James Beard's American Cookery,* with the emphasis on "James Beard's," it was every bit the magnum opus that James himself was.

By early 1972 Beard seemed well-recovered from his heart attack, and in its wake he found much to feel positive about. The revised edition of *How to Eat Better for Less Money* had done surprisingly well, so well in fact that James instructed John Schaffner to award José a four-thousand-dollar bonus from its mounting royalties. James had negotiated an arrangement with Phillip Weill (of *Homemaking with a Flair*), Shasta Beverages, and Schaffner whereby Shasta bought fifty thousand copies of *Hors d'Oeuvre and Canapés* and advertised them for sale in the coupon magazine at the price of one dollar plus a Shasta bottle cap. Consulting deals were also struck with Silver Floss Sauerkraut, Planter's Peanuts, and Swift & Co., even as he consolidated his relationships with Du Pont and American Airlines. Sometimes his consulting work overlapped with projects closer to his heart: During the time he was checking the galleys for *American Cookery,* Green Giant proposed in a letter that he untangle the following conundrum on their behalf:

Problem: The Green Giant Company has developed several frozen vegetable line concepts. One of these will reflect regional recipes made from a combination of vegetables, sauce and varying degrees of flavoring. This line is called Taste America. To date we have had great difficulty in isolating the appropriate combination of vegetables, sauce and flavoring which is *perceived* by consumers as being authentic to that region.

For the author of *American Cookery*, which had been uncharacteristically impassioned about the disappearance of regional ingredients and traditions, the manipulation of regional foodways into mere consumer "perceptions" might be an anathema, but James took the assignment despite that, hoping—if he thought about it at all—perhaps to be a positive influence within a negative trend.

Other business propositions were much more appealing: Beard made detailed plans for seasonal cooking schools in London and Port Townsend, Washington, the latter to be conducted at the weekend home of his Seattle friends John and Dorothy Conway, who had photographed him and Helen Brown eighteen years before. Cooking for an audience, whether teaching or demonstrating, never palled for Beard, and although he could earn thousands for consulting jobs, he remained willing to fly to Boulder, Odessa, or Dubuque for two to five hundred dollars to appear before clubs, institutions, and vocational schools. Given the demands such appearances made on his time, they were hardly cost-effective even when book sales and publicity were factored in. Moreover, appliances, pots and utensils, ingredients, props like overhead mirrors, and printed recipes had to be arranged for, and the toll on his health was incalculable.

He was also ready to begin work on another book. The attraction of Judith Jones as his new editor was based not only on the status and breeding she and Knopf projected but on the inherent promise that they might create books together that embodied the best aspects of his classes. For her part Jones understood the possibilities of playing on Beard's reputation as the "dean of American cooking." As had been the case with Julia Child, Jones knew how to market the magisterial. At Knopf, Beard was not an anachronism whose interest to the public had been exhausted but the possessor of the same sort of veneer as good eighteenth-century furniture, duck prints, and discreetly monogrammed Oxford cloth button-down shirts. Beard and Jones's first book together, conceived two years before, would be a modestly proportioned volume whose title, *Beard on Bread*, would nonetheless suggest not another name-above-the-title work from the Grub Street of service magazines and women's pages but the pedigreed and impeccable expertise of Roberts on order or Hoyle on cards. Researchers and recipe testers were enlisted, with John Ferrone serving as chief collaborator rather than José, who, despite the success of *How to Eat Better for Less Money,* remained banished to the less crucial work of the newspaper and *Gourmet* columns.

Gino had meanwhile decided to quit architecture for good, having held one too many jobs that ended in tears, whether through his employer's financial demise or his own incompetence and temperamental behavior. Once again James was obliged to find some diversion for him and, having little desire to collaborate with him again on a book, packed him off to Paris and a course at the Cordon Bleu. As Gino flew to Europe, James went west to Oregon to launch *American Cookery*, with demonstrations and signings in Portland and Eugene. Afterward, he drove down to Gearhart with Mary Hamblet for "three beautiful but incredibly cold days for this time of year," where, he wrote Julia Child, there were "fields of daffodils growing wild and more people out at 7 a.m. than you could possibly count digging clams and fishing for crabs. We indulged in wondrous ocean fresh cod, fresh crab, clams, and the delicious little Petite Point oysters." From Portland, they motored down the new interstate at eighty miles per hour along the Columbia, through the once rugged gorge and past ancient Indian salmon grounds now flooded by the backwaters of dams: "I remembered that my own father at age five struggled down this same route with his parents in a covered wagon. It gave me great cause for thought as to where we have been and where we are going."

It was a realm at some physical and temporal remove from Child, who wrote James in painstaking detail of Paris cooking schools and restaurants; their cottony bread, limp pommes soufflés, frozen and thawed pâtés, and service running the gamut from glacial to slapstick. Beard himself left for Europe in May and settled in with the Childs at Plascassier, where he awaited reaction to *American Cookery* like a candidate on election night. Gael Greene, also a guest at the Child-Beck compound, had already lauded the book in New York, and by and large so too did the rest of the media. *American Cookery* also prompted an extraordinary outpouring of praise and affection from readers, ranging from housewives ("an average cook, five children, peanut butter and jelly and all that," as one described herself) to others who were moved by Beard's celebration of the nation's culinary heritage ("I am an old man, and the eloquent testimony of *American Cookery* evoked childhood memories of a time almost forgotten; of bacon sweet and smoked, and Smithfield hams and Pennsylvania scrapple called ponhaus; of cream, heavy cream in shiny tinned farm milk pails that wrinkled in thick, yellow folds)."

One review, however, mattered more than most, that of the *New York Times*. But Craig Claiborne—weary of deadlines, restaurant reviewing, and the *Times*'s refusal to acknowledge the contribution of Pierre Franey to his work—had resigned in May in order to launch a newsletter and enjoy the royalties that surged in from his books. Thus the *Times* review was written not by Claiborne—who even at his least attentive was never an enemy—but by his successor, Raymond Sokolov, a thirty-one-year-old *Times* foreign correspondent with a strong interest in food and a scholarly bent. Sokolov took the stated ambitions of *American Cookery* at face value and found the book "all over the lot" due to an approach "that homogenizes an apparently orderly food heritage for Americans out of the most heterogeneous possible pool of recipes." Despite this flaw—"a desire to delineate a national cuisine in one volume, to show that America has a cooking style of its own"—Sokolov found the book "fundamentally impressive and useful."

Beard was devastated. He wrote Ferrone, "What can he have against me? It still hurts and humiliates me very much and not even the *Life* story can take that sting away." The *Life* story was not a review but a celebratory photo spread and interview larded with admiring comments from Claiborne and Elizabeth David, among others. The concept of objective appraisal was alien to Beard: There was in his mind no difference between liking him and liking what he did. Only personal animosity could explain the public criticism of another's work, a notion instinctive to Beard and regularly reinforced by the incessant logrolling and mutual back scratching of the food community. That ethos was one Beard had, as "dean of American cooking," played a major role in creating and fostering: If, as Julia Child and others liked to say, "In the beginning there was Beard," James created the culinary universe in his own image—a universe in which person and performance, substance and appearance, and love and attention were frequently confused.

That old order was changing, however, primarily as a result of the *Times* and of Craig Claiborne's tenure there, during which food stories were subject for the first time to journalistic standards and ethics, and reviews of restaurants, products, and books were expected to be genuinely objective and evaluative rather than mere extensions of public relations. Sokolov's review was rooted in that tradition and, ironically, in a temperament probably much more interested in and well disposed to American food than that of his predecessor. Still, Beard remained upset enough about what he viewed as an attack on his most important work to contact Sokolov, who, while withdrawing nothing, responded with assurances of his admiration for Beard, explaining that he had written only "in the spirit of a zealous acolyte."

James himself was confronted with the ethical constraints of the new food journalism when the Washington Star Syndicate complained about his penchant for dispensing plugs in his column: As the syndicate's president delicately put the matter to Betty Ward, "He is obviously a kind and generous man and it seems to me that sometimes his compassion and generosity to people and institutions with which he has empathy have a tendency to depreciate the value of the column." The fact that readers often responded favorably— his pieces on the microwave oven and food processors he received gratis from their manufacturers produced torrents of enthusiastic and curious mail—only served to make James feel yet more confused.

Friends, though, were friends, and hosannas and commiserations for *American Cookery* arrived from M. F. K. Fisher, Elizabeth David, and others. But the news from the wider world was not good: Sales turned out to be disappointing—steady but not earthshaking (as they would in fact remain for nearly the next two decades). Commercially *American Cookery* would not, it seemed, be a blockbuster on the scale of *Mastering the Art of French Cooking, The New York Times Cook Book,* or even *The James Beard Cookbook.* James was inclined to blame Little, Brown both for lackluster publicity efforts and a more general lack of faith in and enthusiasm for the book. Whatever ties he felt to his principal publisher of the past twenty years were irrevocably severed, and those he already felt to Judith Jones at Knopf were bolstered.

The more likely explanation for the reception accorded *American Cookery* was that for perhaps the first time James had failed to gauge the public taste of the moment. The best selling cookbook of 1972 was *Better Homes and Gardens Menu Cook Book,* a contender whose sales were unreflective of cookbooks generally since its publisher, Meredith, sold copies not only through traditional outlets but extensively through the mails and at outlets like hardware stores and supermarkets. In fact, the last cookbook not produced by Meredith to make the top ten was from television antipodean Antichrist, *The Graham Kerr Cookbook*, published in 1969. In truth the bestselling food-related titles of the year continued to be diet books. Beyond that there were trends, although it was anyone's guess which one of them might ignite and for how long: 1972 saw a concentration of natural foods and counterculture-based titles, including *The Whole Earth Cook Book*, *The Commune Cookbook*, *The Organic Yenta*, and even *The New York Times Natural Foods Cookbook*. Few of these titles proved to have much staying power, although two, *Diet for a Small Planet* by Frances Moore Lappé and *The Vegetarian Epicure* by Anna Thomas, became classics, the former by virtue of its political significance and the latter because of its intelligent and delicious recipes.

Other fashions were less obvious in 1972, but would become clear in retrospect; in particular that for the rigorously authentic yet personal national or regional book such as Diana Kennedy's *The Cuisines of Mexico* or, the following year, Madhur Jaffrey's *An Invitation to Indian Cooking*, Marcella Hazan's *The Classic Italian Cook Book*, and one-time Beard debutante Paula Wolfert's *Couscous and Other Good Food from Morocco*. Three of the authors had been much aided and promoted by Craig Claiborne, but in stylistic terms their books' common ancestor was the work of Elizabeth David. David herself remained much admired if little read in the United States, and the simpler, regionally based cooking she favored had not garnered much attention here, except perhaps among the self-taught chefs of a ramshackle café called Chez Panisse, started in 1971 in the college town of Berkeley, California.

An approach to French cooking very much like David's did have one influential American advocate, although he lived in France, without a car, on a rocky, viper-infested hilltop some distance from the naval port of Toulon on the Mediterranean coast. Richard Olney was an Iowa-born painter who had moved to France in the early 1950s and had not only learned to cook but become part of France's gastronomic establishment, writing for French food publications and breaking bread with leading chefs and winemakers. His first book, *The French Menu Cookbook* (1970), had instantly gained him recognition as a genuine cook's cook, and Beard had lauded it in print. Olney for his part wrote a rather formal note of appreciation:

> The tight little world of American gastronomic journalism is, as I understand it, highly competitive and newcomers are not always welcomed with open arms. In view of that, I feel that I may, indeed, thank you whole-heartedly for your generosity in expressing publicly those thoughts that others might have jealously guarded for themselves.

Such lush, latinate, but almost classically decorous prose was, in Olney's book, joined to a style of cooking that was at once austere and sensual. Olney knew and respected French cuisine, both *haute* and regional, as well as anyone, and brought to them a painter's regard for order, balance, and proportion as well as an understanding of the creative possibilities of working within, rather than attempting to overturn, a great tradition. Moreover, he applied these principles not just to the preparation of individual dishes but to the construction of menus and the selection of wines to accompany them. The point was not adherence to fusty rules of service and protocol but the orchestration of a meal of Mozartian deftness and profundity, as in an elegant but warming autumn menu of crayfish mousse, ravioli of chicken breasts with fines herbes, roast leg of venison with poivrade sauce, sweet potato purée, endive-and-mâche salad, Pont l'Évêque cheese, and molded coffee custard.

But Olney was no aesthete concerned only with effects and surfaces: Flavor was paramount, and in particular the taste of the ingredients themselves in all their various earthinesses and essences. Olney was not interested in richness or the baroque piling on of flavors as much as in gastronomic quiddities and fundamentals, and his tasting vocabulary favored words like *simple, direct,* and *agrestic.* He was an avid gardener who made his own vinegar, a forager in the hills around his home in Provence, and an assiduous cultivator of artisanal food and wine producers. As a result his was a cooking conceived at an agricultural level and then brought to the table with an artist's concern for integrity, harmony, and nuance. In Olney the tension between style and substance and between techniques and materials—between mastery over versus communion with the earth and its bounty—was resolved.

• • •

These were not concepts easily grasped by the adamantine mind of Gino Cofacci, who arrived at Olney's home after his Cordon Bleu course in Paris. Olney was to offer the first of what would be a legendary series of cooking classes that summer in Avignon, and Beard—whose requests Olney was as yet in no position to refuse—had arranged for Gino to be his assistant. Olney's kind of cooking made little sense to Gino, whose obsessive-compulsive temperament found the linear, canonical approach of the Cordon Bleu much more congenial. Gino in turn drove Olney—much accustomed to the easy, pastoral rhythms of his Provençal aerie—to distraction, clinging to him one minute and sulking the next. To complicate matters, Gino had also determined that he was in love with Olney and attempted to send away all visitors to the hilltop, the only escape from Gino's attentions available to the carless Olney. For the several weeks until Beard arrived to retrieve Gino, Olney often felt like a shipwreck survivor sharing a small piece of wreckage with an infatuated lunatic.

Beard did not savor his reunion with Gino and in fact made clear to him that from now on they would lead increasingly separate lives, although James would provide him with pocket money and they would continue to share the same roof at home. With that Gino left for London, James for New York, and Olney was allowed to return to his garden, his cellar of antique burgundies and sauternes, and work on his next book, to be called *Simple French Food,* which James had helped place with Pat Knopf at Atheneum.

James's own book, *Beard on Bread,* was going forward almost effortlessly, a relief after the agonies of *American Cookery:* Recipes worked on the first try, and testers reported the results as among the best breads they'd ever tasted. A relatively modest book in comparison to some of his previous efforts, *Beard on Bread* was a straightforward collection of favorite recipes introduced by a short course in the general principles of breadmaking. Jones's decision to employ illustrator Karl Stuecklen, whose line drawings had something of the rough-hewn kineticism of a Leonardo sketch, served a practical pedagogical purpose but also contributed a homespun, undaunting elegance to the book. Beard tried to persuade Elizabeth David, who had been at work on a monumental and near-scholarly work on English baking for some time, to write a preface, but she declined. Despite the genuine depth of their friendship, David was kind rather than enthusiastic about Beard's books and was never much impressed by any of them. She begged off, citing a very real depression exacerbated by the recent loss of her business to several backers who had seized control of its operations. James was genuinely concerned and wrote Julia Child in France to urge her to check on David, although the two were not much acquainted. In the end, James dedicated *Beard on Bread* to David, "who loves bread."

That autumn Beard found himself embroiled in the first of a succession of unpleasant business entanglements that would plague him over the remainder of the decade. His summer trip to Europe had been in part a tour of leading hotels conducted in aid of a promotional piece for *Homemaking with a Flair*, and James had been joined en route by its proprietor, Phillip Weil, along with John Ferrone and a photographer. Despite the quite-lucrative contract Weil had given him—thousands in fees plus expenses for little more than the use of his name—by the end of the trip Beard loathed Weil, and became furious when Weil was late in paying him and Ferrone. Angry, hectoring letters were catapulted from Tenth Street to Weil's office in San Francisco: "I certainly will not put up with this kind of treatment. . . . You're a big person, Phillip, until you come to the place where you like to wield your power and at that point you become petty over certain infinitesimal details, such as paying for drinks in Europe and you become unpleasant—certainly not up to your position nor what you would like to be as a person."

Nonetheless, Beard remained under contract to Weil, just as he also signed up that fall to promote iceberg lettuce, a commodity he had publicly scorned as "watery and tasteless" in *The James Beard Cookbook,* among other venues. The careless cynicism of these deals and of his current arrangement with Gino seemed to be reflected in James's increasingly caustic and pessimistic moods. In a year-end letter to Child, Beard, who loathed Richard Nixon with uncharacteristic vehemence, mused on the election results and the state of Vietnam peace negotiations with sour and weary resignation:

Well, every day we read the various papers we become more aware of the fact that we are entering into the great period of American fascism. With the American royal family in command and the great collection of inept assistants being appointed for the next four years and Mr. Kissinger's messages having led to further bombings— lovely, wonderful New Year.

For the first time in some years, Beard spent Christmas at home rather than in Europe. But there were consolations: Judith Jones's enthusiastic reaction to the *Beard on Bread* manuscript; a Christmas Eve dinner of baked ham and brandade of cod with Helen McCully and Cecily Brownstone; and the comforting minutiae of his daily life—additions to the house's profusion of majolica, new suits from Toronto, shirts from Barcelona, and Darjeeling tea and Maldon salt from Fortnum & Mason. He broke the diet he had wrestled with since September, whose tenets he had recorded like a mantra in his datebook: "No spirits/No Snacks/No fats/No Seconds," each phrase furiously underlined.

As the administration James had ranted against began to crumble over the Watergate summer of 1973, so too did it begin to seem that his own life contained closet on closet of heretofore-hidden mischief, duplicity, intrigue, and confidence trickery. James's fame had achieved a kind of critical mass, a point at which there was more work, more attention, more offers, and even conceivably more money than he could absorb, a state of affairs that rendered him at once greedy, generous, and gullible. It was hard to say no to offers of large sums of money for the mere use of his name, face, or signature, and it was harder still to refuse the adulation of others; of people, many of them interesting and attractive, who seemed only to want to be near him, expecting little or nothing in return. Moreover, beyond his celebrity and expertise, Beard's own attractions remained real: He was by instinct highly attentive to the needs of others (at least on a selective basis), and to be the recipient not only of the honey and balm of his charm but of his letters and gifts was for many a kind of bliss worth fighting for.

James was never too busy for his fans, patiently replying to letters that in a week typically ran to one hundred varieties of personal reminiscence or trivia, vapid praise, genuinely useful information or corrections, heartfelt and touching appreciations, and not a few inanities. Not all, such as this letter to the editor of a paper that carried his column, were approving:

So Beard had a great dinner at Maxwell's Plum in New York. Did he go incognito like the rest of the slobs? Not at all. He and the super chef got together first and "planned a handsome meal." What kind of a joker is this? If you knew the maitre d', even at McDon-

ald's, you and he could cook up "a handsome meal" too. Grease his
palm, and you could probably even arrange for enough time to suck
the succulent marrow.

Despite such criticisms, on his entry into the seventieth year of his
life, Beard remained unstoppably curious and, until he made up his
mind otherwise, was disposed to giving most persons and their ideas
and enthusiasms the benefit of the doubt. The previous autumn, for
example, he had received a letter from an American based in
Geneva, named Burton Richard Wolf, with an idea for a line of
cooking tools to be designed and endorsed by the leading chefs of
France.

Beard loved the idea, and promptly drafted a letter to twenty-
seven chefs, from Paul Bocuse to the Troisgros brothers, urging their
involvement. It was the kind of project—international in scale, prestigious, and, with 4 percent of the receipts going to James, lucrative—that Beard loved, and he loved it still more when he at last met
Wolf, a bundle of warmth and energy with a grin like a crescent
moon and the well-oiled sheen of antique leather. James was captivated by Wolf's tales of his grandmother's cookware shop, and by
the cachet of the people and places he knew from years abroad. Yet
to James's mind there was something elusive about Wolf, who
seemed to be representing not one but two companies, Bonnier International Design and Artex S.A., both located in Geneva.

In 1973 the mention of Geneva—one of the stock settings for the
seventies international sex, business, and conspiracy novels of
Jacqueline Susann and Robert Ludlum—evoked a veiled world of
secret bank accounts and gold bullion. According to allegations
made by his wife, Wolf had been associated with one of Geneva's
most notorious denizens, Bernard Cornfeld of Investors Overseas
Services, who had scandalized the world financial community. But as
of 1972, Wolf styled himself a publisher and specialist in art and
technology whose most recent project, similar to the one proposed to
James, was a line of toys designed by famous artists.

In the course of his forays into the world of design and graphics,
Wolf became acquainted with Milton Glaser, the founding art director of *New York* magazine and the creator of perhaps the quintessential graphics look of the sixties and seventies. Glaser had a strong
interest in food, and when Wolf brought him and Beard together at

Alfredo's, Beard's favorite Village trattoria, sparks flew. By February, what had begun as Wolf's modest proposal for a line of knives, whisks, and lemon zesters had metastasized into Beard Glaser Wolf Ltd., incorporated in Delaware with a parent holding company in the Bahamas. In the page on page of contracts, agreements, and addenda Wolf produced for their signatures on February 28, Beard, Glaser, and Wolf were each to be shareholders in and consultants— paid in Swiss francs—to Beard Glaser Wolf, whose purpose was "to become the strongest company in the food business in terms of the amount of experience, talent and reputation it can bring to any single aspect of the industry."

Beard Glaser Wolf would, under Wolf's plan, have five subsidiaries: The Good Cooking School, a New York–based academy of cooking with branches around the country; a media group that would produce books, catalogs, and audiovisual materials; a mail-order business selling the products of the media group; retail shops tied to the New York school and its branches; and a consulting group that would marshal the talents of Beard, Elizabeth David, Joe Baum, John Clancy, restaurateur and consultant George Lang, Jacques Pépin, and others for food-related businesses and industries. It would be, in Wolf's phrase, "a knowledge company." It also seemed at first glance to James like a wonderful idea whose time had come: a gastronomic conglomerate of the best and the brightest, whose prestige and importance would surely mark the culmination of his career in food. It would also apparently earn all concerned considerable money at very little risk.

Glaser quickly designed a logo that perhaps said more about Beard Glaser Wolf than anyone intended: A triangle, each of whose three points was overlaid by an enormous star. As winter turned to spring Beard Glaser Wolf looked more and more like a grandiose and hollow fantasy: As long as Wolf kept talking, the project seemed infinitely feasible, profitable, and fun, but in his absence—or under the scrutiny of persons with some distance from the seductiveness of the fantasy—doubts quickly emerged. For one, why did such an undertaking need to be so complex, with offshore holding companies, a stock issue, and a paper purchase by Beard Glaser Wolf of Wolf's home in Larchmont, which Beard Glaser Wolf then leased back to Wolf? For another, why was the cavalcade of culinary stars being rounded up as teachers and consultants asked to sign such

lengthy, Byzantine, and restrictive contracts? Beard grew more confused and concerned.

Meanwhile, he continued to teach classes, filmed commercials
for Corning electric ranges, and speculated in letters and on the
phone about Raymond Sokolov's future as food editor at the *Times,*
both spreading and escalating rumors of apparent dissatisfaction
with Sokolov among the paper's senior editors. James had also
become embroiled in a house purchase he was beginning to regret
even before he took occupancy. His old Portland friend Agnes
Crowther had located a four-story brick town house on Twelfth
Street that she insisted would be ideal for James, his professional
activities, and for Gino, who could be installed on a separate floor,
in relative isolation from the rest of the house. He felt inclined to
rely on Crowther's judgment in the matter, even though he had privately confessed to friends that he had doubts about her mental balance. But by spring he found himself inextricably locked into the
purchase of 167 West Twelfth Street at a price he was uncomfortable
with and a long list of renovations that could not be put off. Just as
his income and expenditures had verged on equilibrium, he found
himself once again short of money, if—happily—not on opportunities to make it.

In April he took a quick trip to the West Coast for demonstrations and to speak to a group of food editors being flown around the
country on a Kraft-sponsored junket called "the Food Heritage
Tour." Although the program indicated the food industry's awareness of the possibility that the vernacular food traditions celebrated
by James in *American Cookery* might represent a trend, it was not
an easy one to marry with Cheez Whiz and Miracle Whip. When
James caught up with the editors in Washington State for a talk on
the food of the Pacific Northwest, the junketeers had already been
addressed on the seemingly incongruous topic of "Food Additives
and Food Heritage" by a Kraft official.

On the heels of his ad campaign for Corning—which would supply cooktops for the new kitchen on Twelfth Street—he had also
been approached by Jenn-Air ranges for a promotion. He was also
asked by Spice Islands to intervene on their behalf with a large
supermarket chain that the company had been unable to persuade to
stock their products. The potency of James's counsel and plugs was
now such that he could not only cause the supermarket shelves to

empty but determine what they would be stocked with in the first place. As the linchpin to so many people's livelihoods and schemes—from Burton Wolf to Phillip Weil, from whom he secured passage on the SS *France* to Europe that April, together with a fistful of first-class air tickets for his travels for the rest of the year—he was himself a powerful and bestselling commodity.

The antidote to the alternately compelling and revolting commerce of New York was, as ever, Gearhart, and in May 1973 James had found a way to combine life on the beach with teaching. The summer cooking classes originally envisioned for Port Townsend, Washington, would take place instead in the home economics department of Seaside High School, a few miles down the highway from Gearhart, beginning June 18. But James arrived at the end of April, dined his first night in Gearhart on salmon cheeks and boiled potatoes, and settled into six weeks of shopping, socializing with old Oregon friends, and leisurely preparation for the classes.

Into the midst of this idyll of long walks down the damp, gusty beach and simple feasts of crab, clams, and salmon—on the sixth day of which James celebrated his seventieth birthday—came a letter from José and reports of vast ructions back in New York. By May 10 Beard, Mary Hamblet, and Beard's Portland lawyer had digested its contents, which boiled with unsubstantiated accusations against Burton Wolf and his "hypnotic charm, completely amoral of course." In particular Wilson alleged that Beard Glaser Wolf was nothing more than a con game based on using James's name to attract investment, and that Wolf and his "sharks" had more or less admitted as much to her at a meeting in Geneva. Her involvement as editor of a Beard Glaser Wolf book project that would eventually become *The Cooks' Catalogue* was promoted by Wolf only "as the pipeline to you, to see that you do what they want and are kept quiet and unquestioning."

Wolf had called on James's birthday—as had Ned Bradford, Joe Baum, and Felipe (but not Gino)—and Beard's initial reaction to José's letter was to dismiss it as yet another of her periodic neurotic, alcohol-induced distempers. After talking to Wolf again, he wrote, "José is being a bitch," in his datebook and returned to his now-unalterable routine of shopping in Seaside or Astoria, long walks on the beach, and a simple dinner with Portland visitors like Mary Hamblet and decorators Jerry Lamb and Harvey Welch, who had loaned James the beach house he occupied at Gearhart. He chatted on the telephone with Judith Jones, with whom two further books were now planned, and visited Portland for social calls and a television appearance. On June 1 Wolf and Milton Glaser arrived in Gearhart. James's lawyer had cautioned him about Beard Glaser Wolf, wondering what the whole point of it really was, but James was still disinclined to make any formal break with Wolf.

Felipe arrived in mid-June to assist Beard with the class, succeeded by a considerably mellowed José a week later. The Seaside High School home economics teacher, Maryon Greenough, had, together with Portland food writer Carl Gohs, done the groundwork, and the classes immediately clicked with an ineffable rightness: Beard—his legs somewhat restored by walking and weight loss—omnisciently prowled the room, and each day the eighteen students turned up earlier and stayed later, never able to get quite enough of Beard or of one another. Beard himself ended each afternoon in a state of exhaustion and elation: As never before he grew in the role of teacher, as though adding layers of nuance and depth to a part he had played dozens of times before and whose every gesture and inflection he until then thought he knew in every possible aspect. But the students came each day not just to practice cooking, but to see what drollery or prank or shtick he might set loose; and the truth was he hardly knew himself what energies and enthusiasms the nondescript classroom down the road from the onetime Gearhart depot might pull out of him.

The students blossomed, too, as though entire childhoods and adolescences could be acted out and transformed on this playground for grown-ups overseen by the most outsize and avuncular Little League coach of all time: A sad and petulant Oregon housewife who was religiously avoided by her classmates evolved into a genial baking superstar; corporate officers and New York media impresarios rubbed elbows with, and deferred to, housewives from Seattle, small-town newspapermen from down the Columbia and dentists from Astoria; and, in that first year, a middle-aged woman from California fell in love with cooking and with James, shedding her diffidence to reveal a countenance as sunny as sweet corn and vine-ripened tomatoes. There were jokes and silly costumes and food that seemed to beget more food; miracles, in retrospect, no more remarkable than the fact that a place that brought Lewis and Clark to tears in winter and spring could become heaven in summer. But this beach, as James had always known, was magic; it was, as Marion Cunningham, the woman from California, wrote James afterward, "the land of Oz and you are the wizard."

Back home in New York, Beard put José Wilson to work on his next book for Judith Jones, a collection of his newspaper columns to be called *Beard on Food*. As an author Beard seemed to be entering a kind of golden age: Despite its paltry sales *American Cookery* had won the 1973 Tastemaker Award as cookbook of the year, and *Beard on Bread* was received with adulation that autumn, effortlessly moving into additional printings and a sale of more than a quarter million copies. Time-Life explored the idea of a multivolume series to written by him and John Clancy called The Art of Cooking, but test marketing results did not reveal the kind of fervent interest Foods of the World had inspired, and there was some question whether Beard's and Clancy's respective agreements with Beard Glaser Wolf would allow their participation.

Beard remained concerned about Wolf but kept his thoughts to himself and did nothing to discourage his friend Elizabeth David from further involvement with him, even while he looked for ways to either remove Wolf from the corporation or reduce his own role in it to that of paid consultant. In fact it was Wolf's elusiveness that rattled James most, and he wanted to flush him out: "He tries, I think, to evade points very purposely. . . . I would like to get Burton out, frankly, in the open for once and see what comes of it." Moreover, he was increasingly alarmed by the contracts being offered—with his participation as a clear inducement to sign—to potential Beard Glaser Wolf consultants: "The contract they have sent out to people is unbelievable! No one in his right mind would ever sign such a contract."

Beard Glaser Wolf was not, however, without concrete achievements: Two books were under contract, *The Cooks' Catalogue* and *The Great Cooks' Cookbook*, the latter consisting of a chapter each on a specific aspect of cooking written by Beard and ten other authorities who had signed up as the core faculty of the Good Cooking School. As for the school itself, Beard Glaser Wolf had retained an architect and put John Clancy to work outlining specifications for a site and the requisite facilities. It was not, in these respects, an unrealistic fantasy, but James felt trapped in a situation about which he knew too little and over which he had too little control. Having reluctantly saddled himself with the new house on Twelfth Street, and having tasted the calm and simplicity of the cooking school on the beach, James was convinced that what he needed was a more autonomous life, free of the complexities and conflict engendered by entourages and delegations of associates, partners, underlings, and hangers-on. He resented his dependence on others and of others on him, but by reason of his profession, his temperament, and, increasingly, his physical infirmity, it was his necessary lot and kept him free of loneliness.

By the beginning of 1974, Beard had signed a deal with Omaha Steaks International, a mail-order seller of filet mignon and other meats. Betty Ward, who now acted as his agent for projects unrelated to books and magazines, obtained ten thousand dollars per year for the use of Beard's name, photo, and endorsement, and although it was by no means his largest commercial contract, over the next few years it became his most visible one, thanks to the ubiquity of Omaha Steaks advertisements. He seemed genuinely to believe in the quality of the product, and Omaha Steaks could hardly contain its delight in having him aboard.

Passive arrangements such as endorsements came James's way with increasing frequency as his celebrity achieved near—if never total—household-word status. He was, in any case, growing less equipped for real consulting work or even personal appearances. In 1974 his health was as poor as it had ever been, beset not so much by a return of the coronary illness of 1972 as by a succession of minor but debilitating ailments: In March he was devastated by fevers and flu, and at the beginning of May he was admitted to hospital owing to the condition of his feet and legs, which now required not only that he wear support hose and bandages but that he move as much as possible by wheelchair, a miserable confinement for one as attached to long walks and ambles as James.

The propeller of his wheelchair and, more and more, his aide-de-camp was Carl Jerome, a small, bearded young man with deep-set eyes and a fast and facile mind who had begun as Beard's occasional driver and had taken to sitting in on his classes. Jerome's background in food was at best sketchy, but he quickly occupied the place in Beard's demonstrations and in the cooking school once held by Felipe Rojas-Lombardi, to whom he bore more than a passing resemblance. With Beard confined to a wheelchair during the first half of the year, Jerome became Beard's double at the school and at demonstrations, carrying out the actual cooking that James described to the audience. They worked well as a team, developing a line of patter that to James's mind increased the theatrical dimension he had always striven for in his demonstrations. James convinced himself that everyone took to Jerome with same enthusiasm as he did, a point of view Jerome took pains to promote.

Jerome also seemed truly to admire and respect James, was a quick and witty gossip, was an efficient and thorough manager, and, most crucially, made few emotional demands. By contrast there was Gino, now closeted in a third-floor apartment, and José Wilson, who sporadically worked on a book based on the *Gourmet* articles on cooking techniques of a few years before. Depressive by nature and now resentful of the increasing influence others—and especially Carl Jerome—were having on James, she became an increasingly trying and enervating presence, as a concerned Beard wrote Julia Child:

> Dear Jose is in a terrible snit and becomes more and more and more depressed all the time and really turns on the water works for practically no reason whatsoever. All she wants to do is sit. She doesn't want to work, she doesn't want to see people, she's just in a terrible depressed state and I feel very sorry for her. But, there's nothing we can do.

Even with James confined to a wheelchair, the second season of Gearhart classes proved a superb and restorative diversion. More than ever James found himself reminded by the Oregon coast of the gastronomic and personal essentials of life:

> I went shopping today and just the size of the fresh vegetables, the rhubarb with its brilliant red stems and its red and green leaves and the magnificent spinach with huge lovely tender leaves and the first little tender peas of the year and tiny new potatoes and exquisite strawberries—all made me think that maybe we'll have to take [care of] and live close to the land again and profit by what the land can produce.

The classes that began in June exceeded his expectations, with a large number of returning students, including Marion Cunningham, whom he had been corresponding with and had visited in California the previous year. The entire class became caught up in James's passion for food and for the food of this place in particular, but Cunningham understood West Coast cooking as perhaps no one in James's life had since Helen Brown. Although the classes dealt largely with preparations like puff pastry, terrines, soufflés, and the rest of the repertoire of high-level cookery, Marion could also appreciate without condescension what less sophisticated inhabitants of the Oregon coast were cooking, the sort of thing you might find in *The Fishwives of Charleston, Oregon, Cookbook,* a community cookbook for sale that summer not far from Gearhart.

It contained, of course, the kind of hybrid creations for which community cookbooks had always provided a home—Coca-Cola Chocolate Cake, Tuna 'n' Macaroni Stuffed Peppers, Weenie Loaf, and Halibut Salad Bunwiches—as well as various trickle-down renditions of dishes promoted by the food establishment: Crab Meat Rarebit, Tuna Stroganoff, and diverse fondues. It was easy enough to mock these and other malformed offspring of national trends and locally abundant materials—for example, Salmon Tamale Pie, Curried Salmon, and Salmon Baked in Potato Shells—but how many cooks in New York could match the women of Charleston for Deviled Crab, Razor Clam Fritters, a North Coast Bouillabaisse, or a dozen recipes for chanterelles and boletus mushrooms? The contents of such a book spoke both to James's influence and his lack of influence; the distance his life and tastes had put between him and Oregon and the fact that, when all was said and done, he lived nowhere else.

Marion Cunningham grasped that truth, as did another student, John Hudspeth, a son of a timber scion who had dabbled in various food businesses around Portland. Cunningham and Hudspeth constituted the innermost ring of a circle of people based primarily in northern California who became, in contrast to his New York ménage and its intrigues and neuroses, a kind of family to James: Chuck Williams of Williams-Sonoma; Chet Rhodes, a San Francisco public relations man; Loni Kuhn, a friend of Cunningham's and a veteran of the Gearhart classes; and James Nassikas, proprietor of the Stanford Court Hotel in San Francisco, Beard's habitual residence in the Bay Area. They might fawn over him as a New Yorker never would and he, lonely, tired, and never sated where affection and praise were concerned, in turn might exploit that fact, but rarely would he have to explain to any of them what he loved about the Pacific Coast or why. They, and in particular Marion and John Hudspeth, kept the embers of Oregon—all the blessings and consolations of his life—alive and, as Marion did, wrote him and reassured him, letting him know that she tended and kept watch over these things:

> I found Portland dressing for winter last week-end. Trees trailing yellow leaves, maples abundant in red and orange, quiet, wet streets. John always a thoughtful, generous host, funny and intriguing too. We made brioche (ate it warm for breakfast with his mother's peach jam) and pie crust for Thanksgiving.

Over the remainder of the year, James's attraction to Carl Jerome swelled into a consuming and heedless infatuation. That summer James had awaited his arrival in Gearhart with a hungry anticipation he had not felt in perhaps fifteen years, and when Carl left, James scrawled "feel lousy" in his datebook. Carl knew how to please him as James himself knew how to please others: When he returned to New York from a short trip to Europe in August, Carl met him with champagne and caviar, and he brought serenity and order to the prattling, hysterical ship of fools that the house on Twelfth Street often seemed to be. When James went on tour to promote *Beard on Food* and *The Great Cooks' Cookbook* that autumn, he insured that Carl would accompany him on virtually every stop of a twenty-three-city schedule.

The trip kept Beard and Jerome on the road through the better part of August and September. But it was a sweet day indeed to be in Portland on September 20, a Friday that Mayor Neil Goldschmidt had proclaimed to be "James Beard Day." Over the last two years, James had found himself the subject of increasing interest among Portland's establishment: He had been approached, not to say importuned, by the Portland Art Museum, the Oregon Historical Society, Oregon Public Broadcasting, and, most gratifyingly, by Reed College and the latter-day successors to the matrons of Trinity Church, each eager for the manna of his presence along the reaches of the Park Blocks, in their clubs, and in the parlors of their Portland Heights homes. Now what had felt so imprisoning and bitter sixty-five years before on these very banks of the Willamette seemed to blur and merge with the waters, as though washed away downstream to the Columbia, to Astoria, and the salmon-fatted sea.

ELEVEN

1975–1979

By the eve of 1975, James had made himself comfortable in the house on Twelfth Street. With decorating counsel from Jerry Lamb in Portland, the living room walls were painted in Chinese red, and a portrait of James in oils that graced the cover of *Beard on Food* was hung over the fireplace. At the south end of the room, elevated a few feet above the floor, was James's bedroom, or rather an alcove fitted with a bed, a telephone, and a mirrored ceiling. Gino occupied the floor above with his own apartment, whose kitchen was outfitted as a full-fledged professional patisserie. His cakes and pastries were sold with some success to a few of New York's better restaurants, thanks to James's intervention. Although Gino had become a baker and pastry chef of some accomplishment, it did not change the nature of his relationship to James. In the morning youngish men might be seen descending from Gino's quarters, letting themselves out the door without introduction, followed by Gino some time later, who, in the now immemorial custom of the house, took morning tea and toast with James and performed the salving and binding of his legs. For all the putative affection and devotion such routines might signify, James had by now resigned himself to the fact that Gino "can never, ever adjust himself to society. . . . I find his behavior at times loathsome and utterly disgusting."

Carl Jerome occupied the floor above Gino and seemed not only to have largely displaced Gino in James's affections but, at least in the eyes of its longest-serving members, to dominate the entire household—a contention Jerome would have denied had anyone made it to his face. The ground floor, where his duties as James's assistant were for the most part carried out, had become a dining room and a handsome kitchen, fitted with a horseshoe of electric cooktops and a separate scullery and utility area, the walls papered with a massively scaled map of the world. It was designed in neither a conventional cooking and dining layout nor as a professional kitchen, but as a classroom, a testimony to the place that teaching now occupied in Beard's life. Two summers at Gearhart had encouraged him to give more time to classes and to the immediate satisfaction and pleasure he gained from them, as well as to attempt a similar course in San Francisco and an intensive, total-immersion course in New York. Carl Jerome was a crucial element in the expansion of James's teaching program as both his assistant and, by this date, director of the James Beard Cooking School, a title many felt he had invented for his own purposes or at least expropriated from José, albeit with James's tacit approval.

The now-prominent position of teaching among Beard's activities reflected not only his own interests but those of the larger public. Where ten or fifteen years before, Dione Lucas and James had had Manhattan to themselves, there were by the mid-seventies at least a dozen major cooking schools in New York and around the nation, not accounting for professional catering and hotel schools and YWCA and university extension courses. Learning to cook—whether in a class, through television or books, or by audiocassette (a series of which James had recorded the previous year to a mixed critical and commercial reception)—was no longer simply an extension of traditional home economics training, through which gastronomically illiterate newlyweds assimilated enough competence in cooking to keep their husbands from grumbling. The agenda advanced by Claiborne and Child—the importation of French cuisine (followed thereafter by Italian, Chinese, and even Mexican and Moroccan) in all its manifold glories into North America—ultimately demanded not just the appreciation of sophisticated cooking but the provision of methods and tools through which Americans might learn to replicate it in their homes, taking for their model the chef and his restaurant kitchen. In growing numbers Americans aspired to professional training and equipment, extending to the commercial ranges whose use in the home Claiborne and others popularized.

The distinction between the home kitchen and that of the restaurant or hotel commissary had in the past been clear, and indeed the founding sisters of domestic science insisted on the unique nature of the home kitchen not only at a practical but at a moral and ethical level: No upright turn-of-the-century Christian woman, however jealous of its efficiency, would care to imitate the suspect and mere-tricious atmosphere of a commercial eating establishment within her kitchen, a chamber sanctified not only by its laboratorylike hygiene but by its roles as the wellspring of feminine emancipation and the bedrock of the traditional family. But the replacement of the decades-old "four F's"("family, food, fashions, furnishings") of the *New York Times* women's page by a section called "Living" suggested that what were once the domestic arts and sciences had been superseded by the very real and serious business of managing a life-style: of reaching, in a new twist on domestic science, toward professional levels of qual-ity, rigor, and authenticity in design, entertainment, and cooking. Home cooks had been served notice first by *New York* and now by the *Times* that their role model was no longer Fannie Farmer but Henri Soulé and his successors. As in sports, the loftiest goal of culi-nary amateurs was to turn, or at least appear, professional.

As a self-described "Fannieite," James found this development somewhat alien. He had always forcefully corrected anyone who referred to him as a chef and was inclined to believe that a home education in cooking such as he had received was every bit a match for that offered by a Swiss hotel school or the Cordon Bleu. In the forties and fifties, he and people like Helen Brown and Helen McCully had replaced home economics with home entertaining as the focus of domestic cookery, but now the image of the knowledge-able-but-relaxed hobby cook they had helped promulgate was being overtaken by the quasiprofessional weekend restaurateur who took food and wine in near-obsessive deadly earnest. James and his col-leagues had wanted Americans to have fun with cooking but also to take it—and them—seriously. Now it seemed that in the latter aim they had succeeded all too well.

That success was evident not only in the popularity of James's classes—now booked two years in advance in New York—but in the sales of Beard Glaser Wolf's *The Cooks' Catalogue,* an exhaustive critical compendium of tools, pots, gadgets, and accessories that every serious cook would covet. The descendent of Wolf's 1972 pro-posal for a line of cooking tools, the catalogue ran to four thousand entries and seventeen hundred illustrations, accompanied by intro-ductory essays on various genera of utensils, amusing quotations and bits of food lore, and recipes assembled in a literate and graphically compelling package of *New York* magazine stylishness. Its production involved dozens of personnel and was largely overseen by Barbara Kafka, an elegant, erudite New Yorker who boasted both a Radcliffe degree and a first-class culinary education.

Kafka had inherited the shambles of José Wilson's preliminary work in 1973 and thereafter found herself facing off Beard Glaser Wolf's numerous creditors and pacifying its disgruntled staff, at one point becoming so frustrated that she left the project entirely. She returned only after being persuaded to do so by Beard, whose involvement in the catalog, though largely ceremonial, was important to its credibility. When introduced to each other by Wolf, Kafka and Beard almost immediately began to argue over a point of culinary arcana—the distinction between larding and barding a piece of meat—and Beard stormed out of the room, bellowing, "I can't work with that woman." But the formidable and self-reliant Kafka was everything the other principal female associate in his life, José Wilson, was not, and she and Beard soon became comfortable partners in work and in literate chat and gossip. Wilson, already resentful of Carl Jerome's position within the Beard ménage, came to detest Kafka and spun further and further out of Beard's core group of favorites into wobbly orbits of drinking and melancholia.

Despite the circumstances under which it was born, *The Cooks' Catalogue* enjoyed impressive sales in both hardcover and paper. It was, moreover, a book that served to mark the status of food in the mid-seventies: Cooking was no longer a means to an end—whether as a form of entertaining, feeding a family, or avoiding drudgery—but an end in itself and one whose accoutrements possessed as much style and inherent interest as the other requisites of a sophisticated, affluent life-style. The right pepper mill or kitchen timer was, properly seen, not just an implement but a design object that gave pleasure to the eye and the mind, and that spoke to and about its owner. Retailers like Design Research and the Pottery Barn had hit on the idea of displaying home furnishings, tableware, and cookware as though they were exhibits in a museum of art and design, and magazines like *New York* and books like *The Cooks' Catalogue* served as reviews and exhibition catalogs. Chief among the function of such publications was to confer "best" status on objects and consumables that were deemed the most laudable or stylish examples of their kind in the eyes of experts, tastemakers, or simply trend-spotting journalists. Listing and rating was a 1970s preoccupation, and although

James had come of age professionally at a time when one did not mention brand names unless one was paid to, he found himself ranking a selection of bottled mustards in the May 1975 *Esquire,* each brand illustrated with a *Cooks' Catalogue*–like mug shot.

In the interim Beard had remained uneasy with his role as a partner in Beard Glaser Wolf and in January 1975, he signed a new contract limiting his participation to consulting and personal appearances and endorsement ties to the Good Cooking School, for which he was paid one thousand dollars plus a portion of the endorsement fees received. It was in fact the opportunity to establish a truly American school of cooking on an institutional basis that had attracted Beard in the first place. But as yet the school existed only as a vehicle for demonstrations on behalf of corporate sponsors like Du Pont Teflon, for whom Beard also filmed commercials under his agreement with Beard Glaser Wolf.

However prescient the approach to cooking it embodied, little good save *The Cooks' Catalogue* came of Beard Glaser Wolf: A sequel, *The International Cooks' Catalogue,* appeared, as did several paperback cookbooks and a restaurant guide called *Where to Eat in America.* But Beard was spared entanglement in the mudslinging of the following year, when Wolf's estranged wife dragged Wolf and his reputed involvement with IOS "commandant" Cornfeld through the courts in an effort to gain title to the Larchmont house.

James and Carl spent the better part of 1975 away from Twelfth Street: to Chicago for a charity appearance, and then on to San Francisco for a set of classes that were to become as much a fixture of James's schedule as those held in Gearhart. In effect the San Francisco classes were an extension of the Gearhart sessions, the result of the energies and persistence of Gearhart students Loni Kuhn and Marion Cunningham. Cunningham was by now not only James's most steadfast and brightest student but a cooking teacher in her own right, who with Kuhn arranged for two weeks of classes at the Stanford Court Hotel. Wines were provided by Gerald Asher, now a member of the California wine trade, cooking equipment supplied by Chuck Williams, and food supplies and a corner suite for James donated by James Nassikas, the hotel's proprietor.

Beard and Carl arrived April 24 and began teaching the following Monday. The students consisted of Napa Valley wine luminaries or their wives joined by Alice Waters of Chez Panisse, whose Elizabeth David and Richard Olney–inspired menus James had dined on the previous autumn and declared in his datebook to be "delightful." By day he and his students—animated, curious, and sophisticated but unjaded—journeyed through filet of beef, salade composé, braised beef, saucisson, beef and kidney pie, rack of lamb, saddle of veal, chicken Provençale, and special sessions on bread, soufflés, and meatless menus. By night James glided through the better reaches of San Francisco society and nightlife, a milieu that for a Portland boy was still every bit as compelling as that of New York, Paris, or London. At dawn in his suite—taking in the bay, marveling over the inexplicable and transcendent chemistry of the classes, and recollecting his recent triumphal receptions in Portland—he felt as John Beard must have felt on his Customs Service inspection tour sixty or so years before, the veritable king of the West Coast.

In the second week of classes he fell ill on Tuesday, was back on Wednesday, and by Thursday was prepared to note "splendid class" in his datebook. He attended parties held by Marion and Loni Kuhn, hosted a reception for the hotel staff by way of thanks for his stay, and flew south to Santa Barbara for a week's rest before going to Portland and Gearhart. He fell quickly into his beach routine, with its shopping trips to Astoria and Seaside, visits to friends down the coast and up along the Columbia in Washington, and gently paced walks up and down the strand. Nothing—including the charmed success of the classes, now expanded to four weeks—varied from previous years except for Carl Jerome's constant presence, which prompted a letter from Mary Hamblet that James described as "nasty," protesting against Carl's near-total dominion over James's time and person and James's apparent willingness to ignore the friendships of a lifetime in favor of this cocky upstart.

The rift with Mary was smoothed over, albeit more by letting tempers cool than by a frank discussion of the emotions at stake. James did not volunteer his feelings to others, and while he was fiercely intelligent and well read, he was by nature unreflective; whether James was Carl's doting victim or whether Carl was in fact as much exploited as he was himself an exploiter was probably not entirely clear even to James. But in any case, however much James enjoyed being accompanied by and working with Carl, Carl was not James's true protégé, to say nothing of being his chosen successor.

That role belonged to Marion Cunningham, a fact that became clear to James during the San Francisco classes and that had solidified in his mind by their end. He had great things planned for Marion, and wrote Judith Jones about them:

> I've been thinking so much since I talked with you about Marion Cunningham, after working with her here for three weeks as my assistant. I feel more and more that she has an infinitely honest approach to good cooking and good food. It's not the approach of the professional food person, it's the approach of the person who loves food for its own sake and who loves its preparation as a way of expressing her own personality. She attacks food with imagination and she gives it a homely quality that I treasure so much in good cooking. . . . It's a combination of naïveté and humility that she projects that I like and I am so impressed with her feeling for tradition and her feeling for thoroughness and her ability to be workmanlike and to tailor things awfully well. It seems to me that, if this project comes off its feet that Marion will give it an honesty, personality and a very sweet quality that it might not have otherwise.

The "project" in question was a complete rewrite of *The Fannie Farmer Cook Book,* which over successive editions and piecemeal revisions had largely lost both its turn-of-the-century roots and its relevance to the contemporary cook. The owner of the title, the Fanny Farmer Candy Company of Boston, was interested in revitalizing what ought to be, as the most famous cookbook in America, a lucrative title. *Fannie Farmer,* or at least what *Fannie Farmer* had become, seemed a rather downmarket enterprise for a publisher of Knopf's pedigree—but so too had the James Beard of Dell paperbacks, Maco books, and innumerable product endorsements. In Jones, however, Knopf had an editor with an extraordinary knack for making classics from what others might see as castoffs.

Jones accepted Beard's recommendation to make Cunningham— untried and clearly no more of a natural writer than James—the author of the new *Fannie Farmer,* with a deal reminiscent of James's contract for *The Fireside Cookbook* nearly thirty years before: She would receive a flat fee with royalties shared between Knopf and Fannie Farmer Candy, and she would accept it, much as James had, in order to have the chance to establish a name for herself. In promoting her with such passionate commitment, Beard put her in a position to become what he had never before permitted anyone to be: an equal and successor in the field that mattered most to him. There was no greater monument in American cooking than *Fannie Farmer*, and to make Marion its custodian was to entrust her with something of the profoundest importance to James. If in 1975 he seemed willing to hand Carl Jerome control of the better part of his life and affairs, he reserved the greatest prize for Marion. It mattered to him desperately to be able influence the new edition of *Fannie Farmer*, and if he could not do it himself—a thought that had more than once tempted him but that he did not pursue—there was no person except the late Helen Brown more suitable or, it must be said, malleable.

Marion's loyalty and devotion were unquestionable in their unremitting and cheerful intensity, but James was less sure about Carl Jerome: James monitored his movements in and out of Gearhart, his health, and his punctuality and recorded them in the datebook. But if Carl was taking advantage of his situation or running amok, as Beard's friends now frequently warned him, James was not yet ready to rein him in. When the two flew to London that July in the first-class nose section of a 747 on a pair of free tickets, insofar as James was concerned Carl was there entirely at his whim and behest. In London Carl, who had been driving a cab a scant two years before, showed himself to the manor born, sharing James's suite at the Berkeley and meals with Elizabeth David and other British food luminaries. On his own Carl surveyed London's gay scene and lunched at a pub called the Pig and Whistle, where he met a man named John to whom he quickly developed an attachment, something James did little to discourage.

From London they flew to Venice for classes at the Gritti Palace Hotel. Carl immersed himself in the city and made a positive impression on all concerned, a fact James reported in letters to friends with the anxious pride of the father of a precocious son. In September, after two weeks at the Child-Beck compound, they returned to New York, to autumn classes and to the signing of a new contract with Omaha Steaks with Carl as a cosignatory. In other respects, James seemed to be loosening many of his ties to New York and its professional food community. With increasing regularity he declined to write book blurbs or attend parties and receptions and turned down opportunities to be photographed by Franceso Scavullo for a collection of portraits of Manhattan's media elite.

The only major commercial project of the year was a James Beard apron to be sold through American Airlines' *American Way* in-flight magazine, for which James continued as a columnist. Beyond that James filmed a "bicentennial minute" for CBS, a commercial-length snippet of life in 1776, in this case relating to George Washington's thoughtful provision of wine to his troops; in a similar vein, he had also discussed doing a joint television show with Julia Child on colonial food, but nothing came of it. With those tasks complete, James abandoned New York and spent a leisured December in San Francisco, living like a pasha at the Stanford Court, where he enjoyed the sexual ministrations and genuine affection of one of the bellmen, dining at Chez Panisse, and giving informal demonstrations at Williams-Sonoma—selling "one hell of a lot of books" in the process, he confided to Child. He spent Christmas with Chuck Williams and returned to New York on New Year's Eve.

James's first appointment of 1976 was with Joe Baum, who was in the final shakedown phase of preparing his restaurants at the World Trade Center for opening in April. Baum had created thirty-five food facilities from coffee stands to delis in the twin towers, but it was Windows on the World, the showpiece dining complex on the 107th floor of the north tower, that totally occupied—not to say possessed—him. Beard had been involved in the project since the beginning and had produced both memos and tapes brimming with a level of ingenuity, passion, and anticipation that suggested that here once again was a chance to create something as brilliant as the Four Seasons:

There must be croissants that float in the air . . . fresh sorbets every half hour . . . fish hash I adore . . . blueberry slump and apple grunt and gooseberry fool . . . crab cakes luscious and hot and wonderful . . . last night I had a lamb ragout so wonderful you just wanted to cuddle it in your arms.

And he was just beginning: There must be deviled crab, lobster rolls, chicken hash with olives and pine nuts, grilled salmon, striped bass, thick-cut lamb chops, and a hamburger with a slice of onion and a dollop of sauce poivrade. In fact, what Baum produced was literally a three-ring circus of food: a dining room, a grill, and a wine cellar in the sky serving a weekly set menu built around a selection of wines. For both Baum, still smarting from the indignities served up to him by RA, and for a near-bankrupt and humiliated New York City, the Trade Center was a triumph of will.

The obstacles were formidable: The lumbering bureaucracy of the Port Authority, citizen critics who felt the entire project was a boondoggle, and the logistics necessary to operate so large and complex an enterprise conspired to push excellence and distinctiveness aside. And while Windows had a show-stopping view that would go a long way to compensate for any deficiencies in the food, Baum was determined to overturn the convention that view restaurants like hotel dining rooms must be gastronomically indifferent. In doing so, he had the help not only of Beard but of Jacques Pépin, and of Barbara Kafka as his menu specialist. He also had the media in his court, and a month after Windows opened a color spread in *New York* written by Gael Greene proclaimed it "the most spectacular restaurant in the world."

In fact the food at Windows on the World consistently hovered at the level of good if never superb, and that, under the circumstances, was an enormous achievement. For reasons often beyond Baum's control and by virtue of its size and ambitions, it was not another Four Seasons, but it was in its own fashion and in its time glorious. It was also, in the scope of its conception and eclecticism, a departure from the inflexible trinity of dining choices available to most Americans: the steak house, the "continental" Franco-Italian restaurant, and, in larger cities, haute-French places pursuing and occasionally attaining Pavillon standards of excellence and exclusiveness. Despite the manifest changes in the nation's gastronomic consciousness, while there may have been more dining rooms at this level of pretension and expense—and a mind-boggling expansion of "ethnic" choices—the fundamental categories available for serious "gourmet" eating remained largely the same as they were in the late 1940s and early 1950s.

One of Beard Glaser Wolf's final projects bore unintended witness to that fact. *Where to Eat in America,* edited by Burton Wolf himself and *Washington Post* food editor William Rice during 1976 and 1977, was a valiant and intelligent attempt to found a gastronomically rigorous guide to restaurants in thirty American cities. Conscious of the futility of imposing a uniform rating system on locales that ranged from New York to Salt Lake City, the editors— with at this point, it might be noted, no help from Beard—cooked up subjective categories that might be applicable anywhere: "Big Deal— Worth It"; "Best Hotel"; "Steak"; "Hamburger"; and the like. But what the guide could propose outside New York, Chicago, San Francisco, and Los Angeles was by and large a coast-to-coast thoroughfare of meat with or without cream sauces, served by gruff hash slingers or cummerbunded dandies peddling rounds of scotch on the rocks and California chablis.

What American restaurants lacked was Americanness—the capacity to enliven traditional restaurant genres and cooking styles with a genuinely and distinctively native twist. Instead they continued in the slavish and Disneyesque pursuit of perfect replication; of the restaurant as a Cinerama travelogue indistinguishable from its parent root stock in Europe or Asia. Despite its vaunted sophistication, New York itself took this exercise in cultural self-abnegation to its greatest heights; and the metropolis's top French restaurants existed in large part to assure its money changers and socialites that their elite and self-involved company constituted a veritable Parisian salon. Farther west of the Hudson, diners had their feet somewhat closer to the ground, if no closer to the virtues of real flavor and culinary excellence.

American restaurants had yet to succeed in the quintessential mission of seventies America: that of finding themselves. Restaurants were and are, of course, as much about artifice as authenticity, and every restaurant has an affinity to the theater. But there was a distinction between acting and imitation—between the interpreter and the impressionist—that was by and large lost on most restaurateurs. Too often, what little creativity found its way into the nation's dining rooms was spent in extending the possibilities of the theme restaurant to often absurd lengths, erecting castles and medieval dining halls in which diners might be attended by waiters in monk's habits or wenches in push-up tops.

In those respects even Joe Baum's most pretentious and overwrought brainstorms were filled with honest conviction, as were James's reveries of floating croissants, schools of grilled striped bass, and cattle drives of burgers spiked with sauce poivrade. But although James was excited by the concept, if not the execution, of Windows and smelled the cordite of culinary revolution at Chez Panisse, his own choice in restaurants was more and more dictated by his health, in 1976 once again in ebb. His physical condition made any outing arduous, and he tended to stick to Village places like the Coach House and Trattoria di Alfredo, old favorites like Quo Vadis, or, most of all, the Four Seasons, whose coproprietor Tom Margittai had now joined the intimate circle of those who received regular dawn phone calls from James.

Fatigue and an array of small illnesses peppered the first several months of the new year with canceled trips, lunches, appointments, classes, and filming sessions for a spate of commercials lined up by Michael Bloom, the new agent handling his nonliterary projects. He was able to hold regular meetings with Judith Jones and José Wilson about *James Beard's Theory & Practice of Good Cooking*, code-named "the Gospel According to St. James" and now lumbering toward completion. They also began to discuss a companion volume of recipes (which would also serve as an update of *The James Beard Cookbook*) with a working title of "The Revised Standard Beard." Jones had little use for Carl Jerome, and her and Beard's sessions with José—whose loathing and resentment of Jerome provided further fuel for her now-habitual funks and benders—were carefully scheduled for those odd moments when he was out of the house. Many of his chores were gradually being assigned to a new assistant named Richard Nimmo, like José inclined to depression and over-drinking, albeit more easygoing in character and without her capacity for effortlessly corrosive banter.

But Carl remained Beard's traveling companion through the first half of the year, to La Jolla, San Antonio, Los Angeles, Bermuda, and, in May, to San Francisco for a month of classes at the Stanford Court. James basked in the warmth and adulation of Marion Cunningham and in the social ether of San Francisco and the Napa Valley's best and richest families. But however sweet California was, Oregon was sweeter still, particularly that June when his assimilation into Portland society was sealed with an honorary doctoral degree from Reed College. The award was arranged by Morris Galen, Beard's Oregon lawyer and a Reed trustee, and while Beard told others it had been offered only "because they thought it would make good fodder for the collectors of money," he was a happy and even eager recipient. Although he might in a hidden gallery within him continue to ache and grieve, he had the better part of what he wanted from Portland—which he described to a reporter the following year as "a city of pleasant homes and what I might call 'reactionary living'"—and his unfinished business with the place seemed at last complete.

From Portland James returned to San Francisco on the Fourth of July, expansive in his mood and in his body, which despite the diets and medical admonitions of the last few years was now in excess of 320 pounds in weight and five feet in girth. But scarcely had he and Carl settled into the Stanford Court than James suffered a pulmonary embolism, the damming of one of the arteries in his lungs by a clot that had dislodged from his thrombosed legs. In critical condition, he was admitted to the hospital for a stay that was to last several weeks, returning to New York at the beginning of August.

The embolism had nearly killed James, and it marked the end of his relationship with Carl Jerome. Jerome's lover of the previous year was due to arrive in New York from London, and despite James's grave condition, it was a rendezvous Carl decided he must make. Inured to James's constant ill health and convinced that he was now out of danger, Jerome left San Francisco, an act his now-innumerable detractors were quick to label a gross betrayal. Beard considered his options over the next few weeks and wrote letters to friends soliciting their views. There was little to commend Carl's continued presence to James: Overweening and increasingly cavalier in every respect, he had in the last year not only refused James sex when he had at last demanded it but had now abandoned him. He decided it was time for Carl to go his own way, a decision greeted with universal relief by the Californians and Oregonians who stood watch by his bed. Beard had been possessed, and now he had been exorcised by a thunderstroke to his body. He belonged to them once again, even as they belonged to him.

On his return to New York in August, James was given a thorough examination by his new physician, Denton Cox, which confirmed James's heart disease and uncovered ailments ranging from ulcers and infections in his legs to prostate enlargement, gout, urinary infection, and a trace of emphysema attributable to James's two-pack-a-day habit from 1918 to 1950. In Cox's view, echoing that of his previous doctors, James must either diet or die. His physician's grim prognosis and his brush with death in San Francisco worked a loud and public conversion in James on the subject of dietary fat and salt intake. James had some experience of the seventies fashion for noisy, uninvited confession, having received a letter on his return home from an acquaintance who had been participating in the highly popular, profitable, and influential est program of psychopurgation. ("The purpose of this communication is to acknowledge you for the great contribution you have made to my life . . . your willingness to share with me who you are allows me to be who I am.") By October he had appeared in the *New York Times, People,* and other media outlets as the chastened former oleophile now full of enthusiasm for healthful eating. Friends who had seen James gazing longingly through a chocolatier's or patisserie's window in the agonies of deprivation during previous diets were, however, unsurprised by Clay's worried admission to *People* that "Mr. B is dying for a frankfurter. You can see it in his face when he opens the refrigerator. He turns up his nose when he hears about the hard-boiled eggs and slice of tomato he's getting for lunch."

Although in most press accounts James was cheerful about his dietary regime, claiming to view it as a challenge and an opportunity to discover subtleties of flavor customarily hidden by butter and salt, in private he took it as a penance. He lost fifty pounds and received a torrent of mail on eating and health, a subject that bored him in the past but on which his embolism had forced him to become an expert. He found himself pursued by authors of natural food and diet books who wanted blurbs, producers of health foods, and various doctors and scientists eager to sign him up as a spokesman for sensible eating. Even former Galloping Gourmet Graham Kerr, now an evangelical Christian and a natural foods zealot, attempted to enlist him in his cause. But James rebuffed all such inquiries, dismissing them as irrelevant to food and cooking as he understood them.

That view was not particular to James but endemic in the food community, for whom the burning question of the mid-seventies was the legitimacy of la nouvelle cuisine, a new style of cooking that seemed to have swept France and was now making its presence felt in the United States. In many respects, however, the question of nouvelle cuisine was less about food than about food journalism:

Although cooking in France had seen various conscious and unconscious moments of innovation and reform over the last three hundred years, this latest "nouvelle cuisine" was the discovery of writers Gault and Millau, who declared it to be a reality in their magazine, *Le Nouveau Guide,* in 1973 and enunciated there what they claimed to be its "ten commandments." In France there was certainly a discernible trend toward lighter sauces, small and more decoratively presented portions, and fish and vegetables, particularly among one-time students of the late Fernand Point. But no matter how real or contrived the movement Gault and Millau claimed to discern, they had if nothing else pulled off with astonishing impact the old food journalism trick of proclaiming their own current project the latest news. Moreover, they owned the paper in which one could read all about it.

As a sister to the fashion and decorating businesses, the food community had been chasing the tail of its own self-proclaimed trends for years and promoting personalities to go with them. But with the proclamation of nouvelle cuisine—the apparent culinary equivalent of the sixties miniskirt revolution—what was in effect little more than a shift in the style of elite restaurant cooking became an international news story. The innovation in cooking apparent in France and now spreading to the United States was as yet amorphous, but food writers became obsessed with it to the exclusion of almost anything else, turning into gastronomic Kremlin watchers, their antennae hypersensitively tuned to what might be the next hot trend. As an adjunct they also became chroniclers and promoters of the chefs who were deemed to be the vanguard of the nouvelle cuisine revolution. By the end of the decade, food writing would seem to have become largely a matter of trend handicapping, celebrity profiles, and gossip—a blend of *Women's Wear Daily* and "Rona Barrett's Hollywood." The public concern about health manifested in the mail Beard received in the wake of his illness, together with the nation's continuing agriculture crisis, were in retrospect the real news stories of the mid- and late seventies but were largely ignored by a food community bent on pursuing evanescent chimeras of style and stoking its own newfound celebrity.

Protests were raised both in jest and in deadly earnest: *New Yorker* writer Calvin Trillin, with his deadpan mockery of the giant-peppermill genre of Continental restaurant and his championing of domestic foods like ribs and chicken, did as much as anyone within the food community—including possibly James—to promulgate an appreciation of American food and a genuinely American gastronomic sensibility. The fieldwork Trillin's essays seemed to propose was carried out in some detail by Jane and Michael Stern, popular-culture journalists who transcribed the culinary glories and horrors of the American highway in 1977's *Roadfood* and succeeding volumes. Whether Trillin or the Sterns were serious or even sincere seemed an unanswerable question, but they were funny and clearly cared about eating: They fawned with Warholesque camp enthusiasm over dishes that members of the food establishment considered beyond the pale, lavishing on unpretentious and unassuming juke joints the same fevered attentions that gourmets once reserved for Le Pavillon.

At the other end of the spectrum were John and Karen Hess, who like Mencken, Mumford, and Hibben before them, linked traditional American foodways and farming with a Jeffersonian progressive agenda. In their view domestic science, corporate agriculture and food processing, and "the gourmet plague" had together conspired to produce a diet that was unhealthy, tasteless, and devoid of cultural meaning, serving only to enrich the same people who were devastating the environment and who had given the country Vietnam and Watergate.

It was a drum that John Hess, as a *Times* correspondent and its food critic during 1973 and 1974, and his wife had been beating for several years in various articles, but publication of their *The Taste of America* in 1977 loosed the sum of their discontents on the public in a vituperative and angry critique of American gastronomy. Most of the Hesses' arguments were well taken: American bread, produce, and chicken were a scandal; much of the food press was far too intimate with industry to truly serve the consumer; and while the raising of public consciousness about cooking was a positive step, the Francophile bent of the nation's leading writers and teachers had, together with these other factors, contributed to the decline and depreciation of American food traditions. Julia Child, Craig Claiborne, and Beard were singled out as the unholy trinity at the center of "the gourmet plague," although the Hesses were somewhat kinder to Beard than Child or Claiborne. Beard was often misinformed about gastronomic history and was a shill for the food industry, but "only Beard seems from his work actually to enjoy cooking and to write well about it."

The Hesses' manifesto raised issues largely identical to those that concerned the political, intellectual, and bohemian gastronomes of the twenties and thirties, and was no less valid for it. Unfortunately the Hesses had spent sufficient time within the food community they decried to pick up some of its worst habits, with which they frequently undermined their own cause: Written in a snide first-person plural, they seemed preoccupied with settling scores and pursuing the nits and trivialities on which gourmets and cooking professionals have always impaled their enemies.

They spent some pages, for example, establishing the not-difficult contention that *James Beard's American Cookery* was as food history a rather loose and sloppy enterprise. The larger point—that the food establishment suffered from the lack of a historical perspective and tended to be drawn to anecdote rather than fact—was worth exploring; so, too, was the contradiction between that establishment's desire to be taken seriously and its intellectual laziness and parochialism, as well as its refusal to consider food from any perspective save that of restaurants and recipes. The deficiencies of the food media and the government agencies that should have been serving consumers rather than industry deserved wide discussion, as did the sad state of America's regional cooking traditions and larders. But *The Taste of America* caused a stir, not a wave. It would have been difficult indeed to cause any shift in the entrenched habits of the food economy and its retainers in the media and in Washington, and that effort was ill-served by the Hesses' own immersion in the bitchy and petty subculture they claimed to deplore.

James's health had remained fragile through the remainder of 1976, and he underwent prostate surgery at the end of the year, recovering much of his strength by March of 1977. Having faced down death at least twice over the past three years, he found the charges leveled against him, Claiborne, and Child by the Hesses in 1977 trifling. In any case, he was hardly the ignorant and shameless hack and huckster they had made him out to be: In the last six months he had done only a single promotional blurb (for K. C. Chang's *Food in Chinese Culture*) at a time he had otherwise declared a moratorium on book endorsements, and he turned down (not once but twice) sponsorship of a line of cooking wines he deemed inferior. And although he remained a consultant to major food companies, the advice he gave them was not inconsistent with the ideals of even the Hesses:

> I went out to Pillsbury's about two weeks ago on a consultation, very much as I used to do in the past, on new products. . . . At a large table we had for tasting I found out they had spent $250,000 on presenting a new product without ever testing it out or having it tested by anyone outside the laboratories. So, I let go and I said that it was just food that had absolutely no human consumption level . . . Fortunately, the executive who had asked me to come out, and with whom I had worked before, agreed with me 100%, but the new products man was upset to a point where he felt that he had something that would revolutionize the world. So, I called back when I got to New York and said that I just felt they should throw the $250,000 down the drain and forget it or they'd lose much more. . . . It was grim!

Over the next few years Beard was to become more forthright about his progressive views than in the past: He was in his mid-seventies, his authority was unassailable, and he found the agrarian and environmental concerns underlying much of the Hesses' book highly sympathetic. He wore his age well: His simplest statements had the sheen of wisdom about them, and his silences seemed oracular; people could hear what they needed to hear in them, a capacity he had always used to his advantage and that now produced not only affection but respect.

As a grand old man, he attracted not only authors disposed like the Hesses to cut him down to size, but a more admiring sort inclined to render him the stuff of legend. A neighbor of Julia Child with several biographies and histories to her credit approached Beard about a book on him and the food establishment. Beard referred the idea to Judith Jones, who pronounced it "boring" and pointed out that it would compete with their own plan for a sequel to *Delights and Prejudices*. That project was at least a few years away, with José just beginning work on "The Revised Standard Beard" and *James Beard's Theory & Practice of Good Cooking* being released in April.

Theory & Practice was in many respects less a book by James than a collaboration between José Wilson and Judith Jones constructed around James's teaching techniques and food preferences. As with the *Gourmet* series on which it was based, the book began with boiling and worked its way through roasting, broiling and grilling, braising, sautéing, and frying to baking. Contemplating the techniques of cooking in the abstract might well have been tedious, but the handsome Karl Stuecklen drawings, Knopf's elegant production, and Jones's knack for tempering Beard the dean of gastronomy with Beard the amiable personality produced an inviting book.

Most of the novelty in *Theory & Practice* could be found in its form rather than in the largely recycled substance of its recipes and advice. It took Beard's passion for teaching and Jones's penchant for dressing cooking up in academic robes to new heights, with the material organized around not only techniques but "master recipes" and variations on them. A reader might indeed work his or her way through it from start to finish and emerge a competent cook, although it is unlikely that many did. What is more impressive is the growing simplicity and directness—as filtered through José—of Beard's approach to eating: a pleasure taken in letting things taste of themselves, born in part, he admits, of having to cut back on salt and fat. Baked potatoes should be savored unsullied by toppings, vegetables cooked in virtually no water, and, above all else, good cooking seen as beginning in the market, as a lengthy concordance of advice on ingredients asserts. Despite its title *Theory & Practice* was a book not about technical mastery but about inculcating a sensibility inclined to leave food well enough alone.

Knopf's publicity department arranged for a promotional tour that would begin with the "Today" show in New York on April 4 and work its way around virtually every significant media outlet in the country. But on April 23 Beard was admitted to hospital for a bowel obstruction that required surgery and confined him to bed until the middle of May. The San Francisco classes scheduled for that month were canceled, but he left for Oregon in mid-June, only to be hospitalized again with abdominal pain and congestive heart failure within a few days of his arrival in Portland. He was finally well enough to hold a week of classes in Gearhart at the beginning of

July. Despite the instability of his health, he insisted on traveling to Europe with Marion Cunningham, flying first to London—where he saw Carl Jerome, with whom he remained on speaking terms—and on to Venice for cooking classes. After two weeks of teaching at the Gritti Palace, he retired to the Austrian schloss of New York cooking teacher Peter Kump, and thence to Michel Guérard's restaurant and spa in southwestern France and to Paris, where he and Marion visited the La Varenne cooking school.

James was still in France when news of Helen McCully's death reached him on August 24. He flew home via London, canceling his passage on the *Queen Elizabeth 2*. McCully had been firm in her wish that there be no funeral or memorial, and there was little to do but get on with the business of living, even as it seemed that the people and fixtures that gave it form and sustenance were dropping away. Michael Field had died in 1971 and Paula Peck a year later, both far too young for their passing to make any sense to James. McCully had been seventy-five, a year older than him, but her death devastated him as no one's had since Helen Brown. She was the mother and protector he could not quite bring himself to confess that he needed, and he was never able to find a way to acknowledge fully to her the place she had held in his life over the previous thirty years.

He filled his calendar with lunches and dinners—gaining back most of the weight he had lost the previous year—and new people: with Michael and Ariane Batterberry, who were planning a new food magazine to be called *Food & Wine;* with restaurateur Stephen Spector; with Peter Kump; and with Barbara Kafka. He had dinner with Ruth Norman and Cheryl Crawford, with whom he had become reconciled at the behest of their mutual friend and his doctor, Denton Cox. He flew to San Francisco and moved into the Stanford Court for Christmas and New Year's, blanketing himself in the attentions of Chuck Williams; Gerald Asher; James Nassikas; Jeremiah Tower, the former chef of Chez Panisse; and Marion Cunningham. On virtually every visit he made to California, James would arrange to be driven north to Sonoma County to the home of M. F. K. Fisher, who alone among his California friends neither chauffeured him nor tied his shoes nor dressed his legs nor dropped everything to do his bidding. They simply talked and cooked.

• • •

The years 1978 and 1979 passed with episodes of illness, classes, and the daily business of sifting offers and requests for appearances, endorsements, and favors. The household now consisted of Gino, José, Clay, Emily Gilder (who had replaced Betty Ward as secretary), and Richard Nimmo. Nimmo did not dominate the household as had Carl Jerome, but his influence on James was detectable. Nimmo was, in the gay argot of the period, a "clone": a lean, mustachioed figure, clad in Levis 501s and a work shirt, whose specific sexual proclivities might be gleaned from the position of the key ring at his waist. James never adopted the full uniform, but made jeans—which hardly flattered him—part of a wardrobe that was increasingly eccentric and for most part all the more delightful for it. Thus attired, Beard was freighted by Nimmo to au courant gay bars at which he took even more than his usual delight in being recognized.

Nimmo's habitual mien was that of even-keeled, alcoholic melancholy in contrast to Wilson's snits, Gino's sulks, and Clay's edgy Pollyannaism. Gilder lived in an apartment in the next building, where she handled James's phone calls on an extension and his correspondence and bookkeeping away from the clutter of the crowded town house. In addition to his core staff, James was represented by two agents, John Schaffner on literary matters and Michael Bloom for purposes of commercials, public appearances, and endorsements. He therefore supported five full- or part-time employees and contributed commissions to two agents. Against this he would earn $190,000 in 1978 from his column, other journalism, and demonstrations, with the expectation of between $30,000 and $50,000 gross from cooking classes. In all he was not a rich man, but given his lack of living expenses outside the Twelfth Street house, neither was he poor. Despite that—or perhaps on its account—he could be counted on never to carry money and to find himself among persons for whom treating James Beard to a meal or drink would be a signal honor. He was generous in the minds of the vast majority of his acquaintances, albeit generous in the fashion that suited him.

His closest friends—those who received phone calls as the blue light of dawn crept across the raised platform of James's bed and bounced off the mirrored ceiling onto his blood orange walls—were for the most part people with whom he had little or no financial congress: Nika Hazelton, Cecily Brownstone, Tom Margittai, and, more and more, Stephen Spector. Spector was a gentleman queen, a former art dealer every bit as cultured and bright as James, who spoke with arcing, swerving intonations, a voice made for gossip, bitchery, and opera postmortems. His restaurant, Le Plaisir, was one of the first examples in New York of a new kind of eating place: founded on European principles not as ends in themselves but as vehicles through which their cooks might express their own personalities and ideals.

Le Plaisir—like an increasing number of small, artisanal restaurants of which Chez Panisse in northern California was the exemplar—had the courage of its own convictions, and to dine there was to be thrilled or sometimes disappointed but never bored. The bohemian-intellectual tendency perennially present in American gastronomy had, in the late 1970s, reentered the restaurant business, encouraged by the agrarian aesthetics of David and Olney and the neoregionalism and utopianism of the American counterculture. Fine dining was no longer the replication of the codified recipes of another country but a transcendent blend of the genius of the cook and the genius of the place, and the place was increasingly acknowledged to be the United States. The well-educated and well-traveled cooks heading the kitchens of such restaurants understood that ingredients—whose freshness and aesthetic rightness could only be guaranteed by flying them in from the place of origin or exploring what grew locally with a purposefulness that had been extinct in most American chefs for years—were as crucial as technique. The melding of European and Asian traditions with domestic materials and the often-too-impatient ingenuity of the new generation of chefs could tend toward the overwrought, but it was a movement in which James detected his own vindication.

Few if any of the people behind such cooking were conventionally trained chefs. Alice Waters and Jeremiah Tower had taken classes from James and from Richard Olney. Elsewhere, Anne Willan's La Varenne in Paris, which James had visited the previous year, was designed to service a student who was neither a hobbyist nor a professional vocational student in the usual sense. While signing new promotional contracts with Sharp appliances and Philip Morris—involving the awarding of eleven plaques in three days to New York restaurants selected for the Benson & Hedges 100's 100

Great Restaurants—James himself expanded the faculty of his cooking school. Guest and associate instructors like Madhur Jaffrey and Barbara Kafka were enlisted, as much to cover for the frequently indisposed Beard as for their very real abilities. Even Gino was enlisted to teach baking.

James's teaching-based *Theory & Practice* won the 1978 Tastemaker Award over an uninspired field led by *Craig Claiborne's Favorites from the New York Times* and Anne Willan's *Great Cooks and Their Recipes: From Taillevent to Escoffier*. The companion to *Theory & Practice,* eventually titled *The New James Beard,* was moving forward under José's care, while she also continued to grind out the weekly newspaper column and James's regular *American Way* features. The column remained influential and at times prescient: In the last week of May James profiled a New Orleans chef named Paul Prudhomme, whose Cajun cuisine and corpulent person became an icon of the next decade.

James's 1978 travel schedule was less demanding than in previous years, in part due to a growing recognition of the physical toll it took on him. He turned down most invitations for demonstrations and speeches unless the venue was either attractive—as in the case of a junket to Hawaii in January—or well paid and prestigious, as was a speech to the food editors at the Food Marketing Institute conference in Dallas in May. The classes traditionally held in San Francisco in the spring were canceled, and James spent the better part of March and April in New York undergoing medical tests. He was now seeing one or more of his doctors a week, although he frequently canceled his appointments with them in order to lunch with Gael Greene, Barbara Kafka, or Carl Sontheimer, the importer of the Cuisinart food processor and publisher of a new food magazine called *The Pleasures of Cooking.* In particular he sought the counsel of Denton Cox, to whom he confided his ongoing depression; his exasperation with the infighting among Emily, Richard, and Clay; his alienation from Gino; and his long-term ambivalence and misgivings about his sexuality. Cox noted in his records that all in all, James was happiest away from New York.

But James managed only two weeks of classes at Gearhart that summer and at the end of October made a brief trip to London and to the Child-Beck compound at Plascassier. In December he flew to San Francisco for Christmas, where he was attended to by his West

Coast entourage and enjoyed a year-end crop of publicity more bountiful and varied than most: He was profiled by Evan Jones, a gastronomic writer and the husband of Judith Jones, in the *New York Times Magazine* and occupied the cover of *Travel & Leisure* dressed in a Santa suit—hatless, so as to reveal the trademark bald head—and adorned with a snowy meringue of whiskers.

James remained in San Francisco for the month of January 1979, conducting classes and demonstrations with as much verve as he had felt in some time. But on his return to New York, his health once again deteriorated, and in March and April he was hospitalized twice for urological and hernia surgery. By June he was well enough to return to California for a further week of classes and to consider attending the twenty-fifth anniversary celebration for Chillingsworth at Brewster on Cape Cod. But that summer's classes in Oregon were canceled and the time at home used to shoot a New Year's party cover story for *Bon Appétit*. On August 1 James hosted the twentieth anniversary of the Four Seasons, whose proprietorship had passed from Restaurant Associates to Paul Kovi and Tom Margittai. The Four Seasons was as good as it had ever been, if not better: Joe Baum's masterpiece had survived the onslaught and inevitable waning of instant celebrity accorded it upon its opening in 1959, as well as the bloodletting at RA in the late sixties, to become one of the nation's truly venerated dining rooms: a genuine original that had the luck—and the talent and determination of Kovi and Margittai—to become a classic.

In 1979, though, it seemed that restaurants just as promising were being born every week in New York. In the later 1970s the dining scene often seemed dominated by the Palace, a place that took the discreetly posh idiom of Lutèce and La Caravelle and applied to it a level of excess, expense, and vulgarity that only New York at its most determinedly aggressive could muster. Among the food press the Palace was the subject of both notoriety and controversy, prompting debate over whether its Lucullan dinners and earthshaking tabs represented a gastronomic triumph or an unconscionable affront to both decency and taste.

The Palace's chef, a veteran of Lutèce named Claude Baills, had made news when he had jumped ship to start his own place in imitation of Le Plaisir. Claude's, together with other newly opened restaurants like Dodin-Bouffant, Chanterelle, and the Quilted Giraffe (then located up the Hudson from New York but soon to be transplanted to Manhattan), received orgasmic commendations from Gael Greene and the better part of her colleagues. Their chefs—or rather cooks— were young, gifted, and American and unlike the midtown and Upper East Side bastions of French dining they traded not in perfect adherence to the time-honored Gallic ideal but in sheer, unexpected, sensual excitement, with dishes like brains and pickled cherries; duck breast with scalloped turnips, sautéed zucchini, and braised onions; or artichoke custard with a tarragon sauce. From such baroque beginnings, New York's new wave of restaurateurs and chefs, like their counterparts in California, had launched themselves from the shores of France and would, over the next ten years, find their way home to the United States.

James's legs landed him in the hospital yet again in September after a three-week trip to England and Plascassier. That same month Marion Cunningham's revision of *The Fannie Farmer Cookbook* was published and finished 1979 in fourteenth position on the best-seller list, a considerable feat for a cooking as opposed to a dieting book. Under Judith Jones's editorship the revision had been made remarkably true to the spirit if not the letter of the original: There were no longer a half dozen recipes for terrapin, more than fifty puddings, and nearly a hundred sauces. But Cunningham and her collaborators—much of the material was written by *Woman's Day* cookbook author Jeri Laber, *Cooks' Catalogue* veteran Irene Sax, journalist Suzanne Hamlin, and Jones—retained the book's emphasis on baking and on the provision of a standard repertoire of universally popular dishes. It was an unapologetically American book, reinforced in the revision by the addition of more material drawn from regions outside Fannie Farmer's turn-of-the-century Boston orbit, such as the Southwest and South.

Cunningham's *Fannie Farmer* also incorporated recipes drawn from foreign cuisines that were by the end of the 1970s well assimilated into the American culinary idiom as well as a more extensive and adventurous selection of pasta dishes than the macaroni familiar to Farmer's original audience. The revision reflected the rise and decline in the popularity or availability of certain ingredients as well: Cunningham increased the quantity of chicken and beef recipes and decreased those for eggs, oysters, and lobster, retaining in the last category Lobster à l'Américaine in an unflamed version, as it had appeared in the first edition. Set against the proliferating flamboyance of late-seventies restaurant cooking—as well as the orgiastic grocery selections and take-out food afforded by shops like New York City's Dean & DeLuca and the Silver Palate whose ilk would gradually infest shopping malls and supermarkets—the food of the revised *Fannie Farmer Cookbook* was straightforward if sometimes bland, but always honest.

In the estimation of an increasing number of people honesty, simplicity, and directness were virtues more and more absent from the business of food in general and from food writing in particular. The Hesses' 1977 book had put the matter with characteristic immoderation: "Short of hard-core pornography there is, we think, no branch of publishing more cynical than that concerned with food." As though to underscore the point, at the end of that same year Paula Wolfert and her soon-to-be husband, the novelist William Bayer, had uncovered at least 165 recipes appropriated from *Gourmet* and other sources in a cookbook by British food writer Lady Harlech. Members of the food community expressed outrage, with James— eight of whose recipes had found their way into Harlech's book— remarking, "I think this is pretty shocking. It just proves there are more typewriter cooks than real cooks out there."

In fact, it was hard to make the claim that recipes constituted intellectual property in the same way that a poem or a patentable device or process might be: Recipes could justifiably be seen as variations on the theme of a given ingredient, process, or tradition rather than original creations produced on a blank canvas. Moreover, recipe writers were generous in sharing and improving on one another's work and, less commendably, in endlessly recasting, recycling, and reselling their favorite recipes. By the accounts of many, Judith Jones was only able to convince Beard to take on further book work by reassuring him that his existing stock of material meant he would not be required to produce any new recipes. If Harlech was averse to the stove, Beard and a sizable portion of his cohorts in food writing were equally averse to the typewriter. In fact, food books that genuinely broke new ground and were arguably worth stealing from—whether by virtue of their assiduous research, like Wolfert's, or on the basis of their sheer creativity, like Richard

Olney's *Simple French Food*—were rare indeed. The real issue was the ingratitude shown in failing to attribute the source of the recipe; of ignoring the rules of mutual aid and protection that allowed the competing factions and individuals that comprised the food community to remain civil to one another; and, most crucially, of giving the lie to the dubious proposition that the food community was a haven of nurturance, honest toil, and generosity in a heartless and hungry world.

Amid the clash of recipes and careers—predicated on the presumption of a bottomless well of gastronomic plenty—hunger itself seemed a question with which at least a few people were preoccupied: If the consumption of food in all its manifold contexts was ultimately a response to the sensation of hunger, what did all these books, restaurants, products, trends, personalities, intrigues, and schemes have to do with it? Food had become a problem; a problem not about the perplexities of having too little but about those of having too much; about the surfeit of information and choice that came with abundance. Hunger seemed to have become not the manifestation of a fundamental need of body and soul but a mere emblem of desire, of appetites that had been teased and manipulated to a state of eternal insatiability by pitchmen, consultants, and experts. The body was jerked marionettelike from eating to dieting and back again, with one new element or another added to the dictates it must follow with each passing week. By the end of the seventies, it was encouraged to ingest goat cheese, bitter salad greens, Buffalo chicken wings, and deep-fat-fried potato skins; it must monitor fat, cholesterol, sugar, and salt; and it must run, jog, or lift weights. If the body had been a mind, it would have been driven insane. An increasing number of people, mostly adolescent girls, opted out entirely and gave themselves over to bulimia or anorexia nervosa or both, the neurasthenias of the late twentieth century.

These discontents were in one form or another pondered by a few writers: A contributor to *New York* magazine summed up the decade with the observation: "Food mavens can win good money and reputations by creating a new kind of vinegar. By *discovering* a new kind of vinegar. Cuisine is big, if sometimes arcane, business, and people are getting fat off it all over town." But "politically, economically we do not seem to be going smiling into the eighties"; in the impending tough times, the writer predicted, people would take comfort in cream and chocolate rather than fitness and diet. The century's perennial consumer conflict between consumption and purgation might at last be at an end.

James's friend M. F. K. Fisher—a person of broader sensibility than most of the food establishment—offered a still more pessimistic view that December in the *New York Review of Books*, arguing that the debased and denatured language of food writing and advertising was an Orwellian expropriation by the marketplace and the media of the body's native hunger and longing for love. "This distortion of values, this insidious numbing of what we once knew without question as either True or False" implied dark and evil days ahead. The editors sent James an advance copy of the article for his comments, but if he had any he did not write them down or voice them publicly. He went about his business and took his comforts where he could. He consented to have his name and recipes affixed to cans of Star-Kist Clams; he appeared on "Today"; he lunched with Sam Aaron, Judith Jones, Jane Montant, Julia Child, Barbara Kafka, and George Lang. Privately he fretted over the waning of his once formidable memory and despaired of both José Wilson's now habitual depression and his own. On December 19 he flew to San Francisco, to the attentions and consolations of the things that he loved and the people who loved him.

James was still settled in his corner suite at the Stanford Court in January 1980 and received his customary visitors there, among them Marion Cunningham, James Nassikas, socialite Denise Hale, Chuck Williams, and the hotel bellman. There were also new young male friends like Clark Wolf, the glib and quick-minded manager of a San Francisco gourmet grocery, and John Carroll, a college student and acquaintance of Cunningham's who was managing the logistical side of the cooking classes being held downstairs in the Stanford Court's restaurant.

As though in response to James's declining powers, enrollment had fallen off from previous years, but despite a smaller number of students, a considerable amount of materials and people had to be marshaled for the classes. It had become James's habit—and now his necessity—to teach seated in a director's chair while a second person carried out the actual demonstration of the recipe under discussion. Given her residence in the Bay Area, her central role in previous classes, her status as Beard's principal West Coast acolyte, and the celebrity she was achieving through *Fannie Farmer,* it would have been natural to employ Marion Cunningham in this capacity. But instead James made the perverse decision to bring in Barbara Kafka from New York.

Kafka and Cunningham were a mix that could not but curdle; where Kafka was an acerbic, intellectual, and worldly Manhattanite, Cunningham was an ingenuous, maternal, and domestic westerner whose cast-iron approach to cooking was at a vast remove from Kafka's big-city culinary sophistication. Kafka was indeed a skilled and forceful teacher, who could at times seem almost to overshadow not only Cunningham but Beard himself, a situation that James was willing to tolerate despite the miasmally foul temper in which he had entered the new year. His appetite for psychological and interpersonal intrigue was sharper than ever—even as some began to notice the ebbing acuity of his legendary palate—and Kafka was the cat he had chosen to set among the pigeons.

Cunningham, who was no stranger to tragedy and abuse, bore her humiliation with uncomplaining dignity, as though she understood that it was what her role in James's life required: to play Portland to New York; to play, in a sense, Mary Beard of the Salmon Street pantry to Mary Beard the cosmopolite. For James's part, the succor and ease he had once found so plentiful in San Francisco and in Gearhart had become more elusive, perhaps in part because he had an unwitting urge to despoil them through gossip and betrayal.

He returned to New York on February 9 to find the household on Twelfth Street a listing hulk on the verge of capsizing: Gino and Clay's mutual contempt was palpable, Richard Nimmo's once-furtive and sporadic binges were coalescing into round-the-clock inebriation, and José Wilson was paralyzed by depression and alcohol. Food, liquor, and cooking equipment seemed to enter and disappear from the house in unaccountable quantities, and Beard worried that his income and finances, largely overseen by Emily Gilder, could not carry him through the rest of his old age.

In fact, despite his inability to teach and give demonstrations as frequently as a few years before, his income was steady: His new contract with Omaha Steaks netted him an effortless $12,000; he could command $2,500 for a day's consulting or personal appearance; and a book of fifty recipes culled for a distiller would be remunerated at $1,000 per dish. But there were irritations and aspersions cast on his reputation: He received complaints from subscribers to a magazine that had used his name in promotional literature without his consent, he was upbraided by an Omaha Steaks customer upset with an order of gristly filets, and his ethics were impugned by a reader troubled by his column's glowing report on a restaurant for which Barbara Kafka had served as a consultant.

He continued to be besieged by individuals, organizations, and businesses that wanted the use of his name, his face, or his body. Although his curiosity about and interest in new developments and emerging stars in the food world remained constant, he was averse to involvement in groups and causes, however apparently benign: He politely rebuffed efforts to involve him more deeply in a program to grant academic degrees in food studies being formed—with the enthusiastic participation of virtually every significant personage in world gastronomy—by an Ohio college professor named John Ronsheim. He claimed he was simply not a "joiner," a proclivity born of his distaste for situations over which he had little control (or that required him to be identified with a particular faction) as well as his memories of the Jeanne Owen–dominated New York Wine & Food Society of the 1940s.

Other invitations were accepted eagerly. As a two-time winner, he attended the Tastemaker cookbook awards, sponsored by French's Mustard, and appeared on a radio program called "This Is My Music," citing Wagner and Stravinsky as his favorite composers. In June he returned briefly to San Francisco before leaving for Europe, where a dinner was held in his honor at the Dorchester in London, and he lectured and hobnobbed on a Mediterranean cruise ship. In July he returned to the United States and to Gearhart, accompanied by John Carroll, who served as his driver, companion, and manservant.

It was a dreary and oppressive summer overhung by a perpetually churning bank of gray clouds, relieved only by walks on the beach and endless—and to Carroll's mind, pointless—car trips up and down Highway 101, where James binged on fast-food hamburgers and fried chicken. He and Carroll occupied not a house on Gearhart Beach but a condominium overlooking the golf course, which James referred to as "a bourgeois dump." As week succeeded week, he grew bitter, petulant, and self-pitying, salving himself with scotch and making slurred sexual advances to Carroll. Classes were a respite from his self-absorption, although they no longer possessed the unlabored perfection of eight years before. Beard had also become preoccupied with the idea of abandoning New York for permanent residence in Oregon, and Carroll shuttled him among properties for sale on the local market, none of which pleased him.

In August, as classes were ending in Gearhart, Beard learned that José Wilson had committed suicide at her cottage in Massachusetts. Within a few days a letter from Wilson arrived calmly setting down her reasons for taking her life and the steps she had taken to put her affairs in order. She had finished work on *The New James Beard,* and other people could and would deal with the column. She was simply unable to bear the interminable malaise that her life had become. The letter did not blame James for that, or for José's solution to it, but the conclusion that he was the author of her travails was inescapable. His despair was unstanchable, and not even the sea and the strand at Gearhart could comfort him.

He was able to put on his customary mask of geniality for interviews with several reporters, but in private his long-standing guardedness about his emotional life gave way to a sad and bitter openness: No one had ever known him or genuinely loved him, he would tell friends, and he was incapable of love himself; he had not achieved what he had wanted, and now it was too late; he was not as famous as he needed and wanted to be. He breached the truce that had prevailed between him and Portland to an interviewer, recollecting "the bitter, biting things" the city had visited on him and the still-harrowing sting of the disapproval and censure of Portlanders long in their graves.

As the days shortened and autumn storms blew off the ocean, Beard spent September and October aimlessly with Carroll in Oregon, making quick forays to Portland and San Francisco for a photographic shoot and a charity event even as his weight ballooned upward toward three hundred pounds again. Carroll drove him back to San Francisco in November, and after almost six months away he returned to New York for a few weeks. He had even less appetite for the Twelfth Street house in December than he had had at the beginning of the year. Its characteristic tension and hysteria were now overlaid by the fact of José's death, which seemed not only a loss but a kind of judgment on the place and its inhabitants. James flew to San Francisco in time for Christmas and in readiness for January classes at the Stanford Court only to discover that they would have to be canceled. There were simply not enough people interested in attending, an event unprecedented in his career and one that capped a bleak and wicked year.

Over the first six months of 1981 something of James's past equilibrium was restored to him. His seventy-eight-year-old body was frail—if, in Denton Cox's view, still dangerously overweight—and he tired easily, but the emotional tempests of the previous year eased. He could become testy, as he did when he insisted that any work done on his behalf by José Wilson be removed from her papers prior to their donation to Antioch College. But students were found for two weeks of classes in March with Barbara Kafka in San Francisco, and he had been fit enough for an appearance for the one-hundredth anniversary promotion for Philadelphia Brand cream cheese in Chicago in February. He and Marion Cunningham traveled to Boston on behalf of "Benson & Hedges Recipes from Great Inns" and received a joint fee of $7,500, a portion of which was predicated on James's promise to devote a newspaper column to the Benson & Hedges promotion.

Enrollments for the three-week-long classes at Gearhart that summer went against the worrisome trend apparent in San Francisco and exceeded all previous years, with twenty-eight students per week at $450 each. The classes were effectively run by Marion Cunningham, who distributed the day's recipes, which the students then prepared and afterward discussed with Beard. James's stamina was quite limited, and his belief in letting his students find their own way left some of them feeling cheated at his comparatively slight participation in the classes. A comparable discontent was felt by those first-time students who felt excluded from the camaraderie and obvious status enjoyed by veterans of previous years, some of whom had attended every session since 1973 and who constituted at least half the enrollment.

James was oblivious to whatever such rumblings may have reached him. That summer he and John Carroll had obtained the use of a house with magnificent views near Tillamook Head. James's visitors arrived in an endless stream; he was rarely alone save to sleep or nap, the weather was good, and he was content and relaxed. He enjoyed the beach, although he told friends he longer entertained the idea of moving there permanently, having perhaps come to understand what Gearhart could and could not do for him. It was to be his penultimate summer there.

He left Oregon in August, returning to New York and the promotional campaign being mounted by Knopf on behalf of *The New James Beard*. Beginning September 14 and continuing through the first week of November, James was flown and chauffeured to interviews, photograph sessions, radio programs, book signings, demonstrations, and television shows in New York, Chicago, Los Angeles, Boston, and Washington. A thousand-recipe successor to James's paperback blockbuster *The James Beard Cookbook, The New James*

Beard was a modestly solid success, selling some 135,000 copies over the next ten years.

In truth the book was neither a basic cookbook like *The James Beard Cookbook* nor did it represent a genuinely "new" approach to cooking beyond continuing in the theme and variation mode of *Theory & Practice*. Both the book and James himself claimed *The New James Beard* represented "the new me," a more easygoing, eclectic, and improvisational dean of American cookery who urged his readers to relax, experiment, and trust their own instincts. But this was the line James had taken with increasing emphasis since *Fireside* and was indeed that of most successful cooking teachers and writers since World War II. *The New James Beard* was an interesting if not compelling collection of recipes that evinced little of the culinary excitement James told interviewers he detected around the country, particularly in the young proprietors of restaurants and food shops. Fashionable ingredients like zucchini blossoms and fiddlehead ferns appeared, and while lip service was paid to the contemporary itch for lighter, less fatty dishes, the text possessed more conviction when discussing recipes like buttery cornmeal gnocchi, a basted Oregon wild duck, and chicken fried in lard.

Unlike *American Cookery* or *Beard on Bread, The New James Beard* was not a book that Beard particularly wanted to write but one that he and José—to whose memory he dedicated it—could produce without much strain, and he had agreed to share a third of its thirty-thousand-dollar advance with her as well as a portion of the royalties. By the time of its publication, James in fact had very little appetite for writing, although two books were in their preliminary stages. The first was to be another small volume in the mold of the highly successful *Beard on Bread*. Knopf editor-in-chief Robert Gottlieb had proposed *Beard on Soup*, an idea that held no attraction for James. Pursuing what proved to be an extremely durable trend, he and Judith Jones instead settled on a book to be called *Beard on Pasta* and retained *Cooks' Catalogue* and *Fannie Farmer* veteran Irene Sax to assemble it.

James had also been urged for some years to write a sequel to *Delights and Prejudices,* an idea to which he began to devote some attention in 1980. James had written the first draft of *Delights and Prejudices* on his own in an exhilarating six weeks, but it seemed that its sequel, provisionally titled *Menus and Memories,* would only be coaxed into existence with considerable effort. James taped interviews with John Ferrone, Barbara Kafka, Judith Jones's husband Evan, and Portland journalist Matt Kramer over the next two years, but nothing resembling a coherent volume of memoirs emerged from them. Although he had already covered the subject exhaustively in *Delights and Prejudices,* Beard's memory was fixed on his childhood and early adulthood, and he seemed reluctant to discuss his life after 1950, the very period that should have been the book's focus. He had little energy for sustained concentration on any project by now, but more than one friend suspected he was simply unwilling either to lay bare the facts of his mature career or to gloss them over in print.

More and more he relished the company of the young, and in particular the reverent attentions of young restaurateurs like Alice Waters, Jeremiah Tower, and Larry Forgione, a classically trained chef bent on establishing a restaurant devoted entirely to American cooking of Lutèce-like seriousness and pretension. In this Beard played the role of dean of American food as proud father of a precocious and gifted brood as well as a prophet who has lived to see his predictions come true. Styling himself in his own eccentric version of a high priest and elder, he frequently dressed in Chinese robes and tunics and surrounded himself with orientalia, posing for *People* in an Asian gown with a rice bowl in his hand, the image of his father, John Beard, the elusive Sinophile burgher of Salmon Street.

Although he was unprepared to display the kind of verbal candor about himself in public that he now occasionally revealed in private, Beard became somewhat more outspoken, an attitude consistent with the liberated sensibility surrounding the marketing of *The New James Beard.* He condemned convenience foods and—with some hypocrisy—junk food and stressed the paramount place of fresh and seasonal ingredients, although these were hardly controversial or unusual positions to take by the early 1980s. What was rarer and more daring was the concern he voiced with increasing regularity during 1981 about the fate of U.S. farms and fisheries, in a period when the gospel of economic growth and the blessings of the free market had led to reckless plundering of the nation's topsoil, wetlands, lakes, and seas. It was a subject he had edged into nervously: He decided to declare his interest in the subject during a panel discussion in San Francisco and before mounting the dais shook with the trepidation of a stage ingenue. While his fellow speakers addressed their habitual gastronomic concerns, Beard declared that there would be no food at all if environmental degradation and the overexploitation of resources did not cease. As he put it to an interviewer, "If we go on with the state of destruction of land for housing and development and polluting the atmosphere and water, there isn't going to be enough food to go around." To another he lamented the despoiling of the great fishery of his home state and the port that had captivated him as a child:

Astoria was a great fishing place and now it's almost fished out. It's sad. That's an almost world-wide tragedy at this point—that waters are being overfished, polluted. I think the Olympia oyster is gone forever; I don't think we'll ever get that back. . . . Then, of course, we are losing so much—they tear up arable land and build the slums of tomorrow. It's just heartbreaking to see this happen. We're going to have a crisis.

James's apocalyptic view was at least partly borne out by the end of the decade: Government and corporate policy encouraged fencerow-to-fencerow planting, and with it topsoil erosion and groundwater pollution, while farmers fended off drought, falling prices, and bankruptcy and their loss of their properties to banks and corporate farmers eager to buy up prime land on the cheap. By the end of the 1980s, more than nine hundred farmers in the upper Midwest alone had committed suicide, their own calamity overshadowed by season upon season of famine in Africa.

It was arguable that James and his colleagues in the food press were, as handmaidens to the food industry, unwitting collaborators in the destruction of American agriculture. But the emphasis placed by the emerging generation of chefs on ingredients over technical mastery was, as James recognized, a potential force for the restoration of the food economy whose loss he mourned. In a restaurant such as Alice Waters's Chez Panisse, food inspired by Elizabeth David and Richard Olney was joined to community activism, ecological awareness, and an understanding that cooking is a product of agriculture as much as of culture. It was, in many respects, a vision descended from the culinary bohemians and regionalists of the 1920s and 1930s, which transcended the immemorial schisms between gourmets and domestic scientists and attempted to restore cooking's rightful context.

Waters and the legion of young cooks and restaurateurs who at one time or another had worked with her—among them soon-to-be celebrated chefs like Joyce Goldstein, Mark Miller, Jeremiah Tower, and Jonathan Waxman—were influential, but the ethic under which they worked did not travel much beyond California and its benign agricultural climate and food-conscious public. Most of the restaurants that came in the wake of Chez Panisse had no ethical context to speak of, but only an ethos that manifested the narcissism of the eighties. If the decade represented the final triumph of American consumerism—of spending sundered from earning and need, of shopping as the ultimate expression of self—and eating is the fundamental act of consumption, it was appropriate that the 1980s, like the 1880s, were food obsessed. Restaurants became the drawing rooms of America's affluent, thirtyish protobourgeosie and the backdrop for socializing and business dealings of every sort. Like the lobster palaces and Delmonico's of a century before, they vied for attention with the size and splendor of their dining rooms, the gloss of their patrons, and the decibels of noise and kilowatts of energy contained within their walls.

Increasingly restaurants also promoted the pedigrees and creative gifts of their cooks, who as owners or star contract players frequently vacated the kitchen in order to prowl the dining room and be ogled by their public. Like any species of celebrity, chefs rose and fell in the public's favor—or at least in the imaginings of the food press and its trend spotters—as did ingredients, tools, and cuisines. Given the need to keep abreast of so much change and innovation, magazines became sources of food information as vital and influential as books, touting chefs, new American cuisine, sun-dried tomatoes, and arugula with the fevered conviction of Wall Street stock tipsters. Two magazines in particular, *Food & Wine* and *Cuisine,* abandoned all connection with the domestic science and women's service magazine traditions of food journalism in favor of monitoring the shifting movements and tastes of celebrity chefs and notable consultants and food authors. A headline in *Cuisine* proclaimed "The World of Chèvre," an unwitting summation of the era's zealous but flighty absorption with the food trend of the moment.

From the myopic and self-regarding media precincts of Manhattan it might have seemed the whole country was greedily feeding on chanterelles and mâche from a single gilded trough stretching from Michael's in Santa Monica to the Quilted Giraffe in New York. In fact, with the exception of the Cajun cuisine popularized by New Orleans cuisinier-behemoth Paul Prudhomme, the trends of the first half of the 1980s were felt only to a limited extent outside the major metropolises of the East and West coasts. In Oregon, a community cookbook called *A Taste of Oregon,* boasting recipes like Frosted Meatloaf, Glazed Burgundy Burgers, and Chili-Ghetti suggested that the members of the Junior League of Eugene had culinary imaginations every bit as fevered as the precocious young cooks being feted in New York, San Francisco, and Los Angeles. But beyond underlining the enduring attraction of such perverse constructions, *A Taste of Oregon*—whose editors sent James a presentation copy—illustrated other trends that James would find gratifying, in particular an interest in local materials and traditions expressed through pioneer recipes and notes on "the usage of foods that are specialties of our state such as seafood, game and fresh fruits and vegetables."

That there existed in Oregon an appetite for this kind of material was borne out by sales of *A Taste of Oregon* in excess of two hundred thousand copies over the course of the decade, nearly double those of *The New James Beard.* It would, of course, have been too much to hope that the popularity of such a book represented the end of the destruction and denaturing of Oregon's cooking that was first detectable in James's youth. But James took pleasure in these developments and a modest measure of credit for them. In interviews he noted that ten years after the publication of *American Cookery,* his championing of American food was at last bearing fruit, albeit perhaps not in exactly the form he had imagined. As 1981 gave way to 1982, magazines from *Metropolitan Home* to *Cuisine* announced the waning influence of nouvelle cuisine and the ascendance of a simpler "New American Cooking."

But the food magazine editors hardly envisioned a nation scouring old community cookbooks or the restoration of pork and pies as the foundation of the American diet. Instead American traditions and ingredients would be but more grist for the superstar-chef-powered trend mill of the last few years. The elegant presentations and amusing juxtapositions of nouvelle cuisine would be brought to bear on American food, moderating its gross and vulgar tendencies: Cranberries, berry fruit, and corn—molded, mounded, or otherwise rendered into artful dollops, disks, columns, or obelisks—would garnish plates of crab cakes and thick-cut lamb chops, and there would be no gravy but only sauces, and sauce *under* the principal component at that.

New American Cooking proved to be for the most part yet another food editor's self-fulfilling prophecy, although the yearning for simpler and more direct food behind it persisted and was addressed over the remainder of the decade largely through the vehicle of Mediterranean and Italian food. The only domestic tradition to attain much long-term recognition was that of the Southwest, whose chile- and spice-laden flavors were for most Americans as foreign as those of France, Italy, or China. Among noteworthy cooks, only Beard's protégé Larry Forgione steadfastly clung to the new American style throughout the 1980s and beyond. Having made a considerable reputation at the River Café, Forgione took over the former site of Stephen Spector's Le Plaisir in 1973. Few disciples were more devoted than Forgione, and it was James that dubbed the new restaurant "An American Place," then as now a shrine to James and his culinary nationalism.

In January 1982 Beard and Barbara Kafka flew west to the Stanford Court for what were to be his final classes in San Francisco. At Kafka's urging, and in keeping with his increasing interest in materials over technique, James had decided to experiment with a class on tasting at which students might assay varieties of pepper, butter, and ham, an exercise to which his students took with surprising enthusiasm. He remained in San Francisco through the rest of the month, leaving only to fly to Los Angeles for a dinner to honor Danny Kaye, an act that required either considerable diplomacy or hypocrisy: Beard loathed Kaye as he did few other people and found the actor's manner overbearing and his much publicized self-immersion in Chinese cooking silly and pretentious.

James returned to New York for the first three weeks of February for classes, a luncheon with the staff of *People,* and work on a piece for the *Reader's Digest* on his childhood Christmas memories. He flew back to California during the last week of February for two weeks of appearances in San Francisco, Los Angeles, and San Diego. In the last city at a culinary competition in which he and Marion

Cunningham were judges, he caused a scene by initially declaring all the entries unworthy of consideration, only to select a dish that was clearly among the most execrable of the lot and insist that it be awarded first place. Beyond the mental strain—exacerbated by alcohol and depression—displayed in such episodes, his travel and his teaching, writing, and media work in New York were an assault on a body growing frailer by the week. By 1982 Richard Nimmo—now assisted at the Twelfth Street house by a talented amateur cook from the South named Caroline Stuart, who was gradually becoming a pivotal part of the cooking school and household staff—had to be called on to drive him to stores and restaurants only a block or two from home. He spent Easter in New York and was visited by John Carroll and Clark Wolf, the latter of whom was about to move to New York to work on a grocery shop specializing in American foods, being developed by Barbara Kafka.

Through the last weeks of April his health deteriorated and by May 2 he was admitted to New York Hospital with pneumonia and intestinal obstruction. He passed his seventy-ninth birthday there and was released five days later with ten prescriptions and instructions to rest at home and to reduce the intensity of his schedule in the future. He forwent the Reed College New York alumni luncheon as well as the presentation of his third R. T. French Tastemaker Award, for *The New James Beard,* which beat out an unimpressive field of contenders. The golden age of food writing of the 1970s, which saw the first works of Richard Olney, Paula Wolfert, Diana Kennedy, and Marcella Hazan, had been succeeded by reworkings of traditional subjects and cuisines as well as a swelling number of titles by celebrity chefs.

In June he left for San Francisco and Portland, where he was to address the National Food Editors' Conference on the cooking and ingredients of the Northwest. But before he could leave California for Oregon, he was compelled to reenter hospital in San Francisco. The gravity and persistence of his maladies, combined with his unwillingness to stay at home, meant that he now had a team of specialists in San Francisco nearly as well acquainted with his condition as their New York counterparts. There had been a time a few years before when he took a certain pleasure in his hospital stays and the stream of visitors, telephone calls, and intriguingly déclassé food that came with them. But now he came to hate them.

Once released, he returned home to a relatively quiet summer in New York, his first away from Gearhart in years. His immobility made him both restive and sullen even as he posed for a *New York* magazine story on the delights of entertaining in his backyard conservatory and garden. The recklessness and cynicism he had displayed at the San Diego cooking competition resurfaced in September when, too sick with respiratory illness to travel, he sent Nimmo in his stead to two engagements in San Antonio. Both were described in his October 22 column as though Beard himself had been present, and he damned the food at one of the events as "horrible" and "an insult to good American ingredients." Despite the sure knowledge that the column would be read in Texas and its falsity exposed, he submitted it to his syndicate. When the discrepancies were uncovered by an editor on the *San Antonio Express*, Beard initially refused to issue a correction and only after some weeks was a revised version distributed by his syndicate.

Throughout the autumn James was restless, ill tempered, and dissatisfied with Nimmo, who had managed to stay in his good graces for over eight years. Projects were begun and abandoned for lack of interest, and dishes were prepared to pass the time of day and ingredients allowed to spoil. His eternal dread of solitude became more pronounced, and he increasingly found comfort in the company of Clark Wolf, for whom he prepared Sunday lunch on an almost weekly basis. Wolf's blend of solicitude and sophistication eased James's craving to be admired and cosseted and to be treated like a contemporary who was au courant with the arts and gay scene. For Wolf James was both mentor and monument, a delightful, witty, and charismatic Dutch uncle who was also the most venerable and accomplished personage in the food business in which Wolf had begun to forge a career.

James's other newfound close companion during this time was a dog given to him by Stephen Spector, a pug that he and Mary Hamblet together named Percy. Initially the dog was little more than an addition to the house's growing collection of orientalia, and Beard resisted its efforts to play or take possession of his lap whenever he sat down in the upstairs parlor. But he was ultimately won over by the unequivocal and unrelenting quality of the animal's affection, just as Gino found purpose in his life by taking over its care and walking it up and down Twelfth Street between Sixth and Seventh avenues. James was restless but incapable of much sustained activity, and the dog in his lap was like a set of beads with which to occupy his huge and fretful hands.

James attained his eightieth birthday in 1983, a day neither his doctors nor friends had expected him to see. But he had an apparently infinite capacity to stage miraculous, phoenixlike recoveries, an ancient and rusty machine shored up with salvaged parts and baling wire, whose gears somehow continued to turn. His eightieth birthday was an event around which the food community could rally and salute both its grand old man and its own history and achievements. But James himself was hardly in retirement: In April, *The James Beard Cookbook* joined *The Fannie Farmer Cook Book*, *The Joy of Cooking*, and *The New York Times Cook Book* in the Cookbook Hall of Fame established at Syracuse University by the R. T. French Company. In the same month *Beard on Pasta* was published and a comparatively light schedule of press, radio, and television interviews arranged on its behalf in New York and Los Angeles.

Beard on Pasta was James's twenty-second book, and although largely assembled and written by Irene Sax, it was a clear reflection of a lifetime of eclecticism, with one hundred recipes drawn not only from Italy but China, Hungary, and the Middle East. Identical in format to *Beard on Bread*, and with illustrations by Karl Stuecklen, the book was neither a major publishing nor culinary event but sold a respectable ninety thousand copies over the next eight years. Its publication and his birthday resulted in a considerable number of interviews and adulatory assessments of his career, although not all treated James in the manner he would have liked. A piece by Phyllis Richman in the *Washington Post* included a survey of his books and both the constants and the changing tastes reflected in them over time. In particular Richman noted the brevity and comparative vagueness of his early recipes and his penchant for including canned and prepared ingredients that no contemporary cook of any seriousness would countenance. It was a mild criticism, if it was a criticism at all, but James felt upbraided by it and alternately sulked and fumed about the piece for weeks.

James's birthday on May 5 was celebrated at the Four Seasons with a Mexican buffet and the better part of his friends and acquaintances from the food business. Mary Hamblet flew in from Oregon

and recalled for those assembled the concoctions of sand and marshmallows James would prepare on the beach during their childhood.
Surrounded in his favorite dining room by friends and by the elite of
the food community, James felt himself momentarily unalone, a star
to whose achievements even the frustratingly inattentive Craig Claiborne was compelled to come and pay homage.

On May 10 James taught a class for winners of the Nestlé Toll-
house Morsels Contest and a few days later flew to Los Angeles to
promote *Beard on Pasta,* in the main through interviews given in his
hotel room, where he could see several journalists a day without
becoming overtired. He then went to Santa Barbara to appear as gastronomy's gray eminence in an episode of Julia Child's new television
series. He continued on to San Francisco, where he gave further
interviews, and lunched on stuffed game hens with M. F. K. Fisher at
her Sonoma County home. At the end of the month he arrived in
Oregon and joined Richard Nimmo at the Gearhart golf course condominium he had inhabited three years before, remaining for a
month under the Oregon coast's sodden, oyster gray sky. He was
tired and irritable—particularly toward Nimmo, who insulated himself from James's nostalgia-stoked ennui with increasing quantities of
vodka—but enjoyed the company of Mary Hamblet and the admiring blandishments of journalists from *The Oregonian.* It was to be
his last summer at Gearhart, and at the beginning of July he shook
its sand from his shoes and flew home to New York and the confines
of his Twelfth Street barracks.

The autumn of 1983 passed in much the same fitful manner as
the spring had, its tedious bouts with low-grade pneumonia and urinary blockages mitigated only by the visits of friends and neighbors
like Lydie Marshall, an energetic and unpretentious French-born
cooking teacher and author who lived a few blocks away. Marshall
had fixed herself in James's affections by virtue not only of her culinary skills and sensibility but by knitting him a sweater that became
a constant in his wardrobe. Together with Clark Wolf, Barbara
Kafka, and Peter Kump, she became one of his regular visitors and
telephone interlocutors during the early eighties and, mindful of both
his physical frailty and his loneliness and discontent, took to looking
in on him regularly. More than most, she was frank with him about
the shortcomings of his staff and professional associates and his fre-

quent obliviousness to how they handled his money and reputation. In his hunger for attention and affection, she felt, he rendered himself far too vulnerable to exploitation.

In late November James received a telephone call from *Daily News* reporter Suzanne Hamlin, who advised him that a cookbook for which he had written a foreword and jacket blurb, *Richard Nelson's American Cooking,* contained at least fifty-six recipes taken almost verbatim and without attribution from other writers' work: specifically, thirty from Richard Olney's *Simple French Food* and twenty-six from Francesco Ghedini's *Northern Italian Cooking.* On closer examination James discovered that not only had he lent his name to a book that would be pilloried for its alleged plagiarism, but that it contained unattributed recipes from his own books and classes. The embarrassment and humiliation he felt in having endorsed the book was doubled by his sense of having been betrayed by Nelson, whom he had known since 1948 and whom he had befriended and assisted in his career. In the late seventies Nelson had helped manage—and some said attempted to dominate totally—the Gearhart summer classes, and no doubt in part through his association with Beard, he had become the proprietor of a successful Portland cooking school, a food columnist for *The Oregonian,* and president of the International Association of Cooking Schools. The jacket of *Richard Nelson's American Cooking* described Nelson as "the first culinary expert in a decade to be admitted to the circle of great American food authorities: James Beard, Julia Child, Craig Claiborne, and Julie Dannenbaum . . . a former protégé of such illustrious American cooks as James Beard and June Platt, [who] has risen to national prominence in a very short time." Whether the pretensions were Nelson's, his publisher's, or both, they were considerable.

The *Daily News* broke its story on December 7, and it indeed became a kind of Pearl Harbor for the food community, of which the Lady Harlech stir of six years before was but a foreshadowing. In the wake of Hamlin's story, the existence of yet more plagiarized recipes in *Richard Nelson's American Cooking* were alleged, including five from books by Craig Claiborne. The food community knit its collective brow, both lamenting and savoring a scandal that garnered the kind of attention it craved and rarely received; as ever, it fought ferociously over what the rest of the world regarded as extremely paltry stakes. But however petty and parochial that outrage might seem to the nongastronomic public, Richard Olney became determined to sue Nelson and his publisher and did so with some justification: Of all the food writers of his generation, Olney's work had the stamp of genuine artistic creation about it. His recipes were not only distinctive in style but truly original in substance. *Simple French Food* was an acknowledged watershed among cookbooks and was perhaps the paramount influence on the leading members of the new generation of American cooks that came of age in California in the seventies and eighties.

Olney reached an out-of-court settlement with Nelson and his book's publisher the following year for what was rumored to be a significant sum. The affair finished James's friendship with Nelson and with Olney as well, as Olney was convinced that Nelson had obtained the recipes in question via Beard. In fact Olney had been sending James copies of the manuscript of *Simple French Food* during the course of its composition in 1972 and 1973, and James apparently copied and distributed recipes from it to his classes at that time and therefore probably to Nelson. Olney felt that Beard had treated his work without the care and respect it had deserved, and, indeed, James had initially misjudged its significance. As he read Olney's first draft, he confided in letters to Julia Child his concern—whether real or merely designed to stir up gossip and rivalry—that Pat Knopf at Atheneum, Olney's publisher, was bound to be dissatisfied with the book. Olney's then junior status in the food world, the amorphous and ill-defined ethics of attribution prevalent among food writers, and James's own failure to grasp what had come into his possession may indeed have resulted in casual treatment of Olney's work, enabling Nelson in all innocence to believe it to be nothing more than generic teaching recipes from Beard's classes.

If James felt culpable in the matter, he gave no indication of it, but told Hamlin of the *Daily News* that "I feel personally transgressed." He was, however, deeply troubled by it. He was by nature highly averse to embarrassment, and with this incident the intrigue, status seeking, and dubious ethics to which he and the food community were habituated seemed at long last to have exceeded his own appetite for them. In food James had found and furthered a profession in which his psychological and professional aptitudes were perfectly melded—a career whose putative substance was based on nurturance, the family, and the communal hearth, but which was at its own table inclined to serve up a bile for which even he now had little stomach.

Even as the Nelson scandal enveloped him, James prepared his Christmas list: pecans for Marion Cunningham; bacon for Sam Aaron; ham for Julia Child; champagne for Elizabeth David; and similar and sundry gifts for Joe and Ruth Baum, Judith and Evan Jones, Philip Brown, Jerry Lamb, John Ferrone, Leon Lianides, John Carroll, James Nassikas, Chuck Williams, Mary Hamblet, and Clark Wolf, among others. He did not give presents to his retinue at Twelfth Street, perhaps by reason of forgetfulness or perhaps out of dissatisfaction with them. But he still remained capable of the cheer, wit, and geniality that had made him a sought-after social companion and continued to enjoy his iconic status as America's king of food, a role epitomized with the fold-out cover of the November issue of *Cuisine*, whose two sides were filled respectively with the back and front of his celebrated bald head.

The early weeks of 1984 passed much as those of the previous year, with trips to Palm Beach in mid-February and to San Francisco a month later, where renal and vascular problems compelled a short hospital stay. Back in New York on April 10, an apparently recovered Beard was honored at a black-tie dinner staged by the Beef Industry Council at which he was presented with a council-published book called *Dear James Beard,* a compendium of recipes and reminiscences from such culinary stars as Julia Child, Alice Waters, and Jeremiah Tower, as well as friends and colleagues like Judith Jones and Chuck Williams. "I really adore it," James said, "but I don't think I'm worth it."

He returned to San Francisco in mid-April to his Stanford Court aerie and what was to be a gala eighty-first birthday party on May 5. But he was hospitalized a few days before that for bronchitis and infections in his legs and appeared at the party in a wheelchair, wizened but smiling gauntly, retreating to his hospital room at the end of the evening. Beard remained there until the middle of the month, when he returned to New York to a relatively quiet summer and a week of classes.

Some months earlier, James had been invited to participate in a gourmet cruise aboard the *Pacific Princess* to the Inside Passage of Alaska, which was also to feature Craig Claiborne and several other less-renowned cooking teachers. Given James's recent hospitalization and worsening condition, both his staff and Denton Cox felt that making the voyage would be extremely ill advised. But James, who more and more responded to disagreement with rages or fits of petulance, was adamant that he would go and that no one would stop him.

He and Nimmo flew to Portland in early August and then to San Francisco, where they boarded the liner on the fourteenth. Even before the ship left San Francisco, the tenor of James's temper was clear. He and Nimmo had been forced to share a cabin that Beard felt was too small and, moreover, inconsistent with his status. In their mutual confinement Nimmo was helpless to escape James's moods and grumbling as well as the endless ministrations his crumbling body required, and sought shelter in a vodka intake that reached two bottles a day. Meanwhile as the ship beat its way northward up the coast, passing Tillamook Head, Gearhart Beach, and the mouth of the Columbia far offshore, James gorged himself with food and liquor. He flouted his prescribed dietary regimen with near-suicidal abandon, stuffing himself with shipboard fare even as he pronounced it disgusting and swilling scotch whiskey.

On the *Pacific Princess*'s return to San Francisco on August 26, he bolted down dinners at Alice Waters's Chez Panisse and Jeremiah Tower's new Stars restaurant. Two days later he flew home to New York, where Caroline Stuart and Clay Triplette were appalled by his condition: He was bloated, his skin was ashen, and his mind and body adrift in lassitude and torpor. They arranged to check him into New York Hospital the following day, where he was diagnosed as having shortness of breath, congestive heart failure, and intestinal bleeding. He remained there until mid-September and was sent home on a strict low-protein diet, subdued in spirit and now incontinent. He returned briefly to Oregon later in the month and picnicked with Mary Hamblet at a cove south of Gearhart. On his return to New York he was still fit enough to hold a party for French chef and cookbook author Madeleine Kamman and to pose for a Christmas photo spread for *New York* magazine. In October he held a week of cooking classes and acted as a judge in the Uncle Ben's Rice Cook-off. He taught a further week of classes in early December and hosted a benefit for the Phoenix House rehabilitation center on the nineteenth.

By Christmas week what little energy he had been able to gather up in the autumn left him, and he passed Christmas Day in bed. Clark Wolf visited him and found him naked save for a towel, his skin a milky, quartzine shroud stretched over his massive bones. His kidney failure was now acute, and the following day he was taken to the hospital to have a shunt for kidney dialysis placed in his arm. Later that week he fell asleep in the midst of a telephone conversation with Lydie Marshall, and two days into the new year tripped over the telephone cord and hit his head on a table. Unable to right himself, he called for Stuart and Triplette, who found him in obvious pain but insisting he required no medical attention. His face was swollen and bruised, and his nose bled for several days thereafter, but he continued to refuse a visit to the doctor and vowed that he would under no circumstances reenter the hospital for his scheduled dialysis or any other treatment.

On January 8 James at last relented and entered New York Hospital, and after a blood transfusion and dialysis regained some of his vigor and a large measure of his once-vibrant capacity for wit and drollery. The blood that had restored him, he announced to his visitors, had belonged to a twenty-one-year-old dancer of obvious balletic and sexual prowess. He critiqued the hospital's cooking and the bland diet he had been placed on, remarking of the chicken broth he had been offered: "I suppose a chicken might have walked through it at some point." A week later, Tom Margittai and Paul Kovi of the Four Seasons sent him a meal of fish and fresh fruit, but his appetite had now diminished considerably, and the hospital discouraged any departure from his prescribed fare. He received visitors, among them Judith Jones, to whom he recounted a dream in which she was a small feral creature alternately darting out from and retreating under a sofa. He offered no interpretation, but Jones believed the figure might represent his conscience.

In mid-January James had one functioning kidney and would require implantation of a cardiac pacemaker, but he had been able to do some work on his newspaper column and sort through his mail. Either Caroline Stuart or Richard Nimmo came to the hospital each afternoon, and Barbara Kafka and Peter Kump were near-daily visitors. Gino, who found James's illness terrifying, went to his bedside only once and fled after ten minutes. By contrast, Larry Forgione passed hours each day in a forlorn vigil just outside the door of James's room. Despite such a constant stream of attention, it often seemed that no one person was clearly in charge of James's care and welfare. Clark Wolf arrived at the hospital one afternoon and was stunned to learn from the hospital staff that although James urgently required another pacemaker, there was no one in attendance to give consent on his behalf.

By the week of January 20, whatever temporary revival in his condition afforded him by his first week in the hospital was at an end, and both his body and his spirits fell into a rapid decline. On the afternoon of Tuesday the twenty-second, Barbara Kafka visited him. After a listless conversation he said, "I can't anymore" and rolled his body away in silence. At 12:45 A.M., his heart—terribly enlarged, as the autopsy would reveal—fluttered and stilled.

Stuart and Nimmo were awakened in the night with the news, and they in turn alerted Peter Kump and others, phone calls spreading, root and branch, across the vast network of James's friends and acquaintances. Nimmo went up to Gino's quarters and told him that Beard was dead. Gino shut the door and remained secreted in his room for several days, unwilling to speak to others and angry that they did not volunteer to speak to him. By midmorning of January 23, the phone began to ring in wave after wave of press inquiries. Stuart, Triplette, and Nimmo were joined at the house by Clark Wolf, Peter Kump, John Ferrone, and Ruth Baum, who attempted to introduce a measure of order and calm into the now-besieged household.

As in his life, not a few people wanted a piece of James in his death: Scarcely a day later, an active figure on the New York food scene stopped a stranger on the street, fingered the checkered silk at his neck, and announced, "This is Jim Beard's bow tie." When the will was read, many were taken aback at its lack of provision for his friends and colleagues: Beard had promised majolica, antiques, books, and a range of the rest of the impedimenta of his life to the people who had been close to him, but the bulk of his estate was given to Reed College. John Ferrone was given the rights within his lifetime to James's book royalties, which would then pass to Henry and Bettina McNulty's daughter and ultimately to Reed. Gino was given a lifetime lease on his apartment at Twelfth Street. There was little else.

James's death was front-page news in the *New York Times* and the subject of a memorial essay by Craig Claiborne, who lauded him as one who "more than any other person helped shape the change in American dining habits . . . an innovator, an experimenter, a missionary in bringing the gospel of good cooking to the home table." In *The Oregonian* he received treatment worthy of Portland's first and finest citizens and was styled "a native son." But the handling of his affairs after his death was too often inept and insensitive: Reed College was anxious to receive the moneys from his estate and the New York bank acting as executor had little awareness of who he was and what might have mattered to him or to his friends. His books and belongings were auctioned off in piecemeal fashion—bow ties, kitchen equipment, antiquarian books, and majolica gaveled away like the relics of a tawdry cult star—and netted $272,000. What remained of the fabric of his life was shoveled into a Dumpster, and the house on Twelfth Street was put on the market for $1 million. However, the stipulation that Gino remain a tenant in the upstairs apartment made the house unsalable, and it was eventually sold to a foundation established by Peter Kump, Barbara Kafka, and others to be maintained as a showplace for American culinary talent. Gino himself died five years later, a few days after James's dog, Percy, was run down near Caroline Stuart's Connecticut home.

Some weeks after James's death, a canister containing his ashes arrived without notice at Mary Hamblet's house in Portland Heights. On a dull and windy day on the cusp of spring, she and Jerry Lamb drove to the coast. At a spot close by Tillamook Head and at another on Gearhart Beach, she scattered his remains along the tide line, sowing them in the sand, feeding them to the hungry sea.

Afterword

or thirty years, James Beard was not only the apotheosis of food but in many respects the exemplar of a good life of which food was the wellspring. The secrets of cooking, eating, and entertaining were disclosed by him; their canons and rules recast by him; and their pleasures were amply expressed and embodied in his corpulence, whether garbed in costumes from Piccadilly or Beijing.

Today it is clear that in a number of ways he moves among us, both in the works he left behind and as a presence not so very different from what he was in life. Of his twenty-two books, at least half remain in print, and many continue to enjoy significant sales. Restaurants and food purveyors still advertise endorsements or mentions he made of them a decade or more before. People frequently express surprise to hear that he is dead; close friends and colleagues slip effortlessly and nearly without notice from past to present tense when they discuss him.

In all this James Beard retains the status of an icon, a man who even in death—perhaps even more so in death—possesses a force that has a kind of necessity about it. Within the food community over which he reigned, his bald head and customary bow tie adorn awards and newsletters, heraldic emblems that confer a kind of historical legitimacy. The job of biographer confers infinite opportunities to assess the depth and nature of one's subject's fame. In my case, few people much under the age of thirty had heard of Beard; few over the age of forty hadn't. To describe who he was to those unacquainted with his name became something of a challenge: Words like *chef*, *cooking teacher*, and *food writer* all came to mind, yet these were all labels that failed to capture entirely what he was, or what he did, and which he himself often detested.

In the end, Beard's measure may now consist less of his achievements or occupations than of the things he came to symbolize; and the meanings they encode continue to resonate like a song or a catchphrase that sweeps the popular consciousness for a summer and is gone, preserved in memory's deepest alluvia for those who were there. That much was true for his public; for his intimates it was all the more so. To know him was to love him and to feel loved—not simply to be appreciated or desired but to feel comprehended; to feel that what one cherished was also cherished by him, and where it was not, that the appreciation was in any case understood. The account rendered in these pages of Beard's own insecurities and dissatisfactions and of his taste for social drama may obscure the depth of the pleasure he took in life and in other human beings, and in particular, the acuity of his insight into them and the instinctive compassion that accompanied it. His pain often estranged him from his fellows, but far more often it moved him to acts of generosity and consideration that were rare in his milieu and that sought no regard for themselves.

In these respects, every encounter with Beard, whether by a follower of his recipes or a member of his entourage, was a personal encounter. Works like *The Complete Book of Outdoor Cookery, The James Beard Cookbook, Delights and Prejudices,* and *James Beard's American Cookery* are the works of a peerless instructor and expert, and also of a unique sensibility that projected itself through and beyond the practical material ostensibly on offer. More than anything he did, Beard deserves—and would doubtless have preferred—to be remembered as a teacher; as one who shared his skills, knowledge, and enthusiasm with irrefutable conviction, as though he were communicating his own essence. Beard's authority was as much a matter of image as expertise, and as dean of American Cookery Beard created a persona to match his breathtakingly wide knowledge of food—a role that he alone could play. That no one today could claim to occupy it as he did—except perhaps for Julia Child, whose fame owes more to French cuisine and a mastery of the television medium than the domestic cooking traditions and homemaking journalism that produced Beard—is testament to the singularity and thoroughness of his performance in it.

But perhaps the role is obsolete, and perhaps Beard himself made it so: He taught us too well for us to need or desire another like him. In any case, those who would succeed him today are hampered not only by their own limitations—most contemporary food celebrities lack Beard's knowledge, taste, and, not least, the dignity and grace of his person—but by the times. Between 1960 and 1989, the American food community and media mined the world's cuisines, cooking techniques, and ingredients, seemingly exhausting every vein from which culinary inspiration or fashion might be extracted. Few will regret the passing of the frenzied trend-making and conspicuous consumption of the 1980s, which reached its peak shortly after Beard's death, a bull market in goat cheese and arugula that crashed with Wall Street at the end of the decade and went the way of the power tie. In its wake the community of food professionals over which he presided seems not only leaderless but directionless. It is often less than clear what purpose is served by the numberless cookbooks, classes, and gastronomic events it continues to produce, or for whom these are intended. Like their predecessors in the food community, Beard's colleagues and heirs find themselves competing for the increasingly limited attentions of a public whose appetite for food lore and products is sated in more ways than one: It appears that since 1985, the passionate and intelligent appreciation of food and drink that was Beard's lifework has become the victim not only of economic recession and a reaction against the excesses of the previous decade but of a public sense of boredom and irrelevance.

It is perhaps of no great consequence if people no longer give their attention to fashionable restaurants and food personalities as they once did and instead turn their energies to home, hearth, and other varieties of cultural activity. But in fact Americans also seem to want to cook less, eating more and more meals prepared by the hands of strangers because they lack not only the time to cook for themselves but the interest. We seem as a people less inclined to gather at our stoves and our tables and take succor in the good things that happen around them. We are in danger of forgetting their magic, their nurture, and the truth of the tales only they can tell; and James Beard would have thought that a tragedy.

Despite his considerable contributions to the commercialization of cooking and eating that has occurred over the last hundred years, Beard's approach to food was fundamentally personal and sensual, grounded in his own past and the communities and traditions he inhabited. He reveled in good produce and the places manifested in it, in recipes both old and new, and in every act of touching, smelling, and tasting food. For Beard the kitchen was a stage of infinite drama and delight, the center of the home that both brings forth our daily bread and memorializes the domestic and agricultural labors and lives of forbears. If we are today less mindful of these things—of the pleasures cooking in the present affords and the voices from the past that speak to us through it—it may be because food has been so thoroughly severed from its context; from the stories, people, rituals, and places that render it psychological and cultural sustenance rather than a mere commodity. That dilemma is partly James Beard's legacy, but so too its solution, and it may be that in the wake of his passing we require only what James Beard himself required: the memory of those sustaining moments that are bound up in the things we eat, those same sweet and bitter seasons bestowed by life and the land that he spent a lifetime remembering and making anew on our behalf.

Ihe following is a list of books and other materials that are cited, quoted, or discussed in *James Beard: A Biography*. It does not include newspaper articles, most magazine articles, or magazine and newspaper articles written by James Beard. Those existing letters and other papers of James Beard that are not in the possession of private individuals can be found at the American Heritage Center of the University of Wyoming and at the library of the Oregon Historical Society.

I also want to acknowledge my debt to the works of social and cultural history and journalism cited below, which have profoundly influenced my discussion. Any errors of interpretation or fact are, of course, my own.

Altman, Dennis. *The Homosexualization of America*. New York: St. Martin's Press, 1982.

Armitage, Merle. *Fit for a King*. New York: Duell, Sloan & Pearce, 1939.

Atkinson, Brooks. *Broadway*. New York: Macmillan, 1970.

Bayer, William, and Paula Wolfert. "A Delicious Little Cookbook Scandal." *New York*, Dec. 12, 1977.

Beard, James. *Hors d'Oeuvre and Canapés, with a Key to the Cocktail Party*. New York: M. Barrows, 1940.

———. *Cook It Outdoors.* New York: M. Barrows, 1941.

———. *Fowl & Game Cookery.* New York: M. Barrows, 1944.

———. *The Fireside Cook Book.* New York: Simon & Schuster, 1949.

———. *Paris Cuisine,* with Alexander Watt. Boston: Little Brown, 1952.

———. *James Beard's Fish Cookery.* Boston: Little, Brown, 1954.

———. *How to Eat Better for Less Money,* with Sam Aaron. New York: Appleton Century Crofts, 1954; rev. ed., New York: Simon & Schuster, 1970.

———. *Jim Beard's Barbecue Cooking.* New York: Maco, 1954.

———. *Jim Beard's Complete Cookbook for Entertaining.* New York: Maco, 1954.

———. *Jim Beard's Casserole Cookbook.* New York: Maco, 1955.

———. *The Complete Book of Outdoor Cookery,* with Helen Evans Brown. New York: Doubleday, 1955.

———. *The James Beard Cookbook,* with Isabel Callvert. New York: Dell, 1959.

———. *James Beard's Treasury of Outdoor Cooking.* New York: Ridge Press, 1960.

———. *James Beard's Menus for Entertaining.* New York: Delacorte, 1965.

———. *Delights and Prejudices.* New York: Atheneum, 1964.

———. *How to Eat (and Drink) Your Way Through a French (and Italian) Menu,* with Gino P. Cofacci. New York: Atheneum, 1971.

———. *James Beard's American Cookery.* Boston: Little, Brown, 1972.

———. *Beard on Bread.* New York: Alfred A. Knopf, 1973.

———. *Beard on Food.* New York: Alfred A. Knopf, 1974.

———. *James Beard's Theory & Practice of Good Cooking.* New York: Alfred A. Knopf, 1977.

———. *The New James Beard.* New York: Alfred A. Knopf, 1981.

———. *Beard on Pasta.* New York: Alfred A. Knopf, 1983.

Beard, James, Milton Glaser, and Burton Richard Wolf, eds., compiled by Barbara Poses Kafka. *The Cooks' Catalogue.* New York: Harper & Row, 1975.

——. *The International Cooks' Catalogue*. New York: Random House, 1977.

Beck, Simone. *Food and Friends: A Memoir with Recipes,* with Suzy Patterson. New York: Viking, 1991.

Belasco, Warren J. *Appetite for Change: How the Counterculture Took on the Food Industry 1966–1988*. New York: Pantheon, 1989.

Bracken, Peg. *The I Hate to Cook Book*. New York: Harcourt Brace, 1960.

Brown, Helen Evans. *The Holiday Cook Book*. Boston: Little, Brown, 1952.

——. *West Coast Cook Book*. Boston: Little Brown, 1952.

——. *Breakfasts and Brunches for Every Occasion,* with Philip Brown. New York: Doubleday, 1961.

Child, Julia, Louisette Bertholle, and Simone Beck. *Mastering the Art of French Cooking*. New York: Alfred A. Knopf, 1961.

Claiborne, Craig. *A Feast Made for Laughter.* New York: Doubleday, 1982.

——. *The New York Times Cook Book*. New York: Harper & Row, 1961.

Council of Women of Trinity Episcopal Church. *Trinity Cook Book*. Portland, Oreg.: n.d., circa 1946.

Crawford, Cheryl. *One Naked Individual: My Fifty Years in the Theatre*. Indianapolis: Bobbs-Merrill, 1977.

Cunningham, Marion. *The Fannie Farmer Cookbook, Twelfth Edition,* with Jeri Laber. New York: Alfred A. Knopf, 1979.

Curnonsky (pseudonym of Maurice-Edmond Sailland). *La France gastronomique: Guide des merveilleuses culinaires et des bonnes auberges françaises*. Paris: F. Rouff, 1921 et seq.

Curtin, Kaier. *"We Can Always Call Them Bulgarians": The Emergence of Lesbians and Gay Men on the American Stage*. Boston: Alyson Publications, 1987.

David, Elizabeth. *Mediterranean Food*. London: Lehmann, 1950.

——. *French Country Cooking*. London: Lehmann, 1951.

——. *French Provincial Cooking*. London: Michael Joseph, 1960.

D'Emilio, John, and Estelle B. Freedman. *Intimate Matters: A History of Sexuality in America*. New York: Harper & Row, 1988.

Doherty, Diane Osgood. *Gearhart By-the-Sea*. Gearhart, Oreg.: Gearhart Homeowners Association, 1985.

Editors of Time-Life Books. *Foods of the World.* New York: Time-Life, 1968 et seq.

Ephron, Nora. *Wallflower at the Orgy.* New York: Viking, 1970.

Erenberg, Lewis A. *Steppin' Out: New York Nightlife and the Transformation of American Culture, 1890–1930.* Chicago: University of Chicago Press, 1981.

Farmer, Fannie. *The Boston Cooking School Cook Book.* Boston: Little Brown, 1896; rev. ed. 1906 et seq.

Favorite Recipes of the Great Northwest. Montgomery, Ala.: Favorite Recipes Press, 1964.

Field, Michael. *Michael Field's Cooking School.* New York: M. Barrows, 1965.

Finck, Henry T. *Food and Flavor: A Gastronomic Guide to Health and Good Living.* New York: Century, 1913.

Fisher, M. F. K. "The Indigestible." *New York Review of Books,* Dec. 20, 1979.

Fishwives of Charleston, Oregon. *Cook Book.* North Bend, Oreg.: Wegferd Publications, 1972.

Fordyce, Eleanor T. "Cookbooks of the 1800s." In *Dining in America 1850–1900,* edited by Kathryn Grover. Amherst: University of Massachusetts Press, 1987.

Fougner, Selmer. *Gourmet Dinners.* New York: M. Barrows, 1941.

Gaige, Crosby. *Dining with My Friends: Adventures with Epicures.* New York: Crown, 1939.

General Mills, Inc. *Betty Crocker's Picture Cook Book.* New York: McGraw-Hill, 1950.

Good Cooking School, Inc. *The Great Cooks Cookbook.* New York: Ferguson/Doubleday, 1974.

Greene, Gael. "The Most Spectacular Restaurant in the World." *New York,* May 31, 1976.

———. "Restaurant Associates: Twilight of the Gods." *New York,* Nov. 2, 1970.

Hess, John L., and Karen Hess. *The Taste of America.* New York: Grossman, 1977.

Hibben, Sheila. *The National Cook Book: A Kitchen Americana.* New York: Harper & Bros., 1932.

Hines, Duncan. *Adventures in Good Eating.* Bowling Green, Ky.: Adventures in Good Eating, Inc., 1936 et seq.

Jacobs, Jay. "James Beard: An American Icon." *Gourmet,* Jan., Feb. 1984.

Jones, Evan. *Epicurean Delight: The Life and Times of James Beard.* New York: Alfred A. Knopf, 1990.

Junior League of Eugene. *A Taste of Oregon.* Eugene, 1980.

Kafka, Barbara, ed. *The James Beard Celebration Cookbook.* New York: Morrow, 1990.

Koenig, Rhoda. "Living to Eat." *New York,* year-end issues, 1979.

Ladies Aid of the First Congregational Church. *Dainty Dishes.* Portland, Oreg.: 1902.

Laughton, Catherine C., ed. *Mary Cullen's Northwest Cook Book.* Portland, Oreg.: Binfords & Mort, 1946.

Levenstein, Harvey. *Revolution at the Table: The Transformation of the American Diet.* Oxford: Oxford University Press, 1988.

MacColl, E. Kimbark. *The Shaping of a City: Business and Politics in Portland, Oregon 1885 to 1915.* Portland: Georgian Press, 1976.

———. *The Growth of a City: Power and Politics in Portland, Oregon 1915 to 1950.* Portland: Georgian Press, 1979.

Mencken, H. L. *The American Mercury,* October 1925.

———. *Chicago Tribune,* June 13, 1925.

Mendelson, Anne. Review of *The New York Times Cook Book, Revised Edition,* in *The Journal of Gastronomy* 6, no. 1 (summer 1990).

Mennell, Stephen. *All Manners of Food: Eating and Taste in England and France from the Middle Ages to the Present.* Oxford: Blackwell, 1985.

Morison, Samuel Eliot. *One Boy's Boston.* Boston: Houghton Mifflin, 1962.

Nelson, Richard. *Richard Nelson's American Cooking.* New York: New American Library, 1983.

Newnham-Davis, A. *The Gourmet's Guide to Europe.* 2nd ed. New York: Brentano's, 1908.

Olney, Richard. *The French Menu Cookbook.* New York: Simon & Schuster, 1970.

———. *Simple French Food.* New York: Atheneum, 1974.

Owen, Jeanne. *A Wine Lover's Cookbook.* New York: M. Barrows, 1940.

Parloa, Maria. *First Principles of Household Management and Cooking.* New ed. Boston: Estes and Lauriar 1888.

Pennell, Elizabeth Robins, ed. *The Feasts of Autolycus: The Diary of a Greedy Woman.* London: Merriam Co., 1896; Chicago: Saalfield, 1900.

Portland Woman's Exchange. *The Portland Woman's Exchange Cook Book 1913.* New edition with introduction and notes by James Beard. Portland: Oregon Historical Society, 1973.

Reed College. *The Quest.* Portland, Oreg.: Reed College, 1920–21.

Rhode, William. *Of Cabbages and Kings.* New York: Stackpole, 1938.

Rice, William, and Burton Wolf, eds. *Where to Eat in America.* New York: Random House, 1977.

Rombauer, Irma S., and Marion R. Becker. *The Joy of Cooking.* Indianapolis: Bobbs-Merrill, 1936; rev. ed. 1943 et seq.

Ronald, Mary. *The Century Cook Book.* New York: Century, 1896.

St. Peter's Guild. *The St. Peter's Guild Cook Book.* La Grande, Oreg.: 1924.

San Grael Society. *The Web-Foot Cook Book.* Portland, Oreg.: First Presbyterian Church, 1885.

Sansbury, Alice. *A Portland Girl at the Chafing Dish.* Portland, Oreg.: 1897.

Schwartz, Hillel. *Never Satisfied: A Cultural History of Diets, Fantasies, and Fat.* Free Press: New York, 1986.

Shapiro, Laura. *Perfection Salad: Women and Cooking at the Turn of the Century.* New York: Farrar, Straus & Giroux, 1986.

Straser, Susan. *Never Done: A History of American Housework.* New York: Pantheon, 1982.

———. *Satisfaction Guaranteed: The Making of the American Mass Market.* New York: Pantheon, 1989.

Susman, Warren. *Culture as History: The Transformation of American Society in the Twentieth Century.* New York: Pantheon, 1984.

Tillamook's Key to the Cupboard. Vol. 11. Tillamook, Oreg.: Tillamook Creamery, n.d., circa 1947.

United Seamen's Service Annual Report 1944. New York: United Seamen's Service, Inc., 1944.

Washington High School. *The Lens*. Portland, Oreg.: Multnomah County Public Schools, 1916–19.

Wechsberg, Joseph. *Dining at the Pavillon*. Boston: Little,
Brown, 1962.

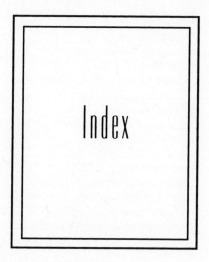

Index

Aaron, Florence, 166
Aaron, Jack, 136
Aaron, Sam, 120, 162, 303, 323
Abbot, Alice, 64
Académie des Gastronomes, 74
Adams, Charlotte, 116, 121, 177
Addams, Jane, 15
Adding Machine, The, 87
Adolph's Meat Tenderizer, 150
Adventures in Good Eating, 164
Agribusiness, rise of, 37
Aladdin oven, 15
Alan Berry (retail store), 120
Alaska, cruise to, 324
Alden, Jerry, 120
Allen, Ida Bailey, 82
Allen, Steve, 211
Alfredo's. *See* Trattoria di Alfredo
Alfred A. Knopf publishers, 123, 199
Algonquin Hotel, 80
Alice B. Toklas Cookbook, The, 163
Alice in Wonderland, 87
American Airlines, 284, 298
American Cookery, 98
America Cooks, 253
American Frugal Housewife, The, 19
American Mercury, 82

An American Place restaurant, 316
American Way, 284, 298
Anatomy of a Murder, 184
Anderson, Edith, 62–63
Anderson, Judith, 102
André (Beard's lover), 163
Angell, Roger, 231
Antrozzo, Delfinio, 31
Apartment Life, 143, 167
Arbuckle, Fatty, 84
Argosy, 136, 139, 149, 167
Armitage, Merle, 100–101, 177
Artex S.A., 264
Artists' and Writers' Cookbook, The,
   207
Art of Simple French Food, The,
   144
Art Theater Players, 83, 84, 85
Asher, Gerald, 246, 280
Asti restaurant, 102
Athena restuarant, 102
Atheneum publisher, 207
"At Home with Jinx and Tex" show,
   121
Atlantic Monthly, The, 10, 145
Auld Lang Syne society, 49, 63
Aurora restaurant, 12

Badger, William, 45
Baills, Claude, 299
Baird, Bil, 121
Balzer's, 147
Baker, George, 63
Baking powder, 57
Bankhead, Tallulah, 102
Barnes, Djuna, 67
Barry, Naomi, 210
Batchelder, Ann, 97, 240
Batterberry, Michael and Ariane, 295
Baum, Joseph: background of, 164; and
    Beard Glaser Wolf, 265; as friend of
    James; 230 323; as restaurant
    designer, 166, 180–81, 186–88, 224,
    249, 284, 285
Baum, Ruth, 230, 323
Beard, Emma, 24
Beard, Genevieve, 24
Beard Glaser Wolf, Ltd., 265–69
Beard, Harold, 25
Beard, James: assignments as consultant,
    139, 169, 208, 222, 235, 249, 251,
    254, 293; attitudes toward food pro-
    fession, 171, 178, 240–41, 262; birth
    of, 30; business ventures of, 86,
    106–7, 114, 152, 265–69, 270; as
    celebrity, 84, 225, 247, 251, 263,
    307; childhood of, 33, 46, 48; child-
    hood remembered, 118–19, 194,
    217, 256; death of, 326; and dieting,
    175, 183, 205–06, 289; education of,
    52, 62–63, 63–66, 86, 110; estate of,
    326–27; as food journalist, 123–26,
    144, 148, 168, 178, 181, 253, 271;
    as food promoter, 134–35, 266, 270,
    297, 310; health of, 166, 193, 210,
    230, 249–50, 252, 270, 288, 292,
    294, 299, 307–8, 317–18, 323–25;
    homosexuality of, 51, 66, 75, 140,
    160; as icon, 267, 293, 319, 323;
    income of, 247, 296, 307; and jour-
    nalism ethics, 258, 321–23; and
    Mary Beard, 1–4, 40, 42, 48–49, 51,
    114; mental health of, 52, 103, 155,
    195, 208, 243, 309; as mentor, 184,
    202, 269, 282, 295; military service
    of, 116–17, 119–20; musical career
    of, 49, 65, 68, 70, 72, 84; personal
    style of, 96, 102, 126, 136, 140, 151,

166, 184, 223, 229–30, 312; resi-
    dences of, 40, 94, 103–104, 116–17,
    189, 266; as teacher, 83, 89, 174,
    208, 255, 268, 278, 304; television
    and radio career of, 83, 121, 169;
    theatrical career of, 51, 62–63, 83,
    86–88, 94; writing style of, 124–25,
    151, 247. See also James Beard
    Cooking School; roles in theater,
    James Beard; travels, James Beard;
    works published, James Beard
Beard, John: avocations of, 49, 50–51;
    career of, 24, 31, 37, 69; death of,
    117; early life of, 24; as father, 3,
    47–48; marriages of, 24, 25, 27, 50
Beard, Lucille: childhood of, 24, 27; as
    adult, 31, 37, 40, 49
Beard, Mary: as businesswoman, 8,
    10–11, 26, 43; death of, 3, 4, 113;
    early life of, 7–8; as homemaker, 21,
    32, 46; marriages of, 11, 25–27; as
    mother, 3, 40, 42, 48–49, 75; per-
    sonal characteristics of, 7, 10, 11,
    14; remembered, 113, 202, 217, 237
Beard on Bread, 255, 261, 269, 311
Beard on Food, 273
Beard on Pasta, 311, 319, 320
Beck, Simone, 199, 222
Beebe, Lucius, 99, 108, 114, 124, 157
Beef Wellington, 227
Benson, Chester, 57, 62, 68, 83
Benson Hotel, 57, 63
Benson, Simon, 57
Bentley, Gladys, 68
Benton, Thomas Hart, 91
Bernstein, Leonard, 198
Bertholle, Louisette, 199
Bertorelli's restaurant, 72
Bess Whitcomb Players, 83
Better Homes and Gardens Cook Book,
    The, 127
Better Homes and Gardens Diet Book,
    The, 176
Better Homes and Gardens Favorite
    Ways with Chicken, 227
Better Homes and Gardens Menu Cook
    Book, The, 258
"Betty Crocker," 97
Betty Crocker's Picture Cook Book, 159
Bird and Bottle restaurant, 114

Birds Eye frozen foods, 121
The Bishop Misbehaves, 88
Bloom, Michael, 296
Bloomingdale's, 173
Bobbs Merrill publishers, 93
Bocuse, Paul, 264
Bohemian restaurant, 41
Bon Appétit, 168, 299
Bonnier International Design, 264
Book of Mediterranean Food, A, 209
Boston Cooking School, 98, 147
Boston Cooking School Cook Book, The, 15, 37
Boulestin, Marcel, 72
Bourbon, Institute, 208
Bracken, Peg, 196, 240, 245
Bradford, Ned, 143, 145, 222
Brennan, John, 11
Brennan's restaurant, 171
Brown, Bob and Cora, 253
Brown, Helen Evans: collaboration with James, 151, 157, 167, 169, 181–82, 202, 205, 208; as cookbook author, 145, 146, 185, 206, 209; death of, 218; as food journalist, 145, 177; friendship with James, 145–47, 151, 153; health of, 175–76, 203, 206; James on, 156, 253
Brown, Philip, 146, 156, 206, 226, 323
Brownstone, Cecily, 147, 240, 263, 296
Buchwald, Art, 171
Bui Van Han, 197
Business Week, 247

California restaurants. *See* Restaurants, California
Callvert, Isabel: assistant to James, 144–45, 149, 168, 185; friend of James, 120, 166; health of, 236
Callvert, Ron, 120, 166
Calories Don't Count, 206
Cannon, Poppy, 163, 169, 173, 177, 240
Can–Opener Cookbook, The, 163, 207
Captain Applejack, 83
Carnegie Tech, 86
Carr, Alvin, 166
Carrier, Robert, 222, 234, 246
Carroll, John, 306, 308, 317, 323
Carson, Rachel, 228

Century Cook Book, The, 60
Chafing dish, 38
Chambord restaurant, 166
Chanterelle restaurant, 300
Charles restaurant, 102
Charley O's restaurant, 224
Chelsea, 79
Chez Panisse, 259, 281, 287, 324
Chicago Opera Company, 41
Chicago Tribune, 82
Chicken jelly, 31
Child, Julia: career of, 122, 199, 205, 211, 225, 232; impact on profession, 212, 225–26, 236, 240, 241–42, 331; as James's friend, 201, 235, 256, 298, 303, 323
Child, Lydia Mary, 18
Child, Paul, 199, 235, 256
Child's restaurant, 80, 102
Chillingsworth restaurant, 183
Chinese Exclusion Act of 1882, 23
Chinese in Portland, 23
Christmas Carol, A, 87
Claasen, Clara, 156, 157, 158
Claiborne, Craig: career of, 154, 173, 180, 199, 227, 257, 321; impact of, 198–99, 240, 246, 257; as James's friend, 166, 189, 208, 320, 324, 327; as journalist, 184, 187, 188, 192, 213, 222, 232–33, 234
Clam chowder, 98
Clancy, John, 183, 232, 265
Clark, Jim, 114
Classic Italian Cook Book, The, 259
Claude's restaurant, 299
Clinique Médicale et Diététique, 250, 252
Coach House restaurant, 238, 239, 287
Cofacci, Gino: deterioration of relationship with James, 222, 223–34, 230, 238, 256, 276; at end of life, 326–27; as James's lover, 175, 177, 181, 189, 204, 208; professional roles, 175, 248, 298, 307; and Richard Olney, 261
Collier's, 145, 167, 170
Colman, Ronald, 95
Colombin restaurant, 75
Commanderie du Bontemps du Médoc, 171

Commercial recipe books, 128
Commune Cookbook, The, 259
Complete Book of Outdoor Cookery, The, 167, 169, 331
Conway, John and Dorothy, 255
Consumer culture, rise of, 14
Cookbooks, community: *Dainty Dishes,* 38, 56; *Favorite Recipes of the Great Northwest,* 215; *The Fishwives of Charleston, Oregon, Cookbook,* 272; *Neighborhood Cook Book,* 146; *The Portland Women's Exchange Cook Book,* 56, 59, 81; *The St. Peter's Guild Cook Book,* 81, 146; *A Taste of Oregon,* 315; *The Trinity Cook Book,* 127; *The Web-Foot Cook Book,* 19–20, 38, 56, 146, 254
Cookbook genres, 259
Cookbook Hall of Fame, 319
Cooking, aesthetics of, 100–101
Cooking schools: Bloomingdale's, 173; Boston Cooking School, 98, 147; Cordon Bleu, 154; Culinary Institute of America, 188; "The French Chef," 211–12; The Good Cooking School, 265; Helen Worth Cooking School, 173; La Varenne, 295; Michael Field's Cooking School, 211; paucity of in fifties, 172–73; proliferation of in seventies, 277. *See also* James Beard Cooking School, and individual entries
Cooking of Provincial France, The, 232–33
Cooking with Helen McCully Beside You, 237
Cook It Outdoors, 114–16
Cooks' Catalogue, The, 269, 278–79
Cook Until Done, 205
Cora vermouth, 170–71
Corbett, Mrs. H. W., 20
Cornell, Katharine, 79
Cornell School of Hotel Management, 109
Corner Bookshop, 253
Cornfeld, Bernard, 264
Costa, Margaret, 246
Courtine, Robert, 234–35

Couscous and Other Good Food from Morocco, 259
Cox, Denton, 288, 295, 298, 324
Craig Claiborne's Favorites from the New York Times, 298
Crawford, Cheryl: friendship with James, 102–3, 115, 166, 181, 251, 295; James guest of, 143, 152, 169, 183
Crowther, Agnes, 88–89, 93, 169, 189, 266
Cuisinart food processor, 298
Cuisine, 314, 323
Cuisines of Mexico, The, 259
Cukor, George, 79
Culinary Institute of America, 188
Cullum, Anne, 104, 115
Cullum, Jim, 103, 106, 114
Cunningham, Marion: and *Fannie Farmer Cook Book,* 282, 300; friendship with James, 272, 295, 306, 323; and James Beard Cooking School, 269, 280, 287, 306–7; James on, 282
Curnonsky. *See* Sailland, Maurice-Edmond
Curtis, Frances, 11, 14
Customs House, Portland, 24
Cyrano de Bergerac, 81

Daily Telegraph (London), 144
Dainty Dishes, 38
Dainty food, 17, 38–39
Daniel, Clifton, 193
Dannenbaum, Julie, 321
David, Elizabeth: as author of cookbooks, 209–10, 259; as food professional, 234, 262, 265, 269; as friend of James, 222, 243, 258, 323
Davis, Adelle, 228
Davis, Mary Houston, 104
Dean and DeLuca, 301
Dear James Beard, festschrift, 323
de Boer, Ate, 140, 142, 163
de Gouy, Louis 27, 253
DeJonge, Dirk, 87
Delights and Prejudices, 113, 202, 209–10, 215–16, 248, 254, 311, 331
Dell publishers, 168

Delmonico's restaurant, 12–13, 165, 187
DeMille, Agnes, 84, 101, 102
DeMille, Cecil B., 84
DeMille, William, 84
Depression, the, 85, 89
Desire Under the Elms, 79
Design Research, 279
DeVoto, Avis, 199
Diet for a Small Planet, 259
Dircks, Helen, 69, 72
Dodin-Bouffant restaurant, 300
Domestic French Cookery, 10
Domestic science movement, 15–16, 17–18, 56, 61, 82, 215
Don the Beachcomber restaurant, 164
Dorris, Nancy, 116
Doubleday publishers, 156
Dyspepsia, 39

Economy Gastronomy, 207
Editors, James Beard's: Bradford, Ned, 143, 145, 222; Claasen, Clara, 156, 157, 158; Ferrone, John, 168, 207, 248, 326; Jones, Judith, 199, 238, 255, 258, 282
Edward Gottlieb Associates, 150, 157, 162, 169, 173, 182, 190
Efficiency in the home, 38
Ehrlich, Paul, 228
1880s: consumerism in, 6, 14; food in, 18; rise of agribusiness in, 7; role of women in, 6, 11, 13–14, 22
Eighties, 313–15
Electric Epicures Cookbook, The, 207
Elizabeth the Queen, 88
Elizabeth II, coronation of, 150
English National Opera, 70
Ephron, Nora, 253
Escoffier, Georges Auguste, 71, 107, 232
Esquire, 280
Ethnic food, 98, 165, 223
Eugene, Oregon, Junior League, 315
Eugénie restaurant, 80
Every Body's Cook and Receipt Book, 19

Falt's Quelle restaurant, 41
Family farm, demise of, 37

Family of Man, The, 176
Fannie Farmer Cook Book, The, 15, 37, 300–301, 319
Farmer, Fannie, 253
Feasts of Autolycus, The: The Diary of a Greedy Woman, 22
Federal Trade Commission, 228
Federal Writers Project, 91
Felix's restaurant, 175
Fenice restaurant, 194
Ferrone, John: as editor, 168, 207, 248; as friend, 166, 323, 326
Field, Michael: as food professional, 211, 223, 231, 232–34; as friend, 230, 240, 295
Fielding, Paul, 84
Fifties, 137–38, 159–60, 164–65, 172, 176–77, 188–89
Finck, Henry, 59–61, 243
Fireside Books, 129
Fireside Cook Book, The, 129–32, 282
Fish chowder, 197
Fisher, M. F. K.: as friend, 151, 185, 258, 295; James on, 240; as writer, 124, 231, 303
Fishwives of Charleston, Oregon, Cookbook, The, 272
Fit for a King, 100–101, 177, 207
Fitzgerald, Scott and Zelda, 67
Fletcher, Horace, 40
Foltz's, 31
Fonda, Jane, 206
Food and Flavor, 59–61
Food & Wine, 295, 314
Food as art, 100–101, 130
Food Editors' Conference, 149, 159, 177
Food journalism: changes in profession of, 233–34, 257, 260, 301; early days of, 18; and la nouvelle cuisine, 290; nexus with food industry, 134, 241; in seventies, 290; in sixties, 213–214; in thirties, 98. *See also* Food Editors' Conference; Food Marketing Insti-tute; Goddard Gala; National Restaurant Show
Food journalists: Adams, Charlotte, 116; Batchelder, Ann, 97; Brown, Helen Evans, 145; Brownstone,

Food journalists *(cont.)*
Cecily, 134; Cannon, Poppy, 163; Courtine, Robert, 234; Dorris, Nancy, 116; Fougner, Selmer, 100; Greene, Gael, 235; Hazelton, Nika, 235; Hess, John and Karen, 291; Hibben, Sheila, 91–92; Jones, Evan, 299; Laughton, Catherine, 128; Lucas, Dione, 154–55; McCully, Helen, 136; Mencken, H.L., 82; Montant, Jane, 231; Nickerson, Jane, 131; Paddleford, Clementine, 96; Richman, Phyllis, 319; Seranne, Anne, 136; Sokolov, Raymond, 256–57; Trillin, Calvin, 290; Waldo, Myra, 178; Watt, Alexander, 144; Wilson, José, 211. *See also*: Beard, James; Claiborne, Craig; and individual entries
Food Marketing Institute, Dallas, 298
Food processing, 16, 36, 90, 254
Food trends: dieting, 39, 176–77, 206; in 80s, 315–316; in 50s, 137, 172, 188; in 40s, 126–27; fresh ingredients, 60, 168; international food, 204, 223, 231, 259, 316; men as cooks, 139; during Prohibition, 56–57; in seventies, 286, 297, 300; in sixties, 196–97, 227, 228, 231, 243; in thirties, 90, 96–97, 98, 100; in 20s, 17, 38–39; use of fat, 239
Food writers: James as, 167, 168; James on, 240; and plagiarism, 321–23
Forgione, Larry, 312, 316, 326
Forties, food trends in, 126–27
Fortnum's, 72
Forum of the Twelve Caesars restaurant, 180
"For You and Yours" TV show, 121
Foster, William Trufant, 64
Fougner, Selmer, 100
Four Seasons restaurant, 186–88, 193, 232, 238, 239, 287
Fowl and Game Cookery, 118
France, S.S., 267
Franco, Gen. Francisco, 95
Franey, Pierre, 189, 234, 257
Fredericks, Carlton, 206
French and Italian Restaurant, The, 12

"The French Chef" TV show, 211–12, 246
French Cook, The, 9
French cooking, 9, 58, 71
French Country Cooking, 209
French Menu Cookbook, The, 259
French Provincial Cooking, 209
Frigidaire, 174
Frozen fish sticks, 177
Furness, Betty, 212

Gabel Country Day School, 83
Gaige, Crosby, 109
Galen, Morris, 287
Galluzo, Joe, 31
Gault, Henri, 229, 290
Gay revolution, 241
Gearhart, Oregon: childhood haven, 43, 45, 68, 72; recollections of, 217; summer course at, 310; visits as adult, 157, 194, 207, 224
Gearhart, Philip, 43
George VI and Queen Elizabeth, 109
Gennaro's restaurant, 72
Gentry, 145
Ghedini, Francesco, 321
Gibbons, Euell, 228
Gilder, Emily, 296, 307
Gin (Mary's servant), 23
Gin Ridge, Gearhart, 43
Gladstone, The, 21
Glaser, Milton, 264
Goddard Gala, 155
God of Vengeance, The, 79
"The Arthur Godfrey Show," 169, 182
Gohs, Carl, 268
Gold Cook Book, The, 127, 253
Goldman, Emma, 55
Goodman, Paul, 207
Goldschmidt, Neil, 273
Goldstein, Joyce, 314
The Good Cooking School, 265
Good Housekeeping Cook Book, The, 127
Good Intent restaurant, 72
Gottlieb, Edward. *See* Edward Gottlieb Associates
Gottlieb, Robert, 311

Gourmet, 116, 123–26, 135, 185, 236
Gourmet in the Low Calorie Kitchen, The, 206
Gourmet's Guide to Europe, 71
Graham, Billy, 176
Grand Dictionnaire de Cuisine, 183
Grauman's Chinese Theater, 84
Great Cooks and Their Recipes: From Taillevent to Escoffier, 298
Great Cooks' Cookbook, The, 273
Greenberg, Clement, 198
Greene, Gael, 233, 256, 298
Green Giant foods, 179, 203, 223
Greenough, Maryon, 268
Greenwich Village, 79
Gruber, Lester and Cleo, 230, 251
Guérard, Michel, 295
Guide Michelin, 74, 141
Gunther, John, 193

Hale, Denise, 306
Hamblet, Harry and Polly, 43, 44, 207, 217
Hamblet, Mary: childhood friend of James, 43, 50, 62, 115, 194; concern for James, 267, 281; at end of James's life, 319, 320, 323, 324, 327; as lifelong friend, 4, 117, 151, 210, 224, 251, 256
Hamlin, Suzanne, 300, 321
Hampden, Walter, 80, 81, 86
Hanes, Bob, 101, 102, 103
Happiness Is a Warm Puppy, 196
Harlech, Lady, 301, 321
Harpers, 207
Harper's Bazaar, 145
Hart, Lorenz, 79
Hatfield, Mark, 215
Haute cuisine, 58
Hawaiian Room restaurant, 164
Hawkins, Harriet, 87, 93, 94, 101, 102, 103
Hawthorne elementary school, 33
Hawthorne Park, 26
Hazan, Marcella, 259
Hazelton, Nika, 235, 296
Helen Worth Cooking School, 173
Hemingway, Ernest, 73
Henry Savage Opera Company, 41

Hess, John and Karen, 235, 291
He Who Gets Slapped, 85
Hibben, Sheila: James on, 153, 240; as journalist, 97–98, 109, 132, 174; as proponent of culinary nationalism, 91–92, 116
Hindley, Catherine Laughton, 229
Hines, Duncan, 158, 164
Holiday Cook Book, The, 145
Hollywood in the twenties, 84
Holt publishers, 156
"Home" TV show, 169
Home economics movement. *See:* Domestic science movement
Home Institute Cookbook, 97
Homosexuality, 67, 79, 241
Hood Valley, Oregon, 12
Hoover, J. Edgar, 78, 95
Horn and Hardart restaurants, 80
Hors d'Oeuvre and Canapes, 111–13, 248, 254
Hors d'Oeuvre, Inc., 108–113
Hotel Continental, Marseilles, 120
House Beautiful, 116, 138
House & Garden, 145, 167
House's restaurant, 40, 41
How to Eat (and Drink) Your Way Through a French (and Italian) Menu, 248
How to Eat Better for Less Money, 162, 237, 247, 254
Huber's restaurant, 41
Hudson, Virginia Cary, 196
Hudspeth, John, 272

I Hate to Cook Book, 196
I Love to Cook Book, 206
"I Love to Eat" show, 121–122
Instant Epicure, The, 207
Instant Haute Cuisine, 207
International Cooks' Catalogue, The, 280
International Wine and Food Society, 109
"In the Kitchen" TV show, 121
Investors Overseas Services, 264
Invitation to Indian Cooking, An, 259
Iowa, University of, 15
Italian Food, 209

Jack's restaurant, 49, 171
Jaffrey, Madhur, 259, 298
James Beard's American Cookery: genesis and publication of, 226, 238, 248, 250, 252–54; reception of, 256–58, 269, 311, 331
James Beard apron, 284
James Beard's Basic Cook Book, 168
James Beard Cookbook, The, 184–86, 201, 225, 258, 311, 319, 331
James Beard Cooking School, consolidation of, 205, 252, 277, 298; early development of, 179, 181, 189, 192; on the road, 208, 267–69, 280, 287, 316
"James Beard's Dollars and Sense Cookery" radio show, 250
James Beard's Fish Cookery, 147, 158
James Beard's International Cookbook, 189
James Beard's Menus for Entertaining, 220–21
"The James Beard Show", TV, 221, 222, 226
James Beard's Theory and Practice of Good Cooking, 287, 293–94, 298
James Beard's Treasury of Outdoor Cooking, 183, 194–95
Jell-O, 128
Jerome, Carl, 270–71, 273, 276–77, 281, 283, 288
Jim Beard's Casserole Cookbook, 169
Jim Beard's Complete Book of Barbecue and Rotisserie Cooking, 156, 158
Johnson, Hugh, 246
Johnson, Nunnally, 91
Jones, Evan, 299, 323
Jones, Fred, 69
Jones, Joseph, 7
Jones, Judith: as James's editor, 199, 238, 255, 258, 282; as James's friend, 263, 287, 303, 323, 325
Journal, Societé des Gentilshommes Chefs de Cuisine (National Premium Beer), 135, 139
Joy of Cooking, The, 37, 92–93, 127, 131, 147, 206, 319
Jue–Let, 23, 26, 31, 48, 217

Kafka, Barbara: as Beard Glaser Wolf editor, 279; on James Beard Cooking Scool faculty, 298, 306–7, 316; as James's friend, 295, 298, 303, 320, 325
Kaye, Danny, 316
Kennedy, Diana, 259
Kennedy, Jacqueline, 197, 198
Kennedy, John F., 197, 198
Kent, Rockwell, 100
Kerr, Graham, 242–43
Klarnet, Phil, 150
Kovacs, Ernie, 211
Kovi, Paul, 238, 299, 325
Knight, Hilary, 196
Knopf, Pat, 207, 209, 248, 322
Kramer, Matt, 312
Krieger, E. R., 25
Kuhn, Loni, 272, 280
Kump, Peter, 295, 320, 325

Laber, Jeri, 300
La Caravelle restaurant, 197, 198, 299
Ladies Aid society, First Congregational church, Portland, 38
Ladies Home Journal, 97, 134
Lafayette restaurant, 94
La Fonda del Sol restaurant, 193, 204
La France Gastronomique, 74
La Grande Creamery, Oregon, 31
La Grande Cuisine Illustrée, 146
Lamb, Jerry, 151, 267, 276, 323
L'Ami Louis restaurant, 141, 238
Lane, Harry, 35
Lang, George, 265, 303
La nouvelle cuisine, 229
Lapérouse restaurant, 141
Lappé, Frances Moore, 259
Larrimore, Earl, 80
La Tour d'Argent, 75, 141
Laughton, Catherine, 128
LaVarenne cooking school, 295
Lebanon, Oregon, 24, 26
Le Caneton restaurant, 75
Le Nouveau Guide, 290
Lens, The, 54, 61
Leo Burnett Agency, 179
Le Pavillon restaurant, 103, 110, 125, 171–72, 189, 206, 234
Le Plaisir restaurant, 297, 299

Leroy, Warner, 224
Les Amis d'Escoffier, 100
Les Chevaliers du Tastevin, 100
Les Halles, 74
Leslie, Eliza, 10, 130, 253
Lettunich, Mateo, 166
Lewis, Alan, 224
Lewis and Clark, 42–43
Lewis and Clark Exposition, 35
Lianides, Leon, 238, 323
Lichine, Alexis, 141, 144, 154
Liebling, A. J., 73
Life, 206, 257
Little, Brown publishers, 143, 146, 250, 258
Lloyd George, David, 82
L'Oasis restaurant, 235
Locke-Ober restaurant, 171
Lolita, 183
London, James's first trip to, 72
London restaurants. See Restaurants, London
London Chop House restaurant, 171
London Ritz, 71
Lone Fir cemetery, 3
Longchamps restaurant, 102, 115
Loria, Gaetano, 70, 71, 72, 75
Lotan, James, 24
Lou Barcarès, 210
Louis Sherry restaurant, 75
Louisville restaurant, 12
Louvre restaurant, 42
Lowenstein, Eleanor, 253
Ludlum, Robert, 264
Lucas, Dione, 154, 173, 184, 211, 240
Luce, Henry and Clare, 181
Lucky Pierre restaurant, 151
Lucullus Club, 100
Lunt, Alfred, 100
Lutèce restaurant, 198, 246, 299

Mabon, Mary Frost, 240
MacAusland, Earle, 124, 135, 236, 240
McCall's, 134, 145
McCully, Helen: confidante of James, 166, 178, 181, 237, 251; death of, 295;, as James's collaborator, 205; as James's student, 174; as journalist, 136, 193, 203–04, 240
McDonald's restaurants, 239

Mack, Ted, 169
McLuhan, Marshall, 233
Maco Magazine company, 154
McNulty, Henry and Bettina, 162–63, 173, 183, 209, 243, 326
McPhee, John, 207
Madama Butterfly, Giacomo Puccini, 134
Magic with Leftovers, 206
Mamma Leone's restaurant, 204
Man Called Peter, A, 196
Margittai, Tom: as James's confidante, 287, 296, 299; and Four Seasons restaurant, 238, 325
Marquand's restaurant, 49
Marshall, Catherine, 196
Marshall, Lydie, 320, 324
Mary Cullen's Northwest Cookbook, 128
"Mary Ellis Ames," 97
Mary Meade's Magic Recipes for the Electric Blender, 207
Mason, Jerry, 136, 152, 169, 183
Massachusetts Institute of Technology, 15
Mastering the Art of French Cooking, 199–200, 225, 246, 254, 258
Maxim's restaurant, 75, 163
Maxwell's Plum restaurant, 224
Mayer's, 31
M. Barrows publishers, 111, 114, 118
Meek, H. B., 109
Meier and Frank, 83, 215
Melba, Nellie, 71
Mencken, H. L., 82, 243
Mercedes (James's Spanish cook), 173
Meredith publishers, 259
Metropolitan Public Market, Portland, 21, 31, 57
Meyer, Fred, 90, 215
Michael Field's Cooking School, 223
Michener, James, 165
Millau, Christian, 229, 290
Miller, Arthur, 207
Miller, Mark, 314
Million Menus for Dining and Entertaining at Home, A, 220
Molnar, Ferenc, 84
Monroe, Marilyn, 169
Montant, Jane, 236, 303

Moses, Robert, 214
Multnomah Hotel, Portland, 41
Mumford, Lewis, 100
Musso and Frank restaurant, 171
Myerson, Bess, 212

Nabokov, Vladimir, 183
Nassikas, James, 272, 280, 306, 323
Nation, The, 82
National brands, rise of, 90
National Cookbook, The: A Kitchen
    Americana, 91
National Premium Beer, 135, 139, 148,
    167
National Restaurant Show, 148
Natural foods, 128
Navarro, Ramon, 84
Necanicum River, 194
Nelson, Richard, 321–23
Nestlé, 182, 193, 205, 211
Neurasthenia, 39
Newarker restaurant, 164
New Family Book, The, 19
New James Beard, The, 308, 310–11,
    312, 315, 317
Newnham-Davis, N., 71
New Republic, 85, 91
Newsweek, 206, 207
New York, 278, 233, 302, 324
New York City, 78, 95
New York Daily News, 321
New Yorker, The, 95, 98, 131, 290–91
New York PM, 121
New York Port Authority, 285
New York Review of Books, The, 232,
    303
New York Times, 94, 200, 278
New York Times Book Review, 241
New York Times Cookbook, The, 199,
    201, 225, 258, 319
New York Times Menu Cookbook, The,
    227
New York Times Natural Foods Cook-
    book, The, 259
Nickerson, Jane, 131, 134, 169, 171,
    180, 240
Nimmo, Richard: and alcohol, 296,
    307; as James's factotum, 287, 317,
    320, 324, 325
Nixon, Richard, 262

No One Ever Tells You These Things,
    237
Norman, Ruth: as author, 205; and
    James Beard Cooking School, 169,
    179, 192, 237; as James's friend,
    115, 166, 181, 251, 295
Northern Italian Cooking, 321

Oaks, The, Portland, 48, 194
Odets, Clifford, 102
Of Cabbages and Kings, 106, 107
Old Crow whiskey, 162
Olds and King, 20
Olney, Richard, 259–61, 297, 301,
    321–23
Omaha steaks, 283, 307
Omelet, 154
119 West Tenth Street, New York, 189
174 Thirteenth Street, Portlamd, 21
167 West Twelfth Street, New York,
    266
126 West Forty-ninth Street, New York, 94
O'Neill, Eugene, 79
1001 Ways to Please a Husband, 178
Orange juice, 137
Oregon, 11, 55, 63, 146
Oregon Trail, 47–48, 63, 81
Oregonian, The, 83, 88, 215, 320, 327
Oregon Journal, 70
Oregon Public Broadcasting, 273
The Organic Yenta, 259
Oscar of the Waldorf, 15, 82
Othello, 81
Oustaù de Baumanière restaurant, 210
Owen, Jeanne: career of, 109, 111; dete-
    rioration of relationship with James,
    123, 160, 178, 240; as mentor to
    and promoter of James, 109–10,
    114–15, 122–23
O Ye Jigs and Juleps, 196

Pacific Princess, cruise ship, 324
Paddleford, Clementine, 96–97, 108,
    134, 240
Paderewski, Ignace Jan, 71
Pagani's restaurant, 72
Palace Hotel restaurant, 49
Pancake House restaurant, 171
Paris, Beard's first trip to, 73–75
Paris restaurants. See Restaurants, Paris

Paris Cuisine, 142–144, 146, 147
Paris Bistro Cooking, 144
Parloa, Maria, 39
Patterson, Fred, 102
Pavlova, Anna, 49
Payne, B. Iden, 86
Peacock Alley, 14
Peale, Norman Vincent, 176
Peck, Paula, 174, 192, 208, 240, 295
People, 312, 316
Pépin, Jacques, 259, 265, 285
Percy (James's dog), 318–19, 327
Perino's restaurant, 171
Philippé, Claudius, 150
Pierce, S. S., 120
Pig & Whistle pub, 283
Pinot (James's lover), 163
Piper, David, 86
Platt, June, 253, 321
Playboy, 136
Playboy Gourmet, The, 206
Plaza Hotel, 123, 155
Pleasures of Cooking, The, 298
Point, Fernand, 290
Poisons in Your Food, The, 197
Pomander Walk, 62
Porter, Cole, 79
Portland, Oregon: and Chinese immi-
    grants, 23, 50; in James's youth, 2,
    35–35, 40–41, 63; in Mary Beard's
    day, 8–10, 12; provincialism and
    conservatism of, 42, 55, 66, 87; tri-
    umphant return to, 151, 215, 273
Portland Art Museum, 273
Portland Civic Theater, 87
Portland Girl at the Chafing Dish, A, 38
Portland Hotel, 21, 41
Portland restaurants. *See* Restaurants,
    Portland
*Portland Women's Exchange Cook
    Book, The*, 56–57, 59
Pottery Barn, 279
Poy (Mary's servant), 23
Prangley, Charlotte, 7
Prisoner of Zenda, The, 95
Prohibition, 55–56, 78, 99–100
Provenson, Alice and Martin, 129
Prudhomme, Paul, 298, 315
Public Market Building, Portland, 89
Publishers' Weekly, 184

Pump Room restaurant, 152
Pure Food and Drug Act of 1906, 35

Quest, The, 64, 65
Quilted Giraffe restaurant, 300, 315
Quo Vadis restaurant, 166, 171, 287

Rainbow Room restaurant, 94
Random House publishers, 193
Ranhoffer, Charles, 15
Reader's Digest, 167–68, 316
"Recipes and Reminiscences", 167
Red Lantern Players, 64
Reed College, 20, 63–66, 273, 287, 326
Reed, John, 55, 87
Reed, Mrs. S. J., 20
Restaurant Associates, 164, 169, 170,
    179, 190, 214
Restaurant Beaux-Arts, 73
Restaurants, California: Chez Panisse,
    259, 281, 284, 324; Don the Beach-
    comber, 164; Jack's, 49, 151, 171;
    Marquand's, 49; Michael's, 315;
    Musso and Frank, 171; Palace Hotel,
    49; Perino's, 171; Solari, 49; Stars,
    324; Tait's, 49; Trader Vic's, 164
Restaurants, London: Bertorelli's, 72;
    Fortnum's picnic hamper, 72; Gen-
    naro's, 72; Good Intent, 72; Ritz, 72;
    Pagani's, 72; Pig & Whistle pub,
    283; Ristorante del Commercio, 72;
    Verrey's bar, 72
Restaurants, New York: Alfredo's, 265,
    287; Algonquin Hotel, 80; An Amer-
    ican Place, 316; Asti, 102; Athena,
    102; Chambord, 166; Chanterelle,
    300; Charles, 102; Charlie O's, 224;
    Child's, 80, 102; Claude's, 299;
    Coach House,238, 287; Dodin-Bouf-
    fant, 300; Eugénie, 80; Felix's, 175;
    Forum of the Twelve Caesars, 180;
    Four Seasons, 186–88, 232, 238,
    249, 287, 299, 319; Hawaiian
    Room, 164; Horn and Hardart, 80;
    La Caravelle, 197, 205, 246,
    299;Lafayette, 94; La Fonda del Sol,
    193, 204; La Grenouille, 246; Le
    Cygne, 246; Le Pavillon, 103, 110,
    125, 171, 189, 206, 234; Le Plaisir,
    297, 299; Longchamps,102, 115;

Restaurants, New York *(cont.)*
  Lutèce, 198, 246, 299; Mamma
  Leone's, 204; Maxwell's Plum, 224,
  263; Palace, 299; Quilted Giraffe,
  300; QuoVadis, 166, 171, 287; River
  Café, 316; Schrafft's, 80; "21" Club,
  103, 136, 166; Waldorf–Astoria, 80;
  Windows on the World, 284
Restaurants, Paris: Colombin, 75; L'Ami
  Louis, 141, 238; Lapérouse, 141; Le
  Cantenon, 75; Les Cigognes, 141;
  Louis Sherry, 75; Maxim's 75, 135,
  163; Restaurant Beaux-Arts, 73;
  Rumpelmayer's, 75; Tour d'Argent,
  75, 141
Restaurants, Portland: Aurora, 12;
  Bohemian Restaurant, 41; Dan and
  Louis's Oyster Bar, 146; Falt's
  Quelle, 41; French and Italian
  Restaurant, 12; Heathman Hotel, 86;
  House's, 40–41; Huber's, 41;
  Louisville, 12; Louvre, 42; Mult-
  nomah Hotel, 41; Pancake House,
  171; Portland Hotel, 41, 63; Royal
  Bakery, 41; Swetland's, 41; Town
  Tavern, 89; Vienna Coffee House, 12
Rhode, Bill, 106–07, 112, 124
Rhode, Irma, 106, 108, 113
Rhodes, Chet, 272
Rice, Elmer, 87
Rice, William, 285
Richard Nelson's American Cooking,
  321–23
Richards, Ellen Swallow, 15
Richman, Phyllis, 319
Ristorante del Commercio, 72
River Café, 316
Roadfood, 291
Rodale, J. I., 228
Rodale, Robert, 228
Rodgers, Richard, and Hammerstein,
  Oscar, 165
Rojas-Lombardi, Felipe, 252
Roles, mostly minor, in theater and film,
  James Beard: *The Adding Machine*,
  87; *Alice in Wonderland*, 87; *The
  Bishop Misbehaves*, 88; *Captain
  Applejack*, 83; *A Christmas Carol*,
  87; *Cyrano de Bergerac*, 81; *He Who
  Gets Slapped*, 85; on KGW, Portland,

86; *King of Kings*, 84; on KOIN,
  Portland, 86; *Othello*, 81; *Pomander
  Walk*, 62; *Queen Kelly*, 84; *The
  Swan*, 84; Taylor Street Comedy
  Team, 87; *The Three Sisters*, 88
Rombauer, Irma, 92–93, 147, 206, 253
Ronald, Mary, 60
Ronsheim, John, 308
Root, Waverley, 73
Rorer, Sarah Tyson, 16, 39
Roy, Mike, 226
Royal Bakery restaurant, 41
Ruff, Clarence, 49
Rumpelmayer's restaurant, 75
Ruley family, 37

Sailland, Maurice-Edmond, 74
Salad, 137
Salinger, Pierre, 197
Salmon Street, Portland, 40
San Carlo Opera company, 41
San Grael Society, First Presbyterian
  Church, Portland, 19
Sanger, Margaret, 55
Sansbury, Alice, 38
Saturday Evening Post, 91, 167
Sax, Irene, 300, 311, 319
Scavullo, Francesco, 284
Schaffner, John: as agent, 154, 156, 168,
  193, 296; as James's friend, 195, 208
School of Hotel Management, Cornell
  University, 164
Schoonmaker, Frank, 144, 173, 193,
  195, 208
Schrafft's restaurant, 80
Schulz, Charles, 197
Scotti Grand Opera company, 64–65
Scribner's publishers, 207
Sealy-Dresser, 31
Seaside, Oregon, 43, 45, 268
Seranne, Anne, 136, 160, 166, 173
Seventies: international trend, 248, 259;
  managing a life-style in, 277, 278,
  279; trend toward simplification,
  259, 286, 289, 302
Seventy-five Receipts, 130
Sheraton, Mimi, 224, 243
Sherry Wine & Spirits, 120, 135, 144,
  169
Shinn, Mack, 108, 109, 113

Shrallow, Freddie, 166
Silver Palate, The, 301
Simon, André, 72, 109, 242
Simon & Schuster publishers, 129
Simple French Cooking for English Homes, 72
Simple French Food, 302, 321, 322
Sinatra, Frank, 198
Sinclair, Upton, 35
Sixties: awareness of hunger, 228; food trends in, 196–97, 204, 206, 220, 223; food writing in, 206–07, 225, 227, 241; Francophilia in, 197–201; homosexuality in, 241; impact of Kennedy on, 197–98, 212; restaurants in, 213, 239
Skotch cooler, 150
Skotch grill, 157
Slenderella Diet Book, The, 178
Societé des Gentilshommes Chefs de Cuisine, 135
Sokolov, Raymond, 257, 266
Solari restaurant, 49
Sontheimer, Carl, 298
Soulé, Henri, 110, 188, 246
South Pacific, 165
Spector, Stephen, 295, 297
Squid, 98
Stanford Court Hotel, 280, 284
Stars restaurant, 324
Stein, Gertrude, 67, 100
Steinbeck, John, 91
Steiner, Rudolph, 228
Stern, Jane and Michael, 291
Stipe, Jack, 94, 102
Stockli, Albert, 166, 179, 193, 205, 225
Stonewall Inn, 241
Strasberg, Lee, 102
Street, Julian, 109
Stroheim, Erich von, 84
Stuart, Caroline, 317, 324, 325
Stuecklen, Karl, 261, 294, 319
Summer Cooking, 209
Summers, Col. Owen, and Clara, 20–21, 24, 26, 217
Sunset, 145, 177
Surmain, André, 169, 173, 178, 198
Susann, Jacqueline, 264
Swan, The, 84
Swanson, Gloria, 84

Swetland's restaurant, 41

Tait's restaurant, 49
Tastemaker Award, 269, 298, 317
Taste memory, 113, 217
Taste of America The, 291–92
Taste of Oregon, A, 315
Taylor, Frank, 168
Tetrazzini, Luisa, 49
Theater Guild, 79
Theme restaurants, 164–66
Thiele, Henri, 57–58, 63
Thirties, 90–91, 95, 97
"This Is My Music" radio show, 308
This Week, 145
Thomas, Anna, 259
Thompson, Kay, 196
Three Sisters, The, 88
Tillamook Valley, 12, 129
Tillamook Head, 194
Time, 206, 207
Time-Life Foods of the World, 231–233, 235
Times, The, London, 71–72
Tobacco Road, 95
"Today" TV show, 303
Toklas, Alice B., 163
Toronto, 8
Tosca, Giacomo Puccini, 64–65
Tower, Jeremiah: as chef, 295, 297, 314; homage to James from, 312, 323; as restaurateur, 324
Trader Vic's restaurant, 164
Trattoria di Alfredo, 265, 287
Travel & Leisure, 299
Travels, James Beard: to Alaska, 324; childhood, 49; in fifties, Europe, 140, 154, 169–70, 173, 183; in fifties, West Coast, 183; first transcontinental train trip, 81; first European trip, 69–75; first wine tour, 135; to Mexico, 169; in seventies, Europe, 250, 256, 283, 295; in seventies, West Coast, 256, 266, 306; in sixties, Europe,193, 202, 208, 209, 218, 222, 225, 229, 235, 243; in sixties, West Coast, 208, 211, 225, 238
Trillin, Calvin, 290–91
Trinity Church, Portland, 20, 49, 127, 273

Trinity Cook Book, The, 127
Triplette, Clay, 237, 307
Troisgros brothers, 264
Truman, Margaret, 193
TV dinners, 137
Twenties, 63, 67, 73, 78–79, 84
"21" Club, The, 103, 166

Ude, Eustace, 9
United Seamen's Service, 119–20
United States, S.S., 193
University of Iowa, Iowa City, 15
University of Washington, Seattle, 86
Untermeyer, Louis, 100

Valentino, Rudolph, 84
Vancouver, British Columbia, 52
van der Rohe, Mies, 186
Varèse, Edgard, 100
Vaudable, Louis, 141, 162, 163
Veach, Bill, 162
Vegetarian Epicure, The, 259
Verdon, René, 198, 246
Verrey's bar, 72
Vichyssoise, 109
Vienna Coffee House restaurant, 12
Virginia City, Nevada, 157
Vogue, 145
Vreeland, Diana, 198

Waldo, Myra, 178, 181, 193, 206, 240
Waldorf-Astoria, 14, 80, 91
Walker, Danton, 108
Ward, Beth, 237, 252, 270
Washington High School, Portland, 27, 52, 54, 57, 62
Washington Park, Portland, 48
Washington Post, 285, 319
Washington Star syndicate, 258
Washington, University of, 86
Waters, Alice, 281, 297, 312–13, 323, 324
Watt, Alexander, 141–42, 144
Waxman, Jonathan, 314
Web-Foot Cookbook, The, 19–20, 254
Wechsberg, Joseph, 228
Weil, Phillip, 254, 262
Weill, Kurt, 102
Welch, Harvey, 87, 101–02, 224, 267

West Coast Cook Book, 145, 146, 185, 209
Western Family, 146, 177
Weston, Edward, 100
Where to Eat in America, 280
Whitcomb, Bess, 83, 87, 157
White House chefs, 197, 198
White sauce, 37
Whole Earth Cook Book, The, 259
Wigmore Hall, London, 70
Wilde, Oscar, 67
Willamette valley, 12
Willan, Anne, 297–98
Williams, Chuck, 211, 272, 280, 306, 323
Williams–Sonoma, 284
Wilson, José: deterioration of, 237, 256, 271, 279, 307–8; as food journalist, 211, 222; as James's amanuensis, 230, 236, 254, 298; reservations about Burton Wolf, 267
Wine and Food society, 72
Wine Lover's Cookbook, A, 111
Wolf, Burton Richard, 264, 265–69, 280
Wolf, Clark: on Christmas list, 323; to New York, 317, 318; in San Francisco, 306; solicitude of James, 320, 324, 326
Wolfert, Paula, 184, 259, 301
Woman's Day, 134, 145, 167
Woollcott, Alexander, 79
Works published, James Beard: Beard on Bread, 255, 269, 311; Beard on Pasta, 311, 319; The Complete Book of Outdoor Cooking, (with Helen Evans Brown), 167, 169, 331; Cook It Outdoors, 114; Delights and Prejudices, 215, 248, 254, 311, 331; The Fireside Cook Book, 129, 248; Fowl and Game Cookery, 118; The Great Cooks' Cookbook, 269, 273; Hors d'Oeuvre and Canapes, 111, 248, 254; How to Eat (and Drink) Your Way Through a French (and Italian) Menu, with Gino Cofacci, 248; How to Eat Better for Less Money, with Sam Aaron, 162, 237, 247, 254; James Beard's American Cookery, 226, 238, 248, 250, 252–54,

256–58, 269, 311, 331; *The James Beard Cookbook*, 184–86, 201, 225, 258, 311, 319, 331; *James Beard's Fish Cookery*, 147, 158; *James Beard's Menus for Entertaining*, 220–21; *James Beard's Theory and Practice of Good Cooking*, 287, 293–94, 298; *James Beard's Treasury of Outdoor Cooking*, 183, 194–95; *Jim Beard's Casserole Cookbook*, 169; *Jim Beard's Complete Book of Barbecue and Rotisserie Cooking*, 156; *Jim Beard's Complete Cookbook for Entertaining*, 169; *The New James Beard*, 308, 311, 315; *Paris Cuisine*, with Alexander Watt, 142, 146, 147

World's Fair, 1939, 97, 109–110
World's Fair, 1964, 209, 214
World War I, 61
World War II, 165
Wright, Richardson, 109, 111
Wynn, Dan, 174
Wynn, Rita, 174

Yamhill Market, 57, 85, 89

Zodiac parties, 220